T0320368

America's Other Automakers

America's Other Automakers

A HISTORY OF THE FOREIGN-OWNED AUTOMOTIVE SECTOR IN THE UNITED STATES

Timothy J. Minchin

The University of Georgia Press

ATHENS

Published by the University of Georgia Press
Athens, Georgia 30602
www.ugapress.org
© 2021 by Timothy J. Minchin
All rights reserved
Set in by 10/13 Kepler Std Regular by Kaelin Chappell Broaddus

Most University of Georgia Press titles are
available from popular e-book vendors.

Printed digitally

Library of Congress Cataloging-in-Publication Data

Names: Minchin, Timothy J., author.
Title: America's other automakers : a history of the foreign-owned sector
    in the United States / Timothy J. Minchin.
Description: Athens : The University of Georgia Press, 2021. |
    Series: 1970: histories of contemporary America |
    Includes bibliographical and index.
Identifiers: LCCN 2020032973 | ISBN 9780820358949 (hardback) |
    ISBN 9780820358956 (paperback) | ISBN 9780820358932 (epub)
Subjects: LCSH: Automobile industry and trade—United States—History.
    | Automobiles, Foreign—United States—History. | Investments,
    Foreign—United States—History.
Classification: LCC HD9710.U52 M556 2021 | DDC 338.8/87292220973—dc23
LC record available at https://lccn.loc.gov/2020032973

CONTENTS

ACKNOWLEDGMENTS

This book grew out of my travels to the United States, especially to the southern states. As I drove around doing research, I noticed the gleaming auto plants operated by foreign companies, many of them positioned in the public eye next to the interstate. (I later learned that this was no accident.) Despite this visibility, I realized that the industry had not received a great deal of attention compared to the domestic companies, especially Ford and General Motors, that are so integrally associated with American identity. I became interested in writing about the history of this vast foreign-owned industry, especially in exploring how large Japanese, German, and Korean automakers had ended up in small-town America.

I started in Georgia. There, archivist and historian Kaye Lanning Minchew helped me to complete valuable early research on the Kia plant in West Point. I would like to thank Kaye and her family for all their assistance and hospitality. I would also like to thank others who assisted me in Georgia, particularly Diethard Lindner in LaGrange and Sheryl Vogt and Jill Severn at the Richard Russell Library for Political Research and Studies in Athens. I completed much of my primary source research on trips to the Russell Library.

As I broadened my research beyond Georgia and became interested in writing a history of the sector, many other people helped me enormously. On a trip to Kentucky, Connie Minch helped arrange interviews with local participants about the history of Toyota's large plant in Georgetown. In Alabama, I was assisted by Ellen McNair of the Montgomery Chamber of Commerce and Steve Murray at the Alabama Department of Archives and History, facilitating the writing of the Mercedes and Hyundai chapters. In Tennessee, my progress was speeded by staff at the Albert Gore Research Center at Middle Tennessee State University, particularly Louis Kyriakoudes and Donna Baker, who uncovered records about Nissan's plant in Smyrna and facilitated interviews in the area. In Ohio, staff at the Ohio History Connection and the Ohio State University Archives, both in Columbus, helped me to gain some valuable information on the foundational Honda plant in Marysville, Ohio, including access to papers that I had previously been unaware of. In Detroit, I found many original records, particularly at the Walter Reuther Library at Wayne State University. I would like to thank the archivists there for all their help. In the Midwest and South, several staff of the United Automobile Workers, particularly Richard Bensinger and Gary Casteel, also assisted me in setting up interviews. My thanks go to all.

I would also like to thank all those who agreed to be interviewed for this project. I conducted ninety interviews in all, over numerous trips. Many people gave generously of their time and records, and I am grateful. While I cannot thank them all individually, I would especially like to acknowledge Al Benchich in Detroit and Dara Longgrear in Tuscaloosa, Alabama, who were particularly generous with their assistance.

Given that this book has a Georgia dimension, I am delighted that the University of Georgia Press is publishing it. At the press, many staff were helpful and supportive; I would especially like to thank Mick Gusinde-Duffy, Bethany Snead, and Rebecca Norton. I would also like to thank the Australian Research Council (ARC), as this book is the main outcome of a three-year discovery grant that the council awarded me. This book could not have been completed without the ARC's generous support.

Several academic colleagues in both the United States and Australia provided valuable mentoring and support. I especially wish to thank Roland Burke, Katie Holmes, Adrian Jones, John David Smith, Kaori Okano, Lane Windham, and Joshua Van Lieu. Bronwyn Hislop and Hiroko Levy provided knowledgeable research assistance, the latter in Japanese sources, while Amanda Rooke did an excellent job of transcribing interviews. Anna Henger helped in accessing German sources. I am grateful to all.

Doing contemporary history is richly rewarding, but it can also be a perilous business. I sent off the final manuscript in February 2020, just before the world economy went into a downturn caused by the coronavirus, at the time a little-known story, especially in the United States. Before completing the manuscript, I updated the epilogue to cover the industry's history through the end of 2019. Like most people, however, I did not anticipate the onset of a global pandemic. It has had a significant impact on the industry, which is experiencing a downturn whose costs are still unfolding. As the manuscript had been completed and entered the editing process, it was not possible to update the epilogue to cover the impact of the virus. In any case, I concluded that it is impossible to ascertain the pandemic's full effects yet, especially as they may last several years. Historians, even contemporary ones, need some perspective, and covering the virus's impact on the industry will be a task for future work. While that impact is likely to be significant, the foreign-owned industry also remains well-placed—for the reasons outlined here—to rebound. So *America's Other Automakers* tells the story of the foreign-owned auto industry through its roots in the 1970s to the end of 2019, an important story of growth, but one that also produced plenty of little-known tensions and costs.

I would also like to acknowledge material used here with permission. Chapter 8 was previously published in a different form as "When Kia Came to Georgia: Southern Transplants and the Growth of America's 'Other' Automakers," *Journal of Southern History* 83, no. 4 (November 2017): 889–930. In addition, a portion of chapter 3 appeared previously as "Showdown at Nissan: The 1989 Campaign to Organize Nissan in Smyrna, Tennessee, and the Rise of the Transplant Sector," *Labor History* 58, no. 3 (July 2017): 396–422. Some early material and ideas, chiefly from chapters 2 and 3, were also previously published in "'They Didn't Want to Be Union': Southern Transplants and the Growth of America's 'Other' Automakers," *Australasian Journal of American Studies* 36, no. 2 (December 2017): 35–65. Thank you to the editors of these journals for their permission.

Finally, I would like to thank my friends, particularly Chris VerPlanck, Abby Bridge, Sara Nosrati, Duncan Nuttall, Rosemary Nuttall, Diane Kraal, Rick Nash, Kerry Nixon, and Kelly Wan, for their continuing support while I wrote this book. My final thanks are to my family, especially my children, Alex, Natasha, and Anton, my sister, Alison, and my parents, Tony and Christine Minchin, for their ongoing love and support.

America's Other
Automakers

INTRODUCTION

On November 1, 1982, the first Honda Accord rolled off the production line at the company's new factory in Ohio. In some respects, there was nothing remarkable about the vehicle, a standard gray sedan built at the warehouse-like facility in Marysville, a small city outside Columbus. Once it came off the line, however, it became clear that this was no ordinary car. The Accord was placed on a podium and then covered in a huge rosette made up of the colors of the Ohio state flag. It was fitted with a special license plate, USA 001, and then was applauded by top company officials, including president Kiyoshi Kawashima, as well as a marching high school band. It was photographed extensively and featured in company advertisements bearing the slogan "Made Over Here." Later, the vehicle was donated to the Henry Ford Museum in Detroit, which documented key moments in the industry's development. As the *Marysville Journal-Tribune* commented, the car "marked the start of a new era in automotive history in the United States." A Japanese company had made its first car on American soil.[1]

From this car a massive industry grew. By the time that USA 001 was made, Nissan was building a $660 million factory in Smyrna, Tennessee, the largest industrial development in that state's history. Eight months later, American-made Nissans were coming off the line. In 1985 Toyota, the biggest Japanese carmaker, located its first North American plant in Georgetown, Kentucky. In terms of volume, Georgetown became the biggest Toyota factory in the world, employing more than eight thousand people.[2] In the 1990s and early 2000s the "transplant" sector grew steadily, with BMW, Hyundai, and Mercedes-Benz among the new arrivals.[3] By 2008 foreign-owned plants employed over seventy-eight thousand workers, turning out a quarter of all vehicles made in the United States, and many more staff were employed by these plants' suppliers.[4]

Even during the Great Recession, foreign companies invested in the United States, a huge automotive market. By 2015 automakers from Germany, Japan, and South Korea operated twenty assembly plants in the United States and Canada. Six of these factories were owned by Toyota, five by Honda, two by Nissan and the Hyundai Motor Group (Hyundai and Kia), and one each by BMW, Mercedes-Benz, Mitsubishi, Subaru, and Volkswagen. Most were located in the lower Midwest or South in a band between I-75 to the east and I-55 to the west. Together they comprised a new automotive corridor that flowed from the upper Midwest, the industry's traditional heartland, all the way to the Deep South. While a short-lived Volkswagen plant in Pennsylvania predated Marysville by a few years, it was Honda that established foundational patterns for the sector, choosing a greenfield site, operating nonunion, and hiring workers without industry experience. It was a successful formula that European and Korean carmakers adopted. By 2018, following a decade of rapid growth, *Automotive News* reported that over 49 percent of the vehicles made in North America were produced at foreign-owned plants, which were on track to manufacture the majority of vehicles made on the continent.[5]

The growth of this sector transformed America's auto industry, challenging the domestically owned Big Three (General Motors, Ford, and Chrysler). As early as 1989, the United Automobile Workers of America (UAW) noted that foreign-owned plants were "fast becoming part of the U.S. industrial landscape," experiencing more rapid growth than the union had anticipated.[6] Twelve years later, *The Harbour Report*, a respected industry publication, termed the arrival of the transplants an "onslaught." In 2008 the *Christian Science Monitor* noted that America's "other" auto industry was booming, while its domestically owned counterparts were struggling. By 2016 the Japanese Big Three (Toyota, Nissan, and Honda) built more cars in America than the at-home Big Three, which were increasingly dubbed the Detroit Three. In the same year, the Japanese Automobile Manufacturers' Association (JAMA) claimed that 75 percent of all Japanese cars and trucks sold in the United States were built in North America, up from 12 percent in 1986.[7] Unlike their domestic counterparts, the transplants—a term that became less common as the industry won acceptance—were significant exporters. Mercedes vehicles built in Alabama were sent to 135 countries, while 70 percent of the BMWs manufactured in South Carolina were shipped overseas.[8] Foreign automakers, summarized the Council of Governments in 2012, were "among the most-successful industries in the country."[9]

Relatively little is known about this large and important industry, and the current narrative has been too positive. The only book on the sector, A. J. Jacobs's *The New Domestic Automakers in the United States and Canada* (2016), is encyclopedic and laudatory, offering little critical analysis.[10] In the areas where the plants are located, the dominant voices are booster-minded elites who see the factories as economic prizes. This is especially true in the South, a region with a long history of recruiting outside investment, first from northern states and then globally. The region's press has also viewed the sector positively. "Rarely," summarizes journalism scholar Joe Atkins, "has a discouraging word been heard in the Southern press in the rise of 'Detroit South.'" Even the national press was overwhelmingly positive. In 2001, for example, the *Washington Post* heralded the arrival of a "New Automotive South" that was providing "high-tech" employment in a region "once known for its low-skilled, low-paying jobs and its isolation from the rest of the world." It was called a "historic shift."[11]

In *America's Other Automakers*, I argue that the industry's growth needs more critical interrogation.[12] Through case studies of key facilities, I demonstrate that there were significant tensions in all the communities where automakers moved, especially over land and the cost of incentives. The money, critics claimed, could have been better spent on poorly performing public services, particularly schools. The arrival of the first Japanese plants produced xenophobia and hostility, especially among older residents. Demand for jobs exceeded supply, ensuring that there were more losers than winners. Wherever carmakers went, they hired from a wide radius, disappointing locals, who also disliked increased congestion. There were major tensions over unionization, culminating in several bitterly contested elections. Clearly, transplant workers were not as contented as boosters claimed.[13]

Many residents also worried that their communities had become too reliant on the industry. As one economic developer admitted, these towns became "heavily dependent" on car factories. In particular, residents feared what would happen when the incentives ran out. As carmakers moved to Mexico, where labor costs were lower, these worries intensified. Between 2011 and 2016 Mexico received nine of the ten assembly plants announced by auto companies. Although it brought carmakers to new parts of the United States, the industry's mobility was a double-edged sword.[14]

As it interrogates the industry's history, *America's Other Automakers* addresses two key questions: Why did these companies locate where they did, and what did their arrival mean—especially in human terms—for the communities involved? In doing so, this study complements and advances scholarship on the auto industry, which has largely focused on other aspects of its development. In particular, the domestic companies have dominated scholars' attention, producing a narrative that concentrates heavily on the upper Midwest (especially Michigan). In seminal works, historians have paid close attention to labor relations at the Michigan-based Big Three, focusing especially on the upsurge in unionization in the 1930s and 1940s and the period of union strength that followed. Autoworkers' experiences on the line have also provided a focus. These works portray the earlier period, when the UAW was strong, as the industry's "heyday," providing the counterpoint for subsequent decline.[15]

Other scholars have duly focused on deindustrialization, particularly in the 1970s and 1980s. Again told from the Big Three's perspective, fine-grained studies by historians and sociologists talk of towns "abandoned," of retrenched autoworkers reaching the "end of the line" and saying "farewell to the factory."[16] Overall, the automobile industry is taken as a prime example of "postindustrial" America, a view furthered by recent studies—principally by journalists and industry insiders—on the industry's problems in the twenty-first century. The events of 2008, when General Motors and Chrysler were saved by a controversial $17 billion government bailout, heavily influenced these works. The transplants challenge this narrative, highlighting that not all of the industry contracted after the 1970s. Foreign-owned plants took off just as their domestic counterparts were declining. The sector also shows that the industry was spreading to new parts of the country, reaching deep into the heartland.[17]

Reflecting on these changes, some scholars have noticed the sector's importance. In the 1990s social scientists contributed management-driven studies looking at Japanese production practices and how they were transferred to other locations.[18] The globalization strategies of large automakers have also been studied, with some works focusing on joint ventures between the Big Three and overseas firms. Most work on the transplants has largely occurred in specialist articles or dissertations, however, and it is generally short on human agency.[19] In contrast, there are a few firsthand accounts, usually from reporters or politicians. They provide close-grained insights into early transplants yet lack wider context. Most of the case studies selected here—particularly the German and Korean firms—have not been examined in detail.[20]

Above all, scholarly examinations of why major automakers chose their locations have yet to be written. When they have addressed this question, most accounts stress the role of economic subsidies, especially in the South. In an overview of the sector's growth, for example, James C. Cobb emphasized the importance of "generous, few-strings-attached subsidies and incentives for new employers." When BMW came to South Carolina, he notes, the $130 million incentive package included a $1 a year lease on a $36 million piece of land, as well as generous worker training provisions.[21] Other accounts made similar observations. As James Rubenstein has written, Georgetown won the Toyota plant because of the "magnitude of Kentucky's incentive package." Rarely, however, has the decision-making process been explored in detail.[22]

The effort to lure automakers with incentives had a deeper historical resonance. As Cobb argued in his classic *The Selling of the South* (1982), starting in the 1930s the South began an organized "crusade" for industrial development, attracting new factories by "selling" the region's low wages and absence of unions. After World War II, boosters used incentives, including tax exemptions, to gain the edge over competing states. These strategies were precedents for the luring of foreign auto plants, which one recruiter termed "one of the prizes of economic development." As this account shows, these tactics were used by many states, not just southern ones. The South, however, had the most success, becoming one of the most globalized regions in the United States as a result.[23]

To be sure, incentives were important, and they increased overtime. While Kentucky's package for Toyota in the 1980s was around $149 million, this paled in comparison to the $325 million that brought Mercedes-Benz to Alabama in the 1990s or the $410 million that lured Kia to Georgia in the early 2000s.[24] Throughout this story, however, less obvious factors also explained why car plants ended up where they did. Location, especially proximity to interstate highways and consumer markets, was crucial. The availability of large numbers of suitable workers was also decisive; in several cases, including those of Toyota and Kia, executives turned down bigger incentive packages largely because of labor force considerations. The desire to avoid unions was also important. It influenced the shift to the Deep South, a region with the lowest levels of union density in the country. Both executives and economic developers admitted as much. According to Nathan Jung, who worked for Kia in Seoul before moving to the United States to manage a major supplier, "in Korea the union is such a big headache for the employers, and always they're asking something more." In contrast, the United States—especially the right-to-work states where the industry gravitated—was attractive because it was "union-free." The industry's move to the South, added Kristin Dziczek at the Center for Automotive Research, "was an anti-union strategy, like get away from the UAW, low wages, no unions."[25]

Human agency was also vital in explaining the industry's growth. The topic of industrial recruitment has usually been viewed in economic terms, yet this was a story about personal connections as much as it was about money. Throughout the rise of the sector, state officials, particularly the governors of the winning states, played a crucial role. In order to secure auto plants, these governors had to go the extra mile, something the winners excelled at. From James Rhodes of Ohio through Lamar Alexander of Tennessee, Martha Layne Collins of Kentucky, Carroll Campbell of South Carolina, and others, one factor was consistent: the winning governor was integrally involved in the recruitment process, forging close bonds with corporate decision makers. Personal contact was "the key," summarized Collins, reflecting on the recruitment of Toyota. "That's what I always stress when talking about economic development," she added. "It's more than just a site, more than the money; it's a relationship that you build, the trust, the expectation, the cooperation."[26]

Our second question—the impact of these plants on local communities—engages with broader debates about globalization. While contentious, globalization is, as Andrew McKevitt has noted, a "ubiquitous buzzword" that has influenced a huge amount of scholarship.[27] As James C. Cobb and William

Stueck have observed, for the South globalization was experienced not as "a fixed universal reality but as an ongoing process of accommodation and interaction between the local and the global." The industry's history illustrates this dynamic well, as residents adjusted to the presence of foreign automakers in their communities, but not without plenty of tension along the way.[28] The sector's history also illuminates the impact of globalization, showing that it extended into every corner of America. In many ways, this story epitomizes an era when "economic globalization" proceeded rapidly, with capital becoming internationalized. Thus, in 1973 12 percent of the world's economic output entered into international trade, but by 1996 this had increased to nearly 24 percent.[29]

This story also raises intriguing questions about globalization, which respected economist Jagdish Bhagwati has called a "defining issue" of our times. As Bhagwati has outlined, globalization has attracted polarizing reactions. Bhagwati is a prominent defender, asserting that globalization has produced economic growth and helped poorer nations. Others argue that the process has proceeded too fast, undermining local rights, feeding mounting social inequality, and leading to a deterioration of the environment. Most of this literature, however, focuses on the underdeveloped world and begins with the assumption that capital moves from the rich world to the poor to exploit workers there. The foreign automakers' story highlights another aspect of globalization that needs to be interrogated further. It demonstrates the messiness of any positive/negative dichotomy, as in this case globalization entailed the shifting of capital and production from a wealthy country to poor areas of the wealthiest country, with mixed consequences for those involved. Even in the areas that secured plants, the impact was complex and ambiguous; while there was economic growth, not all citizens welcomed the plants, and jobs were demanding and hard to secure.[30]

Driven by the need to be more critical, *America's Other Automakers* provides a history of the transplant sector that is based around studies of key facilities. The main focus is on seven big assembly plants that represented pivotal moments in the industry's development. The industry's growth occurred in waves; the Japanese arrived first in the 1980s, followed by luxury German carmakers in the 1990s, and then Korean manufacturers after 2000. Choosing examples from each wave, *America's Other Automakers* looks at foundational factories that paved the way for other companies, especially from the same country, to follow.[31]

Apart from Honda's Ohio plant—the first Japanese transplant—attention is centered on Nissan's factory in Tennessee, the first transplant to locate in the South and one that witnessed nationally publicized battles over unionization.[32] Also significant is Toyota's plant in Georgetown, Kentucky; Toyota became the largest carmaker in the world, and Georgetown was a flagship facility that was widely watched. In 1992, for example, the *New York Times* called the factory a "showcase" that had transplanted Japanese work habits to America. The plant was foundational. By 2017 Toyota had established four more assembly plants in North America, along with two engine plants (more than any other overseas carmaker). It had all, however, started in Georgetown.[33]

From the second wave, BMW's plant in Greer, South Carolina, is particularly important, as it represented the arrival of luxury European carmakers onto the scene.[34] It took the sector in a new direction, paving the way for other German—and European—carmakers to follow. As the *Associated Press* put it, while Honda, Nissan, and Toyota represented the first part of the story, "the second wave of transplants began with BMW's 1992 decision to build a plant near Spartanburg, S.C."[35] For company and state, the plant was a big deal; it represented the largest economic development project in South Carolina's history and was described by BMW CEO Eberhard von Kuenheim as "of great significance," especially as it was his firm's first plant outside Germany.[36]

Also from the second wave, another key development occurred in 1993, when Mercedes chose to locate a $300 million plant in Vance, Alabama. The move shocked observers due to Alabama's poverty, lack of automaking experience, and lingering associations with racial intolerance. Even in Alabama, few thought that Mercedes-Benz, a company with a closely guarded reputation for engineering excellence, would choose their state. "It would have been a *win* for Alabama just to have been mentioned as a finalist," admitted Dara Longgrear, an economic developer who worked on the bid.[37]

The plant thrived, putting Alabama on the map as an industry location. The factory paved the way for the state to secure other automaking facilities, including Toyota, Honda, and Hyundai plants. Other automakers subsequently located in neighboring Georgia and Mississippi. Mercedes's arrival, summarized Montgomery business leader Ellen McNair, was "a ground-breaking event," especially for Alabama. By 2017 that state—which had never produced a vehicle until Mercedes arrived—was one of the top five automaking states. Industry groups calculated that foreign automakers had created 81,715 jobs in the state. In 2016 the sector contributed $9.4 billion to Alabama's economy, 4.5 percent of its gross state product.[38]

America's Other Automakers concludes by examining the arrival of Korean automakers, focusing on Hyundai's plant in Montgomery, Alabama, which was established in 2002, and Kia's factory in West Point, Georgia, announced four years later. As Hyundai and Kia were sister companies—Hyundai was the major shareholder in Kia—their U.S. plants were linked. In order to share parts, the two plants were located eighty miles apart. There were, however, differences between the stories, especially as Kia chose to locate in Georgia, giving that state its first automotive transplant. Both factories epitomized the industry's move into new parts of the Deep South and the increasing importance of economic incentives. With initial investments of $1 billion and $1.2 billion, respectively, they were also massive operations. Their impact was considerable; in 2018, for example, Montgomery mayor Todd Strange described the Hyundai plant as "huge," adding that "in Montgomery we talk about before Hyundai, and after Hyundai, BH and AH."[39]

The Korean automakers grew at a time when most of the industry—particularly the Big Three—was contracting, epitomizing the strength and maturity of the transplant sector. For the Korean firms, it was a remarkable—and unique—turnaround. In the 1970s Hyundai Motors tottered on the brink of bankruptcy, surviving by making rebranded Fords and Mitsubishis. In 1997 Kia did go bankrupt, an outcome that led to its partnership with Hyundai. From small beginnings, both companies achieved astonishing growth, and their ability to manufacture in the United States was crucial. Helped by their U.S. plants, between 2007 and 2017 the Hyundai-Kia group more than doubled its North American production output. By 2018 it was South Korea's largest automaker and the second largest in Asia.[40]

No issue better illustrated the tension that these factories produced than the battle over unionization. Boosters—and the press—repeatedly portrayed the transplants as model factories staffed by contented workers. In 2003 a detailed article by Knight Ridder reporter Jamie Butters was typical. "The plants have had almost no labor strife to speak of," he claimed. "Highly paid workers embrace the strategies of automakers that have brought the jobs to their communities." Within the communities where plants were located, the press also suppressed criticism. "As Nissan goes, so goes Rutherford County," warned the *Rutherford County Daily News Journal* in 2000 as the UAW organized. "People should remember what that company means to our economic well-being." Workers who were interested in the union faced an uphill battle. "The newspapers and television treated Nissan like heroes," summarized Smyrna worker Tracy Reed. "They glorified them."[41]

The union issue illustrates why the transplant sector needs to be approached critically. From the industry's earliest days, unionization was contested. This reflected the fact that when the first transplants were established, the U.S. industry was overwhelmingly organized. In April 1982 the UAW had over 1.2 million members, making it one of the largest and most powerful unions in America. "Our membership is concentrated in automobile manufacturing and it's [sic] parts suppliers," wrote UAW leader Douglas Fraser to Honda's Kawashima. "*We represent virtually 100% of all car assembly workers in North America.*" Confident of its powers, the UAW pressed Japanese automakers to establish plants in the United States rather than relying on imports because it thought it could organize those plants.[42]

Organizing the transplants was vital to the UAW, which could not afford to have nonunion factories undercutting conditions at the Big Three. Behind the scenes, UAW leaders pressured the top management of Honda and then Toyota to recognize the union without elections. In protracted negotiations that are uncovered here, both companies intimated that they would work with the UAW but then went back on their promises. In contrast, Nissan's North American managers, given more autonomy by the Japanese, declared from the beginning that their Tennessee plant would be nonunion. In response, the union launched a high-profile campaign to organize Smyrna, culminating in a hard-fought election in July 1989. This was a climactic battle, and *America's Other Automakers* uses new records, including the UAW's files, to expose that apart from corporate opposition, which the union blamed publicly, its defeat reflected internal divisions, unanticipated staffing problems, and the logistical challenge of organizing a big new facility. Although Nissan workers had many grievances, the company also fostered loyalty by not laying off workers and by expanding the plant.[43] In October 2001 the union contested another election but lost again, hurt by the unexpected economic downturn that occurred after 9/11.[44]

Organizing continued both at Nissan and elsewhere. UAW staff were buoyed by the support they received from workers, who were not the happy team members that industry supporters portrayed. The UAW reported strong demand for organization among workers, despite corporate and community opposition. "All across these assemblies in the South we literally can't keep up, because there's so much interest, with workers," declared UAW southern director Gary Casteel in 2016. "I've never seen more interested workers," added lead organizer Richard Bensinger in the same year. While the union may have overstated its support, there was more to the transplant experience than the dominant narrative of contented communities and grateful workers.[45]

A more analytical approach is also important because it focuses attention on both the industry's costs and its benefits. Stressing that automotive jobs were well-paid and highlighting the industry's considerable symbolic value, elites justified the incentive packages. Their powerful voices dominated perceptions. According to Ellen McNair, a vice president of the Montgomery Chamber of Commerce who was integrally involved in attracting car plants, "whatever" the cost of incentive packages, "it was worth every dime." Auto plants, added Steve Sewell of the Economic Development Partnership of Alabama (EDPA), were the "crown jewel in economic development." They created a massive initial investment, especially with the need for construction jobs, as well as a "tremendous ripple effect" from suppliers. Almost no other industry created as many jobs in related sectors, a point illustrated by industry-sponsored studies. Prepared by the University of Alabama for the EDPA, one 2006 study claimed that Mercedes's plant had created 4,376 jobs plus more than 18,000 jobs in other sectors. The company was also Alabama's largest exporter.[46]

Industry supporters made legitimate points. Transplants brought economic growth to the areas they located in, and most factories expanded significantly. Mercedes had pledged to create fifteen hundred jobs, yet it soon exceeded these projections. With most workers earning more than they ever had, jobs were highly prized.[47] Benefits, however, had a cost. There were usually at least twenty applicants for each position. Transplant workers were time-poor and endured heavy workloads, with high rates of occupational injury. Assembly workers were overwhelmingly young, a telling sign, and workers related that they could only survive a few years on the line. Over time, companies hired more "temps," who were paid less and excluded from the benefits given to permanent workers.[48]

In a broader context, there were other costs. Manufacturing in the United States allowed foreign automakers to gain market share, hurting the Big Three. By 2003, overseas manufacturers, through imports and domestic production, accounted for almost half of the American market, and Toyota was bigger than Chrysler. By 2009, the sector was so large that it was mentioned in President Obama's framework agreement, which specified how GM and Chrysler should restructure following federal bailouts. The plan was even designed to help these companies achieve "full competitiveness with foreign transplants." In order to compete, the domestics insisted that they had to outsource more jobs, especially to Mexico. During the 2016 presidential election, Donald Trump made car production a "key part" of his campaign to "Make America Great Again." Criticizing companies who outsourced, Trump promised to bring automotive jobs back to the United States. As was often the case, the industry was at the heart of American history.[49]

Ultimately, the rise of this industry is an important story with far-reaching consequences. Within forty years, the sector grew to occupy a prominent place in American life. When foreign-owned firms first established factories, few could have imagined that the sector would become so big. The first transplant, Volkswagen's plant in Westmoreland, Pennsylvania, closed after a few years. Set up slightly later, it was Honda's factory in Ohio that endured. As UAW president Owen Bieber recalled, Honda was significant because it was the first transplant that "really got going." Still, VW's example was significant partly because Honda—and others—learned from it. VW was one of the many precedents that the industry drew upon. Although the sector took off in the 1980s, its roots went deeper, reflecting strong forces that pushed companies to manufacture in the biggest auto market in the world.[50]

CHAPTER ONE

Build It Here
The Sector's Roots

In 1955 Volkswagen began examining sites for a U.S. assembly plant. The factory was needed to produce the Beetle, the first imported car to gain mass appeal in America. When the 25-horsepower subcompact was introduced into the United States in 1949, just two were sold. In 1955, however, almost twenty-nine thousand were sold. As Leslie Kendall of the Petersen Automotive Museum put it, after a slow start the car "burst like wildfire. It was the right car for the time. It did for a lot of Americans what the Model T did for generations before." Foreign sales soon exceeded domestic ones, and the United States was a lead market. With its Wolfsburg factory unable to satisfy demand, Volkswagen acquired a hardly used plant from the Studebaker-Packard Corporation in North Brunswick, New Jersey, and got ready to make cars. Everything seemed to be on track; VW announced plans to produce up to one hundred thousand Beetles at the site, negotiated contracts with suppliers, and predicted that it would sell sixty thousand vehicles in the United States in 1956. At the last minute, however, following a feasibility study, the company claimed that American production costs were too high. Plans to build VWs in New Jersey were abandoned.[1]

The episode highlighted important points. It showed that while VW's plant in Westmoreland, Pennsylvania—which began production in 1978—was often seen as the first foreign-owned car plant, the industry's roots went back further.[2] Even before VW's failed attempt, European craft manufacturers had assembled cars in the United States, often from imported kits. After World War II, when car ownership became a mass phenomenon, establishing a U.S. factory was related to levels of import penetration. Volkswagen was the first foreign automaker to achieve mass success in the United States; in 1966, for example, it sold over four hundred thousand cars in the country, securing a bigger market share than American Motors Corporation (AMC), America's fourth largest automaker. Thus, it would be Volkswagen that first explored—and achieved—U.S. production. Operating for a decade, Westmoreland was an important and little-known chapter in the industry's history. Its fate—especially the multiple problems it experienced in maintaining quality and dealing with labor strife—influenced other automakers, which learned from its reputation as a "flop" and did things differently. The failed precedents highlight that the sector's history was not—as its promoters portrayed—one of constant growth and success. From the start, tension and failure were part of the mix.[3]

The Japanese automakers that followed VW did so after many years of investigation, including feasibility studies that were soon shelved. As the North Brunswick and Westmoreland episodes highlighted, committing to American production was risky, and foreign automakers soon got cold feet. By the late 1970s, however, a range of pressures—especially a sustained rise in import sales, the introduction of quota legislation in the U.S. congress, and UAW calls for the Japanese to "build it here"—made American production possible. The most innovative of the Japanese Big Three, Honda, broke the mold. Once its plant was running, Nissan and Toyota tentatively followed.[4]

VW built on little-known precedents, some of them from the industry's earliest days. Building cars started with groundbreaking developments in Europe, especially Germany. In 1885, Karl Benz built the first practical car powered by an internal-combustion engine, patenting the design. In 1893, production of four-wheeled Benz models followed. Helped by Benz's example, European manufacturers dominated early production. A luxury car industry developed, serving the rich in major European cities. Americans—especially East Coast elites—also wanted these cars. Responding to this, at the turn of the twentieth century, four French companies—De Dion–Bouton; Charron, Girardot et Voigt; Mors; and Berliet—built small numbers of cars in the United States, mainly in the Northeast. Between 1904 and 1907, the British Napier Motor Car Company also assembled cars under license in Boston, while Daimler made a few "American Mercedes" vehicles at a plant in Astoria, New York. While all of these ventures were small and short-lived, they highlighted the advantages of producing vehicles in the market where they were sold.[5]

A few years later, other precedents followed. From 1910 to 1918, Fiat built cars and trucks in Poughkeepsie, New York, before it fell victim to the economic turmoil that hit Italy at the end of World War I. More significantly, in 1921 British carmaker Rolls-Royce started making cars in Springfield, Massachusetts. Within four years, 1,701 Springfield Ghosts had been assembled at the Massachusetts factory, which employed 1,200 people. In 1931, however, production ended. As the *New York Times* reported, Rolls was hurt by the cost of converting vehicles to left-hand drive, along with financial problems at its U.S. coach builder (Brewster) and the impact of the 1929 stock market crash. Even after the crash, other companies tried American production. Between 1930 and 1934, for example, Austin Motor Company built cars at a plant near

Pittsburgh. Retailing for $445, the Austin Bantam initially did well, but the company became another victim of the Great Depression.[6]

The early ventures were concentrated in the industrialized Northeast. Here, plenty of workers and suppliers were available, and vehicles could be delivered to customers nearby. The importance of labor force availability, along with proximity to the consumer, was already clear. There were other parallels with subsequent developments. A major impetus for these early factories was the desire to lower production costs; in the 1910s, for example, imported cars faced a 45 percent tariff, but domestic assembly—even of imported kits—avoided this tax. These early automakers also helped to establish foreign cars as aspirational goods, a reputation that postwar importers, particularly from Europe, capitalized on.[7]

Compared to the domestic auto industry, the foreign-owned ventures were tiny. America has long been a land shaped—and defined—by the automobile, and Americans led the way in putting the car into the hands of the people. In 1908, Michigan entrepreneur Henry Ford launched the Model T, the first mass-market car in the world. "I am going to democratize the automobile," declared Ford. "When I'm through, everybody will be able to afford one, and about everyone will have one." True to his word, in 1913 Ford revolutionized American society by introducing the moving assembly line and the five-dollar workday. By 1923, the company was selling 1.8 million Model Ts in the United States and sending many overseas. Workers—largely a combination of poor European immigrants and impoverished whites and blacks from the South—flocked to Detroit to work in the burgeoning auto industry. Founded in 1908, General Motors soon emerged as a major competitor for Ford, spurring both companies to new heights. Under the stewardship of Alfred P. Sloan Jr., who became president and CEO in 1923, GM grew rapidly, promising to "build a car for every purse and purpose." GM and Ford were joined by Chrysler, which was incorporated in 1925 under the stewardship of Walter Chrysler, a former GM executive. By 1929, the United States produced 85 percent of the world's cars, and half of American families owned one, a figure that would not be reached in the U.K. until 1980. "The automobile," wrote historian Eric Foner in reference to interwar America, "was the backbone of economic growth." Although the Great Depression of the 1930s hurt the Big Three, it also allowed them to solidify their grip on the market, as many smaller competitors went out of business.[8]

During World War II, most auto plants were converted to military production, but after the war the United States enjoyed two decades of economic growth, helping the industry. Between 1946 and 1960, the gross national product doubled, and many of the benefits flowed to ordinary citizens through rising wages and increasing car ownership. By 1960, 80 percent of American families owned at least one car, and 14 percent had two or more. Virtually all of them were manufactured in the United States, chiefly in the upper Midwest, where a vast industry powered Detroit, a city that reached its peak population of almost two million in the 1950s. The Big Three dominated the market, with GM—still guided by Sloan—being a major force in American life. In the early 1960s, GM's market share climbed past 50 percent, prompting antitrust authorities to warn the company to "settle for no more than 50% of the market and keep out of trouble." The biggest corporation in the world, GM was often viewed as emblematic of the United States, a phenomenon summed up by the famous dictum of company president "Engine Charlie" Wilson: "I thought what was good for our country was good for General Motors, and vice versa."[9]

Prosperity facilitated stable labor relations. Founded in 1935, the UAW set about organizing the Big Three, bringing GM to heel through the famous sit-down strike of 1936–37 in Flint, Michigan. Shortly afterward, sit-downs also organized Chrysler, but Ford held out until 1941. Following World War II, the UAW used the industry's prosperity to win high wages and good benefits. In 1949 and 1950, the union—now one of the strongest and most influential in America—negotiated pension and insurance funds that were free of employer control. It also secured an escalator clause that provided for automatic wage increases, protecting workers from inflation. In its 1955 contracts with Ford, the UAW added a modified form of annual income. In the years that followed, these supplementary unemployment benefits were increased to replace as much as 95 percent of lost weekly income, providing close to a guaranteed annual wage. After 1955, when pattern-setting negotiations with the big companies were conducted every three years, the UAW used the strong economic conditions to secure further wage and benefit improvements. As the union's executive board summarized in 1964, its "historic policy" was "to win for UAW members and their families a greater equity out of the fruits of advancing technology and the profitability of the industry and not out of the pockets of American consumers." With the industry in an "extremely favorable economic position," it could afford to share the wealth.[10]

During the long postwar boom, the Big Three were so dominant that they found it hard to satisfy demand. For workers, jobs were easy to come by. The story of nineteen-year-old Al Benchich, who started at a Chevrolet plant in Detroit in 1970, was indicative. "I was going to school here at Wayne State [University], and I was running out of money, and it was really easy then to get a job," he recalled. "My car broke down, I coasted into the personnel parking lot in Chevrolet One, and I was waiting for my friend to come help me get my car going. I put in an application, and they called me in three days later." It would be the start of a thirty-seven-year career at GM. In his early years, Benchich remembered high wages and generous benefits—including the ability to retire after thirty years—but also saw warning signs. "I started at production, and if there was a defect and you brought it to the supervisor's attention, he'd just say: 'Keep running 'em,' because the numbers were what was important, not the quality, but the numbers. And we were building crappy cars."[11]

Beneath a facade of market dominance, there were other vulnerabilities. The Big Three made large, gas-guzzling cars—which were profitable—restricting consumer choice. "Whatever Detroit built, America bought," summarized industry writer Paul Ingrassia, "partly because it didn't have much choice." The strategy left domestic automakers vulnerable to competitors who operated differently, especially when fuel prices increased. Even in the 1950s—often seen as the Big Three's heyday—some consumers, particularly young people, demanded something different. The Beetle, which VW imported to help its factory in cash-strapped West Germany, led the way. In 1959, VW became the first foreign automaker to sell over one hundred thousand cars in America in a year.[12]

Japanese competition followed. In October 1957, Japan's largest car producer, Toyota, entered the U.S. market. Eight months later, Nissan followed suit. For a while, both companies struggled, as their products were underpowered and poorly adapted to American conditions. Nissan sold just 123 cars in its first year in the United States, Toyota 288. Both companies, which had been rebuilt after the devastation of World War II, adapted. Between 1960 and 1963, Toyota even halted imports, investing in new technology and improving its production processes. The company returned with the Corona, a car that— as *The Harbour Report* put it—"met all the demands of the American market." The subcompact Corolla, which acquired a reputation for reliability and affordability, was introduced a few years later. Fueled by the company's philosophy of continuous improvement (*kaizen*), U.S. sales took off. In 1965, Toyota sold 6,404 cars, jumping to 309,363 in 1971. Nissan's sales reached 331,203 in 1975, making it the top importer in the country. In the early 1970s, other Japanese automakers, including Honda and Mitsubishi, joined the fray. By 1971, Japan had a $3.2 billion trade surplus with the United States.[13]

A fuel crisis also helped the Japanese. The energy shocks of 1974 and 1979 reduced demand for big, large-engined cars, leading to a market in the United States that was more like the rest of the world. In 1974, a time when America imported one-third of its oil, Arab states retaliated for Western support of Israel in its war with Egypt and Syria by quadrupling the price of oil and freezing exports to the United States for several months. The shock for many Americans—who had to line up for gas that often ran out—was immense. The second oil crisis, related to the Iranian revolution of 1979, further transformed consumer preferences. Well-established in the market, foreign brands that made small cars, particularly Honda, Nissan, Toyota, and Volkswagen, were the chief beneficiaries. Imports rose sharply, reaching 15 percent of the market in 1978 and 28 percent in the third quarter of 1980. After producing the same types of cars for decades, the U.S. manufacturers struggled to adapt. "In its heart-of-hearts Detroit didn't like small cars," summarized *The Harbour Report.* "'Small cars equal small profits,' the thinking went."[14]

Even before the first crisis, the leading importers were considering U.S. production. In January 1973—over twelve years before Toyota committed to a U.S. plant—the *Industrial Review of Japan* reported that the Aichi-based firm was conducting a feasibility study of American production, especially for the popular Corona. The article noted that while setting up an American factory would require "long, meticulous calculations," it was Toyota's "long-range policy line" to do so.[15]

From the beginning, the UAW privately encouraged these moves. An internationalist who later became the first U.S. ambassador to the People's Republic of China, Leonard Woodcock, led the way. President of the UAW from 1970 to 1977, Woodcock called the proposed Toyota plant "a most desirable development" that could reduce "protectionist" sentiment in the United States and help avert an "international trade war."[16] In August 1973, Woodcock wrote Toyota president Eiji Toyoda and Nissan boss Katsuji Kawamata—who was also considering U.S. production—and encouraged them to build cars in America. "As you will recall from our conversations last October in Tokyo," he summarized, "the UAW would look with considerable favour on the establishment of Japanese-owned automobile productive facilities in the United States." The union pointed to precedents, noting that between 1968 and 1970 Japanese companies—especially steel mills and electronics firms—invested more than $100 million in the United States, two to three times more than in preceding years. At a time when all auto plants in the United States were unionized, the UAW reasoned that foreign-owned factories would be too. To ensure that this was the case, they sought dialogue. As staffer Herman Rebhan put it, the UAW offered Toyota and Nissan "full cooperation in establishing assembly facilities in North America, at least in the labor relations field."[17]

Despite the encouragement, these little-known moves fell flat. For several reasons, neither Nissan nor Toyota was ready for U.S. production at this time. In 1971, the "Nixon Shock," a White House–driven initiative that devalued the dollar against the yen for the first time since 1949, hurt both companies. As the yen-to-dollar exchange value fell from 360 to 300, the export-oriented car industry was hit hard. Between 1971 and 1972, Toyota's American sales stagnated, barely increasing from 309,363 to 311,278. While it helped them penetrate the U.S. market, the 1973–74 oil crisis also hurt both companies' global earnings. For other reasons, Toyota and Nissan needed time. It was only in 1966, for example, that Toyota had produced more cars than commercial vehicles. There were concerns about margins, as the average car cost between $1,000 and $1,500 more to produce in the United States than in Japan. The Japanese also doubted the quality of American labor and worried that workers would not accept Japanese production methods. Furthermore, neither company was known for risk-taking. Reflecting its rural roots and tight family control of decision-making, Toyota had a particularly conservative corporate culture. Replying to Woodcock, Toyoda admitted that his company had not committed to U.S. production. "Although much discussion has been made," he noted, "it is still continuing, on the matter, I have to confess that we have not yet arrived at the decision to make a substantial investment in the US for a local production of vehicles." Instead, Toyota would continue to prepare for the "milestone" of local production.[18]

After 1974, sales rebounded, and Nissan and Toyota again investigated making cars in the United States. In June 1976, Woodcock was told by the JAMA that the two firms were exploring the possibility of establishing American factories. Both companies, however, wanted to increase their U.S. sales and "rationalize their model mix" before committing. In November, the UAW also received confidential reports that top Toyota officials had met with their American legal counsel, as well as with Volkswagen managers, to discuss "VW's experience in dealing with state governments" in the United States. By this time, Toyota and Nissan were importing five models, and their sales through October were 292,602 and 234,000 units, respectively. Looking at these figures, the UAW predicted that American plants were only a matter of time. "Current estimates by various sources agree that 400,000 units is the minimum efficient scale for subcompact car assembly," reported staffer Helen Kramer. "The Japanese could reach this now if they could run the compact pickup trucks on the same line as passenger cars."[19]

Other factors paved the way for the sector. Unlike most consumer goods—such as shoes, clothes, electronics, or even household appliances—cars were very heavy, making shipping costs prohibitive. Producing vehicles in the market that bought them also avoided damaging currency fluctuations, a factor that was easily overlooked. "It's a huge issue, especially with the Japanese producers," summarized one analyst at the Center for Automotive Research. "You could be making vehicles very cost effectively in Japan, but the currency's out of whack, so you're selling them at a loss." While the United States was a relatively high-wage economy, wage costs were not a huge deterrent, comprising only 10 percent of production costs. Manufacturing in the United States could also help foreign automakers—particularly the Japanese—gain consumer acceptance, especially as it could be used in advertising.[20]

In the 1970s, an era in which economic globalization took off, large automakers began to establish factories outside their home countries. The first overseas factories were generally established in lower-wage markets, especially those with less domestic competition. In 1975, Toyota set up a plant in Algeria, while Honda established motorcycle assembly operations in Iran, New Zealand, Peru, and Yugoslavia. In 1975 alone, Japanese companies invested $879 million in overseas manufacturing operations, a symptom of the era that Woodcock grasped. "We live today in an age of international business," he told a Japanese audience in October, "that is to say, dominated by international commerce, international finance, and, lastly, international production." By 1975, Nissan was assembling cars in twenty-seven foreign countries, Toyota in seventeen.[21]

Within the United States, mounting anti-Japanese sentiment also increased the pressure to "build it here." As the American industry hit hard times during the oil crisis, many citizens blamed imported cars, especially from Japan. Between February 1973 and February 1974, sales of Japanese cars in the United States jumped 54 percent, largely because the fuel shortage increased demand for economical cars. In March 1974, Woodcock told Japanese counterpart Ichiro Shioji that the UAW was facing "severe problems." GM's sales had dropped 35 percent in a few months, and 160,000 UAW members were unemployed. In early 1974, the UAW's executive board responded by voting for emergency import quota legislation. The union proposed that until September 1975, importers' share of the U.S. market be held to the same average share it had commanded between 1971 and 1973 (about 15 percent). As Woodcock acknowledged in a subsequent speech in Japan, the action exposed the limits of international solidarity. "Our unions operate in a national context," he admitted.[22]

This action was viewed dimly in Japan, where executives wanted to avoid trade friction. Woodcock was caught in the middle. In an awkward letter to Shioji, he admitted that there was a lot of "insular" feeling in his union. "Rest assured," he added, "that such sentiments will not reflect my own deep sympathies for you or the long-term interests of Japanese auto workers."[23] At the UAW's international executive board meeting in January 1974, however, Woodcock explained that members were experiencing "terrible layoffs," and he had to react. "The membership of the Union is in considerable distress," he noted. At the grassroots level, anti-Japanese sentiment also increased. "Many union people, you couldn't pull a Toyota in their driveway," summarized Al Benchich, recalling these years. "They would run you off." Some local unions even bought old Japanese cars, usually Toyotas, parking them outside. Members and bystanders would then pay one or two dollars each to hit the car with a sledgehammer. "It was a way to let their anger out on the Japanese," recalled Benchich.[24]

Despite Woodcock's efforts, the UAW's policies strained relations. The JAMA worried about "the growth of protectionist sentiment by the UAW." When Herman Rebhan, the UAW's director of international affairs, visited Japan in April 1974 to explain the union's position, he received a lot of publicity. The Japanese Ministry of International Trade and Industry, for example, noted that it was keeping a "careful watch" on developments. Rebhan could not stop the UAW being cast in a negative light, especially as the U.S. government and American automakers were not—at this stage—seeking curbs on Japanese cars. For a union that wanted to secure recognition from Japanese automakers, it was a damaging precedent.[25]

The biggest automakers were particularly alienated, with even publicity-shy Toyota criticizing the UAW. As the *Wall Street Journal* reported, the union's actions were "especially upsetting" to Japanese carmakers, who counted on exports to offset the effects of a domestic slump. Largely because of the oil crisis, car registrations in Japan dropped 34 percent in March 1974 compared to a year before. Japanese automakers believed that their products were at a competitive disadvantage in the United States due to successive dollar devaluations and sharp inflation in Japan. Between September 1973 and September 1974, the inflation level in the United States was 12 percent, but in Japan it was twice that. The Japanese pointed out that domestic labor laws did not allow companies to lay off workers during slack periods. As a result of all these factors, corporate profits had nosedived. Japanese executives were also annoyed that members of Congress from the Midwest, particularly Michigan, supported quotas. Refuting arguments put forward by these politicians, the Japanese insisted that American cars sold poorly in Japan not because of import barriers but because of their poor quality, large size, and lack of right-hand-drive models.[26]

Further tensions followed. In the spring of 1976, the UAW supported a Treasury Department investigation into allegations that cars from Japan—as well as from Europe and Canada—had been sold in the United States "at prices lower than their home country sales." When the enquiry made a "tentative negative determination" against Toyota and Nissan, these firms pressed the UAW not to support the case.[27] In April, JAMA managing director Toshio Nakamura also wrote Woodcock to express concern about the "posture of the UAW" in the dumping enquiry. The union, he urged, should not "in any way join forces with those who are pushing these allegations against Japanese imports." In response, Woodcock defended his union. "We continue to stand for essentially free trade," he wrote. "But that trade must be carried on in a fair and legal way." These events highlight how the UAW, long a supporter of free trade, began to change as imports increased.[28]

In 1979–80, as fallout from the second oil crisis led to recession in the United States, the Japanese automakers faced renewed pressure to restrict imports and establish American plants. In February 1980, more than 170,000 U.S. autoworkers were on indefinite layoff, and sales of foreign cars were at their highest level in history. "The domestic industry is going through one of its worst sales slumps since the mid-1970s," summarized the *New York Times*. Between 1978 and 1979, Big Three sales dropped by more than 1 million. The situation was acute at Chrysler, which had to be rescued from bankruptcy by a $1.5 billion federal bailout. Citing the crisis, industry leaders now called for quotas if the Japanese did not accept "voluntary" restrictions. The Japanese, summarized GM boss Roger Smith in 1980, should "examine their export policies very carefully in the light of the current political and economic situation and act accordingly."[29]

Reflecting the industry's lobbying power, politicians took up the case. Among them was Charles A. Vanik (D-OH), the influential chair of the House Trade Subcommittee, who headed calls for the Japanese to impose "voluntary" curbs or face quotas. After the Big Three reported losses of over $4 billion in 1980, pressure increased. In that year, import penetration reached 29 percent, another high. In early 1981, both the chair of the Senate Trade Subcommittee, Senator John C. Danforth (R-MO), and the ranking Democrat, Lloyd Bentsen of Texas, pledged to introduce legislation to restrict Japanese auto imports. A couple of months later, Senator Bob Dole (R-KS), who chaired the Senate Finance Committee, told the Japanese parliament that between sixty-five and seventy senators—a clear majority—would back a bill to cut annual imports to 1.6 million cars.[30]

The industry's size and its talismanic importance help explain this response. In 1981, automobile production and services accounted for 8.5 percent of America's gross national product. More than four million Americans owed their employment to the car, including around eight hundred thousand in manufacturing. The industry's production capacity was also vital for defense capability and a symbol of America's global power. "The problems of the auto industry," summarized an adviser to Ohio senator John Glenn that year, "are of fundamental importance to the State of Ohio, the economic strength of the U.S., and the future shape of international trade."[31] The White House also responded. In 1980, President Carter set up the Automobile Industry Committee, bringing together representatives of government, industry, and labor to tackle the industry's problems. During the presidential election, Carter also promised autoworkers that he would meet with Japanese prime minister Zenko Suzuki and secure import limits. After Carter lost the election—partly because of perceived ineffectiveness in tackling America's economic problems—Ronald Reagan took up the issue.[32]

The new administration needed to respond to industry concerns, especially as many "Reagan Democrats" were autoworkers. As a result, Reagan allowed the auto industry more protection than less emblematic industries such as textiles and electronics, which were also hit hard by Asian imports.[33] In May 1981, following a visit to Tokyo by U.S. trade representative Bill Brock, the Japanese agreed to limit auto exports. The decision was made shortly before Suzuki was due to meet with Reagan. It also came after trade minister Rokusuke Tanaka—citing the UAW's actions—appealed to automakers to hold exports to the level of the previous year.[34] As a result, in May 1981 the auto companies and the Japanese government agreed to a voluntary export restraint (VER) quota. In return for a presidential veto of a congressional local content bill—a

UAW-endorsed measure that limited the foreign content of cars sold in America—the Japanese agreed to restrict their annual number of U.S. imports to 1.68 million in fiscal 1981–82, a number that was retroactive to April 1, 1981. After this, imports were limited to no more than 17.5 percent of the annual demand for cars between 1981 and 1989. In 1982, as the American industry reported its lowest sales in two decades, the agreement was extended for a third year. (Similar restrictions were introduced in Canada.) As a result, the Japanese lost between 250,000 and 500,000 U.S. sales a year.[35]

In Japan, there was concern. Many doubted whether the restrictions would help the American industry, which was viewed as inefficient and uncompetitive. The press also referred to the power imbalance between the two nations, suggesting that the United States had pressured—or bullied—Japan to accept quotas. *Asahi Shimbun* (Asahi evening news) thought that the agreement "left a bad precedent in solving trade problems," while economic daily *Nihon Keizai Shimbun* (Japan economics newspaper) claimed that the terms of the deal had been "forced on us by Washington." Even Eiji Toyoda claimed that his company had "no choice but to comply."[36] Ironically, in practice the quotas often made Japanese cars more attractive. Some customers paid premiums to secure popular models, particularly the Honda Accord and Toyota Camry. The outcome further illustrated the advantage of producing these models locally.[37]

The Japanese now faced intense pressure to build assembly plants in the United States. As *The Harbour Report* observed, the UAW "demanded" that the Japanese build cars in America. Imports were eroding its membership, and the union hoped to organize the new plants. According to the union, jobs would also be created for its members. While they had different motives, the domestic firms took a similar position. "The Big Three also wanted the Japanese to build cars in the U.S., fully expecting that the transplants would have trouble competing on a 'level playing field,'" noted *The Harbour Report*. Believing that the Japanese advantage primarily derived from lower wage rates, the Big Three supported transplant production.[38]

The UAW led the charge. Born in Scotland into a family of union activists, Douglas Fraser was more adversarial than Woodcock, whom he replaced in 1977. Early in his presidency, Fraser declared that he would "take off the gloves" and force the Japanese to build factories in America. The comments concerned Toyota and Nissan, which argued that the Big Three's problems were primarily due to their failure to anticipate demand for smaller cars. Both companies, however, confirmed that they were considering American production.[39] In 1980, Fraser spent a week in Japan talking with major carmakers about building plants in the United States. Just before he left, he promised union members that he would demand that "foreign companies that benefit from our markets contribute to them by building products here." Traveling to Japan at the invitation of U.S. ambassador Mike Mansfield, Fraser met with top executives of Honda, Mitsubishi, Nissan, and Toyota.[40]

For Fraser, the issue was simple; an increase in Japanese-made cars had been responsible for widespread job losses, and it had to stop. In April 1980, the UAW's figures showed that sixty thousand Chrysler and AMC workers were receiving adjustment assistance under the 1974 Trade Act, and petitions were pending for over two hundred thousand GM and Ford workers.[41] Responding to these figures, Fraser accused the Japanese of "a callous display of economic vulturism" by continuing to import heavily. "We have repeatedly urged the Japanese to follow the lead of Volkswagen and build plants here in the United States," he wrote. Fraser promised members that he would get action. "We intend to raise our voices in Washington loud enough for the echoes to bounce off the walls in Tokyo," he declared.[42] Privately, Fraser went further, calling the Japanese untrustworthy and claiming that their culture was "too homogenous." Because they had achieved significant market penetration, the idea of driving them out was "idiotic." U.S. factories were the answer.[43]

Within Japan, there were also calls to establish plants in the United States. As the conservative magazine *Shokun!* (Gentlemen!) noted, building these factories offered "one of the promising ways to mitigate the Japan-US trade friction." Following lobbying by the UAW, Japan's Confederation of Japan Automobile Workers' Unions also supported the move, though in less forceful terms. In February 1980, Shioji called on Toyota and Nissan to build plants in the United States. "Internationalization of Japan's auto industry is unavoidable," he declared. "An advance to the U.S. will benefit the entire auto industry in Japan."[44]

Along with quotas, the UAW pressed for domestic content legislation. Accusing Toyota and Nissan of "absolutely outrageous" conduct, Fraser declared that the UAW would push for strict restrictions on foreign content.[45] In 1981 and 1982, the UAW was the major promoter of the Fair Practices in Automotive Products Act, which required all manufacturers selling more than one hundred thousand cars a year in the United States to use an increasing percentage of American parts and labor, rising to a maximum of 90 percent by 1986. The bill attracted more than 220 cosponsors, including House Speaker Tip O'Neill. According to the *New York Times*, it was "the most bitterly contested trade bill to hit Congress in years," especially as the Reagan administration was opposed. The bill was resisted by Honda of Ohio and by most domestic manufacturers (who were increasingly outsourcing parts jobs), as well as by top Japanese-based executives. In 1982 and 1983, the House passed the bill, triggering "deep concern" in Japan, but it fell short in the Republican-controlled Senate. As a result, the Japanese were able to establish assembly plants free of content restrictions, addressing a major concern.[46]

The biggest Japanese manufacturer, however, still hung back. Just weeks after Nissan finally announced it would build its first American plant, UAW staffer Howard Young reported that he had met with consultants "doing one of Toyota's studies regarding possible production in the U.S." Toyota, whose team production structure was very different from the single job classifications used in the United States, was concerned about "the feasibility of using the Japanese system here." Worried that American workers could not adjust, Toyota was not ready to take the plunge.[47]

In retrospect, the call to "build it here" appears ironic. UAW leaders, in particular, failed to appreciate that foreign-owned factories would be run differently, with team production systems that increased productivity and lowered costs. The Japanese Big Three took their time because they wanted to ensure they could transplant these ideas to America, operating the Toyota, Honda, or Nissan "way." To boost their chances of success, all three companies located in rural areas and hired inexperienced workers whom they could train from scratch. Even at the time, studies highlighted that it was the production system rather than wage rates that gave the Japanese the edge. As a 1982 *Harbour Report* investigation found, the Japanese automakers only required 84 hours of labor to produce a subcompact car, compared to 145 hours for the Big Three. The study contradicted the "widely held" belief that lower wages were the reason for the Japanese advantage. Rather, they only accounted for one-third of the difference. By locating in nontraditional states and avoiding unionization, the Japanese extended their cost advantage, transforming the industry.[48]

UAW hopes that foreign-owned plants would help their members proved misplaced in other ways. Even at the time, there were warning signs. Privately, union officials who toured Japanese car plants admitted that quality was higher than in American factories, giving these vehicles a compelling advantage. In the early 1980s, notes in the UAW's files following a visit to a Toyota factory in Japan were representative. Comments included "Quality—Fits—Finish beautiful" and "metal finish quality excellent." In terms of overall productivity, the unidentified observer noted candidly, "They whip us."[49] Away from the public eye, even Fraser acknowledged the problem. The Japanese, he noted in 1981, had done well "because of the quality and engineering, design of those cars and based upon the way consumers behave in domestic sales." Once cars of a comparable quality were made in America, the challenge for domestic automakers would be immense.[50]

As they pondered U.S. production, the Japanese kept a close eye on Volkswagen's Pennsylvania plant, which opened in 1978. "Other foreign companies are shopping for U.S. manufacturing sites, and other states are competing to attract them," summarized *Business Week*. "Both groups are watching the Volkswagen experience for clues to what to expect—and whether or not to chance it." An important experiment, the Westmoreland plant would shape the industry's future.[51]

On October 5, 1976, VW chair Toni Schmücker traveled from Germany to attend the opening of the company's first U.S. plant. As part of the dedication ceremony, Schmücker rode in a caravan of yellow VW Rabbits, accompanied by Pennsylvania governor Milton Shapp and a host of dignitaries. At the plant gate, Shapp presented Schmücker with a 30-inch gold key to the site, while the VW boss gave the governor a Rabbit car. The two men also autographed stuffed rabbits. "I'm sure the Volkswagen Rabbit will multiply rapidly here," quipped Shapp. Schmücker, however, remained serious. "We are entering the largest single car market in the world and competing with the three largest and most able car producers that exist," he warned. "It is not going to be easy, but we are confident of our success."[52]

Eighteen months later, the first Rabbit rolled off the six-mile-long assembly line in Westmoreland, the newest auto plant in America. As a result, VW became the first foreign company to manufacture brand-name cars in the United States since Rolls-Royce in the 1930s. While often unaware of the British precedent, the press grasped the moment's significance. Volkswagen, summarized the *New York Times*, was "the first foreign automobile company to build cars in the United States since the end of World War II."[53] Proud of the achievement, Volkswagen also commemorated it. The first car, a white Rabbit, was placed on a gold-carpeted stage, where two company officials ceremonially inserted its plastic grill with the VW badge. Rather than going to a customer, the car was sent to the company's museum in Wolfsburg, West Germany. With production under way, Schmücker hoped that VW's share of the U.S. market—less than 2 percent in 1977—would more than double within eight years. To help achieve this, he committed $250 million to the plant.[54]

Westmoreland was important in other ways. By the 1970s Volkswagen was a recognized global brand name, largely due to the Beetle. The company also had deep symbolic importance. During World War II, the Wolfsburg plant was part of the Nazi military machine and had used forced labor. On the eve of the war, the plant's dedication had been presided over by Hitler, who also made design suggestions for the car. In April 1945, the labor force was liberated by American troops, and soon afterward the occupying British forces began Beetle production using military parts. When local authorities took control of the factory in 1949, they made rapid progress, attracting international praise. "For foreigners," observed the U.K.'s *Financial Times* in 1976, "Volkswagen has become established as a microcosm of German industry." Overseen by managing director Heinz Nordhoff, VW became a "symbol" of West Germany's "economic miracle." Eliding its wartime past, the company—and the Beetle—even became an emblem of the counterculture, especially in the United States.[55] The Pennsylvania factory also attracted interest, with Fraser describing it as an "in" plant. "Since it is the first major effort in the American auto industry of an overseas firm," he added, "it has apparently a certain glamour for newspeople."[56]

The plant's roots went back many years. Just six years after taking over in Wolfsburg, executives began looking for a factory in the United States. While plans to start production in New Jersey were abandoned, over the next twenty years VW's American sales grew, surpassing five hundred thousand a year between 1968 and 1971. By 1970 the company outsold AMC, Toyota, and Nissan. In September 1973, a delegation of top officials, led by manager Hans Schomers, traveled to the United States to "explore the feasibility" of building an assembly plant. Meeting with UAW leaders in Detroit, they related plans to build a factory that would employ up to five thousand workers. The delegation also had meetings at the White House and the Department of Commerce, relating concerns about transportation and distribution costs. They also sought information about wage rates and benefit plans, particularly from the UAW, as well as worker training.[57]

Following further investigation, in April 1976 Volkswagen announced that it would establish an assembly plant in the United States. Explaining the move, the company stressed the need to increase access to the American market, the largest in the world. As Chairman Carl H. Hahn explained, the United States was "indispensable" to VW, and starting production there was a "logical step" in the company's evolution. VW also wanted to try and reverse negative perceptions of its build quality. These had increased since 1967, when VW began producing U.S.-bound Beetles in Puebla, Mexico.[58]

The move was also linked to VW's desire to reduce trade frictions. These had mounted since the 1960s, and producing Beetles in Mexico had not solved the problem. In the months before the decision, tensions escalated. Several midwestern congressmen accused VW of "dumping," especially after bosses admitted in 1975 that they were making losses on "all models" in the United States. At this time, a VW Rabbit retailed for $650 more in West Germany than in the United States.[59] In February 1975, several members of Congress wrote Treasury secretary William E. Simon to complain that Volkswagens sold in the United States were cheaper than those in Germany yet contained more equipment and larger engines. The company's pricing policy, alleged Ohio congressman Charles Vanik, represented "an attempt to export unemployment abroad by creating an artificially low price for the Volkswagen." Also voiced by labor groups, these criticisms hurt VW, especially as a falling dollar meant that German production costs were 20 percent higher than in the United States. "The increasing American vigilance on the anti-dumping front," concluded the *Financial Times*, "was a decisive factor in forcing Volkswagen to consider the American car assembly plant."[60]

The announcement that VW had committed to a U.S. plant set off a scramble to land the facility, particularly between governors James Rhodes of Ohio and Milton Shapp of Pennsylvania. These states emerged as front-runners when VW showed a preference for an existing industrial site, reducing costs.

Both states had strong industrial bases but were losing jobs, making them keen suitors. Ohio offered two sites: a former Westinghouse appliance factory in Columbus and a federal tank plant in Brook Park, a Cleveland suburb. Located thirty miles south of Pittsburgh, Westmoreland was Pennsylvania's pick. Chrysler began building this plant between 1969 and 1971 but abandoned it due to poor sales.[61]

Aware of the loss of industry in Ohio, Rhodes's administration made a strong push. "Ohio's manufacturing base is deteriorating at a rapid pace and we are pledged to do everything we can to reverse this trend," wrote James A. Duerk, director of the Department of Economic and Community Development. Rhodes also recognized VW's value. "We have worked long and hard trying to bring Volkswagen facilities into the State which in turn would create many jobs," he wrote in 1976. "We hope our good efforts with Volkswagen will attract other industries to Ohio in the near future."[62] Duerk's department had an office in Düsseldorf, and officials there were in regular contact with VW. They pushed Brook Park, which was located in an area with high unemployment. According to the Ohio team, the state also had "location advantages" over Pennsylvania: it offered proximity to Lake Erie and the Ohio River for shipping, a location within five hundred miles of two-thirds of the American population, and a workforce with automotive experience (the state already had Ford and GM plants).[63]

Pennsylvania, however, was the surprise winner. As would be the case later, the governor played a crucial role in securing the deal. In April 1976, as VW's supervisory board met to decide where to build the U.S. plant, Shapp jetted to Wolfsburg. According to the *Financial Times*, Brook Park was the "hot tip" prior to the meeting. The day before the gathering, one of Duerk's staffers reported from Germany that there was extensive media coverage of the deal. "The odds are 4:1 that the tank plant gets the nod, according to press," he noted. One of the two major German networks, ZDF, even stated that Volkswagen had chosen Cleveland. On April 22, however, another Ohio staffer noted that Pennsylvania was undertaking a "flurry of last-minute efforts to persuade Volkswagen to locate in their state."[64]

A self-made millionaire, Shapp understood business and offered some vital incentives to VW. In the four counties around the site, unemployment exceeded 40 percent, and the prospect of jobs led Pennsylvania to build a four-lane freeway into the plant, as well as a rail spur valued at $65 million. The state also bought the unfinished plant from Chrysler and leased it to VW, offering low-cost loans and deferred and minimal taxes. Like his successors, Shapp defended the subsidies, claiming that the plant would produce forty-five hundred jobs, plus many more at suppliers.[65] Those close to the bid saw Shapp's intervention as decisive. "Volkswagen wanted two rail lines to the plant, and the governor got that for them, and we got another highway to provide them an excellent road system," recalled Turnpike Commission chair Jack Green-blat. "It happened because we had a governor interested in bringing indus-try to Pennsylvania." Seeing an auto plant as a massive prize both economi-cally and symbolically, Shapp never gave up, and his personal diplomacy also played a role. He later termed the announcement "one of the most important events in my eight years in Harrisburg."[66]

The notion that Pennsylvania had outbid Ohio was not the whole story. Proffered especially in the Buckeye State, it reflected the frustration of the los-ing team. Although the details were not specified in his papers, Rhodes had also promised VW tax breaks and had pushed business tax incentive legisla-tion.[67] It is not clear that these changes would have swung the deal, however, as location was key. VW liked the Pennsylvania site because it was closer to the East Coast ports, reflecting its concerns about transportation costs, and because suitable labor was plentiful in the steel and coal-mining area. Seeking general industrial experience rather than automotive knowledge, VW planned to train these workers. "We're looking for honest people who are willing to work," explained James W. McLernon, the president of Volkswagen Manufac-turing Corporation America. "The three factors we consider are previous ex-perience, educational background, and aptitude for assembly-line work." A more rural location than Brook Park, Westmoreland also attracted VW be-cause there was space for expansion.[68]

Westmoreland, however, was troubled from the start. Highlighting the ad-vantages of a greenfield location, which allowed automakers to build a fac-tory and install new equipment, many of the problems related to the plant it-self, which Chrysler had vacated with $100 million still to be spent. Visiting the factory in 1978, a *Washington Post* reporter described it as a "39-acre shell" that had been "abandoned by Chrysler Corp." By the time VW took over, noted an-other observer, the plant was "severely outdated." Trying to distinguish itself from Chrysler, which had called the struggling facility New Stanton, VW re-named it Westmoreland. More than a name change was needed, however.[69]

In other ways, VW started at a disadvantage. Unlike its foreign-owned suc-cessors, it opened a U.S. factory when sales were falling. Between 1973 and 1978, VW's share of the American market dropped from 5 percent to 2.5 per-cent. A major cause was the stronger deutsche mark, which appreciated from 25 cents to 49 cents over this period. As the *Washington Post* noted, given these problems, the plant was always a "gamble." Hurt by the strong mark, VW strug-gled to keep the Rabbit competitive. The $4,000 car was priced higher than its competitors, including the imported Toyota Tercel and the American-made Chevrolet Citation. The high price also reflected the fact that 75 percent of the Rabbit's parts were imported, reaffirming the need for local suppliers. VW paid a 3 percent duty on imported parts, undercutting the advantages of U.S. production.[70] The automaker also experienced volatility at home. In

April 1975, Schmücker announced that VW would lay off twenty-five thousand workers over the next two years, a move prompted by losses of DM 807 million after the oil crisis. Although the company subsequently rebounded in Germany, its U.S. sales remained slow. Despite this, the board, blaming the mark for low volume, agreed to Westmoreland.[71]

There were also problems with the product itself. From the start, the U.S.-built Rabbit was riddled with mechanical defects. Unlike the much-loved Beetle, which the Rabbit replaced in 1974, the car could not be repaired by the average owner, and it did not have as much character. In a broader context, VW's cars lacked the reputation for reliability that the Japanese had acquired. In an interview with *Ward's Auto World* in 1978, even McLernon "unequivocally" agreed with an interviewer's comment that Japanese cars were "the best-built cars sold in this country right now." "That's a tough thing to say," added the VW boss, "but it's true." Furthermore, McLernon acknowledged that the strong mark had hurt operations in Westmoreland. "Our major concern is cost," he commented, "having to make up for the German mark's strength compared with the dollar's."[72]

Once the plant was established, it also epitomized the stresses that transplants produced. As *Business Week* summarized in 1978, "What seemed to be the perfect marriage of employer and region is encountering problems that neither had anticipated. Tensions and suspicions have replaced the early euphoria." There were significant labor and civil rights disputes, along with resistance to the company's presence. This story deserves exploration, especially as it influenced the sector's history.[73]

From the start, the plant produced opposition. Many residents worried that the area would grow too fast and become "another Detroit." Reports of increased crime were blamed on the plant. "That wouldn't have happened if Volkswagen hadn't moved in," commented one resident, referring to a local robbery. Many were anxious about outsiders moving to their area, especially—although none voiced it openly—black workers from big cities. "I'd just as soon VW had gone to Ohio," commented Victor Glancy, a Greensburg resident. "I don't know how many outside people will be moving in—2,000 . . . 3,000—but I definitely know that will increase crime. We're having trouble with the NAACP picketing already." These reactions were not isolated. "A lot of our people didn't want to see this plant open," summarized Mount Pleasant mayor William Potoka. "This is a small town, where people are content. They see change, and they don't like it."[74]

In an area with high unemployment, many residents applied for jobs at the plant, where wages and benefits exceeded local norms. This led to other problems. Jobs at the plant were hard to get; in February 1978, VW had hired just six hundred workers yet had received thirty-six thousand applicants. Residents complained that the company should concentrate its efforts on the five closest counties, but VW refused to make promises. Overall, expectations that the plant would solve the economic woes of a declining area, where fifty-five hundred jobs were lost in nearby Johnstown just as Westmoreland opened, were not met, partly because they were exaggerated. "We thought that VW would be a savior for every unemployed person here," summarized one local.[75]

Like later foreign-owned plants, Westmoreland was located in a heavily white area but within commuting distance of a racially diverse city (Pittsburgh). This also created tension. Less than 9 percent of the early workforce, almost all of whom were hired locally, derived from minority groups. In VW's case, the company was not trying to avoid unionization, but it did set the pattern of locating in rural areas away from other auto factories. Like its successors, moreover, the company's hiring drew complaints. In July 1977, the Pittsburgh branch of the Urban League complained about the lack of opportunities for minorities in the plant. The Urban League, which had joined with the NAACP and several other organizations, was not satisfied. "Our efforts have been concerned with seeing that a fair number of blacks and other minorities are included in the group but if the current hiring pattern prevails this will not be the case," wrote Arthur J. Edmonds. According to Edmonds, 195 workers had been hired, and just 8 were black.[76]

Government organizations made similar complaints. In 1978, the Pennsylvania Human Relations Commission, which investigated violations of state and federal antidiscrimination laws, declared that VW was "not in compliance with affirmative-action requirements." As the commission showed, VW's hiring process disadvantaged black applicants. In order to cope with a massive number of applicants, VW asked the state Bureau of Employment Security to handle preliminary screening. In the summer of 1977, the bureau ran a recruitment program in five surrounding counties. No recruiting, however, occurred in Allegheny County (Pittsburgh), where most African Americans lived. Instead, blacks from the city had to travel to one of the rural counties to apply. Made up of the NAACP and other civil rights groups, the Volkswagen Coalition wanted VW to provide transport for Pittsburgh blacks and help for them to relocate to Westmoreland County. In response, company officials refused to meet with the coalition, claiming they needed time to address the issues. Frustrated by the lack of action, in October 1977 and January 1978 the coalition picketed outside the plant. VW faced conflicting demands: while local whites pressed for jobs and disliked outsiders, civil rights groups wanted to focus hiring efforts on Pittsburgh.[77]

With VW unable to resolve this conundrum, racial tensions continued. By January 1983, eight present and former black employees, together with one unsuccessful applicant, had filed a Title VII civil rights suit against the company. It claimed that "virtually every employment practice" at the plant, including hiring, job assignments, pay, and discipline, was racially discriminatory. After several years of proceedings, Volkswagen tried to settle the case, which was brought on behalf of all black applicants and employees. In a deal reached just before the plant closed, twenty-two plaintiffs received payments varying from $7,500 to $50,000. In the settlement, Volkswagen acknowledged that its "initial hiring practices" had been "unfair to minorities" yet insisted that it had not broken the law. More blacks, it noted, were hired later.[78]

Private records told a different story. According to UAW general counsel Jordan Rossen, both VW and the union had "serious exposure" in the case. The UAW was a codefendant because forty-eight discharges of black workers had not been pursued through the grievance procedure. UAW records showed that the plant discharge rate for blacks was five times higher than for whites. Furthermore, white reinstatements were "traded" for black discharges. "There is also evidence that some UAW officials participated in conduct that arguably contributed to a racially hostile work environment," admitted attorney Daniel W. Cooper in internal correspondence. Aware of its culpability, the UAW tried to settle, offering the forty-eight workers $1,000 each. The case highlighted how the movement of auto plants away from urban areas increased the likelihood of racial discrimination.[79]

The plant also experienced labor conflict. Even before hiring was complete, the UAW was organizing. Helped by the company's acceptance of unions in Germany, efforts proceeded rapidly. In Wolfsburg, labor representatives sat on VW's supervisory board, which was responsible for monitoring management and approving important decisions. Partly as a result, the company stayed neutral throughout the campaign. Organizing was also helped by the plant's location in an area with a strong union tradition, especially among former coalminers and steelworkers, and by the UAW's contract at a small VW stamping plant in West Virginia. Although only one organizer was assigned to Westmoreland, in April 1978 the UAW reported that 87 percent of production workers had signed union cards. On June 9, VW workers voted 865 to 17 in favor of the UAW. For the union, it was a foundational moment. "This is one of the most important organized victories in years for the UAW," summarized Fraser. "We believe there will be other foreign automakers deciding to open plants in the U.S. and we intend to organize those workers as well."[80]

Tensions escalated when the first contract was negotiated, as the local UAW pressed VW to absorb more costs than it was comfortable with. In October 1978, the plant was idled for a week by an unauthorized strike, as many workers felt that the proposed three-year deal was inferior to a Big Three contract. The strike was also triggered by disciplinary action against two workers, including one who was fired for stopping the assembly line. In response to the walkout, VW obtained an injunction that limited picketing. According to the *Washington Post*, the dispute still "depleted" parts of the assembly line. "Developments have been watched closely by other foreign auto manufacturers eager to build cars in the United States," it warned. In December, McLernon admitted to an industry publication that the company had "lost a little" after two strikes that year. Although VW-America was not "in the red," it could not yet "pay the bills."[81]

Private records show that the disputes took a toll. Shortly before the walkout, Schmücker pleaded with Fraser to moderate the UAW's demands. The union wanted VW to follow—or be close to—the Big Three "pattern," but Schmücker insisted that such "demands" would have "catastrophic cost implications for our operations still in their formative stages."[82] While UAW leaders seemed somewhat sympathetic, they struggled to control militant members. On October 9, local attorney Dan Cooper reported that the picket line was "completely out of hand," with violence aimed at salaried workers. In addition, staffer Cecil Hampton related that Autoworkers for Rank and File, a grassroots group, was accusing the international union of "keeping them in the dark." On October 16, workers voted 699 to 390 to return to work, yet staffers worried about a group of "militants" who were reluctant to accept the agreement. According to Hampton, some even threatened to "get themselves fired today in order to lead another walkout out of the plant."[83]

As a result of the strike, workers won some improvements. Pay increased slightly, with production workers starting on $6.50 an hour and progressing to $8.20 within two years. Workers also received a range of benefits, including shift premiums, fully paid health care, seniority protections, and inclusion in the UAW pension plan.[84] Despite these gains, the international union continued to have problems with militant members. Many were former coalminers and steelworkers, both industries with strong traditions of activist unionism, especially in southwestern Pennsylvania.[85] In January 1979, staffers reported that a wildcat strike had broken out. Workers were upset about a range of issues, including "failure to promote people during the build up in employment" and alleged safety violations. They also felt that the plant had poor "production standards." In March, workers engaged in another wildcat, with staffer Frank James relating that they had a "laundry list" of grievances, including thirty-four health and safety complaints. Their action annoyed management, especially in Wolfsburg. "The Germans are all upset and don't understand what's happening and feel if they are threatened with strikes the situation is impossible," wrote James.[86]

Anxious not to jeopardize the plant, Fraser was conciliatory. "Rest assured we as a union believe in resolving problems across the bargaining table," he wrote a local business leader. He accused the media of sensationalizing the March wildcat strike, which he termed an "unauthorized work stoppage." Such interruptions, he insisted, were "routine" in the industry when grievances were not resolved quickly.[87] Despite Fraser's assurances, the UAW's internal reports continued to tell a different story. In June 1979, another unauthorized strike occurred, and the union admitted that a large group of workers were "trouble." Terming the walkout "a serious breach of our collective bargaining agreement," VW obtained a restraining order.[88]

In addition to labor issues, Westmoreland had other problems. Unlike subsequent Japanese-owned plants, which manufactured established and well-priced models, VW trialed new cars and priced them high. In addition to the Rabbit, Westmoreland built the Jetta sedan. Introduced in 1980, the Jetta cost $1,000 more than the similarly equipped Honda Accord and $1,000 to $1,500 more than the larger Toyota Corona and Datsun Stanza, all of which were more reliable. The Rabbit's overdue replacement, the Golf, also struggled to meet ambitious sales targets.[89] Unlike the Japanese companies, which expanded slowly, VW overextended itself. In 1980, it announced plans for a second U.S. assembly plant, a 2.1-million-square-foot operation in Sterling Heights, Michigan. VW's confidence was overstated; between 1980 and 1982, its sales slumped, and Westmoreland hemorrhaged money. As a result, managers cut production in Pennsylvania and halted renovations of Sterling Heights, which was hastily sold to Chrysler in 1983. As chairman Hahn admitted, VW had to accept "considerable losses" in 1982, partly because the second oil crisis had not lasted as long as it had expected. In that year, its U.S. sales fell by a third. "Volkswagen was basically hit three times, i.e., not only by the fall of the market as a whole but also by the move from small to large vehicles, and finally, the fall-off in diesels," he commented in 1983.[90]

VW made other mistakes. Declining gas prices hurt the fuel-efficient Rabbit, but VW's strategy was also criticized by industry analysts, who noted that the company had been "essentially selling the same car for six years." Even after America emerged from the recession of the early 1980s, VW struggled. In the first three months of 1987, its sales declined by 40 percent, forcing another temporary shutdown in Pennsylvania. With sales failing to recover, the plant's fate was sealed. Announcing the plant's permanent closure in November 1987, VW admitted that Westmoreland had been losing money for five years. During this time, the plant operated at less than half of capacity.[91]

Although there were many reasons for the closure, problems with the products were particularly important. As a detailed analysis in the *New York Times* showed, the Rabbit was an uninspiring successor to the Beetle, and as its Japanese competition improved, VW lost market share. The Golf and Jetta—essentially a Golf with a trunk—also failed to capture the Beetle's magic. "They owned the baby boom generation, but they didn't follow up," summarized Thomas O'Grady, a leading industry consultant. "They designed cars for Germany and then tried to sell them here. Meanwhile, the Japanese grabbed their market away from them." Even VW admitted that its cars had struggled, noting in a statement that the U.S. small car market had become "increasingly proliferated and competitive." In tough conditions, loss-making Westmoreland had to go.[92] On July 14, 1988, the factory was closed. Over seventeen hundred workers lost their jobs, and the site was sold to the state. The Chinese government bought most of the equipment, using it in a subsequent joint venture with VW. After the shutdown, the company switched production of Golfs and some Jettas to Mexico.[93] The plant itself was adapted to other uses; from 1990 to 2008, for example, it was used by Sony to manufacture televisions, but few jobs resulted. In a depressed area, many displaced workers ended up in lower-paying positions, while others suffered long-term unemployment. "There was plenty of hardship," concluded a *Pittsburgh Tribune-Review* investigation twenty years later.[94]

The closure had important consequences. With VW's problems being widely reported, Japanese automakers learned the need for careful planning and a diverse model lineup. They saw the advantages of greenfield sites, especially farther south, where states offered bigger incentive packages and production costs were lower. Despite—and because of—its problems, Westmoreland was an important precedent. As *Automotive News* reporter Lindsay Chappell recalled, Volkswagen was "sort of dismissed as a flop, but it was around for ten years or so." In all, VW made 1.15 million cars at the factory, showing that mass production by foreign automakers in the United States was feasible. With more preparation, a stronger product, and a better location, foreign-owned plants could thrive.[95]

The plant also influenced labor relations. The factory encouraged the UAW to believe that it could organize foreign-owned plants, which influenced its strategy of encouraging the sector's growth. According to the union, VW was "a beacon to other foreign-based vehicle builders that production here could be successfully achieved using a UAW workforce." Many industry observers, however, drew different lessons. Noting the union problems at the plant, they claimed that the UAW was largely responsible for the closure. As the *Pittsburgh Tribune* put it, the plant's shutdown was related to "chronic labor issues," including regular strikes and the cost of union wages.[96] The company and union refuted this view. They reiterated that the plant's lack of volume— and the ultracompetitive small car market—had been the main problems. In May 1988, VW's public relations manager, Chester B. Bahn, addressed the problem publicly. "I am writing," he noted, "about the perception among so many people that organized labor somehow played a part in our plant's forthcoming closing. Nothing could be further from the truth." In reality, the plant closing was a "simple matter of volume." According to Bahn, the plant had only lost forty-seven days because of strikes. Despite these denials and the evidence of market-related problems, many insiders believed otherwise. This was a "UAW plant," and the union became linked with its closing. As Bieber related privately in 1988, for the union the plant shutdown was "tricky." For decades, the association lingered.[97]

Events in Pennsylvania were closely watched by Honda, which announced its Ohio plant as VW was gearing up to make Rabbits. Illustrating the company's anxiety, Honda managers asked the UAW for a copy of the Westmoreland labor contract. Frank James advised that the union should "be nice" and agree to the request.[98] In Ohio, Rhodes's staff were also aware that VW was likely to be succeeded by a Japanese automaker. As one state official wrote from Germany in 1976, "Papers all mention that the Japanese will probably follow the VW example and start up USA assembly production operations." After missing out on VW, Rhodes was determined to hook Honda. The next episode in the industry's history, this story evoked both tension and celebration.[99]

CHAPTER TWO

Land Only

Building Acceptance at
Honda in Marysville, Ohio

In October 1977, Tokyo-based Honda Motor Company cre-
ated Honda of America Manufacturing (HAM) and publicized plans to build
a $35 million plant in Marysville, Ohio. Although the smallest and youngest of
Japan's Big Three, Honda—guided by founder Soichiro Honda, a former auto
mechanic who established the company in 1948—was known as the most innovative. Just seven years after entering the U.S. market, and after seeing its
early cars struggle, Honda committed to a U.S. plant, the first Japanese automaker to do so. The factory was also built from the ground up in a part of central Ohio with little industrial heritage. Originally producing motorcycles, it
soon switched to cars. Surprising many, Marysville thrived, cementing a positive era in the United States for Honda.[1]

The experience was foundational. As *Automotive News* reporter Lindsay
Chappell put it, Honda's establishment in Ohio was "the watershed event"
for the industry, showing that foreign-owned factories could thrive. In 1985,
Honda added an engine plant in nearby Anna, and in 1989 it opened a second
assembly plant in East Liberty. Further expansions followed in Ohio and beyond. By 1996, Honda was making more cars in America—over 634,000—than
either Chevrolet or Chrysler. The company had also become the leading exporter of cars from North America. In subsequent years, growth continued.
By 2015, Honda employed almost seven thousand workers at two Ohio plants,
while another eighty-two hundred worked at factories in Alabama and On-
tario. These four plants turned out the vast majority of Hondas sold in North
America.[2]

The story of how Honda came to Ohio is remarkable. Compounding conventional wisdom that car plants needed to be located in industrial areas,
Honda chose a greenfield site outside the upper Midwest. Using overlooked
archival records, this account shows how Ohio's leaders, especially Governor
James Rhodes and James A. Duerk, director of the Department of Economic
and Community Development, played a key role. According to Duerk, Honda

was important because it would "create tremendous public benefits for the entire state of Ohio," which was suffering from industrial job losses. Spending several years courting Honda, the Ohio team realized that personal contact—backed up by generous incentives—could win them the prize. Behind the scenes, however, reaction to the automaker's arrival was mixed, and not everybody—in Ohio and beyond—was delighted.[3]

Part of the reason for this was that the plant was nonunion. After initially seeming to follow VW's example, Honda unexpectedly took a different path. Once the plant was established, managers declared that they sought a "personal relationship" with their "associates," a relationship that a union would disrupt. Although UAW leader Douglas Fraser declared that the unionization of the plant was a "high priority," Honda opposed these efforts. In December 1985, following conflict behind the scenes between the two sides, the UAW abandoned plans to contest an election at Marysville due to lack of support. Honda had shown that it was possible to run a nonunion auto plant in the United States.[4]

It was a crucial moment in the industry's history. As UAW lawyer Leonard Page wrote about the case, any "attempt to abuse the NLRA [National Labor Relations Act of 1935] and operate non-UAW strikes at the very heart of the UAW," and it affected the union's relations with "all other U.S. companies." The implications were enormous. "If Honda's anti-union strategy succeeds in building non-union cars this summer," Fraser added in 1982, "it is obvious that Datsun, Kawasaki, and possible other auto companies may follow. *We cannot let this happen.*" Fraser called on the entire union to mobilize behind a campaign to change Honda's mind. It was a massive—and little-known—effort.[5]

Featuring negative publicity and a threatened boycott, the campaign worried Honda executives, but they held firm. Top managers did a partial volteface on the union issue, making an initial "memorandum" to recognize the UAW without an election but then refusing to honor it. According to Chappell, who covered the sector, Honda had "changed courses" based on off-the-record advice from American managers that they "might have some squirming-room" on the union issue. Honda's actions led to years of tension with the UAW, which worked behind the scenes to get the company to grant voluntary recognition. Bolstered by support from Ohio's political leaders, however, the company refused. By 1986, it had essentially banished the UAW from its plants. Honda's story was crucial in the establishment of a nonunion auto industry. It ensured that the relationship between the new industry and the UAW, which the union envisaged as one of cooperation and recognition, was instead defined by conflict and failure. The UAW was rocked. "Every part of the Union became somewhat traumatized by our subject at hand, the transplants, and the new situation," recalled former staffer Peter Laarman.[6]

Honda entered the U.S. market late. It sold its first cars there in 1970, thirteen years after Toyota and twelve years later than Nissan. Early vehicles struggled, with the diminutive N600 sedan being viewed by Americans as too small and unsafe. Managers learned quickly, and the subcompact Civic, introduced in 1974, and the compact Accord, which debuted two years later, were bigger and better built. They sold well, making American production a possibility, especially when fuel prices rose. During the two oil crises, Honda became the fastest-growing automaker in the United States, its sales jumping from 9,509 cars in 1971 to 353,291 in 1979.[7]

American production also reflected corporate culture. In contrast to Nissan and Toyota, which were established before World War II, Honda was a newcomer, an identity that managers embraced. "Honda is not a typical Japanese company," explained top executive Shoichiro Irimajiri. "Consider our basic philosophy: That we must always hold our own torch, that we must develop fresh ideas of our own, that we must not copy others." Emphasizing innovation, Honda wanted to be the first Japanese automaker to establish a plant in the United States. According to Eiichi Nobe, who worked on the project, many of those involved were "excited" about building the first Japanese cars in America. Years later, Honda celebrated its "historic announcement," boasting that it had set up its factory "long before international economics and talk of trade restraints suggested such action to others." In many ways, it was a brave move. In 1977, when Honda committed to the plant, its share of the U.S. car market was just 1.51 percent, less than half that of Toyota and Nissan, which were still debating the move.[8]

As an internal company history summarized, the decision was "years in the making." In the fall of 1974, company president Kiyoshi Kawashima, who had just taken over from elderly founders Soichiro Honda and Takeo Fujisawa, authorized a feasibility study of American manufacturing that included cost comparisons of imported and locally made cars. According to company records, Honda's interest in American manufacturing partly reflected the oil crisis of 1973, which encouraged the decentralization of manufacturing outside Japan. (The Asian nation relied heavily on foreign oil.) In the early 1970s, Honda was also hurt by the Nixon administration's efforts to protect the dollar against the yen. As it derived 60 percent of its revenue from exports, Honda considered American production. In addition, Honda had what it termed "a long-standing policy to build products in the market where they are sold." Kawashima felt strongly that the company should make cars in its largest overseas market. "This one-way traffic, only exporting finished vehicles, cannot last long," he commented. After receiving the feasibility study, however, Kawashima shelved it due to concerns about the quality and profitability of American-made cars. "Let me hold onto this project for the time being," he explained. "But keep the research data handy so that it can be used whenever the need arises."[9]

That need came in November 1975, when Honda conducted another feasibility study. The move was driven by the popularity of the Civic, a car that forged Honda's reputation for innovation, low emissions, and fuel economy. The Civic was fitted with the CVCC engine, the first to pass the strict emissions standards of the U.S. Clean Air Act of 1970. At a time when the Big Three were lagging in small car development, the Civic's fuel economy—it won an EPA mileage test in 1974—led to strong demand in the United States. As Honda was only a small player at home, Kawashima also felt that it made sense to pioneer manufacturing in America. "Rather than compete domestically to no avail," he explained, "I would like to use this opportunity to take a chance in America, the world's largest market. I would like to build a motorcycle factory and eventually an automobile factory in the United States, where no [Japanese auto manufacturer] has yet done so."[10]

Acting on Kawashima's instructions, in January 1976 managing director Masami Suzuki traveled to the United States and held a series of meetings with industry leaders, including Ford president Lee Iacocca. Iacocca, who drove a Honda Accord and was impressed by the vehicle's quality, was interested in purchasing CVCC engines. After visiting Big Three plants, however, Suzuki continued to have doubts about American-made cars, and these were only reinforced by conversations with local managers. American vehicles, the company noted in its records, suffered from "intrinsic quality problems." The company also had misgivings about American workers, who were perceived in Japan—as one reporter put it—as "unfocused and careless at their work."[11]

For Suzuki and Kawashima, the solution lay not in abandoning plans but in locating in a nontraditional area and operating in a new way. As the company's account of the Marysville project put it, in America "it was not a matter of people intentionally producing bad cars. Rather, it was because the management systems deprived workers of their natural motivation to excel." In May 1976, Honda hired American consultants to find sites where the company could operate differently, training workers in the company's ideas from the bottom up. These locations had to be able to produce one hundred thousand Civics and Accords a year and transport them by road or rail. While the official account made no mention of the union issue, Honda settled on the region "from Ohio to Kentucky," based on its central location and the fact that it offered a "low rate of job turnover, along with highly motivated workers." Wanting a "high-quality labor force," Honda sought to avoid the crime and social problems of the big cities, particularly Detroit. These problems were particularly alien to the Japanese, who were accustomed to low crime rates and high levels of social cohesion, as well as ethnic homogeneity. With these criteria in mind, Suzuki decided that Ohio was Honda's top choice. The managing director visited more than fifty sites in the Buckeye state. Picking a winner, however, would take time.[12]

Hearing that Honda was a prospect, the governor sprang into action. A Republican, Rhodes was determined to attract new business, especially to the region around Columbus, his home city.[13] In May 1976, as Honda began looking at American sites, he traveled to Tokyo and met with top managers, including Soichiro Honda and Kawashima. On the trip, Rhodes offered a lot of help, including implicit support for union avoidance. "While we understand that you are in the very preliminary stages of evaluating a possible manufacturing facility," he wrote Kawashima, "we want to offer our assistance to you in any way that would be helpful in your deliberations." In particular, the state would "do [our] best to help you start operations at the lowest possible cost and would alleviate any difficulties you might encounter." There were also personal touches. During the trip, Rhodes gave Soichiro Honda a reproduction of the Ohio state bird (the cardinal). Clearly pleased, the executive displayed the artwork in his living room.[14]

Following the visit, Rhodes's staff kept up the charm offensive. In confidential correspondence, state officials reassured Honda that Ohio was an attractive place to do business, refuting press coverage that focused on deindustrialization. "Ohio is not experiencing a net loss of industry," wrote official Frederick A. Sexton, adding that the number of companies that had moved away, especially to the "'sunbelt' states," had been exaggerated. Officials were also committed to making the state business-friendly. "Our Ohio business climate is extremely conducive to attracting industry and our department is making every effort to make things even better," added Sexton. Assuaging the company's "concerns," officials stressed that they would do everything they could to help.[15]

Rhodes backed up these words. In the spring of 1977, he pushed a bill through the Ohio General Assembly that created the Water Development Authority (WDA) and the Air Quality Development Authority, two new bodies designed to "assist industry financially" in meeting pollution standards through the sale of revenue bonds. "The bonds are a tax-free issue and reflect a savings in financing cost to the industry," explained WDA director E. B. Ransom.[16] Also in 1977, the assembly passed legislation helping corporations to apply for foreign trade zone status, providing significant tariff and tax relief. "The advantages to Honda with a location in Ohio could be significant if parts are to be imported," Sexton wrote executive Kiyoshi Ikemi. "We in Ohio want to do everything we can to welcome Honda and to see that Honda has every opportunity to prosper and grow in our State."[17]

State officials even helped Honda apply for foreign trade zone status. In August 1977, Duerk wrote Charles E. Webb, the director of the Cincinnati Chamber of Commerce, to support the inclusion of Honda, which was only named as a "major industrial prospect," within the Greater Cincinnati Foreign Trade Zone, Inc., even though Marysville was 120 miles away. "It is my understanding that the jurisdiction of the proposed Greater Cincinnati Foreign Trade Zone is not limited to any specific geographic boundaries," he explained. "Further, because of the nature of the prospect's business, a foreign trade zone status is of utmost importance." These efforts came to fruition in the project agreement that the state offered Honda, in which the government designated the plant as a subzone of a foreign trade zone, reducing duties on imported parts.[18]

Personal contacts were also important, especially in assuaging Honda's doubts. In the spring of 1977, Rhodes and Duerk went on another trade mission to Japan, visiting Honda's headquarters and several manufacturing facilities. While there, Duerk met with Kazuo Nakagawa, the director of Honda's board, as well as several other top executives, discussing the company's plans in detail. After the meeting, Duerk wrote Nakagawa in flattering terms. "We would be honoured to have Honda as a new corporate citizen in the state of Ohio," he gushed, adding that the state would "help in whatever way possible." He also called Honda's production methods "very sophisticated." Company executives lapped up the praise. "It was our great pleasure that our staffs could exchange useful information with the representatives of your trade mission when they visited our factory," Nakamura replied.[19]

Doing his homework, Duerk compiled lists of the key players within Honda, facilitating both official "discussions" and personal visits. On April 26, 1977, for example, he had dinner with Masahiko Obi, the planning manager in the Foreign Sales Division, further building trust.[20] At an important—and confidential—meeting between Honda and Duerk's staff in early May, key concerns were then hammered out. Company representatives reported that transportation costs were "crucial," as was proximity to parts makers. "In general, meeting excellent," noted Duerk's office. "They definitely want to work closely with us over the next several months."[21]

As they looked at sites, Honda's managers showed a preference for rural locations, especially in the southern half of Ohio, which was whiter—and more conservative—than the northern part of the state. Here, African Americans had flocked to work in industrial cities, particularly Akron, Cleveland, and Youngstown. In negotiations with Rhodes, Honda rejected efforts to steer the company to the Brook Park site in Cleveland, a prepared industrial location. As state officials reported, Honda wanted "land only" and preferred the "southern half of Ohio." The company would avoid the mistakes of Volkswagen, which had inherited a factory near a postindustrial city. "Think they would like to build their own," summarized staffer Kaye Evans. In July 1977, Honda vice president Shigeyoshi Yoshida, accompanied by Nakagawa and Suzuki, visited the Columbus area and saw a number of sites, including the one near Marysville. As the *Ohio Report* put it, at the time Marysville was a "small, plains-like city west of Columbus." Home to just seven thousand people, it was located thirty-five miles from Columbus, whose economy was based on education, government, and health care rather than industry. Honda immediately liked the site, which offered a large, flat space and good transportation links. Local officials promised to extend water, sewer, and gas lines from Marysville, seven miles away. Well before the announcement, Honda had a front-runner.[22]

Rhodes continued to pay close attention to detail. When Yoshida and his colleagues visited Columbus in July, the governor hosted a lavish dinner. "My colleagues and I thank you very much for your kind hospitality," Suzuki wrote Rhodes, "and we also enjoyed the nice dinner at the beautiful country club." After the visit, Rhodes left the company in no doubt about his support. "As Governor of Ohio," he wrote Yoshida, "I would do everything in my power to assure your company total success in our state." Insisting that his career had been devoted to "industrial development," the governor put Honda in touch with helpful local contacts. The whole emphasis was on Honda's success. There was no discussion of labor or environmental standards, and few binding commitments from the company.[23]

Rhodes also arranged incentives. Following the July 1977 visit, he talked with key state politicians, particularly Senate President Pro Tempore Oliver Ocasek, House Speaker Vernal G. Riffe, and Senator Harry Meshel about the project. A long-serving Democrat, Meshel was the "key member" of the controlling board, which authorized extraordinary state appropriations. These leaders agreed to provide Honda with up to $2.5 million in public improvements, including funds for a railroad spur. The state also pledged to sell the company 250 acres of land at no more than $800 an acre and to widen U.S. Route 33 near the plant. Furthermore, it committed over $1 million in Comprehensive Employment and Training Act funds for on-site manpower training. Together with Ocasek, Riffe, and Meshel, Rhodes even offered to go to Tokyo "at a moment's notice" if needed.[24] Following Rhodes's offer, Nakagawa wrote back with a project agreement. "We have come to think that it would be beneficial to both the State Government of Ohio and our company to enter into an agreement at an early date so that a close cooperative relationship may be established between the two parties for constructing our contemplated plant in your State," he explained. As part of the deal, Honda received fifteen-year property tax abatements from the state and county, saving it at least $300,000 a year. Although full details were not publicized, industry sources estimated that incentives totaled around $22 million.[25]

Honda's preference for southern Ohio also reflected union avoidance. In early 1977, it was revealing that Yoshida asked Duerk for information on the "union-organize [sic] status" of eight major factories located near Marysville. Duerk's office noted on the letter that six of the facilities were nonunion; the other two only had small craft unions. The information was then apparently relayed back to the company. The union plants were also located in Wilmington, seventy miles away. Prior to the announcement, Honda established that there were few unions in the area. Although the UAW represented workers at several Big Three facilities, these plants were in northern Ohio. The company also rebuffed appeals from Douglas Fraser, who expressed "strong support" for the plant to be located in California. Although the union leader insisted that a West Coast location would facilitate parts shipments from Japan, Honda was unmoved. As he lured Honda, Rhodes also ignored the UAW.[26] In October 1977, when Honda announced its decision, it was clear that labor issues were important. As Kawashima explained, if the motorcycle plant was successful, especially in terms of "relations with labor," it would expand to produce cars. The company also liked the site's proximity to the state-run Transportation Research Center (TRC), a large proving ground with a 7.5-mile test track. Visiting the area in a state-owned airplane, Yoshida and Suzuki were impressed by the work ethic of the test drivers and by the "industrious" nature of the local population. In this area, they could find "a large number of quality workers."[27]

In the local area, reaction to Honda's arrival was mixed. Citing high unemployment, Mayor Thomas Nuckles proclaimed that Marysville was the "luckiest city in Ohio." Among the broader population, however, there was unease, especially about the cost of the concessions. Anti-Japanese sentiment was also prevalent. In November 1982, even the boosterish *Marysville Journal-Tribune* admitted that some locals "resent the company's presence here." The paper aimed to squash such sentiment. "We feel Marysville, as a whole, is proud to have a company like Honda as a part of our community," it asserted.[28] Opposition centered on the town's new wastewater treatment plant. This went ahead after the city council approved an 82.5 percent increase in sewer bills to pay for the facility. Many locals blamed Honda for the increase, as wastewater facilities had to be expanded to handle its needs. Civic leaders responded that Honda would pay for the 500,000-gallon-per-day capacity committed to it. Still, residents disliked higher bills. "Nobody can afford to water their lawns anymore," summarized one. "The only thing we're going to get out of this is jobs. And we're not sure we're going to get many of those," declared another.[29]

There were other concerns. Some residents disliked Rhodes's intervention, especially when the governor bypassed local opinion—including the Marysville Chamber of Commerce—to negotiate with Honda. Business groups wanted to be consulted. After the site was purchased from Ralph Stolle, the brother-in-law of one of Rhodes's business partners, there were rumors that the governor had profited from the sale. Although Rhodes rebuffed the allegations, there were other criticisms. Widening Route 33, for example, proved controversial. A group called Committee Against Route 33 Expansion claimed that the state plan failed to include a steel-and-concrete divider, putting the lives of local schoolchildren at risk. Mobilizing support, they put up billboards declaring "Say No to Rhodes." In the end, it took six years for the road to reach the plant.[30]

Some residents expressed a deeper disquiet. In a November 1982 letter to the *Journal-Tribune*, L. E. Grimes complained that "city hall" monopolized coverage of Honda's arrival. Grimes called for the "true facts" about local reaction, "not just what he (the Mayor) and the local media wants [*sic*] you to hear." Noting the generous concessions that Honda had received and expressing concern that not many jobs were going to locals, Grimes concluded, "I'll grant you the county and state are very fortunate that Honda is here but I don't feel that the city of Marysville is going to benefit for at least 15 years." These were not isolated views. Mayor Nuckles received hate mail because of his support for Honda. Residents were uneasy about a friendship center for the Japanese, many of whom—including Yoshida and his family—settled in Marysville. There were local jealousies, especially after other towns received more suppliers. In 1982, the concerns were even publicized by the *Wall Street Journal*. Entitled "Honda's U.S. Plant Brings Trouble, Not Prosperity, to Small Ohio Town," the story focused heavily on the wastewater plant controversy. Overall, many Marysville residents felt that they bore the costs of growth—especially increased traffic and a higher cost of living—while outsiders monopolized the jobs.[31]

Keeping a low profile, Honda went about its business. Following its announcement, the company began building the motorcycle plant and locating workers. From the start, Honda operated differently from American manufacturers, establishing processes that discouraged unionization. Seeking to assuage worries about the quality of American workers, Honda looked to build loyalty and make staff feel invested in their jobs. One of its first decisions was that all workers would be called "associates," a term that meant "members of a team working on behalf of a common goal." Job descriptions were designed to include responsibility for product quality, and there was a flat wage rate based on a job rotation system. Honda also rejected a traditional "preferential management system." Instead, all staff used the same cafeterias and wore the same uniforms, and parking spaces were allocated on a first come, first served basis. As it selected "associates," Honda privileged those without industry experience; they lacked preconceptions and were more receptive to the company's ideas. Like employees, managers were also hired from other industries. "Honda of America Manufacturing Inc. is led overwhelmingly by managers who came to auto manufacturing from jobs outside the industry," summarized *Automotive News*. Despite this, a "pool of lifelong Honda executives and advisers from Japan" were "ever present," indicating that most authority rested with foreign-born supervisors. Although it had not advertised, Honda received more than three thousand applicants for the first fifty jobs. On September 10, 1979, the plant made its first motorcycle.[32]

Four months later, Honda announced that it would build an auto plant on the same site. The company invested $250 million into the factory, which had a production capacity of nearly 150,000 units. It set about hiring two thousand more workers, with manufacturing to begin in two years. Many workers from the motorcycle factory were transferred to the car plant, which was run along the same lines. Again, "associates" were encouraged to identify with the company, and traditional lines between management and labor were blurred. It also proved easy to fill these jobs. As the Japanese press noted, the company benefited from the depressed economic climate, which hit Ohio hard. "When Honda started manufacturing motorcycles in 1979 and expanded production to cars in 1982, the employees were happy just getting a job," wrote Misato Yasunobu in *Shokun!* When the first car was produced on November 1, 1982, Honda was satisfied that it had achieved "the promised quality in Production." With Japanese managers overseeing operations, a second shift was added eighteen months later.[33]

The rapid expansion highlighted the project's importance. Anxious to prove that American workers could meet its standards, HAM president Shoichiro Irimajiri boldly predicted that Marysville would outproduce Japanese factories. The plant was also central to Honda's plans for the U.S. market. Following the success of the Accord and Civic, the company declared that it wanted to sell one million cars a year in the United States by the end of the 1980s and overtake Toyota as the leading Japanese brand in the country. For a small company, this was ambitious. In 1984, Honda sold 843,807 cars in Japan, whereas Toyota retailed over 2.4 million.[34]

Before the company could realize its dreams, the union question had to be resolved. The auto industry was one of the most unionized in America, and the UAW was one of the most powerful unions in the country. As historian Robert H. Zieger has written, the UAW was a "mass industrial union that had achieved splendid contracts for hundreds of thousands of auto and other industrial workers." Since the early 1940s, no company had run an auto plant in the United States without recognizing the UAW. What happened in Marysville, where the union was assaulting what one Japanese observer termed the "Honda Castle," had huge ramifications.[35]

Even before the motorbike plant was running, UAW staff were meeting with Honda executives, hoping to extract a recognition agreement. In the spring of 1979, regional UAW director Joe Tomasi met Honda officials at the Detroit airport to discuss the question. Dan Minor, a management attorney, represented Honda. It did not go well. "In the meeting they outlined to us what they hoped to have in the Marysville plant," Tomasi told the UAW's executive board. "The whole outline to us was a Right-to-Work, union-free environment. They wanted a Honda environment as far as Marysville was concerned." At the second gathering, Tomasi pressed Honda to "use practices like we do in General Motors, Ford, and Chrysler." He submitted names of laid-off Big Three workers as possible hires, but Honda ignored the suggestions, selecting local applicants instead. "They took them into the plant and totally indoctrinated them into the Honda system," Tomasi charged.[36]

The poor start was illustrative. The UAW expected Honda to act like the Big Three, but the company wanted to be different. Tomasi charged that Honda used the hiring process to avoid union influence, selecting workers from "within 30 miles of Marysville, where there are no unions." Potential hires went through four rounds of interviews and could be rejected for "attitude." "It is kind of a screening process," he asserted. When further efforts to get jobs for UAW members failed, Tomasi sent in organizers. Frustrated with Honda's refusal to hire "our people," he also became abusive in meetings, accusing managers of peddling "the same crap" to avoid the union. "If they get the auto plant under production with 500 of these type characters to start off with, we would be years ever trying to organize their auto plant," he admitted. Tomasi estimated that the UAW would get "two votes" from the first 250 workers.[37]

As negotiations continued, the gap between the sides increased. Influenced by its collaborative relationship with the Japanese Automobile Workers' Union (JAW), Honda saw the UAW as confrontational. Tomasi's abrasiveness fed this perception. Honda's "whole argument," Tomasi told the executive board, was that "the adversary relationship between the Auto Workers and the plants in this country tends to make for a bad product." Rejecting this view, the UAW viewed the JAW as too passive. "I have deep, deep suspicions about the trade unions in Japan," Fraser admitted. In retrospect, however, some staffers felt that Tomasi should have been more conciliatory, as Honda might have accepted a nontraditional contract. As former aide Frank Joyce put it, Tomasi "made all manner of hostile comments, about Honda and about the Japanese in general," sending a "very mixed message" to the company. The negotiations were difficult for Tomasi, a veteran who had received the Purple Heart after being injured at the Battle of Okinawa.[38]

Honda watched the UAW very carefully. In June 1980, an internal memorandum—obtained by the union—outlined the "UAW Arsenal." Managers feared that a raft of NLRB charges might be filed against them and worried that the union might launch a boycott, a tactic that labor had used in high-profile campaigns to organize textile workers and farmworkers in the 1970s.[39] "It is unclear how far they would go here," noted the memorandum, "but they could attempt to make 'Honda' the 'lettuce issue of the 1980's.'" A boycott could draw on "the full range of public relations options" and be very effective, especially as Honda's consumer profile was "heavily weighted towards the liberal side of the spectrum." Cooperation with other unions, particularly the International Longshoremen's Association and the International Brotherhood of Teamsters, could disrupt deliveries. Used to a system based on dialogue and collaboration, managers feared conflict with a union that was capable of "nailing" it.[40]

In the months that followed, UAW actions, although designed to pressure

Honda to recognize the union, made managers more fearful. In 1981, Tomasi stepped up organizing efforts, holding meetings with workers and encouraging them to wear UAW hats and badges in the plant. The move violated Honda's uniform policy, which required all employees to wear unadorned company garments. Although managers admitted that the policy met "resistance," they refused to budge. The company even banned the wearing of buttons, ostensibly because they might scratch the vehicles.[41] Viewing the rules as "anti-union," the UAW filed NLRB charges, arguing that the law protected employees' rights to wear union insignia. In 1981, the UAW won the case before the national NLRB, but the company appealed to the circuit court. As Tomasi admitted, Honda was "disturbed" by the union's willingness to file charges against it.[42]

Following this, relations remained strained. In 1981, the UAW won an election among the four boilerworkers at the plant. The union believed they had a foothold, but Honda insisted that the unit was too small to recognize. Again, the union won this case before the NLRB, but Honda appealed to the circuit court. In September, Tomasi reported that officials had told him that they were "willing to go as far as the Supreme Court to get a decision on the appropriateness of that particular unit." Feeling that its credibility was at stake, the UAW organized a mass rally in front of the plant. Hiring a venue, Tomasi ordered a large tent, big quantities of food, and portable toilets. At the national level, the UAW also began to organize a boycott to force the company to recognize the union. Staffers ordered thousands of hats bearing the slogan "Boycott Honda," made an agreement with West Coast dockworkers not to unload Honda cars, and prepared a national advertising campaign.[43]

Honda was very concerned. A boycott could unleash anti-Japanese sentiment at a time when most members of the World War II generation were still alive. Tensions were increased by the economic conditions of the early 1980s, a time when imported cars—mainly from Japan—reached record levels of market penetration. In 1980, with the American auto industry in what officials described as a "parlous condition," Japan exported 1.8 million cars to the United States, taking around a quarter of the market. Across the Midwest, including Ohio, imports were blamed for job losses. "In the early 1980s," wrote journalist David Gelsanliter, "in parts of Ohio, Japan was still the enemy." In northern Ohio, where thousands of steel and autoworkers sat idle, Japanese cars had their tires slashed, and rocks were thrown through the windows of dealers who sold them.[44] In southern Michigan, one domestic car dealer offered visitors a chance to smash a Japanese car with a sledgehammer, while some angry residents even shot at passing Japanese-brand cars. Politicians fanned the flames. In early 1982, Democratic presidential nomination Walter Mondale told American workers that there was only one way domestic auto dealers could sell cars made in Japan: "You better have the United States Army with you when they land on the docks." At this time, many U.S. union members displayed bumper stickers that read: "Hungry? Eat your foreign car." As the recession deepened and unemployment reached double-digit levels, anti-Japanese sentiment intensified. Honda also moved hundreds of Japanese nationals to the Marysville plant, which it viewed as what *The Harbour Report* called "a primary test lab for both the products and manufacturing techniques it would employ world-wide."[45]

To avert a boycott, Honda talked. At meetings on April 15 and 21, 1982, the two sides met in Findlay, Ohio, to work out a memorandum of agreement. Yoshida led the HAM team, while Tomasi headed a small UAW delegation. Citing the threat of a national boycott, Honda agreed to remain neutral in any UAW organizing campaign and to give ground on the uniform case. In return, the union pledged to be more supportive of Honda's philosophy. "Your representatives stated that the UAW wanted to establish a cooperative relationship with Honda which would recognize the Honda way of operating," summarized Yoshida in a letter to Bieber. "Because of all these things, and because of possible UAW actions which would have affected Honda's operations in the U.S., we agreed to drop our appeal and to remain neutral." To avoid being seen as a company union, the UAW rejected Yoshida's offer that—in exchange for a peaceful start-up—HAM would "help the UAW organize the plant." Rather, the UAW believed it could achieve this outcome.[46]

On paper, optimism was justified. Reached on April 21, the memorandum spoke of avoiding "confrontation," of establishing "a new and harmonious relationship." Honda agreed to recognize the UAW by authorization cards, on which workers declared that they wanted the UAW to represent them, if it signed up a "substantial majority" of employees by the first week of June 1983. In return, the UAW would avoid picketing, demonstrations, or boycotts, and it pledged to organize in a "pro-UAW manner and not an anti-Honda manner." Both sides arranged to "promptly" begin the negotiation of a labor agreement and to hold "regular private meetings" to discuss their relationship. They also decided that there should be "no dissemination" of the agreement's provisions, even to workers. Instead, they prepared a bland statement for subsequent release. Stressing the mutual desire for a "cooperative" relationship, the statement made no mention of specific terms.[47] The union's confidence was increased by an April 23 story in the *New York Times*. Headlined "Honda Ends Opposition to Auto Union's Efforts," it claimed that Honda would "no longer resist" the UAW, instead undertaking what it called a "new era of cooperation." Although reporter Clyde Farnsworth cited "industry sources," local managers claimed that they were "as surprised as anybody" to read the article. The company, they noted, would not be encouraging union activity.[48]

The ambiguity about what was said in Findlay—there was no detailed record of the meetings—was instructive. Over the succeeding months, the UAW expected Honda to recognize it, yet the company insisted that the decision was up to its employees. This position firmed as American managers exerted more influence. In response, the union's position hardened. The agreement provided some justification for its interpretation. In it, Honda pledged that by April 1 it would "advise its Associates" that it was "not opposed" to the union and would "guide" them to "recognize the need for UAW representation." The deadline passed, however, and nothing had changed.[49]

Other issues strained relations. In the early 1980s, the Big Three were hit hard by the recession; in January 1982, for example, more than two hundred thousand autoworkers had been laid off indefinitely. Instead of taking on these workers, many of whom were willing to move, Honda favored local employees. In November 1982, the UAW reported that Honda had hired "very few of our laid off autoworkers."[50] Defending the policy, Yoshida claimed it was vital to be "good neighbors and be welcomed by the local community." Even managers were chosen from workers at the motorcycle factory. While the company failed to mention the union issue, the UAW felt that Honda was avoiding workers who had been "contaminated by an adversarial labor-management relationship," as organizing director Stephen Yokich put it. "If they are unwilling to hire laid off UAW members and continue hiring highly screened and 'uncontaminated' workers, it may be a long time before we can bring this drive to a successful conclusion," he told Bieber in August 1983. Honda showed how the hiring process could be used to avoid unionization, a crucial lesson.[51]

Disagreement over domestic content legislation created further problems. In December 1982, the House passed the Fair Practices in Automotive Products Act, which limited the amount of foreign parts in cars sold in the United States. Honda claimed that the UAW-supported legislation would devastate its Ohio operations, which relied on imported parts. In the plant, managers held meetings to inform workers about this, annoying the union. "Anytime workers are threatened with a plant closing," wrote Page, "it is taken seriously." By November—with relations strained as the UAW pushed the bill—the labor attorney claimed that Honda had "apparently reneged on their commitment to us to assist their 'associates' to understand the need for union representation." Searching for answers, Page discussed ways of convincing Honda to honor the agreement, including filing a legal case, renewing picketing and boycotting, and organizing a key supplier. All of these options were risky, however; a boycott would be hard to maintain, while legal action would lead to disclosure of the document, which could be "embarrassing to the UAW as well as Honda." Because Honda had few links with American companies that recognized the UAW, the union also lacked financial leverage.[52]

On the ground, the union pressed on. Working out of a small office on the edge of Marysville, organizers contacted workers, making the most progress among skilled employees. "If we can win representation rights for the 50 Honda skilled tradesmen," argued Page, "we can once again be in a better bargaining position to force Honda to abide by the 1982 settlement agreement." Arguing that any election should involve the entire workforce, Honda saw it differently.[53] Over the spring and summer of 1984, the company's stance hardened. "It is clear that they intend to fight our attempts to organize Honda workers," Page wrote in March. When the UAW tried to organize a seat manufacturer that was part owned by Honda, managers threatened to close the plant. The UAW filed NLRB charges, but delays cost it momentum. Seeking a foothold, the UAW also organized employees of the Port Service Company, who drove finished cars to the railroad depot. Probably influenced by Honda, the company objected to an election.[54]

In the plant, where two shifts were running, Honda strove to build identification with its employees, policies that—intentionally or not—kept the UAW at bay. Core rules were indicative. All new employees, including executives, were required to work on the assembly line for fourteen weeks before starting their permanent positions. All staff, including executives, wore white overalls that were labeled with their Christian names, along with green caps. Uniforms were packed up by an outside company and washed each day, saving workers money. All employees were required to park in the same areas and eat in the same cafeterias. There was also just one wage rate for all associates in the assembly, weld, paint, tow driver, material services, and quality areas. The job of building identification was continuous and began early. When a worker was hired, he or she even received a small pine tree, which Honda planted in a field next to the plant, signifying each individual's "growth" with the company.[55]

These policies were backed up by concrete rewards. The VIP Program allowed workers to earn points for safety, quality, and productivity (the most common category), and these points led to the most successful workers earning free Honda cars. Each year, "high associates" also received two weeks of additional vacation, a pair of airline tickets to anywhere in the world, and a salary bonus. The points program, which was only available to nonsalaried workers, proved popular, as many wanted to come to work to increase their balance. Honda claimed that attendance exceeded 97 percent, an excellent result. All workers were also allowed to buy one Honda motorcycle, car, and power product at a substantial discount each year. In the longer term, workers received a company-funded pension, as well as a 401(k) savings plan and a profit-sharing plan.[56]

There were other benefits, both in cash and in kind. For just $12 per year, workers and their families could use the $15 million Associate Sports Center, which included a 25-meter swimming pool and fully equipped gym, as well as a Jacuzzi, sauna, and basketball court. There was a meeting room equipped with large-screen TVs, which were rare at the time. During their breaks, workers could eat in several well-stocked cafeterias, where meals cost no more than $2.25.[57] Early on, workers also enjoyed a series of wage and benefit hikes. In September 1984, when the plant celebrated its fifth anniversary, Irimajiri claimed that workers had received three achievement bonuses, as well as attendance bonuses and increases in weekly accident and sickness insurance. Over the five years, the company asserted that wages had risen 57 percent. "Our steady growth has consistently allowed security for all associates and their families," summarized a Honda document. "Through past wage improvements and benefit updates, we continue to be a highly competitive manufacturing company."[58]

Observers who toured the plant were impressed. "It was a scene of quite orderly assembly line work," wrote Japanese reporter Misato Yasunobu in 1985. "The way the employees were moving their hands and bodies in silence seemed quite skilful to me." The plant did not fulfill Japanese perceptions of American factories, which were often associated with unmotivated workers and poor quality. Good pay, especially by local standards, had allowed the company to carefully select workers and overcome these problems while also deterring the union. "As the UAW admits, the wages at Honda are very high in the area," explained journalist Nobuyoshi Yoshida. "So, there are few problems in terms of payments." In 1985, the average starting pay was ten dollars an hour, progressing to twelve dollars after eighteen months. This was well above local norms.[59] American visitors were similarly positive. Expecting auto factories to be dirty and congested, many were surprised by HAM. The rural location of the factory—seven miles out of town in the midst of farmland— also drew comment. As one reporter put it, the Marysville plant was an attractive "self-contained community" that had sprung up on "the flat fields of corn and soybeans of rural central Ohio." Perhaps seduced by these surroundings, even the liberal press gave Honda glowing praise. Following a visit in April 1985, *Washington Post* reporter Warren Brown imbibed the company's message. "A full day in HAM's 1-million-square-foot automobile factory indicates what Irimajiri and other Honda officials mean when they speak about 'togetherness,'" he concluded. "There is nothing mystical about it when observed first hand. It simply translates into one 'associate' pitching in to help another to get a particular job done." Honda was thriving because it was "doing everything right."[60]

The plant also grew because it made a proven product. When it opened, Accord sales were booming, and the factory, which began assembly with Japanese parts, did well. Assuaging fears of a quality drop, outside accolades for HAM-built cars poured in. From 1983 to 1991, the Ohio-made Accord was selected by *Car and Driver* as one of the ten best cars of the year. The public agreed, making the model one of the best selling in the country. In 1986, the plant also began producing the Civic, another established nameplate. Around this time, Honda's sales surpassed Nissan's, and some analysts predicted that the company could fulfill its goal of becoming the number one Japanese automaker in the United States.[61]

Based heavily on company sources—and reflecting early excitement—these reports went too far. In reality, building cars was physically demanding, even at Honda. From the beginning, workers suffered fatigue and workplace injuries but could only see company-approved doctors. "With a union, I could ask to see a doctor of my own choice," explained Gordon Kunkler, an injured lift driver. "I didn't know that." HAM workers were also not as well paid as their Big Three counterparts. Production workers at GM and Ford earned $13.29 an hour, while skilled trades workers earned an average of $15.68. For some, this gap of at least one dollar an hour was unfair.[62] Aware of workers' grievances, the UAW hoped to capitalize. In early 1985—with voluntary recognition unlikely—Bieber told Kawashima that he was authorizing "a more traditional and aggressive organizing drive." The goal was to call an election by the end of the year.[63]

The effort soon ran into problems. Organizers found it hard to penetrate the plant, even to find out workers' names and addresses. In September, Tomasi related that staff were still compiling an "accurate . . . listing of the employees." Another report noted that the "wide geographical area" that workers commuted from was a problem. To try and contact workers, the union had to buy airtime in several cities, including Columbus and Dayton. Furthermore, workers' youth created difficulties. In 1985, the average age of HAM employees was just twenty-nine, and most had yet to get hurt.[64] The union also accused Honda of opposing the drive to organize, alleging that managers had attended seminars entitled "Defending a Union-Free Status." In a May 1985 letter to Kawashima, Bieber was resolute—and scathing. "The UAW will become the bargaining agent for the Marysville workforce," he pledged. "It is just a matter of time. HAM's repudiation of the agreement may have delayed that eventuality, but it cannot change the result. However, where deceit is the cornerstone, it will be most difficult for the parties to forge a mutually beneficial relationship." Kawashima did not reply.[65]

Organizers pressed on. They reported that the lack of job posting, the violation of seniority in shift assignments, and the absence of an impartial grievance procedure were big issues. The central complaint, however, was high workloads. "Honda Associates are fed up with their lack of input into line speed at the Honda operations," summarized Tomasi. Without mentioning the memorandum, the UAW implored Honda to conduct a "high-level, fair campaign." On October 30, the union petitioned for an election, and the NLRB ruled that a vote would be held on December 19.[66] In private, the union was less confident. "We should hold the election—win or lose," Yokich wrote Bieber in September. "Then we will know what we have to do for the next year."

If the union could mount a "full swing drive," Honda might agree to recognize the UAW based on the number of authorization cards signed by workers. A worried Bieber agreed.[67]

Honda, however, was in no mood to compromise. Spurning the UAW's appeals, it cited the results of an internal questionnaire in which over 73 percent of workers agreed "strongly" or "somewhat" with the assertion that HAM should "reject the UAW request" and hold a secret ballot election. Although the UAW claimed that the October 29 poll was unreliable, Honda was emboldened. In a letter to employees, Yoshida pictured the UAW as an outsider whose campaign focused on "how bad things are at Honda." Intimating that the union would hurt HAM, Yoshida added that every worker had a "major stake" in the election. "We all want the kind of job security that comes from producing quality products at competitive prices," he added.[68] Although the company maintained that the issue was up to workers, managers were becoming involved. In another letter to staff, Yoshida illustrated this contradiction well. While claiming to be neutral, the executive added that he was "pleased that most of our associates support what we have been trying to do together."[69]

Other trends boded poorly for the UAW. By 1985, the plant still had many Japanese managers, but top positions were being given to Americans. When Misato Yasunobu visited the plant in 1985, she found that out of 3,038 employees, 158 were Japanese (still a sizeable number). Keen to secure acceptance, Honda appointed Robert Watson as its first American plant manager. When Watson died of a brain hemorrhage in August 1984, his replacement was Scott Whitlock, a "combative" corporate lawyer. In one detailed document, supervisors were now instructed to stress the cost of union dues and the prevalence of strikes at organized firms, familiar tropes of the union avoidance industry. They also claimed that the UAW would make HAM "noncompetitive," a powerful threat.[70] As the vote neared, managers took an even harder line. In the plant, supervisors posted information sheets that portrayed the UAW as an outside force with little to offer. As wages and benefits were "subject to negotiation," workers risked a lot by supporting the union.[71] Funded largely by local businesses, the Associates Alliance—an employee group designed to "keep Honda union-free"—also became active. The group's combative materials, including its symbol of the UAW logo with a black line through it, linked the union to the Big Three's problems. "UAW Loses Jobs While Honda Gains," summarized one flyer.[72]

As the vote loomed, the UAW knew it was in trouble. Writing to Tomasi, Page was unable to find a path to victory. The recognition agreement, he noted, was "extremely difficult to enforce." The Associates Alliance was probably receiving "illegal assistance," yet proving it was tricky. Because the alliance used the UAW's logo, an infringement action was considered, but this would be time-consuming. As a result, Page recommended abandoning the election.

"I understand our own poll indicates that a clear majority of the Honda employees are likely to vote against us on December 19," he noted. "If this cannot be changed dramatically in the near future, I would urge that we not proceed with the election. I have never seen any positive results from taking a loss in an NLRB election."[73] To save face, the UAW filed unfair labor practice charges, alleging that the preelection survey had interrogated employees in order to "chill" organizing. According to the union, Honda had also granted employees improved benefits, including extra holidays, in order to "discourage" unionization and had illegally supported the Associates Alliance.[74]

Honda's Japanese managers were appalled by the charges, which confirmed their view that the UAW was too adversarial. Top executives were piqued by the UAW's criticisms, especially its claim that the company was a "patriarchal monarchy." Workers—and their unions—should be loyal. Identifying with Honda, Japanese reporters described a cultural discomfort with the labor board. "Whatever the truth is, if the UAW tells the NLRB that there is some doubt, the NLRB has to start an investigation," wrote reporter Nobuyoshi Yoshida. "Furthermore, troubles between the employer and the employees tend to happen at such occasions. The situation turned into what the company feared."[75]

Assuaging Honda's fears, the NLRB dismissed the charges. Disappointed UAW leaders saw the decision as symptomatic of the Reagan era, in which the NLRB became less supportive of labor rights.[76] Following this, the UAW withdrew its petition. On March 14, Yokich told Bieber that fewer than 650 workers out of "at least" 2,800 had signed cards. Explaining its deteriorating position, the UAW again blamed the NLRB, management opposition, and the Associates Alliance. In September, Honda also announced a major expansion, increasing employment to thirty-five hundred jobs. As the UAW noted, this created "a poor climate for a representation election." Along with being hard to contact, new hires were young and optimistic.[77]

The expansion helped Honda in other ways. It generated positive headlines, validating claims that the plant was thriving without a union. As Japan's *Shokun!* magazine put it, "That announcement seemed to symbolize Honda's determination not to be swayed by the UAW incidents." Honda boasted that after just three years of production, it had become the fourth largest automaker in the United States and the only one to build car and motorbike engines domestically. The expansion was impressive, increasing the size of the assembly plant from 1 million to 2.2 million square feet and leading to the establishment of two production lines. Costing $532 million, these changes increased annual production to 360,000 vehicles.[78]

Calling off the election left the UAW in a weak position. Announcing the move, leaders put on a brave face. "This is not an admission of defeat—far from it," Tomasi told the press. "We intend to continue the drive at Honda and to put even more people and resources into the campaign." In private, however, leaders were sanguine. Organizing Honda was "very, very difficult," admitted Bieber, especially as the company was expanding.[79]

Campaign records reveal that the defeat reflected more than Honda's opposition—or the plant expansion. Both Page and Yokich argued that the UAW needed stronger central direction, including a public relations strategy overseen by a dedicated staffer. This would counteract the positive press coverage that Honda enjoyed.[80] In September 1986, Yokich also told the executive board that while the UAW was doing more organizing than most unions, his staff was small. Over the previous year, a small minority of organizers had called the majority of elections. Others spent much of their time servicing members, especially displaced Big Three workers.[81] There were also tensions between national and regional staff. Bieber, Page, and Yokich complained that Tomasi did a poor job of managing the drive. The union's decentralized structure proved problematic, as Tomasi resisted central direction. Pushing for more confrontational tactics, Tomasi disagreed with the decision to postpone the election, and he encouraged workers to believe that the UAW would sue the Associates Alliance. This never occurred.[82]

The UAW, whose twenty-five-member executive board included just one woman, Odessa Komer, also struggled to mobilize women workers.[83] Internal files showed that women comprised about 15 percent of Honda's production employees. Tomasi stressed that the UAW, along with needing "a few more organizers," required a female staffer "to coordinate activities for the women employees." The culture of the union continued to be male-dominated. (Despite his suggestion, Tomasi also recommended that a "young lady" be hired for clerical tasks.) Staffer Jim Turner related that all of the Honda organizers were men, and they struggled to mobilize females. In a confidential memorandum, he wrote, "384 identified women; very little UAW support."[84] This was a lost opportunity, especially as early managers were unused to women workers: in Japan, labor laws banned women from working in factories after 10:00 p.m. There were complaints of sexism in Marysville, where women performed a wide variety of production jobs.[85]

The union made other mistakes. Rather than spending time in Marysville, Bieber and Yokich focused on negotiations with top executives, especially lengthy efforts to implement the memorandum. According to Turner, the campaign became a "fight between the UAW and Honda," with workers left as "bystanders."[86] In other ways, the agreement—which the UAW had envisaged as the key to a breakthrough—had the opposite effect. By signing it, the union lost leverage, especially as the document's key terms were so difficult to enforce. Publicizing the agreement was problematic, as it could be portrayed as a "sweetheart deal." Left "extremely frustrated" that they had been unable to "make Honda pay," UAW strategists placed too much faith in the memorandum.[87]

After winning at the NLRB, Honda was on a high. In February 1986, Yoshida informed Bieber that it was the UAW that had violated the memorandum, in which it had agreed that it would not organize in an "anti-Honda manner." UAW materials, charged Yoshida, had been designed "not really to promote the UAW but to criticize Honda and its management." Top Japanese executives also rejected accusations that they were antiunion. The policy of letting associates decide, explained Honda's chairman, Noburo Okamura, was "in line with Honda's global corporate philosophy of neutrality, which emphatically is not one of anti-unionism and not one of anti-unionism at Honda of America Mfg., Inc."[88] In contrast, the UAW was in a difficult position. In early 1986, it tried to restart the drive. Placed in charge, Turner was told by Yokich to "start from scratch if necessary." The veteran staffer reported that it remained very difficult to organize Honda, which was taking on new hires and attracting positive headlines. HAM also used organized tours to bolster its position. "The facilities are impressive," wrote industry guru Jim Harbour in 1987 after a company-endorsed visit, "but more impressive is the totally dedicated workforce. This just isn't employee involvement or quality of worklife, this is total commitment to building a car for the Everlasting Customer." Amid the acclaim, the UAW struggled to be heard.[89]

The positive reports contained some validity. In November 1986, one group of UAW members that visited HAM portrayed it as a place where employees worked hard but enjoyed a quiet, clean, and spacious environment. While workers were "busy," they were not resentful. "Everyone is proud of their plant, their company and their job," they concluded in a report sent to Bieber. In February 1987, a tour by a group of workers from the Saturn plant in Spring Hill, Tennessee—a UAW facility—reached similar conclusions. "The Honda work force appeared youthful, active, and self-assured," they asserted.[90]

Not all of Honda's practices were praiseworthy. The Marysville workforce was overwhelmingly white, especially compared to Big Three plants. For generations, the automotive industry had served as an important source of upward mobility for African Americans. In 1984, blacks comprised about 11 percent of the U.S. labor force but made up over 17 percent of Big Three workers. Data from *Automotive News* showed that Honda's early workforce in Marysville was just 2.8 percent black, while the surrounding area was 10.5 percent African American. The workforce at suppliers was also heavily white. Touring the plant in 1985, Yasunobu noted the disparity. "Another thing that was striking to me was that 98–99% of the employees were white people," she wrote. "There were only a few black people." The outcome reflected Honda's policy of hiring from a thirty-five-mile radius, excluding the urban areas (mainly Columbus) where most blacks lived. Keeping the policy quiet, Honda claimed that few minorities were available.[91] Given that African Americans were more likely to organize—in the 1980s, one out of every four black workers was a union member—critics charged that the move had ulterior motives.[92]

They had a point. When it looked at the Marysville site, Honda sought information about the racial makeup of the area. As Rhodes's files indicate, state officials sent Honda data showing that the area was 90 percent white. While the matter was not explicitly discussed, both sides knew that whites were less likely to organize.[93] Some industry analysts felt that Honda's executives—used to racial homogeneity—sought the same in America. According to Sean McAlinden at the Center for Automotive Research, Honda wanted "rural American counties with primarily German ethnicity," giving it a workforce that would accept its ideas. As the *Japan Times* reported, when Honda looked at sites, it dismissed the idea of locating in racially diverse California.[94]

The situation came to a head in March 1988, when Honda agreed to pay $6 million to 377 blacks and women who had been denied jobs at HAM. Managers settled the charges by the Equal Employment Opportunity Commission (EEOC) after a federal investigation. Although the company was hit with a heavy fine, the case was not widely reported, and managers maintained a heavily white—and male—workforce.[95] The UAW tried to capitalize on the situation, but as most blacks and women were applicants rather than employees, it was difficult. After the 1985 campaign, the union supported Urban League programs to send minority applicants to HAM. The union hoped that having more blacks in the plants would boost organizing, yet Honda still picked workers carefully. "It seems that this may be a way to get UAW people into that facility *if* Honda does not screen out minorities that would normally be pro-union and selectively hire those who are not," wrote staffer Dick Shoemaker. Observers who toured the plant continued to comment on the absence of minorities and women, as well as the dominance of youth. "Honda associates average 27 years of age," noted the Saturn delegation in 1987. "There are many more men than women and almost all were white. One minority was seen working on the assembly line."[96]

At the UAW, there was also room for improvement. Under Turner, a female organizer was hired but was soon reassigned, angering women workers. "It certainly doesn't make much impression on the women to see an organizing drive for a plant this size, with no women on the organizing front," HAM worker Linda Woods wrote Bieber. According to Woods, women employees suffered "discrimination and harassment," and this was "a major point in favour of the UAW." Although organizing the plant would be a "slow struggle," Woods pleaded with the union to stay active. In reply, Bieber expressed "concern," but there was no evidence of action.[97] By the spring of 1987, a year after Turner's arrival, the drive had petered out. When the Saturn group toured the plant, they observed "about twelve" employees wearing UAW hats, a tiny fraction. In October 1988, Bieber told *Automotive News* that the union remained "in touch" with supporters at Honda. Refusing to elaborate, he discussed campaigns at Toyota and Nissan instead.[98]

In the 1990s, there were sporadic efforts to organize HAM. The union claimed that it was "building up members gradually," but reality was more sobering. As a thriving employer, Honda was in a more powerful position than it had been a decade earlier, when it anxiously established the plant. In 1993, the UAW considered restarting the drive but knew it would be difficult, especially as Honda's community support had increased (helped by regular corporate donations). As regional director Jack Sizemore reported, work needed to be done to "enhance the image of the UAW in the largely non-union areas surrounding the Honda plants."[99] Union-commissioned research highlighted the difficulties. In 1991, the consulting firm Greer, Margolis, and Mitchell concluded that HAM was a "poor target" for organizing, partly because of the lack of unions in the area. Two years later, confidential polling by other consultants reached a bleak conclusion. "The polls at Marysville were among the most anti-union the firm has ever found in its long experience in polling worksites," it noted.[100] The establishment of the East Liberty plant in 1989, which followed the "land only" formula, complicated the union's task, especially as NLRB rulings increasingly forced unions to organize multiple units rather than single facilities. "You couldn't just zero in," recalled Bieber. By 1995, when he retired, Bieber was philosophical about Honda. "We were never able to get the support that we thought was sufficient to go to election," he admitted.[101]

As it expanded, Honda won over critics. In 1993, Senator John Glenn, who had earlier supported import quotas on Japanese cars, visited the Honda plant, describing it as "an impressive operation." By this time, Glenn—aware of Honda's contribution to Ohio's economy—backed the company's claims that its cars were American. Other politicians praised the plant, cementing its reputation as a model operation. In April 1993, President Bill Clinton commented, "I just love that Marysville plant and I'd really love to visit it sometime." For Clinton, the factory showed that Americans could build high-quality products for global corporations. By 1994, the Honda Accord was exported in larger numbers than any other American-made car, winning many admirers. "Honda still knows how to build cars as well, or better than anyone else in the world," admitted the *Detroit Free Press*. Thriving on the good news, Honda claimed that it had no labor problems. "The spirit of teamwork and participatory management . . . is the foundation upon which our quality vehicles are built," asserted manager Barbara Nocera.[102]

There remained another side to the story. Behind the headlines, workers had grievances, especially about workloads and injury rates. In early 1995, HAM increased the speed of the line and required workers to work on Saturdays. The union's Harold Cassel reported that many workers were "very upset" over the changes, with some scrawling "UAW" on management proposal cards, on which workers were supposed to choose which of three plans to further increase output they preferred. The move came after complaints from Japanese management that HAM was not meeting its "production schedule."[103] In 2001, the UAW renewed its organizing efforts after receiving complaints from workers, especially about injuries. As part of its campaign, the union used federal safety logs to charge that HAM's injury rates were more than double the average for the industry, releasing the data to the *New York Times*. In a detailed *Times* story, many workers backed up the charges with candid testimony. "You can walk down our assembly line and ask anybody what their injury is, they all have one," claimed Daniel Lowe, an air force veteran. "It was the fastest work I ever had to do in my life," he added. "The first three months, ice packs on my wrists, my ankles and my lower back, not to mention the endless amounts of Tylenol, Ibuprofen, Alleve [*sic*], painkillers by the bucket." Honda refused to release its OSHA 200 logs, adding that its injury rate was high because it reported minor incidents. Industry sources, however, also suggested that these were demanding jobs. In 2002, *The Harbour Report* ranked the East Liberty and Marysville plants as requiring less time than average to build a car. The plants achieved this despite launching new models, which usually slowed production. While HAM's efficiency was praised, this also meant that line speeds were high.[104]

There were also disputes about how "American" HAM's cars were. Critics charged that Honda exaggerated the number of domestic parts in each car, a number that was partly a matter of definition. In November 1991, even *Business Week* threw doubt on HAM's claims. "Honda, Is It an American Car?" it asked. Honda was accused of trying to "roll up" the North American content of its Ohio-made engines, with the Bush administration's Commerce Department asserting that most Honda parts came from Japan. In response, managers gave a vigorous defense, Whitlock insisting that the amount of domestic parts had increased. Certainly, Honda was using more American parts than it had. In 1990, the *New York Times* reported that HAM had contracts with 194 U.S. parts suppliers, up from 27 when it opened. It was wrong, Whitlock concluded, "to treat the work of 1,927 Americans employed at our Ohio engine plant as foreign content." Nevertheless, Honda—like the Japanese carmakers that followed—opposed domestic content laws, suggesting that the benefit to local suppliers and workers was more limited than the industry portrayed. In 1994, even Department of Commerce undersecretary Jeffrey Garten called on the Japanese companies to "make good on what they have said publicly, that they intend to achieve significantly higher levels of parts made in the United States." Strict numerical targets, managers responded, were unfair.[105]

It was also difficult for workers to change conditions, a reality many accepted. Honda maintained decisive advantages, especially in deciding where plants were located and who got jobs. By building factories in semirural areas, Honda offered pay and benefits that exceeded local norms, meaning its jobs were always in demand. As one HAM worker put it, he thought he had "hit the lottery" when he got hired. Although the work was hard, many workers reasoned that they would enjoy the pay and benefits for a while, giving them the chance to create a cushion for the future. Others rationalized that injuries were a trade-off for good wages and benefits. "You're going to have that [injuries] in any plant," summarized Stan Parshall, who had worked at Ford. "Factory work is factory work."[106]

Events in Ohio had wide-ranging ramifications. For Honda, Marysville gave it the confidence to expand globally and follow the "land-only" formula. In 1990, the company opened a $600 million greenfield factory in Swindon, England. Copying many ideas from HAM, Honda ensured that Swindon became Europe's first nonunion car factory. (Managers even called workers "associates.") The UAW also learned a lot from events in Marysville. Leaders reflected that the union should have done more to accept a "flexible" contract, as a foot in the door of the new industry would have been invaluable.[107] Hoping for a new "starting point," the UAW now focused on other companies, particularly Nissan, which was building a plant four hundred miles away. Events in Tennessee would comprise another decisive chapter in the industry's history, one with similarities—but also sharp differences—from what had occurred in Ohio.[108]

CHAPTER THREE

The Jewel in Tennessee?
Critiquing Nissan's Arrival
and Growth in Smyrna

On October 30, 1980, Nissan announced that it had chosen a tract of farmland near Smyrna, Tennessee, as the site for a multi-million-dollar assembly plant, its first in the United States. This was an important moment in the automotive industry's history, and the news secured global headlines.[1] It was the first time that a transplant had been established in the South, a region with little record of building cars.[2] It was also the largest investment— over $660 million—ever made by a Japanese company in the United States and the biggest by a private enterprise in Tennessee. According to Governor Lamar Alexander, this was a "watershed" event for Tennessee that would create economic and demographic growth. Unlike Ohio, which attracted Honda to replace lost industry, Tennessee, a more rural state, would build a new industry from scratch.[3]

In June 1983, the plant produced its first light truck on time, and in subsequent years it expanded steadily. By 1992, Smyrna was the largest car plant under one roof in the country. Located just off Interstate 24, it covered 6.8 million square feet—or more than 151 football fields. Some sixty-three hundred people worked there, with many driving long distances to do so. In 1999, Nissan CEO Carlos Ghosn, citing the plant's efficiency, called Smyrna "one of the top factories in North America." By 2015, following continued growth, Smyrna was the biggest-producing car factory in North America.[4]

The plant played a crucial role in encouraging the sector's growth, especially in the South. By 2015, BMW, Honda, Hyundai, Kia, Mercedes-Benz, Toyota, and Volkswagen had all built plants in the region, which had become an automaking powerhouse. As the *Atlanta Journal-Constitution* put it, "The trend line toward the South supplanting Detroit began . . . when Nissan selected Smyrna, Tenn., for a truck manufacturing facility." By 2015, the Center for Automotive Research documented that five of the top ten auto-producing states—Alabama, Kentucky, Mississippi, Tennessee, and Texas—were in the South. The region, declared the *Washington Post*, had a "new car smell."[5]

Because of this growth, Smyrna's story has usually been told in positive terms. The new factory, summarized the *Chicago Tribune*, was "the jewel in Tennessee." Even the liberal *New York Times* and *Washington Post* pictured the plant as an egalitarian place where workers—or "technicians," as Nissan called them—had a role in decision-making. Reporters also claimed that residents welcomed the Japanese; tensions seemed absent. In Smyrna, summarized the *Times*, "the US and Japan mesh."[6] Led by Alexander, who went on to chair the Senate Republican Conference, influential leaders trumpeted the plant's success. As the *Post* observed, Tennessee's politicians held up the factory as "a shining example of success in the global economy."[7]

The plant's growth, however, also generated little-known costs. Using new archival records and interviews, this account explores the other side of the story. Nissan's arrival in Tennessee created significant tension and opposition, including anti-Japanese sentiment. When the plant opened, labor groups protested vociferously, even disrupting ground-breaking ceremonies. Later, Nissan workers complained repeatedly about conditions, leading to high-profile organizing campaigns. Although Nissan vehemently opposed the union, around one-third of the workforce still voted for the UAW in 1989 and 2001. Smyrna was not a "non-union 'utopia.'"[8]

The story of how Nissan came to Tennessee also warrants investigation. The plant's arrival is commonly linked to a $33 million state incentive package, yet many other factors—particularly locational advantages, lower manufacturing costs, the popularity of pickup trucks in the area, and the personal intervention of Alexander—played little-known roles. Primary sources throw new light on the story, showing that it had deeper roots than many realized.[9]

For Nissan, Smyrna was an important chapter in its history. The automaker began selling vehicles in the United States in 1958 and was the first Japanese firm to develop a light-duty pickup. Nissan introduced the model into the United States in 1960 and sold more than 1 million over the next two decades. By 1980, light trucks comprised 20 percent of its American sales. Proud of its role as a "pioneer" in this segment, in April 1980 Nissan announced plans to build these "historically significant" vehicles in the United States. As president Takashi Ishihara explained, the move was designed to allow Nissan to "be a much larger part of the U.S. scene and to assure the already well-established brand name." In deciding where to site the plant, the company immediately looked at Tennessee and Georgia because these states accounted for 36 percent of light truck sales.[10]

The plant also reflected the industry's globalization. Nissan already had factories in Mexico and Australia and was planning them in Italy and Spain.[11] Japanese automakers were under particular pressure to build their vehicles in the United States. In the 1970s, every small pickup that was made in Japan faced a 25 percent tariff from the U.S. government. Introduced in 1963 by President Johnson in reaction to foreign duties on American poultry, this tariff was known as the "chicken tax." Nissan's decision also came after its lineup of smaller vehicles did well during the global fuel crises. Between 1970 and 1980, Nissan's U.S. sales increased from 151,509 to 628,136, and in 1975, the company overtook Volkswagen as the leading import brand. By 1980, Nissan had the necessary sales volume—and brand recognition—to justify U.S. production. As it was making the move, the company adopted the Nissan name (rather than Datsun) to increase global recognition.[12]

Nissan's decision was a long time coming. As Ishihara related, executives began feasibility studies for the plant in 1974. Over the next six years, a wide range of states wooed Nissan, particularly in the closing stages. "Every state east of the Mississippi River has been doing everything it can to locate this plant in its state for the past 15 months," claimed Alexander in 1980. Nissan looked at sixty-four sites in eight states before narrowing its choice to Smyrna, Tennessee, and Cartersville, Georgia.[13] Alexander's Democratic predecessor, Ray Blanton, also played a little-known role. In 1977, Blanton made a crucial change when he moved the Industrial Training Service from the state Department of Education to the Department of Economic and Community Development following a consultant's recommendation. The move allowed Tennessee to offer worker training at state expense. Economic commissioner James Cotham, who helped recruit Nissan, called the training service "the most valuable tool we have in attracting new industry." Later, Nissan cited it as a central reason for choosing Tennessee. In Smyrna, some local officials remembered Blanton's efforts. According to former city clerk Mike Woods, while Alexander got "all of the credit" for Nissan's arrival, Blanton laid important "groundwork," developing bonds with "tentative" executives. "They just didn't show up and say, 'I want to be here,'" explained Woods. "It was a relationship-building process."[14]

Blanton's political demise ensured that his role was forgotten. His administration ended in controversy over the selling of pardons and liquor licenses, forcing him to retire in disgrace. Although Blanton's papers are incomplete, they show that he helped convince Nissan Industrial Equipment Company, a subsidiary of Nissan Motors, to open a plant in Memphis, which also became the national headquarters and distribution center for Datsun forklifts. The move created an important precedent. In 1981, the Tennessee House of Representatives passed a resolution to celebrate the Smyrna announcement. It noted the importance of the five-year-old forklift plant, adding that Nissan was "an excellent corporate citizen." Alexander also recognized the facility's significance, especially in establishing a Japanese corporate presence in the state.[15]

Building on Blanton's work, Alexander was determined to land more Japanese investment. Elected governor in 1978 under the slogan "Come Along with Alexander," the thirty-eight-year-old Republican traveled frequently to Japan. Explaining his motives, Alexander credited an early White House dinner where President Carter told him, "Go to Japan. Persuade them to make here what they sell here." At the time, Tennessee's family income ranked forty-seventh in the nation. A much poorer state than Ohio, Tennessee would have to work hard to attract an automaker, but Alexander felt he had nothing to lose.[16] "The best thing the Governor can do for Tennessee is everything he can think of to help raise every family's income," he wrote, referring to Nissan. Alexander's interest in Japan also reflected his responsiveness to agricultural interests; the state's farmers exported 40 percent of their products, and Japan was their number one market. His "first priority," however, was attracting good-paying jobs.[17]

In office, Alexander gave a high priority to Japanese investment. During his first term, he visited Japan eight times. On these trips, Alexander had four audiences with the Japanese prime minister and met "dozens of times" with ambassadors, government leaders, and top business executives. In the process, he developed a pitch that downplayed differences between the Japanese and Tennesseans. Instead, Alexander emphasized that Tokyo and Nashville shared a similar altitude, climate, and terrain. "Their maples turn in November just after ours do in October," he explained. In response, Nissan executives expressed affinity for Tennessee's flora and fauna, including its dogwoods, cherry blossoms, and chrysanthemums. Tennessee's state flower, the iris, was even the favourite flower of most Japanese. These personal connections were important. "When I come here, I feel at home," declared Nissan chairman Masahiko Zaitsu on a visit to Smyrna.[18]

Drawing on these travels, Alexander liaised closely with Nissan's top managers as they selected a site. Between July 14 and 16, 1980, Ishihara undertook a secret visit to the Nashville area. During the trip, Alexander accompanied the president on clandestine tours of "the site." The pair also explored the Smyrna area by helicopter, apparently using state facilities to facilitate arrangements. Throughout the visit, Alexander was a courteous host. On July 15, he lunched with Mr. and Mrs. Ishihara at the Governor's Mansion. Before the meal Cotham reminded his boss, "Mrs. Ishihara will be there, so it will be important that Honey [Alexander's wife] be there as well," advice the governor heeded.[19] Alexander also liaised with T. F. Yukawa, Ishihara's personal assistant, describing him later as "a major figure in Nissan coming to Tennessee." Yukawa subsequently thanked the governor "for all the courtesies, assistance and advice" he had "thoughtfully extended" during the long recruitment process. In all, Alexander spent sixteen months in direct negotiations with Nissan, assisted by several aides. Zaitsu alone was received at the Governor's Mansion eleven times.[20]

Other evidence suggests that Alexander's relationship with Nissan's managers influenced the company's decision. As the *Nashville Banner* reported, state officials were particularly important in the final stages. "Smyrna and Georgia were in heated competition for the site," it noted, "and Smyrna was chosen after strong personal persuasion by Gov. Alexander, State Commissioner of Economic and Community Development James C. Cotham III, the Nashville Area Chamber of Commerce and others." When Ishihara was ready to make up his mind, he even called Alexander before alerting the media. At the plant's ground-breaking, Nissan vice president Masataka Okuma—one of the world's top auto executives and the man overseeing Nissan's overseas operations—recalled a meeting during which Alexander offered to "join" with the automaker in a "partnership for success." The metaphor stayed with Okuma. "Partners work together," he added. They "contribute their resources, talents and knowledge to a common goal."[21]

Perhaps Alexander's most decisive contribution, however, was securing the land. On their visits to Tennessee, Nissan executives found an ideal site, a 437-acre dairy farm that had once been a cotton plantation. Close to major highways and railroads, the site was completely flat, slashing the company's preparation costs. The land, however, was not for sale, and its owners resisted state overtures. When he found that Maymee Cantrell was refusing to sell, Alexander caught a plane and was then driven to her Waverly home. At 8:00 p.m. one Friday, the two sat down to iced tea and homemade key lime pie. "Maymee, I hope you will let Nissan buy your land," implored the governor. "It will tell the whole world that Tennessee is the best place to do business and bring jobs to people who need them." Feeling obliged to a caretaker whom she had promised could live on the farm, Cantrell refused to budge. For several weeks, the retired schoolteacher had also rebuffed local and state agencies. Aware that the deal was in jeopardy—Smyrna was the only Tennessee site that Nissan would accept—local leaders contacted the governor. After Alexander personally arranged for the caretaker to move to a new farm ten miles away, Cantrell signed the deeds. As officials recalled, it also helped that she was a Republican.[22]

A few days later, Alexander found out that Nissan also wanted a 260-acre farm that had been owned by the McClary family for over one hundred years. He paid another visit, talking the situation over on the family's porch "one hot June night" and persuading them to sell. Mrs. McClary later explained that she had done the right thing for local people but added, "I can't say it makes me happy to lose our farm." Alexander relied on more than moral pressure. He agreed that the state would pay over $8,000 an acre, well above market value. Receiving the same price, the third farm that made up the site was acquired more easily. Alexander stayed in touch with the residents, who were a "vital link" in the Nissan story, calling them when the news broke. In February 1981, the Cantrells attended the ground-breaking ceremony as guests of the state. The incidents, however, showed that there was resistance to Nissan's arrival.[23]

As he was securing the land, Alexander was putting together a $33 million incentive package. The state contributed $7 million to help Nissan train workers and pledged to spend even more to build a five-lane road to the plant. Furthermore, the Louisville and Nashville railroad agreed to construct a spur to the plant. The plant was also financed by $450 million in low-interest industrial bonds from Rutherford County that Nissan would gradually pay back. Rutherford County had other advantages; taxes were lower than in Nashville, and the cost of living was less. Moreover, Tennessee did not have a corporate income tax.[24] Not surprisingly, a state analysis justified the incentives, claiming that revenues from the plant would exceed expenditures by the end of 1983. Nissan estimated that its plant would create more than nine thousand direct and related jobs by 1984, producing a payroll exceeding $70 million.[25]

The incentives, however, were not decisive. Announcing the company's choice of Smyrna, Ishihara admitted that there were "no substantial differences" between the financial offers of Tennessee and Georgia, adding that the company had made its final decision based on "the actual conditions of the sites." Smyrna, he noted, was "excellent and quite satisfactory to Nissan Motor Co. in terms of location and physical features, zoning, and good access to highways." Because the plant was fully "integrated," consisting of stamping, welding, body assembly, painting, and final assembly, the soil conditions were particularly important, and in this area Smyrna excelled. Ishihara also termed the location "excellent from the standpoint of distribution," both for importing components and for shipping vehicles.[26]

In a broader sense, location was crucial. For a company that depended heavily on the U.S. market, Tennessee's central geographical position was vital. Smyrna was located near Tennessee's geographical center and within one day's delivery by road of 76 percent of U.S. consumers. Nissan liked Smyrna because it was centrally located for customers in the populous eastern third of the country, while parts could be easily shipped from the Pacific Coast by train. As an analysis in the *New York Times* concluded, the Smyrna site was also just off Interstate 24 and close to Interstates 40 and 65. Nissan's soil testing found that a bed of limestone just beneath the topsoil provided an excellent foundation for the company's stamping presses and other heavy equipment. "They were looking for an area that had good solid bedrock, well [*laugh*] we've got a lot of rock here," recalled Mike Woods. Alexander knew he was fortunate. "There are things God gave us and we can't take the credit for," he admitted, referring to the location and soil.[27]

Also drawn to Tennessee's central location, other Japanese firms had provided precedents. In 1978, Sharp and Toshiba began operations in the state, making television sets and microwave ovens in Memphis and Lebanon, respectively. Tabuchi Electrical Company had a plant in Jackson, while Matsushita was completing new factories in Fayetteville and Knoxville. When Nissan made its decision, fourteen Japanese-owned or joint-venture firms had already invested $433 million in Tennessee. "We certainly have more capital investments from Japan than any other southern state, and very likely, more than any other state in the United States," Alexander wrote.[28]

The state also had low labor costs. The average wage was $7.49 an hour, below national norms ($8.84). Tennessee had been a right-to-work state since 1947, reducing union influence. While Nissan avoided comment, many observers saw the union issue as significant. According to the *Chicago Tribune*, the "non-union atmosphere" was important in attracting the automaker. The right-to-work law, agreed an analysis in the *Nashville Banner*, was a "major inducement" for Japanese firms, which valued "close family-like ties with their employees" and feared adversarial labor relations. As Ishihara related, Nissan initially considered sites in the Great Lakes states, but they were discounted.[29] A Tennessee House resolution that welcomed Nissan recognized that the company liked "the work ethic and productivity of Tennessee workers," as well as the state's positive "business climate."[30]

Occasionally, state officials addressed the issue directly. In subsequent correspondence with Ishihara, Alexander stressed the importance of Tennessee's right-to-work law, especially in comparison to Kentucky. "There is a very different labor situation in Kentucky than in Tennessee," he noted. "Kentucky does not have a right-to-work law." As a result, the "Tennessee work environment" was "superior to the Kentucky work environment," as well as that of the midwestern states. In a detailed account of the Nissan recruitment process, Alexander also spoke to the topic. "More than anything else," he explained, "the Japanese decision makers like the Tennessee labor force." Tennesseans had good "work habits," and executives from Sharp and Toshiba praised their employees' productivity to Nissan. Toshiba, he noted, had expanded twice before Nissan arrived.[31]

Local leaders also helped to recruit Nissan. Known for his diminutive stature and sharp dress sense, Sam Ridley had been mayor of Smyrna since 1949. "He was a very strong force in the community," recalled Woods. As mayor, Ridley invested in community facilities, and he wanted more industry. When Nissan showed an interest, Ridley coordinated relations between state and local leaders, earning praise from above. "The civic and elected leadership of Rutherford County is to be highly commended for responding quickly in such a responsible way to the challenge presented them by Nissan," exclaimed Cotham. The mayor even allowed for Nissan's name to be emblazoned on the town's 1.5-million-gallon water storage tank, a symbol of local appreciation. Delighted, Ridley described Nissan's arrival as "the most eventful and outstanding event that has taken place in Smyrna," as well as "one of the biggest in the State of Tennessee."[32]

Still, many residents were not pleased about Nissan's arrival. As Alexander acknowledged, at the time Smyrna was a "sleepy" town with few visitors. For many, it was only known as a speed trap on the interstate between Nashville and Chattanooga. In many ways, Smyrna was representative of Tennessee, an inland state with just three thousand citizens of Japanese ancestry. According to Keel Hunt, an Alexander aide, local reaction to Nissan's arrival was "mixed." He explained: "The economic benefits were clearly understood by so many of the policy-makers in Tennessee, but there was resentment of this relocation, growing out of hard feelings from World War II with respect to Japan." Adding to the tension, Smyrna had been home to a U.S. Air Force base, and many locals had gone off to fight the Japanese from the facility. Although the base closed in the 1970s, hard feelings lingered. Reacting to Nissan's arrival, one group of residents even led a campaign to name the road to the plant the Pearl Harbor Memorial Highway. Ironically, a group of Nissan executives from Japan were housed in the old base while the plant was built. Alexander admitted that memories of the war overshadowed the project. "In all of my meetings," he wrote, "I notice how the War lingers, especially on our side, helping to spoil America's alliance with Japan." As a result, he avoided the topic.[33] Despite these efforts, some Tennesseans brought up the issue. In early 1981, business executive Jim Gentry was typical, writing the governor to oppose Nissan's arrival on the grounds of Japan's wartime record. In response, Alexander claimed that "things change in the world," adding that Japan had become an important ally. After receiving similar letters, however, the governor admitted that he understood citizens' "frustration."[34]

Opposition centered in Rutherford County, where many residents relied on farming. Along with the Japanese issue, citizens worried about the costs of unchecked growth, including the strain on local services that occurred when a large multinational corporation moved in. The plant was projected to produce an influx of twenty-two hundred workers, plus another ten thousand people to provide them with services. Reflecting local anxieties, even Ridley hoped that Smyrna would not lose its small-town feel and become a "small Detroit." In September 1980, the Rutherford County Farm Bureau—a major force in the county—was one of the groups to record its opposition to the plant, concerned that it would lead to unsustainable population growth, burden the county school system, and increase the cost of living. "It's one of the worst things that could happen to Rutherford County," claimed bureau director Dan Mitchell. Mitchell questioned why public officials called the plant "the best thing" and something that would "take care of the county's problems"; in reality, public services would be strained and fertile land lost to development. As the plant was built, traffic increased and services were strained, largely due to the influx of construction workers. As even Ridley admitted, the building process "inconvenienced us to some extent."[35]

Residents also opposed the construction of a connector road to the plant, part of the incentive package. Although at least one home was "displaced," the road went ahead. One of those forced to move, Jamie Johns, complained to Alexander. Her family, she wrote, liked their farm and did not want to leave. While defending the move, the governor understood Johns's frustration. "I am sure that there is very little I can say that can make you happy about the fact that your parents will have to relocate their home as a result of the decision made by the Transportation Department," he acknowledged. In January 1981, the department also chose the route for the connector road after just one public meeting. Citing the need to get the road built quickly, officials disputed residents' claims that a second gathering had been "promised."[36]

Alexander tried to assuage residents' concerns. In written responses, he acknowledged that Nissan's arrival posed "potential problems," including fears of rapid industrialization, pollution, and the erosion of southern hospitality and culture. Nevertheless, the governor downplayed the negatives. "Will such big new plants create a 'little Detroit'?" he pondered. "It shouldn't." He argued that Nissan had to adhere to federal environmental laws, and only small numbers of Japanese would move to the area. Most workers would be Tennesseans, and they would spend their paychecks locally. Reinforcing his jobs message, the governor insisted that southern culture would be strengthened, not undermined, by the automaker's arrival. "Conversation and intact family life comes more easily when parents have one good job instead of two bad ones that keep them absent from home and still poor," he asserted.[37]

The cost of the incentive package also generated concern, especially in Nashville. At a state budget meeting on December 5, 1980, Ned McWherter, the Democratic Speaker of the House, criticized the deal. "We are paying too much for what we are getting," he asserted. "Hell, we gave the Capitol away on Nissan." Even some business leaders voiced similar views. "I think it was too high and it cost us too much," asserted Walt Griffin of the Clarksville Chamber of Commerce. "We don't need another one." There was particular opposition to tax breaks. The director of the state Fiscal Review Committee, Don Morton, spoke out against a bill that allowed Nissan to receive the same tax benefits on leased and bought equipment and another that exempted the automaker's water and air pollution equipment from the state franchise tax. According to Morton, these concessions had a "substantial" impact on state revenues.[38]

The training package also attracted criticism. The chair of the Education Committee in the Tennessee House of Representatives, Frank Lashlee, asserted that the $4.4 million allocated to train Nissan workers should have been awarded to poorly performing schools. "Why should we spend money to train people in Japan and take it away from our kids right here in Tennessee?" he asked. The question was pertinent, as finance commissioner Lewis Donelson reported that the money came from a fund that was used to buy high school equipment. Lashlee tried to get the Industrial Training Service moved back to the Department of Education, a change resisted by the Alexander admin-istration, which described it as a crucial "sales tool." According to the *Knox-ville Journal*, funding Nissan's training package turned into a "major scrap" be-tween House Democrats and the administration. The fight was fueled by the state's labor movement, which opposed Nissan's decision to build the plant with Daniel Construction Company, a nonunion contractor from South Caro-lina. Deeply angered, the state Labor Council lobbied lawmakers to block Al-exander's spending plans. Council president James Neeley even declared that he was prepared to take "part of the blame" if Nissan pulled out.[39]

With many Democrats behind him, Lashlee raised further concerns about the incentive package. In February 1981, he scheduled hearings to explore how Nissan spending was linked to what the *Knoxville Journal* termed Alex-ander's "austere budgets" for education. Lashlee also led opposition to the taxpayer-funded training of 250 workers at a Nissan factory in Kyushu. "Why train them in Japan?" he asked. "Why can't they do it in Tennessee?" The gov-ernor's record on education was questionable. Privileging the attraction of in-dustry, Alexander cut basic aid for public schools, reduced funding for voca-tional education, and failed to propose a salary increase for Tennessee's forty thousand public school teachers. He also delayed a requirement that high school seniors had to pass sixth-grade literacy and numeracy tests in order to graduate, a provision that was not introduced until 1982. The cuts angered parents and teachers, with the Tennessee Education Association pressing for a 12 percent salary boost for its members, who had missed out on numerous increases. Some Tennessee newspapers also spoke out. Slashing funding for education, summarized the *Athens Post-Athenian*, was an "error."[40]

As legislators pointed out, the incentive package also hurt the state bud-get. Unveiled in February 1981, just as Nissan was breaking ground, Alexander's budget for the upcoming fiscal year was, as the *Johnson City Press-Chronicle* put it, a "lean" one. At a time when inflation stood at 12 percent, Alexander's budget was up only 5.5 percent. Over four hundred state employees lost their jobs, and there was no pay increase for those that remained. The bud-get slashed $18 million from basic aid to public schools, while East Tennessee State University had its funding reduced by $221,300. Gasoline taxes were also increased.[41]

The cuts were partly necessitated by the costs of industrial recruitment. In Tennessee's Democratically controlled House, representatives called for a probe of the Nissan deal, with some alleging that Alexander had made "secret deals" to secure the investment. In addition, influential Democrats criticized administration plans to cut "people-oriented programs" such as Medicaid and primary and vocational education while proposing a $20 million package of industrial training and road construction for Nissan. Senators also spoke out. "I think we ought to honor the [Nissan] commitments where we can," commented William Ortwein (D-Chattanooga). "But I come from an industrial area and vocational education is very important to us. I do not intend to sit by and see vocational education ruined." Others voiced similar concerns. "I'm not sure I'm going to vote for all these taxes and fees until I find out that we're not sacrificing services to our districts for industrial access roads," added Riley Darnell (D-Clarksville).[42]

A lot of opposition came from other parts of Tennessee, where citizens worried that they were paying for the plant but would not enjoy the benefits. The Senate Democratic Caucus even accused Alexander of ruining vocational education in many areas in order to train Nissan workers in middle Tennessee. Lawmakers also worried that other industries, along with new arrivals, would expect similar help, an unsustainable situation. "The question is whether we got a good buy," claimed Lieutenant Governor John Wilder, a Memphis native, "and whether we can afford to do it for other industries in the future." In response, Alexander reiterated that the economic benefits justified the incentives.[43]

In other ways, the plant provoked criticism. Nissan located in a largely white area, producing complaints that black applicants found it hard to get jobs. Before production began, Nissan America CEO Marvin Runyon even told a Japanese journalist that Nissan had chosen Smyrna because of "the homogeneity of the labor force." Black residents of Nashville were particularly affected, especially when salaried employees were hired. African American state senator Avon Williams accused Runyon of "bypassing qualified black citizens" in hiring managers. A civil rights attorney, Williams forwarded Nissan thirty-four applications from minority candidates for management positions. Despite receiving assurances from the company that they would receive "favorable and sympathetic attention," Williams reported that nearly half of his applicants had been rejected outright, while the rest had not received commitments. Nissan, he charged, was not honoring its pledge to "ensure equal employment opportunity to black citizens."[44]

Civil rights groups got involved. As Nissan hired more managers, the Urban League and NAACP sought a meeting with Alexander to complain about poor job opportunities at the plant, but the governor wanted to decide who attended. When Nissan began hiring for production positions, allegations of racial bias resurfaced, pushing Runyon to respond. By 1990—after the EEOC case against Honda threw light on that company's even worse record—Nissan claimed that 17 percent of production employees and 14 percent of all employees were African American. Managers now denied that they had been attracted by the racial composition of the local population. Critics saw the situation differently. In resolutions passed at the 1989 and 1992 conventions, the UAW charged that Nissan had a "poor record" of providing jobs to racial minorities.[45]

Tennessee's labor movement also opposed the plant. In early 1981, union groups organized a protest at the plant's ground-breaking ceremony, which was attended by the governor and top company executives. They were upset with Nissan's plans to build the plant—as well as its attached U.S. corporate headquarters—with Daniel Construction. "We have building trades capable of building the plant and I think it is important that organized labor be in on the construction," declared Neeley. On January 28, the Tennessee Labor Council declared that February 3, the day of the ground-breaking, would be a "public holiday." The move was designed to allow union members from across the state to converge on Smyrna.[46]

The unions delivered on their promises. Despite 20-degree weather, some fifteen hundred protesters disrupted the ground-breaking ceremony. Many carried placards calling for a boycott of Nissan's vehicles, while an airplane unfurled a banner that proclaimed, "Boycott Datsun . . . Put America back to work." Union placards were visible to prominent guests; one that read "Boycott Datsun: Quality Products Are Built by Skilled UNION Craftsmen" was even attached to a Nissan pickup displayed for the ceremony. Explaining their motives, protesters stressed their desperate need for work—the recession had hit the construction sector hard—as well as concerns about labor standards. "They'll bring Cuban refugees or Mexicans up here that are not citizens of the United States," summarized S. E. Shane of Hendersonville. "They'll camp in their buses and not pay any taxes. All we want is a job for us to provide food for our families."[47] The scale of the protest—and the angry mood—caught officials off-guard. "Though Nissan had some warning that trouble might be brewing Tuesday," reported the *Wall Street Journal*, "the size and conduct of the crowd surprised it." At one point, Nissan general manager Mitsuya Goto was handed a placard proclaiming, "Union Craftsmen Boycott Datsun." Press images showed that Goto's right hand was held on the sign by one of the protesters. The crowd also booed and heckled the governor, forcing him to raise his voice.[48]

When the time came for the ceremonial ground-breaking, there was further disruption. As part of the ritual, Okuma was supposed to drive the small pickup, but he found the vehicle had three flat tires and was covered in protest stickers. Okuma passed the task to Runyon, who moved gingerly toward the truck. Police were guarding the vehicle when the protesters started to throw rocks, one of which struck officer Virgil Gammon. "He was hit behind the head and was unconscious for a short time," reported chief deputy Truman Jones. In addition, the cables of three radio stations reporting the event were cut. With the state police struggling to control the crowd, Runyon was only able to drive the truck a few feet. Nissan, observed the *Wall Street Journal*, had "labor trouble" before it had a plant.[49]

The protest had important consequences, especially in hardening Nissan's opposition to unions. This was particularly true for Runyon, a Texan who had previously worked for Ford. In a clear signal of intent, Runyon defended his choice of Daniel Construction. He also invited Daniel president Currie Spivey to be a "distinguished guest" at the ground-breaking, which was attended by over three thousand people. Subsequently, Runyon awarded big contracts to other nonunion companies. Shortly after the protest, Nissan executive Jerry L. Benefield, who later took over from Runyon, was forthright on the union issue, telling a management gathering that the company expected a "massive" UAW organizing effort but would prevail. "The only employees who need unions are bad employees, and we don't expect to hire any of them," he declared.[50]

Within Tennessee, the protest strengthened Nissan's position, especially as the state press condemned the violence. The *Chattanooga News Free Press* called the protest a "disgraceful spectacle," while the *Nashville Banner* termed it "deplorable." Mayor Ridley declared that local citizens were "embarrassed" by the scenes, which had "done much to discredit union efforts in this area."[51] The demonstration was also criticized by the state legislature, which insisted that many demonstrators were outside "agitators" (an allegation refuted by Deputy Jones). Clearly embarrassed, Alexander received support from many constituents, some of whom mailed in money to help repair the truck. On February 25, Alexander wrote Runyon and apologized. He visited Japan soon afterward, praising the company's operations there.[52]

In the months that followed, the charm offensive continued. In January 1983, Alexander met with top company officials in Japan, including personal visits with Goto.[53] Later that year, the governor helped plan the plant's official opening. When Ishihara and his wife arrived for the occasion, Alexander arranged for them to be the "state's guest" at the Blackberry Farm, a luxury eight-bedroom residence in the Great Smoky Mountains. Ishihara accepted the invitation, calling it a "great honor." Other executives also stayed at the farm, all at state expense. The Alexanders arranged itineraries for the Ishiharas that included shopping and sightseeing. They also oversaw the provision of vehicles to transport the couple around the picturesque mountains, where they viewed the changing maple trees. On October 21, the plant opening concluded with a lavish dinner at the Governor's Mansion.[54]

By then, the first trucks had been produced, two months ahead of schedule. On June 16, Job 1 rolled off the line in front of cameras from TV stations around the world, including Japan. A 1983 model with a white exterior and a blue interior, it was driven off the line by Runyon, who gave a thumbs-up to cheering workers. Declared a "historically significant" vehicle by Ishihara, the truck was donated to the State Museum in Nashville, where it became part of their "Made in Tennessee" collection. As the plant began full production, Alexander stressed the importance of the moment. "The Tennessee men and women

An aerial view of the huge Nissan Motor Manufacturing Corporation USA plant in Smyrna, Tennessee, taken at the time of the factory's grand opening in October 1983. Courtesy of Albert Gore Research Center, Middle Tennessee State University.

who work at this plant have a lot more riding on their broad shoulders than the success of this plant," he declared. "Their success has a lot to do with how well all of Tennessee succeeds in the next few years."[55]

The start of production also renewed labor tensions. Just two days after Job 1 was produced, the UAW promised an "aggressive campaign" to organize Smyrna, calling it a "high priority." In response, Runyon told the *New York Times* that a union was an unwanted "third party." The Japanese press even reported that Runyon "hates the UAW" as a result of his time managing Ford's Dearborn plant.[56] Observing these developments, Owen Bieber sounded a warning shot. "The UAW is disappointed ... by Nissan's announced intention to operate on a non-union basis," he declared. The new UAW leader disliked Runyon's statement that the conditions of Smyrna workers "absolutely cannot be improved on." In the 1930s, he noted, Henry Ford had made similar declarations, yet the union had prevailed. "History proved Henry Ford wrong, and history will likewise prove Marvin Runyon wrong," he proclaimed.[57]

The battle in Tennessee was very different from what happened at Honda. As *The Harbour Report* noted, while both plants used Japanese production methods, there were "wide differences" in staffing. Honda had moved hundreds of Japanese nationals to Ohio, whereas Nissan had only a "handful." Instead, American executives, many of them hired from Ford, were given "significant autonomy." Nissan's opposition had a hard-nosed, American edge, and organizers saw the firm as unique. "Nissan I think has the worst practice of all the transnationals," summarized organizer Richard Bensinger, and was "really anti-union." There would be no neutrality agreement in Smyrna.[58]

There were other reasons for these differences. Although Nissan was organized in Japan, the All Nissan Motor Workers' Union lacked autonomy and rarely struck. With no pressure being exerted by the Japanese union, Ishihara was happy to delegate labor questions to his American managers, and their position was clear. As Ishihara explained in 1980, Runyon and "his American managers" would "take charge of operating the plant with the management philosophies befitting an American corporation." Even in the plant's early days, less than 2 percent of the workforce were from Japan, and they were all technical staff.[59] Alexander claimed that only "10 or 12" Japanese stayed in Smyrna for long. In April 1984 Ridley wrote that there were few Japanese managers left, and they had been accepted locally.[60]

Having pledged to organize Nissan, the UAW began its campaign. Early efforts struggled. The first group of workers were "starry-eyed, blank-looking people" who believed in the company's promises, staffer Martin Gerber reported in March 1983, especially as many assembled prototypes rather than experiencing full-speed production.[61] The weak state of the national economy—combined with the location of the plant in a rural area—also helped the company. Nissan carried out extensive vetting too; by March 1983, applicants had been screened six times and were waiting with "bated breath" to see who had made it. In all, the company received 60,000 applicants for the first 2,650 jobs, and workers were questioned to ensure they were flexible "team" players. Bieber alleged that interviewers probed union backgrounds as far back as grandparents. Those taken on were optimistic and young—the average age was just twenty-five.[62]

The UAW pressed on. A small group of organizers—led by veteran Jim Turner and assisted by Gladys Holmes and C. E. Strickland—laid the groundwork by talking to workers and looking for grievances. In August 1986, Turner reported that the union was supported by 190 employees. Many were beginning to complain about workloads, which had increased as the plant reached full capacity and began producing a car, the Sentra compact, as well as pickups. Announced in 1985, the Sentra expansion increased Nissan's investment in the site to $745 million, which the company claimed was "the largest to date by a Japanese company outside of Japan."[63]

In 1987, the company's honeymoon ended abruptly. In May, the climate changed when journalist John Junkerman published an article in *The Progressive* that was very critical of the company. In "Nissan, Tennessee: It Ain't What It's Cracked Up to Be," Junkerman—a freelance writer from Massachusetts who had earlier written positively about the plant—drew on interviews with former workers and managers to claim that things had gone dramatically wrong. In one recent one-year period, more than 235 employees had left or been fired, including several top managers. Workers—many of them given pseudonyms—detailed allegations of favoritism and sexual harassment by supervisors. They also claimed that it was dangerous to speak out.[64]

The main focus of the piece, however, was the fast pace of the production line. One described working on the line as "eight-hour aerobics." Another claimed, "You don't have time to unwrap a piece of chewing gum and stick it in your mouth until the line stops." Denied bathroom breaks, workers were also told not to drink (some even wetted themselves). Nissan had not achieved its success through innovative management and an open-door policy, Junkerman concluded, but through an "old-fashioned" speed-up. Following the article's release, a wide range of publications, including *Newsweek*, the *Chicago Sun-Times*, the *Detroit Free Press*, and *Pravda*, sent reporters to Smyrna, producing a spate of anti-Nissan stories. While Junkerman's article was somewhat sensationalized, these journalists heard similar complaints of an overpaced line, demanding and abusive supervisors, and high rates of injury. Even the pro-company *Tennessean* ran a piece entitled "Overwork, Intimidation Claimed at Nissan." Denying the allegations, Nissan entered damage control.[65]

The UAW benefited from the publicity, which validated the complaints it had received from workers. In May, Frank Joyce reported to Bieber that the "powerful article" had attracted local and national attention, undermining Nissan's "carefully crafted" reputation. In June, secretary-treasurer Bill Casstevens also told the executive board that Junkerman's piece had produced "accelerated activity" in the Nissan drive.[66] Responding to this, the UAW rented an office near the plant, assigning four full-time organizers, including Turner, to run it. Complaining of arduous working conditions, workers began stopping by, leading Turner to argue that the time was ripe to make "major organizing gains." In January 1988, Bieber committed to calling an election once a majority of the twenty-four hundred hourly workers had signed authorization cards.[67]

Getting the cards signed was painstaking work, especially as Nissan refused to supply contact lists. The company's policy of putting employees' first names on their uniforms—while appearing egalitarian—also hindered workers' ability to connect (many did not know each other's surnames). Organizers spent many hours working through city directories to gain contact details.[68] By August 1988, they had secured the names and addresses of 1,505 workers, and the number of signed cards had increased to 704. Still, over 500 employees remained out of reach. By January 1989, the number of cards had crept up to 841.[69]

Other problems—many of them structural factors unique to the plant— also hurt the effort. The company's organization of workers into small teams was problematic; it created pressure to conform, especially as Nissan awarded merit points to work groups for accident-free production (a practice that discouraged the reporting of accidents). As the plant was located in a rural area, the distances that workers drove also inhibited organizing. "They live all over, which is one of the big problems," admitted Casstevens. "They live within maybe a hundred mile radius of the plant. They even come over from Alabama and there are some from Kentucky. They live all over so it is a little difficult to run them all down." Above all, the plant's isolation undermined a sense of community among workers.[70]

Managers also thwarted the card-signing drive. As part of a multipronged attack, executives encouraged workers who had signed cards to change their mind, sending all twenty-four hundred employees prepaid envelopes and card revocation forms. In June 1988, workers opposed to the union began picketing outside the plant, catching the UAW off-guard. Nissan's managers claimed that they were not involved. "Many of our employees are sick and tired of UAW activities for the past six months," declared Gail Neuman, Nissan's head of human resources. "Enough is enough. They [the workers] want them to go home." The company welcomed the group's activities, however, and the UAW alleged that many picketers were office employees. The professionally prepared materials used by the "antis," including signs declaring "Nissan: Free and Proud of It" and "UAW—Go Back Home," also suggested corporate involvement. Again, Nissan was more aggressive than Honda.[71]

Despite these problems, the campaign gathered momentum. Organizers related that workers had plenty of complaints, especially over health and safety, an issue the union emphasized. As vice president Don Elphin summarized, staff visits with Nissan workers indicated that injuries were "the number one item." According to the UAW, Nissan had sped up the line without using proper precautions, causing multiple injuries. Between 1985 and 1988, according to figures from the Tennessee Workers' Compensation Department, Nissan reported 372 cases involving more than eight days of worker absence, six times more than Ford's unionized Glass Plant in Nashville. It was also higher than any other large organized workplace in Tennessee. Publicizing the issue, the union handed out testimonials from maimed workers. "When people get hurt in that plant," claimed staffer Maxey Irwin, "there's no place for them to go. At a UAW-organized plant, there's other jobs for them to do. But at this place, they give their bodies to Nissan, and Nissan does not have a job for them." Because many workers had suffered injuries, the UAW believed that the issue could be decisive.[72] Capitalizing on the progress—and buoyed by its April 1989 victory at a Mack Truck plant in Winnsboro, South Carolina—the UAW got ready to call an election. In May, Yokich reported that more than half of Nissan's twenty-four hundred workers had signed authorization cards. Receiving this news, UAW leaders agreed to contact the NLRB. In early June, the board ruled that the vote would take place between 1:00 p.m. on Wednesday, July 26, and 1:30 a.m. on Thursday, July 27. Pleased that workers on medical leave were allowed to vote, organizers accelerated their efforts.[73]

When the results came in, however, it was Nissan that prevailed, securing 1,622 votes compared to the UAW's 711. There were several reasons for the outcome. In particular, the union's efforts to capitalize on the safety issue were never as pivotal as it wished. There were disputes with the Tennessee Occupational Safety and Health Administration (TOSHA), the UAW complaining that the agency was reluctant to carry out a "forceful inspection" of the important employer. TOSHA also lacked the resources it needed to perform rigorous investigations. Furthermore, Nissan fought back, claiming that unionized plants also had safety problems. Observing these developments, some workers doubted whether the UAW could tackle the injury problem. "We would still have to build cars if the union came in," summarized Joan Williams. "We would still have back pains. They want us to think these things would go away." The health and safety push also struggled because the plant was relatively new, and most workers were young. "You must remember in eighty-nine that was a new plant," recalled former organizer Larry Steele. "That work had not started to cripple the workers yet."[74]

Continuing its hostile stance, Nissan also prevented the UAW from gaining a decisive advantage in the safety area. In response to a complaint from four prounion employees, the company refused to release its OSHA 200 logs—which detailed all injuries by name, date, and time, not just those resulting in more than eight days of lost work time—ostensibly because disclosure would have violated workers' privacy. Inside the plant, however, the company announced that it would not provide the "damn logs" to "UAW agents," its term for workers who supported the union. Although TOSHA fined Nissan $5,000 for noncompliance, the company appealed, and the records remained closed. Without the logs, the issues remained muddied. In *Beyond Mass Production*, a study of Japanese firms in the United States, Martin Kenney and Richard Florida showed that injuries at these companies were often underreported. As a result, obtaining reliable data was "difficult." In 1988, however, even the Tennessee Department of Labor recorded 151 injuries at Nissan that had caused employees to miss more than a week of work, a significant number. Overall, the UAW had identified a good issue, but it was unable to turn it into a winner.[75]

Nissan also kept wages and benefits competitive with the Big Three, another important factor. In 1989, the average base hourly wage was $13.95, 16 percent lower than at Chrysler and GM and 20 percent less than at Ford. A relatively generous profit-sharing program, however, ensured that annual take-home pay was $32,579, just 9 percent lower than at Chrysler and GM and 15 percent below Ford. The company also stressed that the cost of living in Tennessee was lower. Largely hired from lower-paying industries, many workers praised Nissan's pay and benefits. "There is no reason this plant should have a union," declared Tammy Graham. "Where else could you make $30,000 with all the benefits we have?" The UAW, thought veteran *Automotive News* reporter Lindsay Chappell, was unable to offer an "immediately clear benefit" to Nissan's workers, whose wages were envied locally.[76]

The campaign suffered from many other problems. Nissan's preelection opposition was extensive and forceful, with the company using its access to the workforce to great effect. Through *Nissan News*, an in-plant newsletter, and the internal television system, which ran twenty-four hours a day and was transmitted in more than 120 locations, workers were bombarded with antiunion material. As the election neared, the company upped the ante. Jerry Benefield, who became CEO in 1988, proved a particularly forceful opponent. Described by *Automotive News* as a "cigar-chewing Georgian with a love for horses and cowboy boots," Benefield portrayed the UAW as an unwanted outsider, publicly challenging it to organize the workers or "go home." Such bullish tactics took a toll. Workers, reported organizer Ben Perkins, were "fearful of talking on the job."[77]

The UAW had problems of its own. Staff complained that the campaign lacked central direction and was too important to be run through the union's regional structure. Bieber, however, only established the Transnational and Joint Ventures Department *after* the Nissan vote. While the UAW had a department for every Big Three automaker, it took time for its structure to adapt to the industry's growth. Among staffers, there were also complaints that not enough resources were being devoted to organizing, a common problem in the labor movement at the time.[78]

There were also significant internal divisions. In 1987–88, Bieber's leadership faced a challenge from the New Directions movement. Coalescing around executive board member Jerry Tucker, the reformers called for more forceful strategies to combat globalization and concessionary bargaining, galvanizing support from Big Three workers. Tucker highlighted how the UAW had been complicit in implementing "team production" systems in domestic plants, especially in the wake of the 1982–83 recession. By the end of the 1980s, the team concept production system, which often copied Japanese methods, had been introduced at fifteen GM and five Chrysler factories. These changes were unpopular with some workers, who complained of higher workloads and injury rates, as well as job losses and a weakening of union influence. According to *Labor Notes* scholars Mike Parker and Jane Slaughter, the much-heralded system, rather than empowering workers, represented "management by stress," a conclusion reinforced by other industrial relations researchers. Although he survived—and insisted that the union had to help Big Three plants become more efficient—Bieber admitted that the challenge was "time consuming" and damaging just as the Nissan election was looming. "It disrupts the family to some degree," he recalled. To some extent, the UAW's support of the team concept system also undermined its appeal to transplant workers.[79]

The fact that the Nissan plant was expanding was also very important. In April 1989 the company declared that it would build a third vehicle—a midsize sedan—in Tennessee, growing the factory by 1.2 million square feet. The third line, Benefield noted, would create two thousand jobs and increase annual production capacity to 440,000 vehicles, making Smyrna the highest-volume auto factory under one roof in the country. The company had chosen Smyrna for the major investment, explained president Yutaka Kume, because it was "very impressed with the quality and productivity levels" of employees.[80] The move hurt the unionization drive, especially as new hires were harder to organize. As it took on staff, Nissan screened carefully. When the UAW filed for the election, massive bulldozers were preparing the plant extension in full view of workers. Many workers worried that Nissan might cancel the investment if they supported the UAW. On the eve of the election, Gail Neuman pointedly refused to rule this out. "If our environment were to change in such a way that we were unable to remain competitive, then, of course, we would have to reassess investment plans," she warned. Nissan's expansion, summarized the *Detroit Free Press*, was "crippling to the UAW because it promised thousands of new jobs if the union was defeated and eliminated the need for protection from layoffs."[81]

In other ways, Nissan workers viewed the UAW as a threat to their economic security. Since establishing Smyrna, Nissan had not idled any workers, running continuously for six years. In internal discussions, the UAW admitted that this helped the company. Organizing the plant, wrote staffer Carlton Horner, would be "virtually impossible" until it experienced "layoffs and all problems that come with layoffs."[82] The Big Three's predicament compounded the problem. After the 1987 contract negotiations, GM and Chrysler enforced a semipermanent "idling" of eight plants that affected more than twenty thousand workers. Some Nissan employees feared that if they voted for the UAW, it would transfer in displaced members from Big Three plants. Validating these anxieties, the nearby Saturn plant in Spring Hill, which was unionized, was staffed by many UAW members from the North. "The Saturn thing, they used that," acknowledged Bieber, "because it was true that we brought people from within."[83]

Trying to hit back, the UAW appealed for political support. Although he enjoyed solid labor backing, Smyrna's Democratic congressman, Bart Gordon, refused to endorse the union's efforts because he did not want to upset the big employer. "We stayed out of it," recalled Kent Syler, Gordon's former chief of staff, referring to the drive. Other state politicians—including Democratic governor Ned McWherter—reacted in a similar way. "The labor-supported governor of Tennessee and most, if not all, other labor-supported elected officials did not publicly back the UAW in the campaign," noted an internal union analysis. Because almost all of Nissan's suppliers were unorganized, the union was robbed of another source of influence. "They had no leverage from the suppliers or customers," summarized Kristen Dziczek at the Center for Automotive Research.[84]

Other politicians helped Nissan—and its suppliers—in any way possible. Leading a charge by southern Republicans, Alexander fought domestic content legislation, which he described as "disastrous" for Nissan. Clearly, Nissan was not using as many local suppliers as it claimed publicly, and real economic development, especially in terms of skilled workers at local entrepreneurial suppliers, was limited. Privately, Alexander admitted that Nissan's goal was to achieve 38 percent domestic content by 1984, yet it was some way off. Alexander mobilized opposition to the Fair Practices in Automotive Products Act, which went through the U.S. House in 1983 but then withered in the Senate. Alexander wrote to all twelve members of Tennessee's congressional delegation to oppose the bill and informed Ishihara that he had done so. He claimed privately that Ishihara had warned that the plant would close if the legislation passed. Once the bill was thwarted, Nissan pressed ahead with the Sentra expansion. The governor also made it clear that the UAW was not welcome in Tennessee.[85]

The union issue, however, refused to die. Even after the election, the UAW received complaints from Nissan's workers. Maintaining a presence in the area, staffers declared that they would keep organizing "for as long as it takes." A year after the loss, the union was holding meetings in Smyrna and staffing an office, and Yokich anticipated that there would be "another election." In response, managers told the union to leave town. "I hope they go to Poland," quipped Neuman.[86] In the plant, however, plenty of problems remained. Nissan remained evasive about its health and safety record, even refusing entry to TOSHA inspectors. Gradually, demands for union representation gathered momentum. In March 1994, Ben Perkins reported that many Nissan workers, unhappy with heavy workloads and autocratic supervisors, were pushing for a new campaign. "Pressure for productivity is probably greater than it has ever been," he explained. In addition, the 401(k) program was being switched to an investment program, upsetting and confusing workers. Despite positive reports about the company in business publications, the pressure to cut costs and maintain the plant's reputation for productivity had taken a toll.[87]

In the late 1990s, the pressure on workers increased further. Nissan hit hard times, hurt by overcapacity in the global auto industry and fallout from the 1997–98 financial crisis. Following its 1999 partnership with Renault—the French automaker rescued Nissan from near bankruptcy by buying 45 percent of its shares—the company, under new CEO Carlos Ghosn, restructured. Known as "Le Cost Killer," the Lebanese Brazilian slashed overheads and increased productivity, alienating workers. Overall, some two hundred thousand jobs were eliminated globally as part of Ghosn's Nissan Revival Plan. While admitting that the cuts were "harsh," Ghosn wrote that they were "the social price" that needed to be paid for "past management mistakes." As the savings took hold, Smyrna workers complained of even higher workloads and more injuries, boosting the union's efforts. Industry sources suggested that these complaints were valid. Between 1995 and 2001, *The Harbour Report* ranked Nissan as the top automotive company for productivity for seven consecutive years. Smyrna was a key reason for this. In 2000, it was the *Report*'s number one plant for labor productivity. In July 2001, the UAW, claiming that high workloads were a major issue, filed for another election. Nissan's cars, summarized Larry Steele, contained a lot of "blood."[88]

By the time the vote was held on October 4, however, the mood had shifted. As Steele recalled, 9/11 unexpectedly created a climate of "insecurity" that hurt the union, especially because it led to a sharp economic downturn. Vigorously opposing the union, the company played on these fears. In a crucial speech before the election, Ghosn—a ruthless opponent—warned workers that "bringing a union into Smyrna could result to making Smyrna not competitive, which is not in your best interest or Nissan's." Coming from a boss who claimed that Nissan had "too many factories," this was no empty threat. The union lost by 3,183 votes to 1,486.[89]

Other factors were also important. Shortly before the election, Nissan announced that production of its flagship Maxima sedan would be transferred from Japan to the United States, creating five hundred jobs in Smyrna. The news reinforced workers' perceptions that they had more economic security without a union. Others noticed that Nissan did not retrench workers when the economy tanked. "Even if the wage is lower than that of the Big Three," concluded the monthly magazine *Kaigai rodo jiho* (International labor information), "the fact that the plant sticks to its 'No Lay-off' policy, leading to few concerns about employment, must have contributed to the voting result." The union also faced the same challenges of contacting a vast and disparate workforce and trying to win over a hostile—or skeptical—community.[90]

The UAW's failure to organize Nissan had significant consequences. Many observers—not to mention the union itself—had thought it would do better. At three joint ventures—a well-publicized GM/Toyota plant in Fremont, California; a Ford/Mazda factory in Flat Rock, Michigan; and a Chrysler/Mitsubishi partnership in Normal, Illinois—Japanese automakers had accepted the UAW. All of these facilities were established in the 1980s, and unionists believed that gains at foreign-owned facilities would follow.[91] After the Nissan elections—particularly the first one—the climate changed. Following the 1989 result, Toyota's position in Kentucky, where the UAW had been working to extract a neutrality pledge, hardened. Meanwhile, Subaru-Isuzu in Lafayette, Indiana, a joint venture that had been established two years earlier, reneged on an earlier promise to be neutral. Both companies said the decision was up to workers. As Benefield commented, executives across the sector were confident that they could keep the union out. "Even if an industry has been traditionally organized," he commented in 1990, "it's not necessary anymore that they be organized now." In retrospect, some UAW staffers were candid about the magnitude of what happened in Smyrna. As former public relations director Peter Laarman put, in Tennessee the UAW suffered a "huge defeat . . . a kind of Waterloo for the union."[92]

The defeats in Smyrna were especially important because they encouraged other foreign automakers to move to the United States. In the final stages of the 1989 campaign, BMW announced its first American factory. The plant led to a wave of expansion by German automakers. In the wake of the 1989 defeat, Toyota also publicized an expansion of the Georgetown plant. With the additions at Georgetown and Smyrna, total transplant and joint venture capacity reached almost 2.9 million vehicles, surpassing Chrysler's output. From 1988 to 1991, moreover, the auto market "virtually died," Big Three sales tumbling by 31 percent. "The big winners," summarized *The Harbour Report*, "were the transplant manufacturers." Between 1988 and 1991, their sales increased 85 percent. Further expansion occurred in the years that followed, with Hyundai announcing its first U.S. plant soon after the second Smyrna election.[93]

The transplants had a number of decisive advantages. Although companies were reluctant to divulge the numbers, it was clear that foreign-owned plants relied heavily on imported parts, particularly early on. Nissan opposed the content legislation because the company could not meet the mandated domestic content level of 90 percent in 1985. Using imported parts slashed production costs. These factories also had a new and young workforce, which enabled the companies to avoid pension outlays. The transplants, summarized the UAW, were "new plants with the very lowest manufacturing costs." In 1992, a study by the Economic Strategy Institute found that the transplants had a $2,000 per car advantage over domestic automakers; wages were lower, health care costs were less, and productivity was higher. As a result, the Big Three were "dying." In 1993, industry analyst David Healy admitted that while transplant wages were similar to those of Big Three workers, "the advantage comes in the fringes, the pensions and the health care." With very young workforces, transplants saved a lot on health care and pension costs. According to Healy, total transplant labor cost was between twenty and twenty-five dollars an hour, compared to forty dollars at the Big Three (despite near-wage parity). The foreign-owned companies were in a powerful position.[94]

By the end of the 1980s, both domestic executives and the UAW knew that the transplants—which they had envisaged as small facilities that would unionize—were a major threat. "In short," Bieber commented in 1990, "the combination of direct imports and transplant vehicles in this market is creating a massive headache both for us as a workers union and for the major employers we deal with." A few months earlier, Chrysler chairman Lee Iacocca had put it plainly. "The transplants," he declared, "are murdering all of us— all of the Big Three." Around the same time, the *Economist* reviewed the transplants' growth, asking whether the Big Three were "headed for the junkyard." Unsure how to respond and "traumatized" by the sector's unexpected growth, the UAW was in a quandary. While it no longer encouraged new transplants, it alienated the workers it wanted to recruit if it criticized the sector.[95]

Governor Alexander saw the situation very differently. For the Blount County native, who easily won reelection in 1982, it was satisfying to turn the tables on northern states. "Tennesseans for three generations have left home for Detroit to get the kind of jobs Nissan now brings here," he boasted. "Nissan is welcome here because it will hire Tennesseans, pay them good wages, pay Tennessee taxes, and help raise our low average family incomes."[96] In the decades that followed, prominent Tennesseans—including Al Gore Jr.—watched proudly as Nissan powered substantial economic growth in Tennessee. Several other Japanese companies followed the automaker to the Nashville area, and the local economy boomed. Things would never be the same for Smyrna, which the *New York Times* had described as an "essentially rural" town of eighty-six hundred people when Nissan arrived. By 2013, more than forty-three thousand people called Smyrna home, and middle Tennessee was one of the fastest-growing areas in the country. Two hundred miles to the north, a similar transformation had occurred in Georgetown, Kentucky, but only after Japan's largest automaker won a long battle for acceptance.[97]

CHAPTER FOUR

"Toyota, a Big Yes"?
Reaction and Resistance in
Georgetown, Kentucky

On December 11, 1985, Toyota Motor Company (TMC) announced that it would invest $800 million to build its first solely owned assembly plant in North America. After receiving offers from thirty-six states, Toyota chose a 1,400-acre site in Georgetown, a small town in central Kentucky. Scheduled to start production in 1989, the new factory would produce two hundred thousand vehicles a year and employ up to three thousand people. State officials were delighted. "Toyota's excellent worldwide reputation and its ability to attract supplier plants make it a great addition to Kentucky's corporate community," declared Governor Martha Layne Collins.[1] Kentucky's first—and only—female governor, Collins played a key role in luring Toyota, pulling off the deal in a male-dominated environment. "After eighteen months of hard work and persistence," she wrote a friend, "the decision was certainly gratifying."[2]

Collins's pride was understandable, especially as Kentucky's rivalry with Tennessee, a finalist for the plant, was intense. Earlier that year, Collins had tried to secure GM's Saturn plant but lost out to Tennessee. "Kentucky and Tennessee will always compete," she reflected, "football, basketball, whatever it is, and that's always a challenge."[3] Now she had turned the tables. The Toyota plant represented the biggest initial investment in the United States by a Japanese firm, surpassing Nissan's record. Clearly piqued, Tennessee governor Lamar Alexander wrote Nissan president Takashi Ishihara on Christmas Eve, urging him to expand Smyrna so that it could remain "the largest Japanese manufacturing plant in the United States." Although Alexander dispatched officials to Tokyo to help Nissan plan an expansion, Kentucky took the record.[4]

Toyota was Japan's largest carmaker, and its arrival in Kentucky was an important moment in the industry's history. Between 1965 and 1985, its U.S. sales ballooned, rising from 6,404 cars to over 1 million. As industry scholar A. J. Jacobs has observed, Toyota became America's "import king." Toyotas were famously reliable, and the brand also acquired a reputation for delivering on its goals. True to form, as early as June 1988, Georgetown produced its first car, a white Camry. Shortly afterward, full production began, ahead of schedule.[5] Subsequent growth was impressive. By 2015, the factory produced several models—including luxury Lexus sedans—and employed seventy-five hundred workers. Based on capacity, Georgetown had become the largest Toyota plant in the world.[6]

Influenced by this growth, Georgetown has consistently been viewed not just as a success story but as a model plant.[7] There are good reasons for this. Between 1990 and 2001, the factory won eight J. D. Power and Associates quality awards, presented to the industry's top-performing factories. Accolades for the Camry—including Power's prestigious Best Quality Car in North America—poured in.[8] The factory was also highly rated by the well-regarded *Harbour Report*, which measured productivity. Georgetown, summarized *The Harbour Report* in 1992, was "one of the best assembly plants in North America."[9] Visitors flocked to the plant. In the late 1980s and early 1990s, "tens of thousands" of guests, including company executives, production engineers, and tourists, traveled to Georgetown to witness the Toyota production system, which emphasized just-in-time inventories, zero defects, and continuous improvement. In 1991 alone, twenty thousand visitors came to the plant. "Anybody who competes with the Japanese has to come and see this," explained James P. Womack, a Boston consultant. "Without a doubt, Toyota has become the benchmark of the world," added business executive Heinz Prechter. Consumers also migrated to Toyota's products. In 1996, Americans bought 360,000 Kentucky-built Camrys, making it one of the most popular models in the country.[10]

Praise extended to the company's treatment of its workers. In 1992, the *New York Times* called the factory a "showcase" that had transplanted Japanese work habits to America. "The U.A.W. has never tried to represent Toyota workers here," added Doron P. Levin. Other portrayals were glowing. Georgetown, declared *Automotive News* in 2006, was the "crown jewel" of Toyota's North American operations, a "mother plant" where the UAW had got nowhere. Toyota's workers were "largely contented," summarized the *New York Times* in 2007, and this was the "biggest obstacle" to union penetration.[11]

Because the plant was so valuable to the region's economy, community reaction to Toyota's arrival was also positive, especially when viewed in retrospect. A couple of *Cincinnati Post* headlines—"Birth of a Plant Meant the Rebirth of a County" and "Toyota's Second Home: Kentucky"—encapsulated the upbeat tone.[12] By the 1990s, the thriving factory was a source of pride, especially for local leaders. Academic studies of the plant's impact, particularly by scholars based in Kentucky, were also glowing. In 1998, Charles F. Haywood, a finance professor at the University of Kentucky, claimed that "once the early success of the venture became apparent, success bred success." Deriving from a Lexington conference that was opened by former Japanese prime minister Morihiro Hosokawa, most of the papers in P. P. Karan's *Japan in the Bluegrass* were similarly favorable. "Twenty years later," summarized Kentucky historian Elizabeth Duffy Fraas in another study, "the all-out recruitment of Toyota seems a 'slam-dunk.'"[13]

In reality, there was more to this story. As archival sources and oral histories document, Toyota's arrival produced plenty of hostility and tension. Some residents were opposed to a Japanese company locating in their community, while others criticized the generous incentives that Toyota received. Even company executives acknowledged the problems. "We had some difficulties," recalled Fujio Cho, who oversaw the plant's launch. Unlike Smyrna, Georgetown was established in a region with low sales—Cho called it "a blank area for us." Toyota battled for acceptance. Privately, executives also doubted the quality of local workers and worried about constructing a supply chain in a region with no automotive history. While the company stressed that it had thrived because of careful decision-making, a heavy reliance on imported parts—one industry researcher claimed that no more than 25 percent of a car's value was added in Georgetown—also explained its success.[14]

It is important to interrogate the mood when Toyota arrived rather than be influenced by subsequent growth.[15] Early on, many Kentuckians worried that the plant would produce unregulated growth, heavy traffic, and pollution. As the factory grew, concerns persisted about the loss of small-town values and familiarity, deeply human reactions. Residents complained that the vast majority of Toyota workers lived outside Scott County, while employees admitted that their jobs were very demanding. Executives acknowledged that subsequent acceptance should not obscure the diverse reaction that occurred at the time. "Toyota is now accepted as part of the fabric of Kentucky," commented manager Dennis Cuneo in 2006, "but it wasn't 20 years ago." Even the *Georgetown News and Times*, which had greeted Toyota with a special edition headlined "Toyota, a Big Yes," recognized this point. "The road to preparation for Toyota's location in Scott County was not necessarily a smooth one," it noted later.[16]

Challenging press observations, the union issue was also fraught. Pointing out that several joint ventures—as well as the Big Three's plants—were unionized, the UAW worked hard to get Toyota to recognize it. "We don't think the foreign-owned companies setting up operations here should be resisting the union," summarized Peter Laarman in 1987. Despite perceptions that the union had not tried to organize the plant, the union pushed hard behind the scenes for bargaining rights. Early on, it looked as though Toyota's managers might compromise, but over time, its position hardened. Citing community opposition to the union and staffing the plant with workers from outside the industry, Toyota stood its ground. Labor tensions, however, remained.[17]

The story of why Toyota chose Kentucky is also more complicated than it appears. The decision has usually been linked to a headline-grabbing $149 million incentive package. As James Rubenstein wrote in *The Changing US Auto Industry* (1992), Toyota had thrown the choice "to the highest bidder," and Georgetown was the surprise winner. "But when the magnitude of Kentucky's incentive package was revealed," he added, "the logic underlying the choice became clear." Other observers drew similar conclusions.[18] Several other states, however, reportedly offered bigger packages. While the incentives were important, a bigger role was played by Collins's intervention and the geographical and logistical advantages of the site. Like other governors, Collins played a critical part, but she had to overcome gender barriers to do so.[19]

Toyota's decision was the culmination of a long journey. Under the influence of Sakichi Toyoda, the company began life in 1891 as a textile manufacturer. As the automotive industry took off in the United States, Japan's industrial strength lay in other areas. After the Great Kanto Earthquake of 1923 devastated the railway network, however, budding entrepreneurs such as Toyoda saw the need to develop the automobile business. In September 1936 Toyoda Automatic Loom Works became the first company in Japan to be granted a license to manufacture cars, beating Nissan by eight days. Shortly afterward, the brand name changed from Toyoda to Toyota. In November 1938, with the opening of the Koromo Assembly Plant in Aichi Prefecture, TMC was founded. Like other Japanese corporations, Toyota was soon consumed by World War II, but in 1949, when an Allied ban on car production was lifted, the company resumed production, quickly becoming Japan's largest auto producer.[20]

Entering the U.S. market in 1957, Toyota learned quickly. After its underpowered Crown model flopped in America, the company improved the quality of its vehicles and fitted them with larger engines. In the 1960s and early 1970s, a time of strong economic growth in Japan, Toyota expanded rapidly, increasing production from 477,643 vehicles in 1965 to 1.61 million in 1970. Sales in the United States grew thirtyfold over the same period, helped by the introduction of the Corolla subcompact (1966). The car did well during the energy crisis of 1973–74, winning the brand recognition. This paved the way for the introduction in 1982 of the slightly bigger Camry, which also proved popular. By 1983, Toyota's share of the U.S. market nudged 6 percent.[21]

This success paved the way for Georgetown. As early as 1973, Toyota commissioned feasibility studies for a U.S. plant, yet cautious executives delayed a decision, instead building market share. Following the second energy crisis, Toyota's exports surged, giving the issue urgency. In 1980, automobile production in Japan topped ten million vehicles, making Japan the world's largest car-producing country. Executives began to look closely at U.S. locations, particularly after Honda and Nissan established their plants. As the biggest Japanese importer, Toyota was also heavily affected by the voluntary export restraint (VER) quota of May 1981. According to an official history, the VER "worried" executives, who disliked "trade friction."[22]

Still, Toyota balked. Managers talked with Ford about creating a joint venture rather than building a solely owned plant. In doing so, Toyota hoped to establish a foothold in America and circumvent the quotas. Held in September 1980, the talks collapsed when the two firms were unable to agree on which vehicle to build. Soon afterward, Toyota began negotiations with General Motors. In March 1982, Eiji Toyoda and GM counterpart Roger Smith agreed to create New United Motor Manufacturing Inc. (NUMMI), based at GM's plant in Fremont, California. Toyota contributed $250 million to the joint venture, which was announced in February 1983, while GM added $20 million plus the $130 million plant. The Fremont factory, which had shut down a few months earlier, would be reopened. The establishment of NUMMI was influential, especially as it gave Toyota the chance to try out its team concept production system in America.[23]

Even after committing to NUMMI, which made the Toyota Corolla and the virtually identical Chevrolet Nova, Toyota needed production capacity in the United States to compete with its main rivals. As early as April 1980, it hired consultants to investigate the establishment of a solely owned factory. Reflecting a conservative corporate culture, Toyota again delayed the decision, largely because of fears that quality and profitability could not be upheld. Over time, however, the move became more attractive. In 1982, TMC and Toyota Motor Sales Company merged to form the Toyota Motor Corporation, helping further growth. Between 1982 and 1985, the yen also appreciated against the dollar, hurting Toyota's imports. In the fiscal year 1982–83, the average yen-to-dollar exchange rate was 248, but this fell to 201 in 1985–86. If it made cars in the United States, Toyota would be insulated from these fluctuations.[24]

Other factors were also important. By 1985, Marysville and Smyrna were building vehicles that were competitive in cost and quality with those made in Japan. Toyota executives were impressed. In 1985, Toyota's sales in North America also reached one million for the first time, and the belief that the company should contribute to the local economy "gained momentum." In the summer of 1985, having received offers of inducements from "numerous states," Toyota threw the process open, inviting applicants to fill in a questionnaire that covered areas such as proximity to suppliers, transport links, and labor force availability. After receiving many responses, Toyota selected sites in Tennessee and Kentucky as front-runners. Both states were within a day's drive of two-thirds of the U.S. population, giving them distribution advantages.[25]

Even before the call for applications, Collins had mobilized. Winning a historic race in 1983, Collins was only the third woman in American history to be elected governor without succeeding her husband. Aware of Kentucky's poverty, she made economic development a priority. Keen to land a large auto plant, Collins took charge of the Toyota project. Almost all of the negotiations to recruit the firm were conducted at the state level, and Georgetown's leaders only found out about the decision when the press did. "There was a group from the state working with them [Toyota]," recalled vice mayor George Lusby, "and it was a state motivation that got it."[26]

Because Honda and Nissan had been given state incentives, Kentucky's officials understood that they would have to offer a similar package to Toyota. At the heart of the state's deal were important commitments to train workers, as well as an agreement to acquire the land, conveying the site to Toyota in fee simple. The Department of Transportation also committed $47 million to upgrade roads. The company was given flexibility about how many jobs it would create. If any part of the agreement was held to be illegal or unenforceable, the remaining provisions would be unaffected. These protections were important to Toyota, which wanted to minimize its risk.[27]

Incentives, however, do not explain why Toyota chose Kentucky. Other states offered equal or bigger subsidies, but Collins's personal role in the negotiations helped put Kentucky ahead. Although many details were kept secret, it was known that the other finalists were Georgia, Indiana, Kansas, Missouri, and Tennessee.[28] In order to beat these bids, Collins built on the efforts of her predecessors, especially fellow Democrat Julian M. Carroll, who had established a state office in Japan in 1979. Commerce secretary Carroll Knicely, who served under both governors, ran the office, which was designed to attract investment. When they announced their choice of Georgetown, Toyota's leading decision makers, including president Shoichiro Toyoda, praised Collins. According to Toyota, the governor had "engaged in active lobbying activities including visiting the TMC head office." Launching an eighteen-month-long campaign to land the plant, Collins made eight trips to Japan, more than any other governor.[29]

Collins went the extra mile, especially when company officials visited Kentucky. On a crucial site selection visit in November 1985, she entertained the Toyota delegation with a lavish dinner at the Governor's Mansion, arranging food and entertainment tailored to Japanese tastes. A former schoolteacher who was used to interacting with people, Collins even arranged a performance of Steven Foster's "My Old Kentucky Home," a favorite of the Japanese visitors. "I had a dinner that night that many people thought probably kind of sealed the deal because of the food I served and because of the entertainment I had," she recalled. The event concluded with an impressive fireworks display outside the mansion. Toyota's decision makers also stressed the importance of that night. "The most decisive factor," explained a company official, "was the dinner party hosted by Governor Collins in November [1985]. Governor

Collins arranged to have many people there—the president of the University of Kentucky, the president of the Kentucky Chamber of Commerce, and all these people. Our people thought that here in Kentucky everybody is united to help Toyota." On other occasions, Collins took company officials to distilleries, shrewdly capitalizing on one of her state's most famous products. "You know as well as I do that the primary Kentucky product our new Japanese friends developed an affinity for wasn't Kentucky Fried Chicken," wrote distillery executive T. W. Samuels Jr. to the governor.[30]

After the deal, Collins maintained contact, especially with the Toyoda family. In March 1986, she entertained Dr. Shoichiro Toyoda and his wife when they visited Kentucky. Two months later, when Toyoda flew in for the groundbreaking ceremony, he attended the Kentucky Derby with the governor. For Collins, these details were "the key" to economic development, which relied heavily on relationship building. In this case, Collins worked extra hard to gain this trust, as the Japanese corporate environment was male dominated (as were Toyota's factories). "The only time you saw females were if they came in to serve and whatever," she recalled of her meetings in Japan. "Most of the time I was the only female in the room, and so that was kind of an adjustment." Illustrating the connections formed, Toyoda started bringing his wife to meetings. "To me that was the greatest compliment he could pay me," remembered Collins. More than three decades later, the pair still stayed in touch.[31]

Other factors also swayed Toyota. Georgetown had strong physical advantages, including access to important highways. The site was two miles from Interstate 75, a major industry artery. Georgetown was only fifteen minutes from Lexington, home of the University of Kentucky and an airport. In addition, the site offered major rail access, allowing Toyota to develop the largest intermodal rail facility in the region. The site was large and flat, with plenty of room to expand, and it was serviced by cheap power. Toyota officials also liked that the location was roughly equidistant between the Nissan and Honda factories. With a Ford plant in Louisville and a GM factory in Bowling Green, Kentucky had a presence in the automotive industry. Unlike Tennessee, however, it did not have any Japanese-owned car plants, avoiding competition for political attention. Once again, location trumped incentives.[32]

Labor force considerations were also important. Explaining Toyota's decision, Carroll Knicely cited the importance of a "very productive labor force," while Georgetown mayor Tom Prather asserted that the area offered a strong "work ethic" and a labor pool that was "very, very broad," with workers willing to commute long distances. The absence of unions was also significant. As one state brochure boasted, there were "no labor organizations representing workers in Scott County manufacturing firms." Although

An architect's rendering of the Toyota plant in Georgetown, Kentucky, before subsequent expansions. Like other foreign-owned car plants, Toyota's was situated on a large and flat site close to interstate highways. This allowed the company to build a big, low-density plant. Courtesy of Kentucky Department for Libraries and Archives.

Toyota had recognized the UAW in Fremont, this was largely because of GM's influence. Privately, its managers worried that union workers would be reluctant to adopt its flexible manufacturing system, which emphasized teamwork.[33]

When Toyota's choice was publicized, it generated lots of positive reaction. In Collins's files, the number of praiseworthy letters outnumbered those opposed to the deal, though this was partly because vocal economic elites were some of the biggest supporters.[34] "Wonderful! Wonderful! Wonderful!" exclaimed James J. Coleman, an industrial development manager, who called the project "the best single achievement for Kentucky in decades." In a similar vein, Bowling Green attorney John David Cole termed the announcement "one of the most significant events in the history of the Commonwealth." Collins also received a warm letter from Dick Mayer, the CEO of Kentucky Fried Chicken. "We applaud your efforts to promote economic development in Kentucky," he wrote. "The future of all Kentuckians will be brighter as a result."[35]

State politicians rushed to take credit. In particular, freshman Republican senator Mitch McConnell, who had narrowly beaten Democrat Walter Dee Huddleston in 1984, attempted to steal Collins's thunder. On December 9, two days before Toyota's announcement—and with Collins respecting the company's confidence—McConnell, who had been told of the decision at a private dinner, publicly released the news. In response, Collins issued a terse statement outlining her displeasure. The governor had reasons to be cautious; early in her term, she had worked hard to land the Saturn plant but was narrowly defeated by Spring Hill, Tennessee. "We don't want to come in second again," she commented. Viewing McConnell's actions as ungracious, many—but not all—citizens saw through them.[36]

From the beginning, not everyone gushed at Toyota's arrival. Even before the plant was confirmed, local leaders were expressing both concern and support. As city-county planner Steve Mooney admitted, a facility of Toyota's size would create serious headaches. "We want to keep the characteristic of Georgetown as much as we can," he noted. "It's going to be a challenge." Once the announcement was made, anxiety mounted. On December 11, mayor-elect Sam Pollock, acknowledging that the plant would create "problems" and "difficulties," announced that he would be visiting Smyrna and Spring Hill to see how they were coping with similar challenges.[37]

In order to understand these worries, it is important to realize that Georgetown was a quiet agricultural community. With a population of just eleven thousand, it was very close-knit, and residents cherished the familiarity and safety of small-town life. "You knew everybody," summarized lifelong resident Price Smith, remembering the town in his youth. "If I picked up the phone to call my dad, I didn't call his number. I said, 'I want my daddy,' and the operator would put me through!" Those who came to the town, even from other parts of Kentucky, recalled that incomers were rare and not easily accepted. Lindsey Apple moved to Georgetown from Louisville in 1960 to attend Georgetown College, the historic Baptist institution, returning a few years later as faculty: "When I was an undergraduate, Dr. Carl Fields, who taught history, said that you had to live in Georgetown or Scott County for three generations before you were home folk, before you belonged. You were *always* an outsider."[38]

Georgetown's closeness also reflected a static economy. In the early 1980s, the area depended heavily on tobacco, a crop that had been declining for decades. Population figures illustrated the depressed economic climate. In the first half of the 1980s, Scott County's population grew by only 0.5 percent, sitting at around twenty-two thousand in 1985. The county suffered a net migration loss in these years, but because births surpassed deaths, the natural increase exceeded outmigration by about a hundred people. Between 1979 and 1986, the number of manufacturing jobs in Scott County fell, from 2,882 to 2,189. Prior to Toyota, the town's chief claim to fame was its assertion that it was the place where, in 1789, Baptist minister Elijah Craig had first produced Kentucky bourbon.[39]

Rather than worrying about the lack of growth, many residents liked the status quo. When Toyota arrived, they were concerned that the area's character would be lost. "This is pretty much a farming community," recalled long-term resident Wayne Robey, "and especially at that time, I think some of the farmers were, 'Gee, they're going to buy up all the land, and [put] houses everywhere, and there's not going to be any more farms.'" In the weeks after the announcement, reports came in of surging land prices near the plant, stoking fears of rapid development. Concerned residents spoke out. "I have to admit I was not all that thrilled when I first heard that Toyota would be moving to Scott County, my home," wrote Daniel T. Brown, speaking for many. Looking back, Collins acknowledged these fears. "The people in Georgetown," she summarized, "there were some who didn't want the plant and were not happy with the fact that we were going to make the town and the county grow."[40]

The state handled the acquisition of the land for the plant, and the process was difficult. As late as December 10, 1985, the day before the announcement, key landowner Marilyn Singer had refused to sell. The Singer family owned 136 acres along I-75, land that Toyota badly wanted. Informed that she had forty-eight hours to agree, Singer complained that she had been "pressured all day long." Eventually, the state found a loophole allowing it to acquire her land without her signature (her husband signed). Although Singer disputed the state's right to acquire her land—even accusing it of "maliciously" violating her "contractual rights"—the deal stuck. As one resident recalled, the Singers were "very much opposed" to selling to Toyota.[41] Other landowners had mixed feelings. The most important was tobacco farmer Price Smith, who owned 900 acres of the proposed site. "Here's land that has been in the family for *years* and years and years, and there is some reluctance to want to give it up," he recalled. In particular, one family member had been wounded on Iwo Jima during World War II and had "bad feelings" about selling to the Japanese. According to Smith, state officials were on a "fast track" and desperately wanted the land. Offered a generous—but undisclosed—sum, the family eventually accepted.[42]

As the site was put together, there were other disruptions. To make way for Toyota, two cemeteries had to be moved, with the costs borne by Scott County. Because the cemeteries were deemed abandoned (the last burial was in the 1870s), the fourteen graves were relocated, with little sentiment. "It's very important we get everything rolling," commented Toyota attorney Mike Slone. U.S. Highway 62 also had to be widened, causing the state to purchase and relocate two businesses and change the access of several others.[43]

Once the land issue was resolved, local concerns focused on several issues, all of them related to growth. At a hearing held by the Planning and Zoning Commission on December 30, "upset residents" voiced their concerns. As the *News and Times* reported, many did not want the Toyota site to be rezoned from agricultural to industrial, the main business of the meeting. They worried that the change would increase traffic and felt that local authorities were too accommodating to Toyota. "I don't think it's right for one man or one group to say they can do this," asserted Bill Beckett of Oxford, opposing the zone change. Others worried about large numbers of Toyota workers commuting on rural roads. "Not everybody will be coming in by way of the bypass," summarized resident Wilma Ewbank.[44] The hearing encapsulated how life had changed quickly for the commission, which was used to "seemingly-quiet, hour-long meetings" once a month. Now it held frequent "marathon" sessions, with every seat filled. "In terms of planning and zoning, we've had tremendous changes since Toyota," explained Mooney.[45]

As part of the Toyota agreement, the Georgetown Water and Sewer Service Board agreed to build a wastewater treatment plant. The large facility caused a lot of tension, with residents worrying about contamination of the water supply. "We stand a chance of creating a hazard for this community," commented Neil Duncliffe, a local attorney. Stuart Muir, who lived near the proposed site, became angry at one meeting, pointing to a model of the sewage plant and knocking pieces of it onto the floor. "You'll see this thing in court," he vowed. Four hundred residents attended a Zoning Commission meeting in mid-January, with many represented by Duncliffe. According to the attorney, the Muirs, who owned 87 acres, would "move away" if the sewage plant went ahead.[46]

Largely due to residents' protests, the issue took more than six months to resolve. At a Zoning Commission meeting on January 27—at which the plant site was rezoned from agricultural to industrial—protesters called for the sewage facility to be built on-site, reducing the impact on residents. In February, the *News and Times* reported that "many" locals felt they had not been consulted about the waste plant's location. "Those people feel it is a problem. I don't know how I would feel having to live next to it," admitted Don Olver, a member of the Georgetown Water and Sewer Service Board. The opposition caused the Scott County Board of Adjustment to delay issuing a permit. In May 1986, after six hours of testimony and questions, the board postponed a decision until the state had held a public hearing. Two months later, the county finally granted the permit, but the water board agreed to spend $2 million on extra piping to assuage concerns.[47]

Residents also worried about air pollution. In June, the Kentucky Natural Resources and Environmental Protection Cabinet held a public hearing to discuss Toyota's air pollution control program. The state argued that Toyota's controls were "state of the art," but some citizens were unconvinced. Resident Randy Maddox called for the state to carry out an environmental impact study before approving the permit, while the local branches of the Audubon Society and the Sierra Club also expressed concern. "The people's right to quality air is essential," commented the Audubon Society's Ruth Housik. "The need for health also." Because Toyota could not begin construction without the permit, however, the state agency was under great pressure, and it gave its approval a week later. Jerry Hammond, a Versailles resident, then filed suit to stop construction of the plant on environmental grounds. In July, however, circuit judge David Knox dismissed the complaint with costs to the plaintiff, who was a local union leader.[48]

Other sources illustrated that local reaction was mixed. Conducted in July 1986 by the Survey Research Center at the University of Kentucky, an impact survey of 1,049 residents—322 in Scott County and 727 in surrounding counties—highlighted in quantitative terms that Toyota's arrival produced a lot of concern. Illustrating the plant's high profile, 89 percent of respondents in Scott County and 78 percent in surrounding counties claimed that they had heard "a lot" about Toyota's arrival. Although most respondents thought that the plant would produce jobs and tax revenue, they had many concerns. Doubting that their families would benefit, many feared that jobs would go to outsiders.[49] The incentives were controversial, with 51.8 percent of respondents disagreeing or strongly disagreeing with "state funding" for the plant. Over 54 percent also felt that the factory would "overload public services." Around 82 percent thought that there would be "crowded schools," while 67 percent worried that crime would increase. Reflecting prevailing anti-Japanese feeling, 46 percent of respondents said they would not like to work "under Japanese managers."[50] Almost 80 percent of respondents felt that the factory would elevate the cost of living, while a compelling 91.3 percent thought that "increased road congestion" would occur. Many also doubted whether Toyota would fulfill its obligations to the community.[51]

These issues deserve further exploration. Anti-Japanese sentiment, for example, was common at the time, especially as most of the World War II generation was still alive. Long-serving Toyota employee Kim Stamper remembered the reaction after the announcement. "Most of the . . . mid-life to younger people were good," she summarized. "The older [generation], that had fought in the war, had family members die in the war with Japan, they weren't real welcoming of it. . . . There was a man that lived down the road from us, and he said he wouldn't even speak the name Toyota, because he was so distraught that it had come there." Local historian Lindsey Apple also recalled antipathy. "There was a holdover of suspicion, hostility, to the Japanese because of Pearl Harbor," he noted. Residents who had served in the Pacific were "broken" when they heard that Toyota—which operated three military aircraft factories during the war—was coming.[52]

The sentiment resonated beyond Scott County. Around three hundred thousand Kentuckians had served in World War II, and more than ten thousand had been killed. Collins's papers demonstrate that many Kentuckians disliked the arrival of a Japanese automaker, and they frequently evoked memories of the war. "December 7, 1941, without any warning or declaration of war, the Japanese cowardly bombed Pearl Harbor," wrote veteran John Connor Sr. from Whitesville. "I feel that the Toyota plant is just another bomb they've dropped on us. This time, it was not only supported but strongly sought after by our politicians." Such belligerence was also expressed by residents of other states. "I have a brother in wheel chair from World War II, where he fought in the war against Japan," wrote Mrs. Pearl Branham from Ohio. "We won so what do we owe Japan? . . . Bring back the passenger trains and buses, we will ride them rather than ride Japan junk. If it isn't made by Americans Co, we don't need it." Less likely to arouse memories of the war, younger correspondents still emphasized Toyota's origins, arguing that Japanese automakers were getting an unfair amount of market access.[53]

Undeterred, Collins replied by insisting that foreign investment was vital, especially as Kentucky had high unemployment. She also argued that most constituents supported Toyota's arrival.[54] Still, the opposition was serious enough for Collins to be probed about it on a trip to Tokyo in February. "Questions were asked us will the people of Kentucky accept Japanese investment and Japanese people," she noted. Even at the ground-breaking, Dr. Toyoda referred to anti-Japanese sentiment. Describing the plant as "a new born child," Toyoda expressed his "hope" that one day the "child" would be "appreciated." In retirement, Collins acknowledged the strength of feeling. "There was just a certain amount of distrust there," she recalled, "because they were foreign. It was a foreign company, and they had different ways of doing things than what Americans do."[55]

Concerns about the incentive package were also widespread. At a meeting of the Planning and Zoning Commission in January, residents spoke out. "I think we do get the cart ahead of the horse," declared local man James Sexton. "Can the American car companies really compete (if foreign companies get the incentives as Toyota has). No, I think they cannot." Many Kentuckians, including legislators in Frankfort, shared this view. In February, the House Appropriations and Revenue Committee raised questions about the Toyota agreement. In the late 1980s, Wallace Wilkinson, the Democrat who succeeded Collins (at the time, Kentucky governors could not be reelected), campaigned against the incentive package as a poor deal. Concerns about the costs were also raised by reporters. One *Lexington Herald-Leader* story, "Toyota Deal: Did Kentucky Give Away Too Much?," was indicative.[56]

Even among business groups, there was considerable concern. In May 1986, the leader of the Paducah Business and Professional Women's Club spoke for many. "The procurement of the land for the plant site was not handled in accordance with the procedure for other business wishing to start operation in KY.," claimed Jean Elkins, "since businesses are required to purchase at least a percent of the land they acquire. This is taxation without representation." Other residents objected to the entire agreement. "They [Toyota] are a business much like state government," wrote Danville's W. Frank Burberry, "and both must be run like a business. No more gifts. No more bending and breaking existing legislation." Collins received a stack of similar letters.[57]

The controversy refused to go away. In 1986, the Property and Buildings Commission, which had issued bonds to buy land for Toyota, filed a friendly lawsuit against the Collins administration, arguing that it had breached the state constitution by giving gifts to a private business. At issue was a 1986 law—passed by the General Assembly at Collins's urging—that authorized the incentives. Several citizens and labor groups joined the suit. In June 1987, following a lengthy battle, the Kentucky Supreme Court upheld the administration's conduct on the grounds that it was designed to reduce unemployment, a public purpose. As the *Herald-Leader* reported, however, the court was "deeply divided," its 4–3 vote reflecting ongoing disquiet. Furthermore, dissenting justice Charles M. Leibson alleged that the court had been pressured to "find some way around the constitution in the name of political expediency."[58]

The plant produced other legal challenges. In one case, landowner Gordon Taub disputed the state's right to use eminent domain to build a four-lane highway near the plant. In order to construct the road, several properties that Taub owned had to be condemned, and he argued that the state should not have acquired the land for a private corporation. Hearing the case, circuit judge David Knox again ruled in the state's favor. Although Taub won an appeal, the Kentucky Supreme Court upheld Knox's ruling. There was "public" benefit to the road, Knox felt, because it served both Kentuckians and Toyota. A complex case, *Taub v. Commonwealth of Kentucky and Martha Layne Collins* stayed before the courts for two years.[59]

Labor issues also generated tension, especially after Toyota announced that Ohbayashi Corporation, a nonunion contractor from Japan, would build the plant. Protesting the move, the AFL-CIO's Building Trades Council and the United Brotherhood of Carpenters led a campaign for the work to be awarded to a unionized American firm. "Toyota simply must not be permitted to profit from its lack of respect for our laws, our working standards, and our traditions," wrote local carpenters' union member Leonard R. Bauer, "particularly at a time when American construction firms are not permitted to bid [on] construction work in Japan." In November 1986, hundreds of construction workers demonstrated outside the Japanese embassy in Washington, D.C., and in front of the Hotel Pierre in New York, where the Japanese ambassador was having business meetings. Their placards—"Got a yen for fairness?" and "Forget Toyota. Stop giveaways to corporations that don't respect American habits"—showed that the case had moved beyond labor issues.[60]

On the national level, the campaign secured other supporters. They were led by the AFL-CIO's Building Trades Council, which saw Toyota as a test of "whether Japanese investors can come to this country and disregard the standards we've worked for." After exposing details of the incentive package, Ralph Nader also described the deal as "corporate freeloading on the backs of taxpayers." Clearly embarrassed, Toyota retreated. Soon after the national protests, Ohbayashi agreed that two thousand construction workers would be hired through union channels. Around one thousand existing workers were also allowed to stay.[61]

There was also conflict with the UAW. Because NUMMI was organized, the union insisted that Georgetown should be too. "Toyota and the UAW today enjoy a relationship based on mutual respect and trust in the joint-venture auto plant operated by Toyota in California," it noted. "We hope and expect to develop a similar relationship with Toyota in Kentucky." The company refused to sign a deal, however. Failing to see NUMMI's example as decisive, managers told the UAW that Georgetown was a different situation and that Toyota Motor Manufacturing (TMM), the new name for its U.S. manufacturing operations, was a separate entity from TMC, which had agreed to the NUMMI deal. The argument frustrated the UAW, which also complained that Toyota was reluctant to hire workers with industry backgrounds. "They [Toyota] are screening out people who have had previous experience and my own idea is this is to eliminate union influence," charged Bieber. In response, Toyota admitted that it preferred "freshmen."[62]

The UAW tried to change the company's position. In 1986 and 1987, Bieber repeatedly sought meetings with TMC's top decision makers to resolve the issue. On one occasion, he even turned up unannounced at Toyota's headquarters in Tokyo after his attempts to get an appointment with Eiji Toyoda were unsuccessful. Bieber was told, however, that the chairman was unavailable. Efforts to meet with vice president Masami Iwasaki in the United States fared no better, even when Bieber offered a wide choice of dates in 1987 and 1988.[63] Iwasaki was evasive, refusing to commit because his schedule was "very tight." Bieber was unimpressed. "I think this cat is using every trick to push our meeting down the road," he wrote an aide.[64]

There were other reasons for Toyota's evasiveness. Rather than recognizing the UAW in advance, managers argued that employees should choose. "Workers themselves decide whether they belong to union or not," declared TMC director Iwao Isomura. The company also insisted that as TMC and TMM were separate entities, TMC could only "advise" TMM about union organization, not "order" it. Toyota's separation of TMC and TMM hurt the UAW, which had hoped for greater centralization. "What they did was to make the Georgetown plant just like a different company," recalled Bieber.[65] In labor relations—seen as a local matter—TMM had considerable autonomy. As Japanese union leader J. Ogiso related, TMM was largely staffed by Americans, some of whom had experienced "bad times with UAW." They were consequently "skeptical about UAW's present cooperative attitude toward management." Toyota's Japanese executives also worried that UAW members would not show the "flexibility" and "good faith" that the company needed. Toyota was under pressure in this regard, with Fujio Cho relating that American dealers were "extremely worried" about the quality of the cars that came out of Kentucky. If customers saw these cars as inferior, dealers could close. To address these concerns, the company wanted to create what one consultant called "the ultimate in plants" in Georgetown.[66]

Workers were chosen carefully. Highlighting how word had spread, by January 1990 the company had received two hundred thousand applications for three thousand positions. Even those seeking entry-level jobs were tested for fourteen hours, compared to an hour at most American companies. Rather than manufacturing experience, Toyota was interested in applicants' "potential to perform, their desire and ability to learn, and their interpersonal skills." Only the very best could make it, and Toyota regarded those who had been laid off from other plants—rightly or wrongly—as wearing a badge of failure, especially as the company rarely closed factories. Toyota wanted to start from scratch with workers who accepted the "Toyota Way" rather than the UAW's "American Way." Avoiding traditional terms such as "supervisor" and "employee," Toyota placed hires into three categories: group leaders (managers), team leaders (supervisors), and team members (workers). For many, these classifications were designed to reduce union sentiment.[67]

As the plant hired more workers, the evidence mounted that managers were reluctant to select applicants with union backgrounds. In early 1988, forty-five laid-off UAW members from Rockwell International in Winchester applied at Toyota, but none were hired. The company told these workers that while they were well-qualified, it would meet its needs with "applicants who have been evaluated at even higher levels."[68] Other workers from union plants complained that they could not get jobs at TMM. According to Donna Mattingly, the wife of a unionized ironworker from Louisville, the project was based on "lies" because only "non-union" workers were hired. Some applicants with union backgrounds even sought the governor's assistance, but Collins was reluctant to get involved. As TMM president Kaneyoshi Kusunoki admitted in 1988, the company preferred workers without industrial experience, despite the challenges. "They've had to be trained in every detail of automaking," admitted Kusunoki, "from learning the names of the parts on up."[69]

In mid-1988, Bieber finally managed to meet with TMC managers. In confidential gatherings at the airport in Los Angeles, he made a last-ditch effort to persuade the company to recognize the UAW. Toyota, however, now cited local opposition to unions. "Our philosophy is spirit of cooperation with community," commented executive Hiroshi Okuda in May. "We think the community activities beneficial and essential to the Company."[70] The argument angered Bieber, who insisted that the UAW was not a "plague." "You are trying to paint a picture that you cannot survive in Georgetown with UAW," he told Isomura in July. "That's a lot of boloney. I won't accept that." Isomura responded that the Georgetown factory would become more "American" over time, increasing the dominance of local mores. Unionization, he added, was up to employees. To Bieber's dismay, production began without a labor agreement.[71]

The state of the local economy compounded the union's problems. In February 1986, Clark Equipment Company closed its Georgetown plant, which employed more than seven hundred people. Ironically, competition from foreign fork-lift truck producers, including Nissan and Toyota, was behind the shutdown. In what the *News and Times* described as the "end of an era," the closure removed around $12 million from a local economy already hurting from the decline of agriculture. "Toyota, when they came, I would call us almost a deprived community," summarized George Lusby. As the numbers indicated, locals were keen to work at Toyota.[72] As wages were kept close to UAW levels, successful applicants often experienced rapid economic progress. Karen Wells recalled that the job changed her family's life. "This was more money than we'd ever seen," she noted. Another early hire, Reuben McIntyre, went from making three dollars an hour to seventeen dollars an hour. "It changed my lifestyle," he recalled. "I never had a whole lot in my life." Like Wells, a struggling horse breeder, many workers came from farming backgrounds. In Japan, where Toyota had rural roots, it had a history of hiring what one industry expert called "agrarian youth." With low-wage backgrounds, these applicants were seen as hardworking, appreciative, and malleable.[73]

The demand for work was especially great among African Americans, who were hit hard by agriculture's decline. In October 1986, a University of Louisville study found that "blacks and other racial minorities" were "more highly represented" among Toyota applicants than in the population of Scott County or the state. Although Scott County was less than 10 percent black, nonwhites made up 15.5 percent of applicants for TMM's production jobs. Despite this demand, only small numbers of blacks were hired. While Toyota refused to give precise numbers, those hired felt isolated inside the plant. Drawing on their history, they persisted. "We were used to being discriminated against," summarized McIntyre.[74]

As part of their training, most early employees went to Japan for four weeks. Although there were cultural differences—especially as Toyota's Japanese plants did not hire women in production jobs—most participants enjoyed the trip, and they learned a lot about the Toyota production system. Illustrating this, in June 1988, early hires produced the plant's first car, a Camry, which was driven through a paper curtain onto a decorated stage. To remind workers of the accomplishment, the vehicle was left at the plant "forever." Wayne

Robey was part of the group that built the car. "That very first white Camry," he recalled. "I installed . . . the left rear axle on that particular car. It was a lot of pride . . . from everything, from Toyota deciding to come into Georgetown, to me actually getting a job there . . . and actually installing parts on the first car. . . . It's historic."[75]

Once celebrations subsided, the start of production generated fresh tensions. Funding the bypass around Georgetown—a road that was now badly needed—proved controversial. As part of the Toyota deal, Collins promised that the state would pay for the first stage of the bypass. The road had been planned since 1974, but efforts to secure state funding had been unsuccessful. In September 1988, there were further complications when Governor Wilkinson, who had come into power criticizing Collins's concessions to Toyota, demanded that local government pay to acquire the land for the project. This was resisted, as many residents felt that the road was mainly for outsiders working at TMM. "A much less number of employees live and work in Georgetown/Scott County and these are the people who will have to pay the additional taxes," wrote one group of residents in 1990. Following heated negotiations between county, city, and state officials, Frankfort approved the project. Wilkinson's successor, Brereton Jones, agreed to state funding and forgave the city its share of the costs. In 1993, the bypass was finally opened.[76]

The controversy exposed deep-seated tensions about who worked at Toyota. In 1990, out of 3,460 plant workers, just 500 lived in Scott County. More than 900 resided in the Lexington area, while many more commuted from Louisville or other parts of Kentucky, as well as neighboring states. This was a significant source of complaint, especially as the community's compensation was largely limited to the occupational tax assessed to each worker in the county. "When most of the Toyota workers go home," noted a *News and Times* editorial, "the rest of that paycheck is spent elsewhere, benefitting merchants outside our community and boosting another community's economy." The influx of outsiders produced complaints about "traffic problems" that never disappeared. Acknowledging the issue, long-serving mayor Tom Prather noted that Cherry Blossom Way, the highway servicing the plant, was often a "fire-hose of traffic."[77]

Aware of the need to win over local opinion, Toyota gradually built acceptance. From the start, the company launched a charm offensive. In one early, full-page message in the *News and Times*, Toyota emphasized that it felt at "home" in Kentucky and was "proud" to be making cars there. In a subsequent full-page ad, Toyota even called the first cars it had sold in the United States a "mistake," adding, "We owe a lot to America. America gave us a chance when we were small and scared. It gave us the challenge that helped us become who we are. This is something we will never forget." In securing approval, Cho, TMM's foundational president, was key. His affable, down-to-earth personality—he usually wore the standard Toyota uniform of khaki trousers and a navy shirt—won him plaudits, as did his love of fishing and the fact that he lived in Georgetown. "People just *loved* him," recalled an early employee.[78]

Some Scott Countians also reached out. In 1986, the *News and Times* started Inside Japan, a weekly column that broke down barriers. The Japanese, noted columnist Bernice Bowers, were not that different from Americans. *Dynasty* was one of the most watched TV shows, baseball was widely played, and Kentucky Fried Chicken was popular. American music was omnipresent— there were even Michael Jackson sing-alike contests. Unlike Honda, the company's path was also smoothed by the fact that most managers were Americans. In the late 1980s, just sixty-five Japanese families had moved to Kentucky to work for TMM, and most lived in Lexington. This choice was not surprising; in 1980, Georgetown had just five residents with Japanese ethnicity. As late as 2016, Scott County's population was just 1.2 percent Asian. Lexington, however, was bigger and more diverse.[79]

Toyota built acceptance in other ways. At the ground-breaking ceremony, it gave $1 million to the county, which was used to fund a community center. In April 1987, following several months of covert meetings with Mayor Prather, Toyota requested that its site be annexed by the city, a move that generated up to $1.7 million in tax revenues. Toyota consequently paid the city's 1 percent payroll and net profits tax, as well as county taxes. Without this income, recalled Prather, Georgetown would have gone "bankrupt," because it had no "revenue-stream" to pay for the extra costs of servicing the plant. A voluntary move by the company, it was widely praised.[80]

Plant expansions also helped. In 1989, Toyota added a $300 million engine factory, creating five hundred jobs. The following year, it built a second assembly plant, generating fifteen hundred jobs and increasing its site investment to $2 billion. The addition made Toyota the largest manufacturing employer in central Kentucky. In 1994, the new factory began to make the Avalon, a 6-cylinder sedan. Other investments led to the production of a Camry wagon and the manufacture of 6-cylinder engines. Georgetown even exported cars to Japan, a source of local pride. Keen to avoid further controversy, Toyota did not seek incentives for the engine plant or the second assembly facility. Domestic content levels increased; by 1994, Cho claimed that TMM had 174 U.S. suppliers.[81] TMM also won awards. In 1990 and 1993, Georgetown nabbed J. D. Power's Gold Plant Quality Award for best car factory in North America. The prizes brought positive national attention to the town, stroking local egos. In 2006, the *New York Times* claimed that Georgetown epitomized how "auto prosperity" had moved away from the upper Midwest, where carmaking was in decline. Toyota also increased local support by featuring Georgetown's attractive downtown in its commercials.[82]

Out at the plant, however, tension persisted. Jobs at Toyota, while well-paid and sought after, came at a price. As even company supporters admitted, working in the plant, especially on the line, was arduous. Jack Conner, the director of the local chamber of commerce, admitted that working at Toyota was "not easy." "It's physically demanding," added Robey, a TMM manager. "I would say that building cars is a young man's game, or a young woman's game." While revealing a clean and orderly environment, Toyota's plant tours confirmed that assembly workers were overwhelmingly young. With the line moving constantly, employees had less than a minute to perform their allotted task, and most worked on their feet. "I mean you earn your money, every day," summarized Karen Wells, who worked at the plant for twenty-one years. "It's just not easy. You don't go in there and think: 'I'll have an easy day today.' Every day you think: 'Phew, I *earned* that money.'" Hours were long, with Toyota requiring employees to stay for up to two and a half hours at the end of their shifts—which lasted almost nine hours—if production targets were not met. Locally, Toyota workers were known to be time-poor. Wells, who ran a plant nursery in retirement, joked that she sold a lot of "Toyota flowers," hardy perennials that could survive long periods without watering.[83]

The work took its toll. Most car plants had high rates of occupational injury, particularly repetitive strain and back injuries, and Toyota, while not releasing data, seemed no different. Veteran Georgetown residents knew as much. Toyota workers, explained Lindsey Apple, suffered "a lot of carpel tunnel, a lot of shoulder injury problems. I've been involved with the local museum, and when these people are injured, while they're recuperating, they often will work as volunteers. . . . Toyota rarely hires them back. They're damaged goods."[84] As researchers in Japan have shown, Toyota's production system, while sold as "people-friendly," was physically demanding, and injuries were common. As in Kentucky, most Japanese workers came from rural areas, undermining their ability to protest or quit.[85]

Hoping to capitalize on workers' complaints, especially over injuries, the UAW tried to organize TMM. In the summer of 1989, following requests by workers, the union rented an office in Georgetown and launched a recruitment drive. Collecting information, organizers found that there were plenty of issues. Vacation benefits were not generous; they operated on a graduated schedule of "up to 20 days" after fifteen years of service, yet the plant was less than five years old. Workers did get three personal illness reimbursement days a year, but these were only paid at 65 percent of the base rate. If a worker took a PIR, they no longer qualified for a perfect attendance award, losing their rights to participate in a drawing to win a free car. Workers also had to use their break time to attend compulsory safety meetings. Crucially, workers had no written job security rights. If they were injured and could not return to production, they became "associate" staff and were paid $7.59 an hour, about half the normal rate.[86] Pointing out that a lot of employees had been terminated, organizer Bill Young told workers that without a union, they had no job security. "As a general rule," he explained in November 1989, "your Company can promote you out of seniority, take away existing benefits, cut wages or even discharge employees.... So the answer about job protection is NONE, Without a *UNION 'Legal Binding Contract.'*" Illustrating the point, several employees who filed wrongful discharge lawsuits had their cases dismissed by the Kentucky Court of Appeals, which ruled that Toyota's handbook did not constitute a contract. Like millions of other "at will" employees, TMM workers could be fired at any time and for any reason, with few exceptions.[87]

The UAW, however, faced a momentous task. In a poor state with high unemployment, Toyota's jobs were prized. Between 1982 and 1987, the income received by Kentucky's tobacco farmers dropped by 48 percent, with further decreases forecast. Other parts of the farming sector, such as grain and corn production, struggled, while the coal industry was in decline. "The Toyota Motor Corporation project comes at a time when the future of two of the state's major economic sectors, agriculture and coal mining, is not very promising," wrote Collins in 1986. In this climate, organizing was tough. "So many people were so grateful for what they had," summarized Robey. "The great majority of the people were making more money... than they ever dreamed they would make in their entire life. And with things being that good, why change it? ... It's got a lot of promises, but what's going to be the end result?"[88] Many shared this perspective. The UAW soon faced the Truth Team, an employee group that argued that workers were doing well without a union.[89] The group was encouraged by events in Smyrna. "It seemed to form prior to the time of the UAW-Nissan election," wrote TMM vice president Alex M. Warren Jr., who denied corporate involvement.[90]

There were other problems. In 1990, regional director Bill Osos called for the UAW to "take the gloves off" at Toyota, a sentiment echoed by other staff. Still hoping for a high-level deal, Bieber was cautious. In the Nissan campaign, he added, union criticisms of the company had a "negative impact." The UAW had to walk a tightrope, especially as criticism of Toyota could reinforce claims that the union favored the Big Three. During the late 1980s and early 1990s, mass layoffs at the domestic automakers further hurt the union. In 1991, GM slashed seventy-four thousand jobs, one of the biggest layoffs in American history. In contrast, TMM—as workers noticed—thrived.[91] As well as job cuts, negative headlines about lost strikes and union decline hampered efforts. Won over by Toyota's donations and plant expansions, community leaders opposed the UAW. Major local employers, including Clark Equipment Company and FMC, had kept unions out, and Toyota hired executives from these firms. It was also hard to contact workers, with organizers having to search for names and addresses over a wide area.[92] Staff on the ground struggled to cope, and the union was unsure of where to focus its efforts. Strategists toyed with the idea of trying to mobilize female employees, especially by publicizing Toyota's failure to hire women in its Japanese plants, but the idea was not adopted by the male-dominated executive board.[93]

Brought in to find a solution, consultants identified other problems. A core drawback was that the union was seen as an outsider, something it needed to be more aware of. In 1992, one memo noted that Toyota workers had been handed business cards with a Detroit address. This type of material, they noted, "should come from Kentucky instead of Detroit." The advisers also pointed out that the UAW repeatedly referred to "Toyota workers," alienating those who embraced the company's team member discourse.[94] The UAW's support for domestic content legislation exacerbated the outsider issue. The union was a major force behind the American Automobile Labeling Act, which required manufacturers of new cars to list domestic content. As the *Washington Post* reported, Toyota saw the law as "patently discriminatory" because it excluded labor as content. With Toyota publicizing the union's position, many employees felt that the union was discounting them. This perception, Bieber admitted, had "dampen[ed] the organizing drive."[95] As the plant expanded, things got harder, especially as new workers were optimistic. At the same time, Big Three layoffs reduced organizing capacity. Between 1980 and 1994, UAW membership fell from 1.49 million to 742,000.[96] By the mid-1990s, the union had turned to other targets. "Unfortunately that didn't work out," Bieber admitted in retirement, his final judgment on the Toyota campaign.[97]

Toyota transformed Scott County. Between 1980 and 2015, its population surged from 21,813 to 52,420. In one of the fastest-growing areas in the state, there were new subdivisions, a state-of-the-art interstate exchange, and fresh industrial development. "Much of the growth is related to the Toyota Motor Manufacturing plant," summarized the *Herald-Leader* in 2017. When the automaker arrived, Georgetown had one McDonald's and a struggling retail sector; two decades later, it had three McDonald's and new stores, including a Walmart Supercenter. Civic elites were reluctant to criticize Toyota, insulating it from further union organizing.[98]

On the ground, growth continued to divide residents. Some stressed that there was a big strain on local services, especially the school system. (In 2017, Scott County still had only one high school.) Others missed the way the town had been. "There are people that will *still* tell you that they wish they had never seen [Toyota], you know, because of the growth that this has caused," admitted Price Smith. Residents also worried about the area's dependence on Toyota, which dwarfed other employers. For good or bad, however, all agreed that their area had been transformed. "Events of this magnitude are history-changing for a community. They changed the course indefinitely," summarized Mayor Prather.[99]

For the auto industry, Georgetown was highly significant. As *Automotive News* reported, this was where Toyota had proved its global credentials, cracking the largest auto market in the world. Georgetown demonstrated to everybody that Toyota could replicate its production system in the United States. Two decades later, the company had nine North American assembly plants.[100] The plant was also very important to Kentucky. In July 2017, the Bluegrass State was third in the nation in car and truck production and number one in terms of vehicles produced per capita. Auto-related facilities employed over one hundred thousand Kentuckians and contributed 4.2 percent of the state's GDP, with Toyota being the biggest player of all. Confirming the plant's importance, in 2017 Governor Matt Bevin authorized $43.5 million in incentives for a $1.3 billion upgrade.[101]

TMM's history highlights other broad themes. While the company's arrival was—and is—seen as a success story, reality was more complex. As other firms followed Toyota and established U.S. plants, residents welcomed the jobs but worried about the costs of growth. Economic benefits were unevenly shared, incentive packages controversial. As states battled to land foreign-owned auto plants, people and location—as well as incentives—also remained decisive. In the early 1990s, Governor Carroll Campbell was instrumental in bringing BMW to South Carolina, opening an important chapter in the sector's history. The second wave had begun.[102]

CHAPTER FIVE

A "Success Story"?

BMW Comes to
Greer, South Carolina

By the end of the 1980s, the foundational Japanese transplants were well-established, showing that successful automobile factories
could be run outside the upper Midwest, the industry's traditional base. All
three Japanese plants were located in what the *New York Times* called the
"budding mid-South automotive corridor." None had strayed far from I-75, the
industry's traditional axis, which stretched from Detroit to Atlanta, passing
near Marysville and through Georgetown in the process. By staying relatively
close to major industrial centers, first-wave plants enjoyed access to suppliers, major distribution markets, and qualified workers. Moving farther south,
where states were poorer and more isolated and where the industry lacked a
presence, was risky. "Well, I suppose it's okay for Toyota to be in Kentucky, but
that's as far south as you want to go, brother," summarized industry reporter
Lindsay Chappell, recalling the mood.[1]

In the 1990s, however, the industry did expand into the Deep South. During
the decade, four major transplants opened: a BMW factory in Greer, South
Carolina; a Mercedes-Benz plant in Vance, Alabama; a Toyota works in Union
Township, Indiana (an exception to the move to the Deep South); and a Honda
facility in Lincoln, Alabama. In 2000, Nissan also announced a big plant in
Canton, Mississippi. Apart from Toyota, which located in southwestern Indiana, near Kentucky, these factories took the industry into new areas. As the
Washington Post reported in 2001, across the "New Automotive South" the
world's best-known automakers were making millions of vehicles, initiating a
"historic shift" in a region blighted by poverty and low wages. Industry sources
recognized the magnitude of the transformation. "Is the South the new home
of U.S. automotive manufacturing?" asked *The Harbour Report* in 2002.[2]

Of the new plants, BMW's was particularly significant. It was the company's
first factory outside of Germany, a major shift for a brand that traded heavily
on a reputation for German engineering. In this sense, it had a greater significance than its Honda, Nissan, and Toyota counterparts, which were subsid-

iary facilities for companies that already manufactured in the United States. It was also the first European transplant and the first car plant in the Carolinas, states synonymous with the low-wage textile industry.[3] BMW's factory was also the first transplant to be built by a luxury carmaker. Industry observers doubted whether the firm could maintain its quality overseas, especially in the Deep South. A quarter of a century later, however, few questioned the plant's success: it employed more than eight thousand people and produced six models. BMW had invested $7.8 billion into the plant, which had helped its share of the U.S. market to quadruple. In 2018, Greer was the largest BMW factory in the world.[4]

State officials were especially proud. The gleaming factory, defined by its striking U-shaped visitor center, dominated state advertising. BMWs built there were displayed in the Greenville-Spartanburg airport, while virtual ones popped up on Spartanburg County's website. As Chappell put it, BMW became a "cheerleader for the state." Attracting press attention, it was seen as a "success story." For many, this narrative was epitomized by the plant's global reach. By 2016, the plant was America's leading vehicle exporter (by value), sending its cars to 140 different countries. Mercedes-Benz in Alabama also became a major exporter, a characteristic that defined the German transplants. They also used their U.S. factories to develop crossover or SUV models that were popular in Europe and Asia, as well as the United States. In contrast, the Japanese and Korean automakers largely manufactured for the North American market, and they relied more on passenger car production.[5]

Continuing the emphasis on firsts, this chapter explores why BMW came to South Carolina and examines the impact that it had on the area. Capturing a lot of media attention, the factory has often been described as pathbreaking. According to Governor Carroll Campbell, BMW's arrival was "a watershed event for the state." Claiming that the project would create "10,000 plus" jobs, Campbell asserted that BMW represented "an economic development coup unequalled in this state's history." The plant was undoubtedly significant for the industry too. A range of companies, including Honda, Hyundai, Kia, Nissan, Toyota, and Volkswagen, all subsequently built plants in the Deep South. Southern auto plants, concluded the *New York Times* in 2005, "set the industry's pace."[6]

BMW's decision to locate in the Deep South shook up the industry. At its heart were unprecedented incentives provided by South Carolina, which was desperate to land the investment. There was, however, more to the story, especially as generous subsidies were offered by other states. Personal bonds between Campbell and BMW executives were crucial, as were infrastructure, location, and the ability to avoid unionization. The prior history of German investment in South Carolina also played an important—and unique—role.[7] The plant's impact was similarly complicated. The incentive package proved controversial, especially in a poor state with acute social needs. Behind the scenes, there was opposition to BMW's arrival, and there were significant labor tensions. Not all South Carolinians were elated, and only a tiny minority got jobs. BMW located in a relatively prosperous part of the state, and economic benefits were unequally distributed. The most disadvantaged areas of South Carolina—especially heavily black eastern counties—stayed poor.[8]

For BMW, the factory was an important moment in its history. In 1968, the company began selling cars in the United States, but it did poorly. Making large-engined, performance-oriented models, BMW was hit hard by the oil crises of the 1970s. In 1975, the Bavarian brand had just 0.17 percent of the U.S. market, and *Fortune* described it as "barely known to American motorists." BMW, however, had just launched its 6-cylinder CS luxury coupe, a stylish car that did better. Helped by this, managers established BMW of North America, Inc., in Montvale, New Jersey, its first sales company to be based outside Europe.[9] Soon afterward, BMW launched the 3 Series, a compact sedan and coupe that brought the brand to a new demographic. Between 1978 and 1986, BMW sales tripled. Although the subsequent depreciation of the dollar against the deutsche mark hurt—and highlighted the advantages of U.S. production— BMW had established itself in the American market.[10]

The decision to set up the American plant took a long time. Despite managers' reluctance to acknowledge them, labor issues were always important. In 1989, BMW began looking at possible locations for their first factory outside Germany. In all, the company considered 250 sites around the world, especially lower-wage locations in Europe. Among top managers, a U.S. location was pushed by manufacturing chief Bernd Pischetsrieder, who had run out of patience with the demands of Germany's unions, which he felt put his company at a competitive disadvantage with Japanese brands. Several of these brands had established factories in the United States, avoiding unionization in the process. In order to increase its U.S. sales, BMW needed to compete with the Japanese, who had moved squarely into the luxury segment. In January 1989, Toyota launched its Lexus brand, a move partly aimed at BMW. By the end of the year, the Lexus LS400 was selling well. Nissan's Infiniti started selling vehicles in the United States a few months later, while Honda's Acura division was already established. As A. J. Jacobs has documented, compared to its Japanese rivals, BMW was "saddled with out-dated, inefficiently built, and over-priced models." Establishing a low-cost greenfield plant outside Germany would allow it to lower costs and develop new models.[11]

From the start, however, the American plant reflected personal journeys, as well as balance sheets. Early in the process, Pischetsrieder bought a Chrysler minivan and, together with planning director Helmut Panke, toured the American South for several weeks in search of a suitable location. Both senior managers in their forties, the two men met with Carroll Campbell, a Greenville native of a similar age. Keen to attract good jobs to a state that depended heavily on the declining textile industry (in which his father had worked), Campbell spent three years convincing BMW that South Carolina could "meet and exceed their demanding specifications." Early on, BMW ruled out states with strong union bases, as well as those with Japanese assembly plants. On these grounds, South Carolina was in a strong position.[12] This was a very personal story, with the governor playing a key role. The *Charlotte Observer* was among those to describe the relationship between Campbell and top BMW executives as a "courtship." All the elements of a romantic pursuit were present, including "quiet inquiries, secret meetings, [and] clandestine journeys." There were also plenty of rumors.[13] When the deal was announced, Pischetsrieder also commented on the importance of personal links, stressing that momentous business decisions could not be separated from the individuals who conducted them. "At the end of the day," he explained, "your success is always determined by people."[14]

From the start, Campbell privileged economic development. In February 1987, just after his inauguration, Campbell undertook trade missions to the U.K. and West Germany, the biggest international investors in South Carolina. "Economic development," he explained, "is one of my top priorities and I am going to take a very personal role in our development activities." According to the governor, it was crucial for South Carolina to explore "all of our opportunities, here and abroad."[15] Campbell's files indicated that the state would need to work hard to attract global investment, especially from Germany. According to one analysis by consultants, Germans were familiar with populous states such as New York, California, Texas, and Florida but had little awareness of South Carolina. If they did know the Palmetto State, they associated it with "cotton plantations" and *Gone with the Wind*, images of the slave past that were hardly synonymous with high-tech investment. It was crucial to "put South Carolina on the map in the minds of the German speaking public." To do so, Campbell traveled widely, documenting his efforts in regular reports. Along the way, he mobilized support from business groups and famous South Carolinians. They included Anna Graham Reynolds, Miss South Carolina, who accompanied the governor on several missions.[16]

There were other obstacles. South Carolina had a shortage of skilled workers, especially in the automotive industry. Firms that located in the state raised this problem. In 1989, French tire maker Michelin, which had opened its first American plant in Greenville, complained that it was "extremely difficult" to recruit technicians and machinists. "Most of these people have been relocated from outside South Carolina," wrote company manager David L. Headrick. For many firms, turnover was also a problem. In 1988, a survey by the state Development Board revealed that 23 percent of manufacturing firms reported difficulties in hiring or retaining workers.[17]

Behind these statistics lay deeper problems. In 1986, a confidential Development Board report documented the prevalence of poverty and low educational standards across South Carolina. The majority of counties (twenty-eight of forty-six) had an unemployment rate above the national average (6.5 percent), while in five counties the figure exceeded 10 percent. In per capita income, South Carolina ranked forty-fourth out of fifty. The report identified the labor force as the state's "greatest weakness," as most workers were "minimum wage and unskilled." The dominance of textiles, which had given jobs to many workers who had not finished high school, compounded these problems. As the report documented, while 73.9 percent of Americans had finished high school, only 66.2 percent of South Carolinians had. Almost half a million residents had not completed ninth grade, and 21 percent were "functionally illiterate." As the board acknowledged, these "overwhelming" statistics were a far cry from Campbell's public pronouncements, which stressed the quality of the state's workers.[18]

Given these problems, landing an automaker—especially a prestigious one—would be a major coup. According to a detailed account of the recruitment process in Campbell's papers, the story started in May 1989, when the governor learned "through intermediaries" that an "international manufacturing concern" was interested in building an American factory. Highly motivated, the state swiftly packaged several sites, and on July 1 Campbell flew to West Germany to open a Development Board office in Frankfurt, an automotive center. In Germany, the governor also held a major press conference to sell South Carolina's "economic climate and quality of life." The effort paid off, as three weeks later Campbell learned that representatives of the firm were scouting the Upstate for sites. Officials suspected that the company was BMW, a hunch that was soon confirmed. The governor then made an unannounced trip to Munich and met with Pischetsrieder, using the occasion to reiterate the advantages of locating in South Carolina. At the time, Campbell was the first leader of a U.S. state to have met with BMW about its plans.[19]

It took time, but Campbell's persistence paid off. The governor worked tirelessly on the BMW deal, maintaining "confidential contact" with Pischetsrieder's office. On March 13 and 14, 1992, top company officials visited South Carolina, touring possible sites in Anderson, Greenville, and Spartanburg Counties. Although managers were particularly drawn to Spartanburg, they had concerns about its "configuration of the site" and "the quality of South Carolina's workers." Campbell's team worked "virtually around the clock" to address these worries, faxing documents back and forth to Germany. Finally, at 8:55 a.m. on June 22, Campbell received notification that BMW had chosen Greer. The following day, the news was announced simultaneously in Munich and Spartanburg County. For Campbell, it was the high point of his political career.[20] State newspapers were full of praise. "South Carolina Wins the

Prize," proclaimed *Appalachia*, a regional journal. "Upstate Wins Race," added the *Greenville News*.[21] Immediately using the deal as advertising, Campbell announced it while seated beneath a giant state license plate that read, "BMW 1." According to the Development Board, BMW's decision represented "the single largest international economic development project in South Carolina's history." The board's modeling estimated that for every public dollar invested, approximately forty-nine dollars would be generated in payroll over a twenty-year period.[22]

The state, however, invested big sums in order to land this prize, details it glossed over. The final deal offered $135 million of incentives, including land purchases, infrastructure improvements, and tax incentives. BMW was granted a one-dollar-a-year lease on the 900-acre site, as well as state-sponsored worker training. State agencies put in a freeway ramp, cleared the land, and were responsible for all sewer and utility connections. There were plenty of other perks, including fifty-five free apartments for company executives.[23] The land purchase was vital. As the board acknowledged, the state's acquisition of land for a site on I-85, as demanded by BMW, was "truly unique." According to state records, the Ports Authority, Spartanburg County, and the state together acquired the land for $36.6 million. It was then leased to BMW for its token price for thirty years, with a twenty-year "renewable option." If BMW decided to own the land, the company could buy it for the original price, avoiding rising values. The automaker was also allowed to sublease the land to its suppliers. In order to house the BMW Communications Center, Spartanburg County leased property on Lake Blalock for one dollar a year for thirty years. Again, there was a renewable twenty-year option.[24]

Several other provisions were crucial. According to state documents, BMW received $70.7 million in tax breaks over a twenty-year period, made up of $29.7 million at the state level and $41 million at the local level. The breaks included a fee-in-lieu of local property taxes, the establishment of a multicounty industrial park with a tax credit for every job created, and a sales tax exemption on industrial electricity and production machinery. Given BMW's concerns about the quality of the labor force, the job training provisions were also important. Under the deal, the state Board for Technical and Comprehensive Education agreed to provide a "customized training program" for BMW. Featuring preemployment screening, on-the-job training, and specialized preparation "as may be required," the program was comprehensive. The state agreed to these provisions despite lacking "full knowledge of precise costs." To help fund the commitment, Campbell sought help from wealthy GOP donors, securing over $3 million from local businesses.[25]

Private correspondence shows that the company pressed for a good deal, intimating that others had offered more. On March 20, Pischetsrieder told Campbell that in addition to concerns about the size of the Greenville-

Spartanburg airport, the company felt the incentive package was not generous enough. "The financial support so far offered by the State of South Carolina does not yet meet the competitive offer," he insisted. If South Carolina could come up with a "financially competitive agreement," then "BMW would definitely decide to set up the new US plant there." Pischetsrieder closed by reminding Campbell of the economic value of the plant, which would export cars globally.[26] Other concerns delayed the deal. In particular, managers continued to worry about local workers. As Campbell's notes put it, BMW devoted "intense scrutiny" to the "quality of South Carolina workers and their output." The company also demanded direct interstate frontage.[27]

Site concerns were rectified more easily. Even before BMW had committed to the deal, the state had acquired the land, overriding local concerns. In the spring of 1992, Spartanburg realtors Johnson Development Associates and Lancaster Realty acted on behalf of the state to secure the land. Most landowners were paid between $15,000 and $20,000 an acre and were told that their land was needed for a "big overseas business." While these deals were conducted, Campbell's office would not confirm that Spartanburg County was a contender or discuss his whereabouts. In all, more than one hundred property owners were convinced to sell. According to the *Spartanburg Herald-Journal*, most were paid two to three times what their properties were worth. When landowners were "hesitant," realtors arranged for friends and neighbors to pressure them. If that did not work, Campbell made personal phone calls. The governor knew that the process had to be conducted quickly, as BMW worried that displacing residents would damage its public image. By May 13, more than 140 parcels of land had been assembled at a total cost of over $36 million. In return, the realtors received more than $200,000 in commissions.[28]

South Carolina also offered BMW other incentives, many of them authorized by enabling legislation that Campbell pushed through the General Assembly. As the governor acknowledged, these details were important. One key component included transferring $25 million in bonds to the Ports Authority to develop a foreign trade zone in Spartanburg County, allowing BMW to import its components duty-free and pay a lower rate of duty on the foreign content in finished vehicles. The legislation also provided $10 million from highway funds for development near the plant and allowed Spartanburg County to issue revenue bonds based on fees BMW would pay in lieu of property taxes. At the local level, Spartanburg and Union Counties created a regional industrial park to host suppliers. State leaders also eliminated inventory taxes and slashed corporate income tax to 5 percent a year.[29]

Still, incentives alone cannot explain BMW's choice. As generous as South Carolina's concessions were, other states offered more.[30] It was Spartanburg's location that gave it crucial advantages over rivals, particularly a site in Omaha, Nebraska, that was closely considered. Nebraska offered BMW a larger incentive package—valued at between $180 and $240 million—but BMW wanted to be close to the eastern seaboard, facilitating domestic deliveries and exports. More than fifty German companies were also located near Charleston, a major port. Offering a large site near Interstate 480, Nebraska made the short list following a visit to Munich by Henry Kissinger and top state officials. In the end, however, Nebraska's leaders recognized that they had been trumped by a better location. "You can't move the Atlantic Ocean," admitted governor Ben Nelson.[31]

BMW also stressed the importance of location. According to the automaker, it was investing in the United States because it wanted to broaden its international competitiveness by exporting more. It also aimed to reduce its dependency on one currency and raise its profile in America, the "largest, most competitive and dynamic consumer market in the world." As a global brand, BMW had to be "fully represented" in this market.[32] In relation to these plans, South Carolina's location was perfect; the state was positioned midway between New York City and Miami, with 70 percent of the U.S. population living within a thousand miles. One of the oldest in the country, the state-funded special schools program was also important, providing training to the company's specifications at little or no cost. According to BMW, the Palmetto State got the nod "because of its established highway, airport and port infrastructure, its technical training system, close cooperation between business and government and the quality of the . . . work force."[33]

BMW's key decision maker, veteran CEO Eberhard von Kuenheim, spoke to the importance of these considerations. According to von Kuenheim, the "most critical" factor was infrastructure. Here, South Carolina's transport links, together with reliable utilities and a strong supply and distribution network, "completely fulfil[led] BMW's requirements." Following a secret visit in March 1992, von Kuenheim selected Greer over a large alternative in Anderson County because the latter lacked a suitable airport. An infrastructure issue thus helped seal the deal, especially as officials promised to extend the runway at the airport.[34] In other ways, South Carolina's location was advantageous. The state's history of textile making gave it a stronger industrial base than most outsiders realized. In the early 1990s, a quarter of South Carolina's workers were employed in manufacturing, one of the highest concentrations in the country. Until the 1960s, textiles thrived. Between 1973 and 1996, however, employment in the state's textile industry halved (from 160,000 to 80,000), creating a huge reservoir of industrial labor. Announcing its choice to the media, BMW recognized the importance of this legacy, as the site was close to the former textile hubs of Greenville and Spartanburg. This ensured a ready supply of workers who were used to factory discipline.[35]

The presence of German companies also gave South Carolina a unique advantage. As historian Marko Maunula has shown in *Guten Tag, Y'All*, since the

1950s Spartanburg County had become a "model community of globalization." Prior to BMW's arrival, the area attracted numerous European companies, including Ciba-Geigy, Michelin, and Hoechst. In 1965, when Hoechst opened its Spartanburg chemical factory, it cited the importance of location, as 80 percent of U.S. textile mills—Hoechst's customers—were within a 250-mile radius. The presence of Michelin, which supplied BMW with tires, was also important.[36] As he negotiated with BMW, Campbell sold this history. Working closely with the Frankfurt office, the governor arranged testimonials from foreign business leaders who had located in South Carolina. By 1992, more than fifty German companies were located in Spartanburg County, including Adidas, BASF, and Bosch. According to some counts, the county was home to more German firms than any other in America. Locals dubbed fast-paced I-85, on which many factories were located, the "Autobahn." In 1993, *Site Selection* magazine rated South Carolina as having the second highest number of foreign investments in the nation. Around the same time, *U.S. News and World Report* found that the state was home to nearly two hundred foreign firms, and they employed 10 percent of the workforce. Because many South Carolinians worked for European firms, BMW's apprehensiveness was assuaged.[37]

In addressing BMW's concerns, Campbell was also very important. While other governors, particularly Nelson, had courted BMW, Campbell's approaches were uniquely detailed and personal. In particular, he forged a close bond with von Kuenheim. Reputedly the longest-tenured chief executive in the industry (he had been in the role since 1970), von Kuenheim had overseen dramatic growth at BMW, where turnover jumped from DM1.4 billion in 1970 to DM30 billion in 1992. Von Kuenheim was heavily invested in BMW's success, and the first overseas factory was a big step. As Campbell recalled, the executive "left no stone unturned in making sure every component was in place to achieve the ultimate goal of enhancing global competitiveness."[38] For several years, the governor went back and forth to meet with von Kuenheim. On March 30 and 31, 1992, for example, he had a personal meeting in Germany with the CEO. "We are providing you all of the resources at our disposal to make Project Pretoria a success," Campbell pledged. "We can discuss these in detail when we meet."[39] Von Kuenheim later paid credit to Campbell's role, commenting that the company had selected South Carolina because "the governor convinced us this is the best place in the world." The company also appreciated Campbell's efforts to preserve its anonymity.[40]

Campbell also intervened to assuage BMW's infrastructure concerns. In March, he flew to Munich after securing an agreement to extend the Greenville-Spartanburg airport runway by half a mile. This allowed it to accommodate the 747 cargo planes that served BMW. Campbell also persuaded the local Airport Commission to sell 100 acres of its property if BMW needed them. "The Development Board is at this time assembling sufficient acreage in the vicinity of the Greenville Spartanburg Airport that will meet your needs," he wrote Pischetsrieder. "You have my assurance that I will do everything within my power to make your project a success in South Carolina."[41]

When BMW executives visited, Campbell rolled out the red carpet. On March 13 and 14, 1992, top company officials jetted in on a decisive excursion, visiting sites in Anderson, Greenville, and Spartanburg Counties. Throughout the visit, state officials were on hand. Aware that the company's decision was up for grabs, later in the month Campbell visited BMW's headquarters in Munich. Reiterating his commitment, he enticed BMW's executives back to South Carolina. On April 10 and May 28–29, Pischetsrieder and Panke were invited to the Governor's Mansion for "private meetings." On the second occasion, the two executives stayed the night at the antebellum residence, where they enjoyed lavish hospitality.[42] Von Kuenheim also received similar treatment. According to an oral history with Campbell's wife and son, the first family wined and dined BMW executives at the mansion, sealing the deal with von Kuenheim on a cocktail napkin after an evening of classical music, wine, and cigars (all at state expense). "You got the two decision makers, the governor and the chairman of the board of BMW, in a relaxed atmosphere, away from everybody else, and they got it done within just a few minutes," recalled Mike Campbell. "They didn't have anything else to write on, so one of them has a pen, they pull it out, and they write it out on the back of a cocktail napkin."[43] The governor claimed that the water and sewer rate was one of the matters settled in this way. Aware that even a small issue could be a "deal-killer," Campbell ensured that every item was resolved.[44]

The lack of unions was also used by Campbell to entice BMW. In the 1980s and early 1990s, the high pay and generous benefits of West German workers were criticized by employers, who complained that their industrial competitiveness had been undermined.[45] Realizing this, Campbell saw an opening. In materials pitched to the company, the state stressed that it offered "a qualified and willing work force (set free from the ailing textile industry), lowest work stoppage rate and lowest unionization." Behind closed doors, these arguments were forcefully propounded to BMW, which was unionized in Germany but keen to break labor's hold. As Campbell asserted in one presentation, South Carolina was a top place to do business "based on the state's competitive labor climate, including availability and cost. . . . The state's labor force prefers to work directly with management, with a union membership rate of just under 3 percent, the lowest in the country."[46]

The pitch worked. Announcing its decision, BMW cited the "positive relationship between business and government" as a primary consideration, perhaps a reference to the state's hostility to unions. According to *Europe* magazine, moreover, one of the attractions that BMW found in South Carolina was "a largely non-union work force." American labor leaders made similar points.

Robert Georgine, president of the AFL-CIO's Building Trades department, related that BMW "made clear it would require a complete non-union environment, even an anti-union environment, before it would agree to build in South Carolina." Helping the company to achieve this, in the Upstate area just 2 percent of the workforce was unionized, even lower than the paltry state average. "It's no accident that BMW chose South Carolina to put its first plant in the United States," recalled the UAW's Frank Joyce.[47]

Avoiding unionization allowed BMW to slash production costs, a big advantage in the increasingly competitive luxury market. South Carolina's wages, which were about 20 percent lower than the national average, were particularly important. In recruiting foreign industry, Campbell justified these wages because the state had a lower cost of living than northern states. This was attractive to BMW, which announced that its pay would be "competitive" with South Carolina's manufacturing industries, where workers earned about ten dollars an hour. In contrast, BMW workers in Germany earned three times as much (including benefits).[48] Following AFL-CIO criticism, BMW backtracked, asserting that its wages would "be competitive within the automotive industry with wages, benefits and training." When the plant opened, workers earned fifteen or sixteen dollars an hour, slightly below Big Three levels. Still, benefit and legacy costs were significantly lower, and the company was cushioned by incentives. Overall, production costs were around half what they were in Germany.[49]

The opening of another unorganized auto factory, especially by a German firm that dealt with unions at home, was a major cause of concern for the UAW. By the early 1990s, the Big Three had been losing market share for thirty years, and the trend was apparent in all market segments, including the luxury category. Rather than welcoming BMW's investment, a chastened UAW now regarded the industry's expansion as a headache. BMW's choice of location also worried the union. As the *Encyclopedia of Southern Culture* put it, for decades the South had been the labor movement's "No. 1 organizing problem." Throughout the postwar era, the region had attracted outside investment by "selling" its low rates of unionization, a strategy South Carolina had perfected.[50]

Still, the UAW hoped that a European carmaker would be open to dialogue. From an early stage, the UAW worked behind the scenes to pressure BMW, using its links with German counterpart IG Metall. In July 1992, staffer Don Stillman traveled to Germany to meet with IG Metall leaders, including Klaus Zwickel, a member of BMW's supervisory board. Stillman asked IG Metall to push BMW to recognize unions in Spartanburg.[51] Von Kuenheim, however, declared that organized labor would be excluded from the plant. "We don't need an outside, third party between management and our employees," he proclaimed. "The prerequisite for the success of the planned investments are satisfied workers who have consultation rights," blasted IG Metall in response. According to Germany's largest industrial union, von Kuenheim, who had dealt with organized labor for decades, had made a "political decision" to "challenge" U.S. unions, which had less power than their German counterparts. Despite the setback, IG Metall, which had 3.6 million members, promised to "work closely" with the UAW to secure a union recognition in Spartanburg.[52]

These efforts struggled. In August, Bieber sought an "informal" meeting with "top BMW management" to discuss the issue, offering to come to Munich or "any other place that might be convenient." There was no record of a response from BMW.[53] Around the same time, von Kuenheim did write Zwickel, but the BMW boss was unrepentant, declaring that it was wrong to "transfer uncritically" German labor relations to South Carolina, which was a different situation. "Unions are no ends in themselves," he added. On December 11, Bieber again wrote von Kuenheim, seeking an informal "get acquainted" session at the upcoming *Automotive News* World Congress in Detroit. According to Bieber, the "off the record" discussion would "give us a chance to begin what hopefully will be a positive and constructive relationship."[54]

The company stalled. On December 17, Zwickel faxed that BMW intended to meet with the UAW later, once all of the American managers at the South Carolina plant were in place. He also stressed that von Kuenheim was about to retire as CEO (although he retained influence as chair of the supervisory board).[55] Von Kuenheim himself wrote back on December 22, stressing that his time in Detroit was "very limited." The CEO suggested that Bieber contact incoming plant manager Al Kinzer, an American who had previously helped steer Honda's Marysville factory down a nonunion path. The UAW knew that it was being brushed aside. "This makes it pretty clear about what we're up against," Stillman wrote his boss.[56]

On the ground, BMW's determination to push unions aside did not go unchallenged. As the plant was being built, local union members picketed the company about its decision to hire Fluor Daniel, a Greenville-based construction company. According to Stillman, Fluor Daniel had a "bad reputation as an anti-union firm."[57] The AFL-CIO also got involved. "The issue is that if BMW is allowed to proceed and exploit workers in a very vulnerable part of the United States in a time of economic hardship, every worker in this nation and every American in any job is going to see his standard of living threatened," declared Georgine. Arguing that the state had promoted an antiunion atmosphere at BMW that would result in "substandard" wages, the AFL-CIO also sent letters to the United States House and Senate labor committees. In other ways, the issue took on national prominence; on April 1, 1993, for example, the AFL-CIO demonstrated outside BMW's U.S. headquarters in New Jersey, claiming that the company was exploiting workers in the South. The Federation also wrote the South Carolina Department of Health and Environmental Control, raising concerns about BMW's air quality controls. Under pressure to keep the project on track, the DHEC ruled that BMW's projected air emissions were "within allowable standards."[58]

As the plant took shape, the campaign intensified. The UAW, pledged Joyce, would make "every effort" to win bargaining rights. According to the union, BMW had become a global force on the back of its organized workers, and the firm should not operate "any differently" in America. Organizer Ben Perkins declared that the union would begin a campaign as soon as the plant was finished. "We definitely have it as a target and we intend to organize it," he declared in March 1993.[59] A few months later, Bieber confirmed the plan, declaring that the UAW would "stake out" its "rights" to the plant. These efforts, however, were immediately undermined by Georgine's claim that the company would pay "third world" wages in South Carolina. "Our workers are world-class, not third-class," responded von Kuenheim, identifying with BMW's adopted state. Claiming that it had "total confidence in the ability of American workers to produce world-class quality," the company skillfully pictured the union—and not itself—as the outsider.[60]

In South Carolina, powerful elites needed little encouragement to fight the union. Even before the plant was operational, the state press came out strongly against the UAW. "Union membership is falling," proclaimed *The State*; "hence, the union bosses are knocking at Southern factory gates." Among the other major papers to editorialize against the union were the *Greenwood Index-Journal* and the *Spartanburg Herald-Journal*, which was widely read by BMW workers. Feeling that northern union leaders were looking down on South Carolina, the state press disliked Georgine's remarks. "If BMW plans to treat its workers like 'Third World' people," wrote columnist Betsy Teter in the *Herald-Journal*, "then why are thousands of resumes piling up at the corporate offices? . . . The absurd rhetoric coming from the union bosses is a perfect example of why BMW didn't go to the Northeast or the Midwest. Who wants to deal with logic like theirs?"[61]

Protecting his cherished achievement, Campbell portrayed the state as under attack from outside unions. "They," he asserted, "can keep their bosses out of here." The governor's spokesman, Tucker Eskew, took on Georgine directly. "The elitist attitude of Northeastern outsiders toward South Carolina speaks volumes of their disdain for South Carolina," he blasted. The play on regional identity was powerful, especially in a state with strong southern characteristics. By portraying the union as an enemy of economic development, state leaders also sent workers the message that they would have more job security without the UAW. With headlines such as "Unions Attack BMW," press coverage reinforced the image of organized labor as an unwanted troublemaker.[62]

The UAW faced other obstacles. Keen to avert what the *New York Times* called a "bruising fight against organized labor," BMW designed the plant to ensure that any organizing campaign was likely to fail. To oversee the running of the plant, BMW hired Kinzer, the former Honda vice president. Under the Virginian, BMW followed a similar approach to Honda, staffing the factory with hardworking agrarian employees instead of displaced autoworkers. Rather than building the factory in the eastern part of South Carolina, which was heavily African American, BMW also located in the Upstate, which was much whiter. According to industry insiders, managers studied Honda's success closely. "BMW when it set up in South Carolina in the early nineties hired Honda people and basically said to them, 'Build us a Honda factory that can make BMWs,'" recalled Lindsay Chappell. "And so it was really done in the image of Honda, of America." As *Automotive News* reported, BMW's "first U.S. management team" came from HAM.[63]

There were plenty of similarities. The uniforms that BMW workers wore were modeled on those from Honda. Everyone at the plant—including Kinzer—wore white lab coats, and managers worked in an open area next to the training floor. There were no walls, private offices, or executive washrooms. The company's aim, declared spokesman Bobby Hitt, was to "promote a feeling of unity." Like Honda, BMW organized its workforce into small groups, describing them as "team members." The company hired Susan E. Conway, who had introduced "self-directed" teams at nonunion textile mills, to oversee human resources. Conway shaped the groups, which were designed to give workers more responsibility and increase their investment in their jobs. To help achieve this, BMW refused to automate some tasks, including welding work. Rather than constantly repeating one or two twenty-second tasks, workers carried out several jobs requiring several minutes each. As such, the plant's design made it very hard for the union to penetrate.[64] The UAW also alleged that BMW used the hiring process against it. As Bieber complained in 1995, BMW "highly screen[ed] people" to keep the union out. These allegations had some validity; in 1994, Hitt told the *Los Angeles Times* that it would give a preference to workers who lived within a fifty-mile radius, areas where almost no union workers lived. Once hired, many workers were sent to Germany, where they were inculcated in BMW's values. Overall, the union complained that the $5 million training program, which was partly funded from private sources, had an "anti-union" animus.[65]

There were also problems in contacting the workforce. Organizers found it hard to get access to the plant, even to distribute materials nearby. Located outside Greer's city limits, the plant's isolated location complicated the union's job, especially as organizers who went near the property were highly visible. Describing the BMW site as a "vertically-integrated, multi-employer complex with little public access," Leonard Page reported to Bieber that organizers could not "effectively handbill." In addition, the South Carolina license bureau refused to give out names and addresses even when organizers obtained employees' plate numbers. Workers commuted from a large number of counties, further complicating the task. Although workers complained about the pace of the line and injury problems, the ready supply of labor—combined with the broader antiunion climate—prevented the UAW from calling a vote.[66]

The union controversy was not the only tension. The generous incentive package also attracted criticism, and not just from outsiders. In 1992, some residents doubted the wisdom of granting $135 million in incentives to BMW. "Sure there were people who questioned the investment," summarized Dennis Hennett, president of Greer State Bank. Many felt that Campbell had been too generous and had kept important details private. In 1992, several leading South Carolina newspapers, including *The State*, the *Greenville News*, and the *Spartanburg Herald-Journal*, requested records of the incentives offered or given to BMW but were told that the information was exempt from the state Freedom of Information Act. According to Mark Elam, Campbell's legal counsel, the law did not provide access to information "relative to efforts or activities of a public body to attract business or industry to invest within South Carolina." The following year, the AFL-CIO also asked for details of the incentives, including how much public money was used to purchase the site and train workers. Campbell's staff responded that they had provided preliminary costing of some incentives. They refused to reveal final specifics, including what BMW had pledged in return. Once the deal was announced, even Democratic congresswoman Liz Patterson, who had supported Campbell's efforts, became suspicious. "We have invested heavily in attracting this international company to our community," she commented. "It is my hope that we will see that investment pay promising dividends in the future." In private notes, Patterson was more direct. "We have given a lot and hope to get a lot in return," she wrote.[67]

On the ground in Greer, there was also opposition. In a series of appeals, Mayor Don Wall expressed citizens' concerns about increased traffic congestion and the strain on municipal services, especially as the plant was located outside city limits.[68] Greer was a small rural community, and many felt that it was unsuited to large industrial development. In August 1992, residents formed the Flatwood Road Area Homeowners' Association to express their views. In a letter to Campbell, members listed eleven objections to the plant, including increased noise levels, the close proximity of high-tension power lines, and more traffic. "One of our concerns," they summarized, "is an agricultural area is to be swept away by heavy industry, high tension power lines, runways, railroads and large cargo planes." They also worried about a fall in property values, with some claiming that their houses had become unsellable because they were located near the factory. At its first meeting, fifty-five families joined the association, with one resident claiming that their lives had become a "nightmare" since the plant announcement.[69] Growth-minded state leaders, however, brushed aside objections. "BMW's operations are extremely clean and quiet," wrote staffer Douglas McKay III, "and a credit to communities fortunate enough to have one."[70]

The deal generated broader tensions. At a time when the textile industry remained a major employer in South Carolina—and when efforts to protect it from global competition were ongoing—not all residents approved of Campbell's aggressive recruitment of foreign companies. Rather, many felt that more should be done to protect existing industries. Opposition to NAFTA, which threatened textiles, was also widespread. A consistent defender of local interests, veteran U.S. senator Ernest Hollings believed that one foreign car plant could never replace the eighty thousand jobs that the textile industry still provided to South Carolinians. Across the state, Hollings led opposition to NAFTA, which the export-focused auto industry supported. "While daddy grows tobacco there in Hartsville," he wrote in 1993, "mama is working in the sewing plant and together they are trying to send that boy to Clemson. NAFTA would ruin this." In November 1993, the controversial treaty passed Congress with active support from Campbell and his Republican colleagues, leaving behind divisions in South Carolina that reflected the chasm between the "old" and "new" economies.[71]

Others pointed out the irony of a luxury European carmaker locating in one of the poorest states in America. As the *Herald-Journal* put it, few locals could afford the cars built in their area, which some jokingly referred to as "Bubba Made Wheels." In 1992, the median annual income in Spartanburg County was $17,000 a year, yet BMW's cars retailed for between $22,900 and $83,000. In 1991, the company sold just 421 cars in the Palmetto State, about the same number of new and used vehicles that a Big Three dealer retailed in a day.[72] One *Herald-Journal* investigation found that even local elites drove American cars. "Spartanburg County leaders may have BMW on their minds these days," summarized reporter Adam C. Smith, "but they tend to have big American gas guzzlers in their driveways." Illustrating the point, local mill-owners Roger Milliken and Walter Montgomery both drove Cadillacs. Others noticed that BMW's arrival had done little to transform the crumbling mill towns dotted around the Spartanburg area, instead generating new inequalities. As *New York Times* reporter Doron P. Levin wrote in a detailed feature: "Gleaming black BMW 740 sedans, costing $60,000 each, glide up and down the broad boulevard that is this city's main street, their elegance a striking contrast to the crumbling buildings and vacant lots, once home to so many knitting mills." One car plant—while a step in the right direction—did not transform South Carolina's economic fortunes, which were tied to an industry that had been declining for decades.[73]

In response, state leaders mounted a vociferous defense. In June 1992, Campbell commissioned a report by the Development Board that concluded—not surprisingly—that the incentives were more than justified. According to Campbell, South Carolina simply "made an investment for a return." Parts of the state press, including some who had earlier questioned the deal, publicized these findings.[74] Defending their conduct, state leaders also cited the large number of applicants for BMW's jobs. According to Campbell, South Carolina badly needed well-paid industrial work. In April 1993, the *New York Times* reported that BMW was expecting one hundred thousand applications—or more—for its first one thousand jobs. As the plant was being built, applicants swamped the company's temporary offices in Spartanburg.[75] When the company issued its first call for applicants, sixty thousand people responded. "Everybody in the area wants a job at BMW. I mean everybody," summarized twenty-nine-year-old Allison Ballenger.[76]

On the surface, the plant's trajectory seemed one of unalloyed success. After a ground-breaking ceremony on September 30, 1992, the giant factory was constructed on time, built on what the *New York Times* described as a "900-acre stretch of red clay halfway between Spartanburg and Greenville." With Campbell under pressure to justify his investment, the plant got off to a good start. On September 8, 1994, following what BMW termed "the fastest factory start-up in automotive history," the first car rolled off the line. The whole process had taken just twenty-three months. When the plant was announced, production was not scheduled until 1995.[77]

Further expansions followed, and state leaders continually praised the plant, which became the poster child of the modern, globally connected South Carolina they wanted to emphasize. Symbolizing this, even under Jim Hodges, a Democrat who served as governor from 1999 to 2003, the state leased two BMW police cruisers for just one dollar a year, an arrangement that began when the plant was announced. The deal gave both company and state valuable publicity, especially as the cars were used to patrol major highways. As Hodges put it, the cruisers signified that BMW was "a significant player in the economy of our Great State." Other state leaders stressed the automaker's symbolic importance. "BMW means even more to the state than the capital investment it has made and the jobs it has created," summarized Charles S. Way Jr., secretary of commerce, in 2002. "It is an international symbol of the quality business climate companies can expect to find in South Carolina." The growth of the plant, which underwent a major expansion in 1998 to build the X5 SUV, also bolstered claims that the incentives had been justified. "There is a consensus that BMW has lived up to and in some ways exceeded its expectations," summarized Hodges.[78]

Not all South Carolinians, however, agreed. "The so called 'consensus' doesn't mean anything," replied Jack F. Mayer of Simpsonville. Some, like Pickens resident Robert J. Edsall, took on the subsidy issue directly. "South Carolina does not have to bribe businesses to come to our state," he claimed in a letter to Hodges. Edsall was particularly incensed that BMW did not pay any corporate income tax. "We hear about our state's dilemma not having enough money for education, buses, roads and more," he wrote. "While the state, cities and counties raise taxes at will, South Carolina looks the other way and lets BMW not pay any corporate income tax to South Carolina. . . . No wonder foreign countries laugh at the United States. We give away the store and they carry off our money, too."[79] In 2007, BMW made a global profit of $4.9 billion but had yet to pay any corporate profits tax in South Carolina. Although employment at the site continued to rise—it reached almost nine thousand workers in 2015—BMW also relied heavily on imported parts, leading critics to claim that employees were assembling cars rather than making them. In 2015, industry expert A. J. Jacobs found that the majority of the parts used in Spartanburg-built vehicles still came from overseas. The plant did not meet Jacobs's definition of a "New Domestic" automaker, which required a domestic content level of at least 62.5 percent.[80]

In the final analysis, BMW's economic impact upon South Carolina also needs to be kept in context. In 1995–96, with the plant in full flow, the United States Census Bureau reported that South Carolina's poverty rate remained virtually unchanged from a year before; some 16.5 percent of residents were poor, above the national average. Poverty rates, moreover, remained high across the South. In 1999, 13.9 percent of southerners lived in poverty, the highest rate in the nation. Like Honda, Nissan, and Toyota before it, BMW also located in a part of the state that was relatively prosperous, meaning that its benefits were not shared by poorer regions, particularly the heavily black counties in the east. In 1992, the state Bureau of Labor Statistics reported that the unemployment rate in Spartanburg County was 5.1 percent, the third lowest in the state. In contrast, Clarendon, Marion, and Barnwell Counties, all located in the east and heavily black, had jobless rates above 12 percent. By 1998, these patterns had not changed; eastern counties were still missing out and were too remote for workers to commute to BMW. With a predominantly white population, many textile-dependent communities in the piedmont also struggled, and most were located some distance from Spartanburg.[81]

After 2000, growth was concentrated in the strongest areas, which knew how to attract industry and assuage the workforce concerns that BMW had expressed. The problems of the textile industry, which collapsed as global textile quotas were eliminated and China joined the World Trade Organization, also created economic needs that BMW could not fully address. Between 2000 and 2010, the industry lost six hundred thousand jobs nationally, a "tidal wave" that hit South Carolina hard. Few new industries, meanwhile, moved into the heavily black and rural counties in the east. By 2016, Spartanburg County had an unemployment rate of just 4.6 percent, one of the lowest in the state, but five counties—Bamberg, Orangeburg, Allendale, Marion, and Marlboro—had jobless rates above 8 percent. All were in the east.[82]

For most in the industry, however, BMW was an overwhelming success, and few could deny its positive impact on the Spartanburg area. In a broader context, the company took America's auto industry forward in important ways: the first German transplant, the first by a luxury carmaker, and the first to be located in the Deep South. The establishment of a nonunion factory by a European firm was also significant. As Frank Joyce admitted, the factory showed that it was possible for a "German employer to establish a nonunion plant in the United States," crushing hopes that European automakers would give the UAW a foothold in the new industry. Watching these developments, BMW's archrival, Mercedes-Benz, looked closely at the Deep South as the location for its first North American plant. The place that Mercedes chose, however, even shocked the winner.[83]

CHAPTER SIX

Surprising the World
Mercedes-Benz Lands
in Vance, Alabama

In April 1993, less than a year after BMW's announcement, Mercedes-Benz declared that it was looking at around thirty states as a location for a $300 million, fifteen-hundred-employee assembly plant. Mercedes's move was inextricably linked to the example set by its German rival and closest competitor. "Once BMW started making products in the local market, they had an advantage over Mercedes, so Mercedes had to follow suit," explained Lindsay Chappell. "BMW's decision helped, of course," acknowledged Kurt Martin, a senior Mercedes executive who worked on the project. "We said, 'Okay, if they are doing it like this, it's the right thing to do it.'" There were other links between the two stories, especially as South Carolina tried hard to land Mercedes-Benz. Ironically, Governor Carroll Campbell ended up criticizing the incentive package offered by Alabama, claiming that it was excessive and unsustainable. South Carolina's bid, he claimed, was more "prudent."[1]

Six months later, when Mercedes announced that it had selected a 966-acre site in Vance, a small town near Tuscaloosa, for its first North American plant, there was widespread shock. Although it had courted Mercedes with an incentive package valued at $325 million or more, Alabama was not expected to win. One of the poorest and most maligned states in America, Alabama had no history of automotive manufacturing. As it bid for Mercedes against well-heeled competitors, Alabama was—as even its economic developers admitted—severely up against it. "The biggest obstacle for us is that we never produced a vehicle," admitted Steve Sewell, an official involved in the bid. "We had no reputation, so you didn't have the credibility. . . . We were an unknown." When the news came down, politicians remembered the widespread astonishment. "Our first [car plant] was Mercedes," recalled Sheila Eckman, a Republican county commissioner, "and everybody just thought that was crazy." As the company admitted, its choice "surprised the world."[2]

Mercedes was a huge catch for Alabama. According to one state analysis, the factory was "one of the largest international economic development projects in Alabama's history." Within five years, it would have an "investment impact" of more than $500 million, creating over ten thousand jobs. The symbolic value of a prestigious carmaker—one with an instantly recognizable logo—was also massive. "The state now has an increased level of national and international visibility in its economic development programs," summarized the report. "The stars are falling on Alabama today, and they have three points on them."[3]

The plant proved foundational for both Alabama and the industry. In succeeding years, Honda, Hyundai, and Toyota built assembly plants in the state, and scores of suppliers also set up shop. By 2015, the Center for Automotive Research ranked Alabama as one of the top ten automotive-producing states in the country. It all started with Mercedes. The company's arrival, summarized Ellen McNair of the Alabama Development Office (ADO), was "really the beginning of a fabulous journey for the state, as far as automotive is concerned." The plant, added local official Dara Longgrear, was "a history-changing event for Alabama." "If Mercedes hadn't come to Alabama," reflected another official, "Honda wouldn't have come to Alabama, Hyundai wouldn't have come, Toyota wouldn't have come. . . . Mercedes opened it up."[4]

Observers, especially in other states, felt that the Mercedes story was simple: officials had bought the plant. "The state of Alabama is paving the street with money, to get that [Mercedes]," summarized one Tennessee-based reporter, recalling the reaction. It was true that incentives played a bigger role in luring Mercedes than they had previous transplants. Other factors, however, were again important, including location, personal connections, and the company's desire to escape high labor costs in Germany. Despite the loud voices celebrating Mercedes's arrival, its impact on the state was similarly complex. There was a lot of opposition and concern, especially about the cost of the incentives. Only a tiny minority of locals got jobs at the plant, and fundamental patterns of inequality were largely untouched.[5]

The plant's roots stretched back several years. In 1990, Ford launched the pioneering Explorer, while a new Chevrolet Suburban came out the following year. Other brands followed suit, and the SUV market took off. Mercedes was keen to get in on the action, yet it lacked a compelling product. Placed in charge of the project team, Dieter Zetsche remembered that in 1991 the company investigated "conventional" options to replace its ageing G-Class wagon, an expensive hard-core off-roader. The solutions, however, either were "too costly" or lacked mass appeal. Assembling a team with an average age of thirty-six, Zetsche, who had been president of the Freightliner Corporation in Oregon, decided that new thinking was required. After four months of investigations, the team proposed building a car-based SUV that would offer high-class quality "at a world-wide competitive price." To achieve this, the vehicle should be manufactured "in a greenfield operation as a separate legal entity" rather than at a

Mercedes factory in Germany. In early 1992, the team received approval for the project from the board of directors, along with a hefty budget of $1 billion. Investigating locations in Europe, the Far East, and the United States, the latter got the nod. "The U.S. is the birthplace of the sport-utility vehicle and provides by far the biggest market," explained Zetsche. "These facts made it easy to focus our search effort here in the U.S." Martin also stressed that the United States was the best place to build an SUV: "We finally had to spend all the money. We said, 'Let's go to the biggest market out there, the biggest market for this kind of SUV.... Let's go to the United States.'"[6]

The decision also reflected broader priorities. It was part of the company's "global strategy to expand production in world markets and move into new vehicle segments." In addition, Mercedes cited a desire to "move closer to its customers," especially as the United States was its largest market outside of Germany.[7] An important precedent had been set by the commercial vehicles division, which had produced vehicles overseas since the 1950s. Explaining its decision, Mercedes also noted that it had already set up an assembly plant in South Africa and was planning factories in South Korea and Mexico. Furthermore, the company acknowledged that moving production to the United States protected it from currency fluctuations and reduced labor costs. Like BMW, Mercedes wanted to escape the expensive unionized environment that prevailed in Germany. "No one in the world wants to pay for the German comfort in costs," admitted chairman Helmut Werner. Symbolizing larger shifts within the company, in October 1993 the Daimler-Benz Group became the first German corporation to be listed on the New York Stock Exchange.[8]

From the start, the plant was designed to build an SUV, a segment that was particularly popular in the United States, where fuel was cheap, roads were wide, and consumers preferred large vehicles. As one of the biggest SUV markets in the world, the United States was a logical place for Mercedes-Benz to set up the plant. SUV buyers, many of them used to driving pickups rather than passenger cars, were also seen as more accepting of lower build quality than luxury car owners. The company acknowledged that the decision to build SUVs might not please Mercedes traditionalists, who were wedded to its high-quality sedans and station wagons. As an internal document asserted, Mercedes now had to "focus on a broader range of products in order to expand its presence and market share throughout the world." It was no longer sufficient to "only specialize in traditional vehicle segments." Martin acknowledged that this was still a "huge step," especially as the company's reputation was closely linked to manufacturing passenger cars in Germany.[9]

Overseen by Zetsche and Andreas Renschler, a senior Mercedes executive, the site selection team comprised members of the original project group, together with American managers from Freightliner and Mercedes-Benz's holding company, Daimler-Benz. Using the code name Rosewood, the team worked in secret as they scouted locations. "The members of the site selection team soon converted into undercover agents for 'Operation Rosewood,'" wrote Zetsche. Competition for the plant was intense, with the team considering more than 150 greenfield sites and some existing factories. As Werner commented, the company was "gratified by the overwhelming response and warm welcome extended to Mercedes by all of the states." After looking at a variety of factors, including transportation costs, the "education and availability" of the workforce, proximity to suppliers, and quality of life, the team narrowed their list to six finalists: Alabama, Georgia, Nebraska, North Carolina, South Carolina, and Tennessee. A site near Mebane, North Carolina, was seen as the favorite, partly because it was close to Freightliner's three truck plants in that state. Also favored was a location near Summerville, South Carolina, that offered excellent access to the Port of Charleston, facilitating parts and vehicle shipments. After an "intensive" selection process, however, Mercedes made a different choice. It also established Mercedes-Benz Project, Inc., an independent company based in Tuscaloosa that was responsible for the development, manufacturing, and marketing of the new vehicle. According to the *Wall Street Journal*, the announcement ended "more than five months of frenetic lobbying and much speculation in five Southern states."[10]

The news was a shock. "You could hear the gasps of astonishment for *years*," recalled Chappell. On September 29, the day before the announcement, the *New York Times* reported that North Carolina was the "heavy favorite," as it had been for months. Even those who worked on the Alabama bid were surprised. "We were sort of the dark horse candidate running at the back of the pack," admitted Sewell. "I did not expect Mercedes to choose Alabama when I came here for my job," added Ed Castile, the director of Alabama Industrial Development Training (AIDT), who was appointed shortly before the Mercedes announcement, having previously worked on Tennessee's bid for the plant. "I worked on it up there. . . . Alabama at best was a distant *anything* and then winds up the winner!" Mercedes, added prominent politician Don Siegelman, had taken a "chance" on his state.[11]

The obstacles facing Alabama were formidable. While the Carolinas were home to more than two hundred German companies, Alabama had twenty. As the *Wall Street Journal* reported in 1993, the state also had a struggling education system, the fifth-highest poverty rate in the country, and a "largely unskilled" labor force. Its reputation for racial intolerance proved hard to shake, hurting efforts to attract industry. As Siegelman aide Lee H. Warner noted, many of the defining events of the civil rights era—including the 1955–56 Montgomery Bus Boycott, the 1963 Birmingham campaign, and the 1965 Selma to Montgomery march—had occurred in Alabama. Unless its leaders did a better job of recognizing the importance of this history, Alabama would be "perceived by many as a state based on racial violence and with a generally negative reputation."[12] Some state newspapers admitted the problem. According to the *Birmingham News*, Alabama had a "reputation for poor state services like education and for racial turmoil." Dubbed "the city too busy to hate," Atlanta, Georgia, had boomed since the 1960s, while Birmingham had languished. Just over two hours apart by road, the two cities had similar populations in the 1950s, but by the early 1990s, Atlanta was well ahead.[13]

Even Mercedes's bosses admitted that they made an unlikely choice. Referring to Alabama's slogan, "The State of Surprises," Werner acknowledged: "To be honest, we didn't know very much about Alabama before we began the site selection process. We were indeed surprised—and extremely impressed—when we saw all that Alabama and, in particular, Tuscaloosa, had to offer." Other managers remembered being probed about their decision. "If anybody still asks why we chose Tuscaloosa," Zetsche quipped later, "my answer will be short and simple—have you ever heard of the State of Surprises." According to the *New York Times*, the announcement was a big deal for "long-suffering Alabama," which was "seldom thought of [as] an industrial mecca." Symbolizing the "exultation" it produced, local business leaders even erected a 5,600-pound Mercedes hood ornament on top of the scoreboard at the Alabama-Tennessee football game a few days later.[14]

As Werner implied, the incentives that Alabama provided were crucial in explaining Mercedes's decision. Press reports concentrated heavily on the package, which was valued at between $300 and $439 million. Even if the lower figure—which the *New York Times* endorsed—was used, the deal dwarfed the $180 million reportedly offered by South Carolina and the $120 million by North Carolina. Reporters in the losing states were especially likely to see the package as the only factor. The *Charleston Post and Courier* thought that "Alabama simply bought the new $300 million plant. While South Carolina's incentive package was far from modest, it couldn't compete with what Alabama was offering." Similarly, the *Spartanburg Herald-Journal* claimed that the Carolinas had been "strong contenders" for the Mercedes plant, and Alabama had only won by offering Mercedes a "horrendous display of attractions."[15]

The package was the work of Governor Jim Folsom Jr., who came into office in April after Guy Hunt was convicted of ethics violations. A few days later, Folsom was approached by Mercedes. The son of legendary governor James E. "Big Jim" Folsom Sr., a colorful "liquor-guzzling" figure who served two terms in the 1940s and 1950s, the new governor was widely known as "Little Jim," even though he stood more than 6 feet tall (his father had been 6 feet 8 inches). Folsom Jr. played an important role, flying to Stuttgart three times and negotiating a complex agreement. The deal was generous, and the workforce training provisions were especially important. According to the AIDT, the state committed "up to $90 million" to "construct and equip" a training facility for Mercedes and prepare workers. The building and equipment were estimated to cost $25 million, while the remaining $65 million was earmarked for training.[16] Dispatched to Germany, supervisory staff even had their international airfares, along with their meals and hotels, paid for by the state. Folsom also agreed to spend $75 million on Mercedes vehicles for use by state employees, along with $7.5 million on "image advertising" and public relations activities. There were many other concessions in the Rosewood agreement, which was several hundred pages long. In this case, incentives were a central factor in explaining an automaker's decision.[17]

Still, the press simplified the issues. Although details remained secret, Mercedes claimed that other finalists offered as much as Alabama. Company officials stressed other influences, including location and infrastructure. "We found that Tuscaloosa provides the best combination of those factors we are seeking," explained Werner. "A quality workforce, a strong transportation network, a university environment, business vitality and favorable quality of life. In addition, Governor Folsom and the state of Alabama are extremely committed to the development of the workforce, through educational reform and worker training." Placing a high value on training and graduate programs, the company was especially attracted by Vance's proximity to the University of Alabama.[18] "Mercedes, one of the criteria they had was to be near a university, research university," remembered Sewell. Access to the Port of Mobile was also crucial, facilitating imports of parts and exports of finished vehicles. Those involved in the bid also stressed that Mercedes liked that Birmingham, a former steel and iron center, had many displaced industrial workers. According to Sewell, this was a "huge" advantage.[19]

Other evidence muddies claims that Mercedes went to the highest bidder. Although Campbell asserted this, his papers show that when Mercedes was looking at his state, the governor stressed that it would not be welcome if jobs were guaranteed to union members from Freightliner, where the UAW represented workers at a plant in Mount Holly, North Carolina, near the South Carolina line. To justify his stance, Campbell cited the example of the Mack Truck plant in Winnsboro, South Carolina, where the UAW had won an election in 1989. The plant was recruited by Dick Riley, Campbell's Democratic predecessor, and the Republican blamed the NLRB result on a transfer clause that allowed unionized workers from Pennsylvania to get jobs in South Carolina. Campbell did not want a repeat of this outcome. In response, Mercedes opted for Alabama, where Folsom, a Democrat, did not interfere in hiring.[20]

Intangible factors also made a difference. As Werner related, after visiting many sites he felt a strong connection with Tuscaloosa County because its foothills reminded him of the picturesque area around Stuttgart, the company's hometown. Renschler also noted that decision makers liked the Tuscaloosa area and felt "at home." With the company having what Kurt Martin called the "luxury" of being able to choose between several bidders, it opted for the place with the "best feeling." Personal connections, agreed well-placed local observers, were important. Mercedes chose Tuscaloosa County, noted local CBS news anchor Lisa Keyes, because "it was similar in topography to the area in Germany . . . where the plants were." In particular, the German visitors liked the area's "rolling hills." Executives also commented on the friendliness and warmth of Alabamians.[21]

Of the finalists, moreover, only Alabama offered Mercedes the chance to put significant distance between itself and archrival BMW, whose Spartanburg plant was just ninety miles from Charlotte. In the Carolinas, especially in South Carolina, Mercedes feared that it would be a "second child" behind BMW. As many experts noted, Mercedes chose Alabama over South Carolina because it did not want to be in the same state as its closest rival. According to Klaus Zehentner, the German consul in Atlanta, in Alabama Mercedes-Benz would be "the top address. It will have a towering position." In the Crimson State, Mercedes could have a fresh start, a fitting place for a manufacturer that did not want to be a "transplant" but rather a new company building its own vehicle. Executives liked the challenge that this presented, and it fitted their bold plans for the M-Class. Imbibing this vision, state leaders also wanted to prove the doubters wrong. "Our message to the company was, 'Your success will be our success,'" remembered Sewell. "We were basically saying, 'Your success is just as important to us as it is to you.'"[22]

Folsom's role was also important. As Martin remembered, the effusive governor persuaded the German decision-makers to take Alabama seriously. The Germans had initially refused to visit the state because they did not see it as a serious contender. "I don't think we will end up in Alabama," Martin told his colleagues. Project members did not know "anything" about the state, which lacked profile in Germany. It was Folsom who changed this. "He was very committed, and we started good personal friendships with them," recalled Martin. "He was really a guy who put the solution in place, to put Alabama on the industrial landscape, because Alabama was, and I know now, more famous for winning the college football games instead of as any industrial area." In some ways, the Germans' lack of knowledge about Alabama was an advantage, as they were not as influenced by negative perceptions as Americans.[23]

Even after the plant announcement, there were obstacles. In early 1994, the planned ground-breaking was washed out twice because of rain. In front of national media, as well as over three hundred government, business, and community leaders, Folsom and Zetsche shoveled the first soil on the third attempt. "I see at this moment a greenfield site; however, in reality it is far more than that," commented Zetsche. "It is the foundation for what will become a world-class plant, producing a world-class vehicle, utilizing the strengths and talents that lie within the state of Alabama." Martin recalled the day with pride—"it was good, and to see it growing"—but emphasized the massive task ahead. "We had no offices then," he noted, with many managers working out of shipping containers. Production was not expected to begin for three years, and many wondered if it would succeed. "The word was that the plant was only going to last five years," recalled Jason Armstrong, a Mercedes worker.[24]

Demand for jobs was keen. On August 17, 1994, just one day after the state began accepting requests, more than seven thousand people had applied for the fifteen hundred jobs on offer, overloading a post-office box in Tuscaloosa. Applicants were not deterred by the fact that they needed to undergo a lengthy period of screening, written tests, and interviews before finalists completed forty-eight hours of training. In all, more than fifty thousand people were expected to apply for the production and technical jobs, which paid between twelve and eighteen dollars an hour. Even this estimate proved conservative, as Mercedes received over sixty thousand applications.[25]

In a state that had never built a car, however, it remained difficult to find qualified workers. Despite the huge demand for work, German managers complained repeatedly about the poor quality of applicants, particularly for skilled positions. "It was a lot of challenges," recalled Martin. "We had a lot of applications, of course, but . . . to educate them, that was a big undertaking. And so there still was a lot of training before we hired them to see how they behaved, how they could adjust to a production system. It was of course one of our big challenges." Even state officials acknowledged the problem. As Castile admitted, workers' lack of automotive experience was "obviously an issue." Although the state promised to spend $90 million on training, Mercedes said this was not enough. In the fall of 1994, the company submitted its estimate of training expenses, claiming that over $127 million was required.[26]

Unlike some of its Japanese predecessors, particularly Honda, Mercedes refused to address the issue by importing skilled staff from overseas. Mercedes expected a lot of the local workforce because it wanted the Tuscaloosa operations to be seen as "American" yet uphold its reputation for quality. "We want an American company with all functions from engineering to sales, with the spirit of Mercedes-Benz and based on the excellence of the company," explained Zetsche. When the plant was announced, Mercedes also called for Alabama-built vehicles to have up to 70 percent local content, another difference from its Japanese predecessors.[27] It proved a challenge, with *Automotive News* reporting that Mercedes complained about the quality of workers at suppliers. Even Sewell acknowledged these problems. "For manufacturing in general in Alabama," he related, "highly skilled positions, again like these maintenance technicians and other high sort of skill sets, are difficult to find." As a result, Mercedes struggled to meet its goals, never reaching—by its own admission—more than 65 percent content from "NAFTA suppliers," many of them based in Mexico. Remaining evasive about exact U.S. content levels, the company imported some major components, including engines. "The main brain of the car is totally German," acknowledged one worker. Despite the company's plans, economic benefits were not as widely distributed as supporters claimed.[28]

Those who secured a position found that conditions were tough. Jason Armstrong, for example, had previously held a production job at a local roofing factory. The work was demanding, but it had not prepared him for life on the line at Mercedes. "It was harder," he recalled. "When you look in the mirror, you say, 'Oh my God, what have I done?' [laughs] Yes, sir . . . it's a lot harder work, hard on your hands, and you're standing on your feet. . . . You used to get a fifteen-minute break every two hours, and you had to stand up, and you're continuously working." Armstrong, who considered himself "one of the lucky ones," remembered that he survived because of "hot baths and prayer, plus my wife wouldn't let me quit." Once again, the reality of these jobs was far removed from industry claims. "You work for every cent you get," summarized Armstrong, who was still at the plant—but no longer on the line—twenty years later. Even plant supporters made similar admissions. "The demands are great," related Lisa Keyes, who noted that Mercedes expected "excellence." Workers had to stay behind when production goals were not met.[29]

Within Alabama the training provisions generated opposition, even at government agencies. In 1993 AIDT opposed wage payments to the Mercedes trainees yet gave way because it understood that "competition for this particular project is such that the Governor and the Alabama Development Office must explore all opportunities for presenting the winning incentive package." Still, unease persisted. In 1994, materials prepared for incoming governor Forrest "Fob" James indicated that aides were concerned about "the legality of paying wages of Mercedes employees" with state funds. "Alabama cannot and should not pay wages for a private company," noted a written report presented to the new administration.[30] Once it had made the commitments, the state had difficulty honoring them. In January 1995, Castile wrote state finance director Jimmy Baker that he needed $26.97 million extra to meet Mercedes's training obligations. In his letter, Castile acknowledged that he was making a "huge request" but made clear that the state had to find the money. The problem was compounded by the fact that, rather than copying the Japanese, Mercedes used a new manufacturing system, necessitating extra training. According to the company, it had developed an "original production system which is a combination of American, Japanese, and German automotive best practices."[31]

In the 1994 race between Folsom and James, the cost of the Mercedes agreement was a major issue. As the *Mobile Register* reported, the governor endured "searing criticism" from his opponents about the deal, which was widely viewed as a "Folsom-led corporate welfare package." According to political analysts, these accusations contributed to Folsom's defeat. To be sure, there were

other factors behind the loss, especially the rising tide of Republican sentiment sweeping the country that year. As a popular former governor, James
was also a formidable challenger. What should have been a big boost to Folsom's reelection, however, became a liability.[32]

Criticism of the package was widespread. "When Mercedes came, everybody complained about the amount of incentives that were being paid," summarized Todd Strange, a Montgomery business leader. As *Automotive News* reported, the deal attracted particular hostility from civil rights groups, which
wanted job targets for minorities. In early 1994, black caucus leaders, led by
state senator Hank Sanders, met with company executives to discuss their
concerns. "Mercedes now has a moral obligation, a duty and a responsibility, to include blacks, women and other groups that are often excluded from
these opportunities," explained Sanders. African American leaders also criticized Mercedes's moves to create a Minority Advisory Board without adequate
consultation.[33]

Others argued that in one of America's poorest states, the incentives should
have gone into social programs. In 1994, Alabama ranked last in elementary
and secondary school spending. Despite this, a well-publicized education reform package failed to pass the state legislature, leaving schools underfunded
while Mercedes enjoyed generous subsidies. Even some company supporters
argued that Alabama should improve its schools, arguing that this would attract industry. "If we had spent more money in the last 20 years on education, we would have a better-trained work force," explained Bo Torbert, a former chief justice of the Alabama Supreme Court. "Maybe we wouldn't have to
give as much in incentives to get Mercedes here." When news surfaced that
the state had used the National Guard to help prepare the plant site, many
residents were angry. "People are asking questions," explained state senator
Mac Parsons. "They've got holes in their roads and school playgrounds that
need fixing. Why does Mercedes get work done by the guard and not everybody else?"[34]

Opposition was not just about money. Many white Alabamians were upset
when Folsom decided to stop flying the Confederate flag over the state capitol, prompted by an aide who suggested that Mercedes might not come to
the state otherwise. Announced in April 1993, as Mercedes was looking at the
state, the flag's removal was another nonfinancial factor that swayed the company. As the *New York Times* reported, ever since 1963, when Governor George
Wallace had started flying the flag over the capitol to protest a visit by Robert Kennedy, Alabama had placed racial defiance above economic development. "We'll never know how many companies it scared off," admitted Robert
Sutton, a spokesman for the Development Office. According to the *Times*, the
flag's removal convinced Mercedes that the "romance of racism had ended" in
Alabama. Despite this, the move triggered howls of protest, including threat-

ening phone calls targeted at Mercedes dealers. Stung by the criticism, Folsom engineered a compromise, allowing the flag to be flown at a ground-level monument.[35]

The costs of the agreement greatly concerned Folsom's Republican successor. Even before taking office, James authorized an analysis of the package that exposed how generous it was. The study concluded that it was "impossible to assess cost per job due to vagueness of deals and effects (future) on tax base." The study's calculations, however, put the cost per job at between $300,000 and $700,000, while associated industries "utilizing MB package benefits" cost over $1 million per job. Under the agreement, suppliers that created at least fifty jobs that paid a minimum of eight to ten dollars an hour, including benefits, received generous tax breaks. While Mercedes was portrayed as a great catch for Alabama, the cost of landing the deal was considerable.[36]

In private, James worried about how the state would pay for the commitments. In one detailed analysis by Chris Bence, James's main staffer, concerns were laid bare. According to Bence, the agreement was "essentially a lengthy list of carte blanche financial and resource commitments on behalf of the state. At best it contained a poorly structured process of funding and resource delivery, no state security interest, and unsound/illegal sources of funding by the state. About the only thing the Folsom Administration didn't give Mercedes was power of attorney over the state comptroller's office." When he ran for governor, James promised that while the agreement's funding commitments would be honored, the "delivery process" would be changed to reflect the state's "fiscal and legal constraints." In November, James began negotiations with Mercedes to change the "flawed and undoable" parts of the agreement. "Fob James," recalled a senior Mercedes executive, "he tried to renegotiate certain things. . . . It was a little bit of a struggle."[37]

The changes also reflected how state agencies and local authorities were struggling to pay their Mercedes commitments—or were resisting doing so. As James came into office, not all funding had been secured. Economic Development Administration monies for water and sewer works had not yet been obtained, while the city of Birmingham and Jefferson County were avoiding their project commitments. Aides also doubted the legality of some parts of the agreement, including the payment of trainee wages and the way that the state Industrial Development Authority had used tax incremental financing bonds to offer Mercedes $42.6 million for plant construction. As two aides reported to James, Ed Castile, who was very knowledgeable about the project, had "grave concern about the method of funding and feels some of it will have to be restructured to be legal."[38] In November 1994, Castile outlined some of his objections in a letter to another official. "Because of the Rosewood agreement we have absolutely no negotiation options as far as cost, etc." he wrote. "I have tried to force some issues, such as airfare costs, and have been beaten each time because of 'the book.' It is frustrating to have to accept some of the costs that we are being asked to pay. We basically cannot say no to anything." The paying of trainee wages remained a sore point. "No state can afford this," asserted Castile, "and, to my knowledge, no other state pays wages of trainees with state funds."[39]

The Rosewood agreement presented particular problems for cash-strapped local authorities. The city of Tuscaloosa was obligated to pay $31 million for the plant but struggled to find the funds. In September 1994, city officials admitted that their financial obligations to the project were much greater than they had anticipated, partly because water and sewer costs had risen from $13 million to $21 million. The city had applied for $7 million in federal and state grants, but they had not been approved. "Even with the $7 million, we have $23 or $24 million out of pocket, which is crippling," commented Finance Committee chair Jerry Plott. Neither Birmingham nor Jefferson County, which had promised $10 million for site preparation, had paid. City officials claimed that they forgot to include the amount in their budget, while Jefferson County waited for the city to pay first.[40] In the spring of 1995, the state's $42.6 million commitment for building costs was due, and it struggled to find the money. James planned to cover the cost by floating a state bond issue, but a threatened lawsuit by teachers' groups stopped him from using the school fund to pay the obligation. The crisis attracted global attention. *Wirtschaftswoche*, a German business publication, termed the situation an "international fiasco," adding that America's "fourth-poorest state" had promised Mercedes "too much." In the *New York Times*, Allen R. Myerson also exposed that the state missed the $42.6 million payment when it was due. In the end, James only covered the amount by borrowing from the state's $16 billion pension fund at an interest rate of 9 percent. This was 2.5 percent above the usual rate.[41]

Insisting that the state should keep its word, Mercedes resisted any weakening of the agreement. It was crucial, Renschler wrote James, "that the Project Rosewood Agreement remains intact." He also urged the governor to show that "the State not only upheld its commitment in full but, also, is committed to economic development in general."[42] According to Mercedes, the company had a "very good" relationship with the Folsom administration, but the situation changed when James took over. "We believe we've begun to establish a good one with the new Governor and his staff and look forward to working with them," noted a company document.[43]

In May 1995, the two sides negotiated a revised agreement that increased state protections. Whereas previously Mercedes was to be paid $5 million a year indefinitely for training costs, now a limit was set at twenty years, and the funding was subject to legislative approval. Provisions for the training center were changed, with Mercedes giving up ownership of the facility to the state and agreeing to repay relevant incentives if the plant never opened. The revised agreement imposed other restrictions, with Mercedes being required to repay the $42.6 million in building costs if the plant failed to materialize. This amount was also converted from a lump-sum gift into a lien on equipment. Furthermore, Mercedes agreed to buy back the state-funded visitor and training center at the market price rather than at a nominal value. Finally, James quashed the planned $75 million fleet of twenty-five hundred Mercedes vehicles for state employees. Despite private misgivings, Renschler declared that Mercedes was "satisfied" with the revised package.[44]

There were also significant tensions over labor issues. Early on, Mercedes rebuffed calls by the UAW for the plant to go to Michigan. Together with the state government and business groups, the union pointed out that Michigan possessed large numbers of experienced workers and an excellent supplier base. In September 1993, the UAW's top leaders wrote Werner and urged him to locate the plant there. "We believe Michigan offers Mercedes more opportunities to build a world class vehicle than any other state," they noted. In other overtures, Bieber stressed that the UAW was used to "cooperative labor-management relations" and would ensure that the plant was "among the most competitive in the world." Mercedes did not respond to these approaches, and Michigan did not make its list of finalists. In Tuscaloosa, some observers felt that the union avoidance was important to the company. Mercedes liked Alabama, noted Lisa Keyes, because it "wouldn't have to deal with unions and everything that goes with that."[45]

The UAW persisted. It hoped to secure a recognition agreement before production began, but the political climate turned against it. The 1994 election was a blow to the union, which related promises from Folsom of "helping us at the Mercedes plant." The UAW could expect little assistance from James. Nationally, moreover, the GOP controlled both chambers of the U.S. Congress for the first time in forty years.[46] Despite the challenging climate, the UAW stepped up organizing efforts. With thousands of hopefuls applying for jobs, early efforts were slow, and it also proved hard to contact a workforce drawn from a wide geographical area. The union saw an opening in 1998, however, when Mercedes-Benz and Chrysler merged to form DaimlerChrysler AG, bringing the German automaker into partnership with an American firm with almost seventy thousand union members. Between 1998 and 2002, Daimler-Chrysler expanded production of Mercedes SUVs in Alabama while shrinking Chrysler's workforce in North America. This made it imperative for the UAW to organize Vance. Union officials insisted that when the plant had opened, managers—most of them Americans, in accordance with the company's localization plans—were antiunion. In contrast, Daimler pledged to stay neutral, partly because managers were eager to avoid a strike. "I feel very confident that those workers, given a free choice, will choose to be U.A.W.," declared organizing director Bob King.[47]

Even with corporate neutrality, the UAW was up against it. There was little community support for the UAW in Alabama, where union density stood at 9.7 percent, compared to 21.6 percent in Michigan. The state had some unions, recalled economic development official Phillip Dunlap, but they were "isolated," and a right-to-work law made it hard for them to thrive. Like most business leaders in the state, Dunlap saw unions as unwanted outsiders. Appealing to the workforce was also difficult. The starting wage of $12.80 an hour was well above average for Alabama, which had some of the lowest wages in the country. By 1999, moreover, the favorable exchange rate had reduced the differential with Germany. Cementing their loyalty, workers received frequent raises. After two years on the job, they were paid between $20.50 and $24.25 an hour, compared to an average of $21.00 an hour at DaimlerChrysler's unionized plants. Workers also received many perks, including 25 percent discounts on Mercedes vehicles. Despite the change of ownership, local managers continued "feel-good" practices to keep workers away from the union, offering free corporate clothing and movie tickets. Even film choices built corporate identity; for example, workers were encouraged to see *The Lost World*, a sequel to *Jurassic Park* that featured the M-Class. Fear of retaliation also held back UAW supporters, especially as there were many union opponents in the plant.[48]

Pay was a key issue. Mercedes kept its wages close to Big Three levels, a powerful weapon across the sector. "No one has gone more than 7 or 8 percent lower than the Big 3 rates," summarized industry expert Sean McAlinden in 2003. "In fact, among the transplants, that gap is actually getting narrower." Foreign automakers, added *Automotive News* in 2004, "traditionally have kept wages close to Big 3 levels." Mercedes still made savings in benefits, while even UAW wages were lower than those received by German car workers. The Alabama plant cost 30 percent less to operate than a comparable German factory, partly because Big Three autoworkers earned about nineteen dollars an hour in wages, compared to twenty-eight dollars in Germany.[49]

At Mercedes, the union faced other problems. On the job, each employee wore "team wear," including a tan golf shirt with the employee's first name embroidered on it. Shared by workers and supervisors, the uniform broke down barriers. When Governor Don Siegelman toured the plant in 2000, even he wore a tan shirt with "Don" on it. Inside the plant, union opponents seized the initiative, forming the Team Members Information Committee, which distributed flyers and stickers that attacked the UAW. Although DaimlerChrysler was not directly involved, local businesses were. The UAW failed to respond to these tactics, instead concentrating on high-level dealings with management. The strategy left its grassroots supporters feeling isolated. The poverty of the area and the newness of the plant also made most employees grateful for their jobs, while work-related health problems had yet to develop. At the time of the 1999 campaign, turnover was only 1 percent a year, and most workers saw little need for the union. "The company gives us very good benefits, and they pay us well," summarized Tonya H. Hallmark, who had previously earned eight dollars an hour in an apparel mill. "If they come in, we're going to lose what we've got." The fact that Mercedes established the plant as a separate company—its formal name was Mercedes-Benz U.S. International (MBUSI)—also hurt the UAW's efforts to secure recognition from DaimlerChrysler. Claiming MBUI was a separate entity, the parent company resisted the union's demands for a card check agreement.[50]

The plant also grew. Capitalizing on the SUV boom that began in the 1990s, the M-Class resonated with buyers. "The vehicle hit a home run," summarized Dara Longgrear, "and they began to sell more than they could make." The $35,000 car, noted the *New York Times*, appealed to drivers "who dream of backwoods rambles but usually venture no farther than the nearest Eddie Bauer store." In 2000, Mercedes announced a $600 million expansion of the plant, creating two thousand jobs. More than 1.5 million square feet were added to the factory, which now produced an expanded range of SUVs. Announcing the move, Mercedes chief Juergen Hubbert proclaimed that the company's bold "vision" in coming to Alabama had been fulfilled. Behind the expansion was another $119 million in state incentives. The plant's success, however, had proven the doubters, many of whom had thought it would never get off the ground, wrong.[51]

The expansion hurt the UAW, which was trying to organize when the news was announced. It created a mood of optimism, especially as workers saw opportunities for advancement without the union. "Everybody that's working here is thinking that somebody in their family may get a job," summarized employee Toby Hicks. "I'm very proud of this place."[52] Although the union put its campaign on the back burner, it understood the imperative of organizing the plant. In 2003, the *Detroit News* termed Mercedes a "UAW battleground," noting that it was a key part of a "monumental labor struggle" to organize in the "growing Southern auto belt." At its 2006 national convention, the UAW made organizing a priority, setting aside $60 million for the purpose. Efforts at Mercedes were stepped up.[53]

By 2006, after nine years of production, more grievances were emerging. "Everything from Mercedes says what I get can be changed at any time—my pay, my benefits, my pension," complained Harold Fleenor, who had worked at the plant for eight years. Another issue was the company's use of "temporary" workers, who could be hired for up to thirty months with no guarantee of becoming full-time. For all production workers, moreover, promotions were not governed by seniority, and the company also frequently scheduled overtime at short notice. Workplace injuries were increasing, and hurt workers were often cast aside.[54]

The structural obstacles, however, remained immense. As *McClatchy-Tribune*

Business News noted in 2006, unions faced a "serious uphill battle" at the site, especially as wages exceeded area averages. Many workers made twenty-seven dollars an hour, about the same as UAW members and more than twice the manufacturing average in Alabama. "Why do we need a union?" summarized Diane Pierson, who had previously earned eight and eleven dollars an hour in two full-time jobs that she held simultaneously. "We have good pay and benefits, and they do not treat us unfairly. There aren't many jobs where you can get paid like this for 40 hours. Some people forget where they came from. We didn't have these kind of jobs before they came here." While the company was officially neutral, union supporters also complained that supervisors, most of them locals, opposed the drive. Some important officials admitted that the company was not impartial, even at the highest levels. Mercedes, acknowledged Dara Longgrear, "certainly didn't want the union, but they couldn't say that publicly."[55]

In the area around the plant, the union struggled for support. "There's just this right-wing 'the boss should have it all' mentality," charged the UAW's Gary Casteel, discussing the Tuscaloosa area. In 2006, both the UAW and the International Association of Machinists abandoned campaigns at Mercedes. Although workers had complaints about workloads and wanted a stronger voice, many were prepared to put up with these problems rather than go against community mores. Unions, added Martin, also had a poor reputation among local people who had witnessed the decline of the iron and steel industry, both of which had been heavily organized. "It's not that the *management* wants that," he claimed, reiterating the public line, "it's a question of the people there. . . . Birmingham lost all the unionized jobs, and so the reputation of the union is *not* that they guarantee jobs." There were other powerful fears. As Jason Armstrong recalled, workers worried that if the union were voted in, UAW members would "come down and take the jobs here." Many workers saw the UAW as an outsider, and its support of the Democratic Party in a state that was overwhelmingly Republican was an obstacle.[56]

The UAW pressed on. "The union's been trying to get in ever since I've been there," summarized Armstrong, a plant veteran. Efforts resurfaced in 2014, when the UAW tried to pressure parent company Daimler, which was no longer in partnership with Chrysler. Seeking to bypass opinion in Alabama, the UAW worked with IG Metall, which represented Daimler workers in Germany, pushing for recognition without a vote. According to Michael Brecht, an IG Metall official and Daimler vice chairman, it was "unacceptable" that the company's workers in Alabama did not have a union. Under new UAW president Dennis Williams, the union oversaw the creation of Local 112 in Tuscaloosa and asked Daimler AG to recognize it. Placing an increased emphasis on organizing, Williams stressed the importance of the Mercedes plant. "What happens here is important to the future of the labor movement," he declared.[57]

Local 112 was an attempt to mirror German works councils, where a committee of workers and managers met and negotiated working conditions. These councils were illegal in the United States unless an outside union represented workers, so UAW participation was required. In an internal union document, IG Metall and the Daimler World Employee Committee pledged their "ultimate support in the immediate formation of a UAW local" in Vance. Although works councils did not have formal bargaining rights, the UAW hoped that if enough workers signed up, Daimler would recognize Local 112 as a legitimate bargaining agent. In response, Zetsche, now Daimler's CEO, claimed that it was up to workers to decide. Pressured by community groups, which associated the UAW with plant closings, Zetsche and other decision makers reasoned that MBUSI could not afford to alienate local opinion. As the union's efforts stalled again, Casteel blamed the influence of local "union avoidance" forces, many of whom felt that the UAW threatened the factory's success.[58]

The plant helped Mercedes achieve strong growth. In 2001, the company set a sales record in the United States that was underpinned by the M-Class's popularity. By 2017, MBUSI employed over thirty-five hundred workers and produced three hundred thousand vehicles a year, far exceeding original projections. It made a range of models, including the C-Class sedan—a vehicle known for exacting quality standards—and AMG models—Mercedes's prestigious performance vehicles. The expanded range reflected managers' confidence in the plant. Between 1993 and 2016, Vance helped Mercedes to increase its share of the U.S. market from 0.76 to 2.84 percent.[59]

The plant was also of enormous strategic value, especially to Alabama. In 1999, the state leased three M-Class vehicles "at no additional charge" because Governor Siegelman wanted to use them for industrial recruitment. Mercedes, explained a staffer, was "a major industrial presence and an important corporate citizen." As such, the company added "strength and credibility to the Governor's efforts to convince other industrial prospects to locate in Alabama." Key state officials felt that Mercedes played a significant role in attracting other car plants during Siegelman's term. "I think that Honda and Hyundai probably came because Mercedes did look, and choose here," summarized Castile. Apart from its economic impact, Mercedes had tremendous symbolic currency. "For us, Mercedes was the ultimate brand and the ultimate industry to say, 'Wait a minute, Mercedes is in Alabama?'" recalled Sewell. "So there was a curiosity factor that attracted a lot of attention to Alabama. It gave us another story to tell and something else to talk about beyond those old images of the past."[60]

There was, however, another side to the story. Despite the confident press releases, Mercedes failed to alter deep-seated economic patterns in Alabama, which remained a very poor state. In 1999, 25.3 percent of the state's children were poor, up from 24.1 percent in 1989. While the poverty rate had declined in Tuscaloosa County, it had failed to improve in most rural counties, including the Black Belt. "Economic development is occurring in the metro counties in this state," summarized Annette Jones Watters, manager of the state Data Center. "It's bypassing the rural counties. The good times are all occurring in the metro counties." As had been the case at BMW, Mercedes chose a relatively prosperous area of the state, and the poor—and predominantly black—parts of both states remained largely unchanged. Even industry supporters acknowledged this. "We still have a lot to do in terms of civil rights work and the poverty level," noted Lisa Keyes. Between 2014 and 2016, almost 17 percent of Alabamians lived in poverty, well above the national average (13.7 percent).[61]

Since the 1970s, Alabama has also been hit hard by the decline of traditional manufacturing industries, particularly textiles, steel, and papermaking. The automotive industry did not replace all the lost jobs; in the 1990s, Alabama lost more than thirty thousand jobs in textiles alone, while steelmaking declined precipitously around Birmingham. The effects were dramatic. "The loss of jobs due to plant closures not only devastates families and their communities, but it is also detrimental to Alabama's economy," wrote Siegelman. The governor admitted that the recruitment of new industries, while welcome, "could be offset by the loss of our mature industries." Sewell also acknowledged as much. "Even with the tremendous success that we had," he noted, "we still had a net loss in terms of manufacturing jobs." Between 2002 and 2017, federal data showed that Alabama lost almost fifty thousand manufacturing jobs.[62]

Ever since Mercedes's arrival, Alabama has scored badly on important indices, especially in terms of educational attainment. In 2000, the state ranked forty-ninth in the percentage of its citizens with high school diplomas. Just 77.5 percent of adult Alabamians held the qualification, compared to a national average of 84 percent. "Thank goodness for West Virginia," noted the *Birmingham News* (the Mountain State came last). Alabama also ranked forty-fourth in the percentage of citizens with bachelor's degrees. The low levels of educational achievement were linked to the high poverty rate, as citizens without formal qualifications struggled to land decent jobs. Bringing in automotive factories meant little to the bulk of citizens, who lacked the skills to secure these positions. Alabama, summarized the *News* in 1999, had a "poverty-ridden past." Growing more slowly than other southern states, it struggled to overcome this. The questions asked earlier, especially about the cost of the Mercedes agreement when educational needs were so great, remained pertinent.[63]

Despite these limitations, Mercedes was very important. Well before the 1990s, the Birmingham area was reorienting its economy to the medical, educational, and financial industries, and Mercedes added much-needed manufacturing jobs.[64] For America's auto industry, the plant was also significant. Throughout the 1990s, foreign-owned manufacturers grew, transforming the industry. Between 1980 and 2000, the production capacity of foreign-owned manufacturers increased twentyfold (from 250,000 to 5 million). By 1995, Honda claimed that one in four domestically made cars were manufactured by these firms. "Transplants," *The Harbour Report* concluded at the end of the 1990s, "continue to fuel growth in North America." Exporting more than Japanese and Korean firms, Mercedes and BMW led the way.[65]

The failure to organize German automakers also had far-reaching consequences. Existing transplants felt vindicated, while new arrivals learned the method. After 2000, more companies, emboldened by Mercedes's example, would come. They pointed to the German firms, which dealt with unions at home but not in the United States. "Although we get an impression that only Japanese manufacturers are refusing unionization, that is not true," noted Japan's *Kaigai rodo jiho* in 2001. The "German transplants" also had "no unions" and followed the model of building on "green fields" and hiring young workers from other industries. Keen to show that they were a major force in the industry, Korean automakers would adopt these practices next. Taking the industry into new areas, growing rapidly, and bringing more suppliers with them, they also made their own mark.[66]

CHAPTER SEVEN

Y'All Come?
Hyundai in Alabama and the
Start of the Korean Wave

In April 2002, Hyundai Motor Company (HMC), Korea's larg-
est automotive manufacturer, announced that it had chosen a site near Montgomery as the location for its first U.S. manufacturing plant. Hyundai invested
$1 billion into the factory, creating over two thousand jobs. Built on a 1,744-
acre site next to Interstate 65, the plant was a clear marker of the industry's
growth, especially as it was the first auto factory in southern Alabama. The
news, summarized the *New York Times*, was "another huge lift to the state's
emerging status in the automotive industry." When the plant enjoyed its
"grand opening" on May 20, 2005, former U.S. president George H. W. Bush, Alabama governor Bob Riley, and Hyundai chairman Chung Mong-Koo were all
on hand to cut the ribbon. The ceremony was publicized around the world.[1]

The plant also represented the first time that a Korean automaker had
built a plant in the United States. Hyundai Motor Manufacturing Alabama
(HMMA) paved the way for the establishment of a sizeable sector, including
Kia's first American plant and the influx of scores of Korean-owned suppliers, many located in Georgia and Alabama. While there were similarities with
earlier developments, the Korean wave had distinctive elements. These automakers brought with them more suppliers than their Japanese predecessors.
When they built their plants, Hyundai and Kia were also much smaller players
and had troubled recent histories. In 2001, Hyundai's share of the U.S. market
was just 2 percent, and the company was dubbed a tier 2 brand by *Automotive
News*. In contrast, the Japanese Big Three established American factories after
securing a much stronger market position.[2]

In the United States, Hyundai faced an uphill battle even after committing
to the plant. The Korean upstart did not have the solid reputation of the Japanese Big Three, which built a loyal following based on their cars' reliability and
quality. It also lacked brand recognition and prestige, crucial advantages for
BMW and Mercedes. A newcomer to the American market, Hyundai was desperate to prove itself to both Americans, the dominant military and economic

influence in South Korea since the 1950s, and the Japanese, Korea's hated prewar colonial ruler. When the company arrived in Alabama, many residents did not even know how to pronounce its name. "I'm trying to teach people it's pronounced 'Hyundai' like 'Sunday,'" explained Governor Siegelman. Local pastor Gary Burton was typical, admitting that he knew "nothing" about Hyundai when the plant was announced. Many residents were surprised, even bemused, by Hyundai's arrival, especially as the Montgomery area had no car-making past and had never been an industrial center. "Whoever thought a car manufacturing factory would come swooping into Montgomery like this?" one asked.[3]

Hyundai also located in a new part of the Deep South, taking greater risks. Eschewing proximity to former industrial centers, which had been important for BMW and Mercedes-Benz, Hyundai located in a rural part of southern Alabama. This made the plant especially significant. "It began to solidify Alabama's role in the automotive industry," summarized Todd Strange, the director of the ADO. "Mercedes started it, and then Honda picked it up, but those were *north*. . . . Hyundai and then subsequently Kia coming *south*, it pulled the automotive paradigm for the entire United States market . . . south." The poorest part of a poor state, south Alabama was widely looked down upon, even within the state. Hoping to change this, most locals welcomed the company—another difference from early transplants. "The Hyundai announcement," summarized regional developer John Clyde Riggs, "was the best economic news for south Alabama since cotton was king." Farmer Jim Henry, who owned land near the plant, was more succinct. "Two words: Y'all come," he declared.[4]

Both company and state officials aimed to turn disadvantages into strengths. Local leaders warmed to the Korean company because they felt that it made the kinds of vehicles that they could afford. Hyundai executives, meanwhile, expressed affinity for the area and the site, open farmland that gave them space to establish themselves away from their German and, particularly, Japanese rivals. They also cited the importance of personal connections and the generous "hospitality" of Alabama's leaders, especially Siegelman.[5]

For Hyundai, the risk paid off. In 2010, the company sold around 538,000 light vehicles in the United States, and HMMA made over half of them. Five years later, the factory employed thirty-three hundred people and could build over four hundred thousand vehicles a year. Three models were made there: the Sonata midsize sedan (the factory's first build), the Elantra compact, and the Santa Fe SUV. By 2017, Hyundai had invested $1.8 billion in the site, which included a 3.2-million-square-foot assembly plant, as well as a stamping facility, paint works, two engine shops, and a two-mile test track. According to Hyundai, thirty-five tier 1 suppliers had also been attracted to Alabama, creating seven thousand jobs.[6]

The plant's benefits, however, came at a cost. Some residents doubted whether the $252 million incentive package was justified, particularly as wider patterns of poverty and economic inequality remained largely unaffected. Alabama was still one of the poorest states in America, and its Black Belt—a heavily African American region of seventeen counties clustered to the south and west of Montgomery—continued to be one of the most deprived parts of the country. As a result, African American activists tended to be skeptical of the company's claims.[7] Even conservative white leaders acknowledged the limitations. They noted that suppliers avoided the Black Belt, clustering instead on the interstate heading to Georgia. "For 75 percent of Alabama it hasn't changed," admitted Sheila Eckman, a Republican county commissioner in Lee County. "Anything west of Montgomery's pretty much poverty." In 2002, Siegelman claimed that the Hyundai plant would help the Black Belt, but most of its residents lived too far from HMMA, and no interstate passed through the poorest counties. A promised car plant in the Black Belt never materialized. In addition, demand for Hyundai's jobs always exceeded supply.[8]

Hyundai's history highlights how remarkable HMMA was. Founded in 1967, HMC was a newcomer to the industry. The Hyundai Group also made its fortune in the construction industry, helping to rebuild the country after the devastation of the Korean War (1950–53). As South Korea struggled to recover— the fledgling nation was in ruins for years, and the gross national product per capita only exceeded $500 a year in 1975—the small carmaking arm could not cut its teeth in a big domestic market, as its German and Japanese rivals had. Between 1972 and 1978, Hyundai Motors teetered on the verge of bankruptcy, only staying afloat because of subsidization from the company's other industrial sectors.[9] HMC survived by making partnerships with foreign automakers, producing rebranded Fords and Mitsubishis for export. In 1976, it began shipping the Pony, which was independently manufactured but based on Mitsubishi's designs, to Latin America and Africa. Two years later, the car was exported to Europe. The North American market was not penetrated until the 1980s, when Hyundai launched the front-wheel-drive Excel, the Pony's replacement. In order to establish itself in a demanding market, Hyundai relied on discount pricing, with the Excel selling for up to $3,000 less than similar Japanese models. Highlighting what a newcomer Hyundai was, in 1986 it sold only 168,000 cars in the United States; at the same time, Toyota was retailing over a million. It was also not until 1991 that Hyundai produced its first engine without foreign assistance.[10]

Hyundai's low prices had a downside. Although sales rose, its cars struggled to be taken seriously. Produced by a company that was chasing volume, the small basic vehicles quickly acquired a negative reputation. Comedian Jay Leno, a respected car enthusiast, famously joked that Hyundai's drivers were the only ones to benefit from high gas prices, because every time they filled up, their car's value doubled. David Letterman joined in, quipping that the best way to scare astronauts would be to put the company's distinctive "H" logo on a spacecraft's control panel. During the 1998 Winter Olympics, Hyundai was a target again, with Leno comparing its cars to a luge sled. "There's no room, you have to push it to get going, and it only goes downhill," he claimed.[11]

In the 1990s, the problems mounted. Hyundai's sales and profitability crashed, largely due to quality concerns. In 1993, the company was forced to close a short-lived $400 million assembly plant in Bromont, Quebec, having to pay back millions in government incentives. The plant was hit by a variety of issues, including far-flung supplier networks, communications problems between Korean managers and French Canadian workers, and what scholar A. J. Jacobs termed "major issues with vehicle reliability and quality." The debacle reinforced what the *Globe and Mail* termed Hyundai's "lower-quality image." In 1997, Hyundai was also hurt by the Asian financial crisis, which led to the collapse of a third of Korea's thirty chaebol, including automaker Daewoo. The year before, in a revealing incident, Todd Strange, who worked as a car dealer before moving to the ADO, turned down the offer of the Hyundai franchise in Montgomery because he did not see it as a viable brand. A few years later, Strange would be flying to Korea to court Hyundai.[12]

In the late 1990s, the comeback began. As a result of the 1997 crisis, Hyundai acquired a 51 percent stake in Kia, helping model development and increasing market share. Another key move came in 1998, when New York attorney Finbarr O'Neill became CEO of Hyundai North America. In a bold move, O'Neill oversaw the introduction of the industry's first 10-year, 100,000-mile warranty, known as the Hyundai challenge. Greatly exceeding industry averages, the warranty attracted new buyers and pushed Hyundai to improve quality, partly to reduce repair claims. Between 1998 and 2001, helped by the warranty, sales of Hyundai and Kia rose from 173,110 to 569,956. Growth was also driven by the Santa Fe, which was introduced in 2000 and captured the growing craze for car-like SUVs. With other initiatives under way to improve quality, the company began to attract positive headlines. Between 1998 and 2002, Hyundai's share of the American market rose from 0.57 to 2.19 percent. "Hyundai Motor Company," declared the *Birmingham News* in 2002, "is the phoenix of world automakers."[13]

Hyundai soon had the sales volume it needed to consider a U.S. plant. The company's growth also increased South Korea's trade surplus with the United States, pushing Hyundai to examine North American production. Learning from its Quebec experience, Hyundai wanted to locate in an English-speaking region with plenty of workers. As a major player in the industry, Alabama was a contender. So too were several other southern states, particularly Georgia, Kentucky, Louisiana, Mississippi, and Tennessee.[14] Hyundai spent more than two years investigating locations in the United States, mostly in secret. In Alabama, the story broke in September 2001, when the press identified the company's interest.[15] By this time, Hyundai was approaching the final stages of the process. As one state document recorded, Hyundai's site selection "involved 2 years of preliminary study and site review and nearly 1 year of concentrated effort." According to the Montgomery Chamber of Commerce, Hyundai looked at "almost 100" sites in the United States, with consultants making their first full visit to Montgomery in July 2001. At this time, there was plenty of competition, especially from Mississippi. According to Mississippi governor Ronnie Musgrove, his state had tried to land a foreign automaker for "fifteen to twenty years" but had failed to "get past the sidewalk."[16]

A young Democrat, Musgrove was determined to change this. Elected in 2000, Musgrove increased investment in education and pushed hard for generous industry subsidies. In November, his efforts paid off when Nissan announced that it would build a $1.43 billion factory near Jackson. Having lured Nissan with a $377 million incentive package—and personal diplomacy—Musgrove hoped to "entice" other automakers, establishing an industry to challenge Alabama.[17] Understanding the importance of individual contact, Musgrove courted Hyundai intensively. According to documents obtained by the Associated Press, between July 2001 and March 2002, Mississippi spent $386,241 trying to land the plant. Expenses included helicopter flights, engineering fees, and gifts for Hyundai executives. In February, Musgrove, Senate minority leader Trent Lott, and U.S. congressmen Chip Pickering and Roger Wicker also traveled to Seoul to meet with Hyundai executives. In early 2002, however, Nissan unexpectedly declared that it did not want to share the Mississippi workforce with another big automaker, presumably because doing so might increase wages. Highlighting the role that luck could play in the story, Mississippi's bid was derailed.[18]

The other main contender was Kentucky. Drawing on the state's automotive presence, Bluegrass officials pushed a site in Glendale, about ninety minutes from Georgetown. Aware of the competition, Alabama's leaders hit back. In March, the legislature approved a $118 million bond issue to offset Hyundai's costs. The amount included $75 million to train workers, a crucial provision. When Hyundai made its announcement, the press argued that these inducements had been decisive. "Incentive Package Enticed Hyundai," declared the *Tuscaloosa News*. Valued at around $123 million, however, Kentucky's bond package was actually bigger, and it included $70 million for the acquisition of property and plant construction.[19]

In reality, other factors were more important. Montgomery got the nod partly because it offered a smooth land deal, with officials obtaining options on all the required property by mid-February. In Kentucky, by contrast, the state was unable to obtain a key 111-acre piece of land within the site from the Howlett family. "The inability of getting an agreement with the Howletts has been a major problem—a very, very serious problem," admitted Governor Paul Patton. "The public relations effect of it has been pretty counterproductive." There was a further dispute with Kenneth Floyd, a local farmer who alleged that he was misled into selling his farm for $3,500 an acre, much lower than his lawyer advised. Following a legal challenge, Floyd settled when the state offered him "significantly" more for his land. Lawsuits also delayed Kentucky's attempts to condemn property that it had purchased options on. As Hyundai was anxious to avoid negative publicity, these difficulties were important. Alabama's team also made sure that Hyundai was aware of Kentucky's difficulties.[20]

There were other reasons for Alabama's success. Again, individual factors and not just incentives made a difference. The state had a positive track record with Mercedes-Benz, whose parent company, DaimlerChrysler, held a 10 percent share in Hyundai following several joint ventures. Unlike Nissan in Mississippi, Mercedes welcomed Hyundai, which competed in a different part of the market. "Mercedes helped, I mean they helped *sell* it," recalled Ed Castile. "The guy that ran that plant then, when Hyundai was coming in, was a fella named Bill Taylor, and . . . he helped us with that. . . . His experience helped sell the Koreans on drawing pictures of what their experience might look like."[21] Mercedes's enthusiasm was important because Hyundai wanted to locate in a state that already hosted a foreign automaker. "Both Kentucky and Alabama have proven records of successfully recently assimilating an assembly plant owned by an overseas automaker, a matter of particular concern as HMC builds its first U.S. facility," noted Governor Don Siegelman's files. The governor sold Mercedes's success to Hyundai. The M-Class, he wrote Chung, was proof that "Alabamians produce only the best," a persuasive argument for a company that wanted to improve quality.[22]

A New South governor who was educated at Georgetown and Oxford Universities, Siegelman also made Alabama more attractive to international investors. Aware that any association with racial intolerance was bad for business, the Mobile native projected forward-looking images. Starting on January 1, 2002, for example, the state changed its long-standing license plate, based on the "Heart of Dixie" slogan, to the neutral "Stars Fell on Alabama" motto. The move symbolized how Alabama was seeking to belong on the global stage.[23] Siegelman was integrally involved in the change, even hiring the graphic artist (Helen Moore) responsible for the new plate.[24]

The site was also important. Alabama offered two locations, with the other contender located in Opelika, a small town in Lee County. Although Opelika was also a finalist, site factors helped Montgomery to get the nod. Conducted in late 2001, Hyundai's confidential assessments of the two sites—contained in Siegelman's files—offered clues about its choice. While the Opelika site had fewer residents, disadvantages included the "irregular" shape of the land, its grading, and large numbers of trees. "The existence of relatively mature trees on this site will require relatively more site preparation than other competitive sites," noted the assessment. "Tree removal also has adverse cost and delay implications." Furthermore, 200–300 acres of the site were in a floodplain, affecting a planned railroad spur that had to traverse it.[25] In contrast, Hyundai described the Montgomery location in glowing terms: "The site has a good shape, is relatively flat and has few trees to clear." Not only was it adjacent to Interstate 65, the land was 2–3 meters higher than the road, giving Hyundai the visibility that it wanted. Five families owned the land, more than in Opelika, but not enough to concern the company. A much bigger workforce also lived near the Montgomery site, addressing managers' anxieties about staffing the plant.[26]

Visiting executives also connected with the site. According to Ellen McNair, an ADO official who worked extensively on the bid, the attractiveness of the Montgomery location appealed to Hyundai's decision makers. "Our site was fabulous," she recalled. "I mean, it's a beautiful rectangular piece of property, had interstate on one side, a four-lane US highway on the other side, a half-mile of rail right there . . . all the utility infrastructure. . . . It is a beautiful site. It just shows extremely well." Replete with bucolic dairy farms, the site had a nostalgic air. "Cattle, hay bales and trees draped in Spanish moss dot the landscape," noted the *Birmingham News*. Pictures taken by McNair's team showed the site covered in grazing livestock. Running in front of the site, Teague Road, named after a local farming family, carried food from the farms to market. A few months later, the scene would be very different.[27]

The intense competition for the plant decreed that Alabama still had to offer generous incentives. At over $252 million, the package equated to $117,317 per job, which officials justified by industry norms. State and local governments agreed to spend $55 million to buy and develop the 1,600-acre site and $29 million to make road improvements. Hyundai also qualified for $76.7 million in tax incentives, including a local abatement of $27 million and a $29 million corporate income tax credit. Those close to the deal, however, stressed that these concessions only mattered in combination with an excellent location. "Incentives don't make a bad site good, they make a good site better," summarized economic developer Lori Hugeley.[28]

Individuals also played a key role. Appointed ADO director in 2001, Todd Strange was particularly important. Working fourteen or fifteen hours a day, he led the Alabama delegation. Referring to Hyundai as "Project Beach" and "V for Victory," Strange maintained the company's anonymity for as long as possible. As the team dealt with Hyundai, they made important personal connections. McNair remembered close bonds with J. H. Kim and Ahn Byung Mo. "We traveled to Korea all the time," she related, "and nurtured those connections. I mean . . . the relationship is extremely important." President of Hyundai's U.S. division, Ahn was an important figure, reporting directly to long-serving chairman Chung Mong-Koo. Reflecting on the recruitment process, Strange also stressed the importance of individual connections, especially with Chung. "It's *always* personal," he recalled. "You try not to make it personal, but it is.... With most negotiations, particularly foreign negotiations, before you delve into the business side of the equation you really have to know the people.... Getting the trust and getting the respect is something that we tried to do and had an opportunity on five or six or seven occasions, over lunches, over dinners." According to Strange, these connections—together with the importance of the site—were more decisive than the incentive package, which was similar between the finalists.[29]

Keen to modernize Alabama, Siegelman got personally involved. Elected in a landslide over Fob James in 1998, the new governor lobbied successfully for automotive investment. In 1999, he persuaded Honda to locate a $400 million plant in Lincoln, Alabama. Aware that the Rosewood agreement had contributed to Folsom's defeat, Siegelman oversaw a smaller, $158 million deal for Honda.[30] Building on this success, he reached out to high-level Hyundai managers. In October 2001, for example, the governor met with CEO Kim Dong-Jin at an undisclosed location in the United States, traveling "a long distance on short notice" to accommodate the executive. Kim came away impressed by Siegelman's "most gracious hospitality" and commitment. "Your command of a wide array of details of your state's ability to host our company conveyed to me a sense that you would be with us for the long term," he wrote. "We will need that ongoing attention and support to succeed." At a time when several states were vying for the plant, the confidential meeting ensured that Alabama was a major contender. "It is clear to me that Alabama is a very impressive state," Kim concluded.[31] After the CEO invited Siegelman back to Korea, further discussions followed. Particularly important was a visit that Siegelman made to Hyundai's headquarters during the Thanksgiving holiday in 2001. Aware of the importance of the remembrance, executives were impressed. Following meetings with Chung in February, Siegelman learned that Alabama was "on the short-list of sites being considered for Project V."[32]

The governor kept up the pressure. In March, as Hyundai was making its final decision, he wrote Chung and assured him of Alabama's commitment. "We are eager to work with you the 'Hyundai Way,' building the best for consumers throughout the world," he enthused. The governor also wrote Kim Dong-Jin—in Korean and English—on behalf of "your friends in Alabama."[33] Siegelman promised Hyundai that if it chose Alabama, he would take state leaders to the company's Korean factories for detailed fact-finding. Illustrating cross-party commitment, U.S. senators Jeff Sessions and Richard Shelby made the same pledge. Once he had landed the deal, Siegelman stayed involved. In May, he wrote Thomas C. Hubbard, the U.S. ambassador to South Korea, requesting the "expeditious granting" of visas for Hyundai managers and their families who were relocating to Alabama. Justifying his action, Siegelman stressed the plant's importance.[34]

Led by Sessions and Shelby, Alabama's congressional delegation also lobbied hard. Politicians interacted with Baker Botts, the Washington, D.C., law firm that represented Hyundai, and KPMG, Hyundai's U.S. consultant. These efforts made a difference. As Baker Botts's Jeff Stonerock wrote confidentially to state official Dave Echols in October, HMC was "continuing" to explore its options in the United States, and Alabama was a strong contender. "HMC appreciates the time, hard work, and cooperative spirit you and other Alabama representatives, as well as the Alabama Congressional Delegation, have shown in providing the information necessary for HMC to make an informed decision," he added.[35]

An experienced senator, Shelby got particularly involved. When the company was making its decision, the Republican threw his office open. "Please know that I stand ready and willing to offer any assistance I can in moving forward your negotiation and selection process," he confidentially wrote Chung in February. Used to securing federal funds for Alabama, the senior senator offered more than words. In March 2002, as Hyundai readied to make an announcement, Shelby arranged for the state's offer of $35 million for training expenses to be boosted by "$15 million out of federal monies available to him." The state hid the source of these funds from Hyundai, which had been pushing for more training assistance. As lawyer Frank D. McPhillips wrote Siegelman, "We do not want to let it be known to Hyundai or to Kentucky that this federal assistance is being made available, so we have characterized this as additional State money."[36] Involved in a tightly contested race for the Republican nomination for governor, Bob Riley also got involved. In November 2001, he traveled to Korea, using the trip—which was also related to his membership of the House Armed Services Committee—to court Hyundai. Along with several other lawmakers, Riley enjoyed a 125 mph ride on the test track at Hyundai's headquarters. "I felt like Dale Earnhardt, Jr.," he declared.[37]

Hyundai's move to Alabama also reflected union avoidance, a particularly urgent need for Korean companies. In contrast to the Japanese, Korean automakers confronted militant unions. In the 1980s and 1990s, South Korea witnessed rapid growth in union membership and frequent strikes, many of them triggered by workers' belief that the national economic miracle was not being equally shared. In 1987, there were almost four thousand strikes across the country, causing the loss of 6.94 million workdays. Many turned violent; in December 1991, for example, a major strike erupted at HMC after managers refused to give employees a bonus. Around a thousand workers seized the factory, evicting managers and smashing up over two thousand cars. While the 1995 Declaration for Industrial Peace, a national framework designed to encourage dialogue, reduced tensions temporarily, they increased after the 1997 economic crisis as companies laid off workers. As Hyundai became a global automaker and increasingly reliant on the North American market, the frequent strikes became problematic. In late 2001, just as it was looking for a location in the United States, HMC was hit by a series of strikes, costing it $554 million in lost production. "In South Korea, labor strife in auto plants, often violent, is as routine as the daily lunch break," summarized reporter Doron Levin.[38]

Not surprisingly, HMC did not declare that it wanted to evade unions. Evidence indicates, however, that Hyundai avoided states where unions were strong. Early on, HMC briefly considered Ohio, which would have given it greater proximity to suppliers, yet the company dismissed the state reportedly because it was home to unionized GM and Ford plants. "Just because Honda has managed to fend off the UAW doesn't mean Hyundai can," commented the *Pittsburgh Post-Gazette*. "Southern states could be a safer choice because of right-to-work laws." Hyundai's finalists were all southern, and industry observers agreed that union avoidance was a key factor.[39]

In Alabama, officials were more candid. According to McNair, it was no accident that Hyundai gravitated to the state. Unions, she insisted, robbed companies of the "flexibility" they needed to respond to market demands. In the battle to land Hyundai, McNair thought that Alabama's right-to-work status gave it an edge over Kentucky, which did not have such a law. McNair's files also document that "Labor"—including union avoidance—was a central HMC concern. In the area around the site, hostility to unions permeated the air. In Auburn, which strongly supported the bid, economic development director Phillip Dunlap felt that domestic automakers had declined because they were "totally captive" to the UAW.[40] Other government officials acknowledged the importance of the issue. "As a right-to-work state . . . I think that helped us," commented Ed Castile, who was heavily involved in the bid. Alabama had attracted foreign automakers, added Sheila Eckman, "because we're not very demanding. They seek us out because we have low wages and no unions, mostly no unions, and we do have a good workforce." Hyundai's decision also came a few months after the UAW's second defeat at Nissan in Tennessee, which confirmed how difficult it was to organize in the region.[41]

Locating in Montgomery also generated cost savings, which were particularly important for a budget automaker. As they assessed the site, executives liked that the manufacturing wage in the area was $10.78 an hour, well below the national average. By offering above-average pay for the area but below par for the industry, Hyundai knew that it would have a ready supply of workers, giving it the upper hand if there was any protest. Looking to reduce labor cost, executives complained to Siegelman that Alabama's workers' compensation rate was "extremely high," demanding an "effective offset." In confidential documents, HMC also pressed for incentives for suppliers, particularly the twenty or so tier 1 Korean companies that planned to locate nearby. In response, the state offered Hyundai reduced workers' compensation rates and promised incentives for suppliers, including help with land acquisition.[42]

In addition to Mercedes's role, prior investment by Asian automakers also helped Alabama. Hyundai's decision closely followed two significant moves by its biggest Japanese rivals. On November 14, 2001, as Hyundai was considering final locations, the Honda plant in Lincoln made its first vehicle six months ahead of schedule, while a second production line was added a few months later. In 2001, Toyota also decided to build a $220 million engine plant in Huntsville.[43] The recruitment of these firms shaped how Hyundai was courted. Understanding the importance of a large greenfield site, the state offered Honda a flat location to accommodate its 1.7-million-square-foot plant. Located forty miles east of Birmingham, the site was close to I-20, the major route to Atlanta. As Sewell recalled, the incentive package also focused on addressing Honda's "training and infrastructure needs."[44] It was a similar story with Toyota's engine plant, for which the state again prioritized site preparation. Both plants gave Alabama strong selling points as officials recruited HMC.[45]

As Hyundai made its decision, Alabama's auto industry was thriving. On November 9, 2000, the industry celebrated two milestones in one day, as Mercedes-Benz broke ground at a second plant in Vance and Honda welcomed its first hourly workers in Lincoln.[46] State officials used these successes to assuage HMC's anxieties and give the company some "peace." "It was their first North American facility," added McNair, "and it's a scary thing to spend a billion dollars on something. So they wanted partnerships that they could depend on." Alabama's recent success gave it an advantage over Kentucky, which had not landed a foreign automaker since the 1980s. Hyundai, whose only other foreign plants were in emerging nations, needed this reassurance, especially as the U.S. market was demanding.[47] In the end, the hard work paid off. At 8:35 p.m. on April 1, 2002, Dong-Jin called Siegelman with the good news. "Hyundai and Alabama have forged a business partnership that will benefit Alabama families for generations to come," declared a delighted governor. "It was a huge thing for our community," added McNair. "It was just an amazing, amazing celebration in our community."[48]

The state press was ebullient. The *Daphne Bulletin* wrote that the "blockbuster announcement" was a "major coup" for the state. Hyundai's plant, added the *Tuscaloosa News*, was a key moment for Alabama, solidifying its "growing international reputation as 'the Detroit of the South.'" Even the *Washington Post*'s Warren Brown, a black southerner who admitted to ambivalent feelings about the region, called the factory "splendiferous."[49] As some writers noted, Hyundai was especially significant because it diversified the industry's presence in Alabama, its lower-priced cars complementing Mercedes-Benz's luxury vehicles and Honda's midrange products. Companies from Japan, Korea, and Germany now produced a full range of vehicles in the state. State officials retained a soft spot for Hyundai because it manufactured affordable vehicles. "They make a good product that even more people within Alabama can afford to buy," summarized the ADO's Billy Joe Camp. Some also remembered that, unlike Germany or Japan, Korea had been a wartime ally.[50]

Hyundai's investment was significant. Apart from two thousand jobs in the plant, the company planned to bring 20 primary suppliers and up to 120 other suppliers to Alabama, producing fifteen thousand jobs within five years. "This is the biggest economic development project in the history of Alabama," declared Siegelman. For Hyundai too, its first U.S. plant was path-breaking. President Kim described the facility as "of great importance" to HMC, especially in advancing its "mission toward quality."[51]

Behind the scenes, there was another side to this story. Even before the announcement, the cost of the package strained the relationship between state and local governments. In March 2002, McPhillips reported to Siegelman that area officials were concerned about how much they were committing to the plant. "The local entities are legitimately concerned about putting substantial up-front money into this project if Hyundai fails to perform," noted McPhillips. "After all, there is the unfortunate example of Hyundai's attempt to manufacture vehicles in Canada, which ended with Hyundai closing its facility." The local authorities pressed for a "right of reversion to the real property" if HMMA closed before the twenty-year bond used to finance its commitment had matured. State officials also looked to rein in site preparation costs and refused to pay for all of the company's third-party legal and consulting expenses and ground-breaking ceremony costs. Although the state did not meet every item on the company's "wish list," Hyundai still chose Alabama.[52]

Outside government circles, many citizens were concerned about the cost of the incentives. Over 51 percent of the package came from taxpayers, diverting funds that could have been spent on Alabama's public schools—among the worst in the nation—or on addressing the state's high poverty rate. "Critics complained that this incentive package was overly generous and an example of corporate welfare," summarized John Mohr in the *Encyclopedia Alabama*. There were also local tensions. "Early on there was some consternation about the incentives package," summarized local pastor Gary Burton. Even some Hyundai workers felt uneasy. "The state bends over backwards for this company and [they] show absolutely no gratitude," wrote one worker later. Even the land deal produced problems. A group of landowners sued the Montgomery Industrial Development Board after finding out that one person had been paid more for his land than the others. The case dragged on until May 2014, when the landowners received $3.45 million in compensation from the board.[53]

There were other tensions. In June 2002, two African American state representatives—Hank Sanders of Selma and John F. Knight Jr. of Montgomery—complained that the state's list of contractors bidding to perform highway work for the plant did not contain any minority-owned companies. "We ask you to instruct ALDOT [Alabama Department of Transportation] to give qualified black-owned businesses the opportunity to bid on the project," they wrote. In reply, Siegelman did not promise to make this commitment.[54] Local authorities also proposed a contract that specified that 30 percent of their site preparation work should be carried out by minority-owned firms, yet this provision did not apply to ALDOT construction.[55] Labor issues were also present. In the fall of 2003, Hyundai began hiring. As Castile recalled, demand was "very huge," and training workers was "more challenging" than it had been at Mercedes and Honda, which were located in industrial areas. The first batch of production workers, admitted production manager Craig Stapley, was "about as inexperienced as you can get when it comes to building cars." Many white-collar staff were also hired from other backgrounds. A lot of the sector's managers, summarized *Automotive News* in 2005, were "people recruited from outside the auto industry." While this trend had always been apparent, it accelerated overtime.[56]

Heavy demand meant that Hyundai could pay slightly less than other automakers and push workers hard. In 2006, Mercedes started its employees at $16.00 an hour, rising to $27.00 after two years. At Hyundai, however, workers began at $14.22 an hour, increasing to $21.34 after the same time. Soon, complaints about the pay differential, as well as the long hours and heavy workloads, were expressed to the UAW. Seeing a potential opportunity, in early 2006 the union conducted a one-day "blitz" at HMMA, with eight organizers passing out handbills and taking names. The effort confirmed that there were many grievances. Along with complaints about wages, workers spoke out about long hours and having to work weekends because of mandatory overtime. "It just wears on you," claimed one. "It would be nice to have some time off." Others cited overbearing managers. "Every time you say something, you get the same response: 'You knew that when you came to work here,'" commented a worker. Cultural differences between Korean executives and American employees were common, especially as most Koreans were on short-term contracts and worked long hours. They expected the same of their staff, even when they had family commitments.[57]

The obstacles to organizing Hyundai were considerable. Given the poverty of the area, jobs were sought-after, and many workers felt they should tolerate the downsides. The company made all employees sign agreements that they would not talk to the media, and most were reluctant to come out as union supporters. Worries about the plant's future were also common, especially as there were few other industries around. "Most people are fearful that if the union comes in, they'll shut down the plant," admitted one. Struggling to overcome these problems, the UAW did not launch a full campaign.[58] At national gatherings, union leaders discussed the obstacles. In 2006, Bob King told the national convention that cracking the transplants, including Hyundai, was one of the UAW's "biggest challenges." Although the task seemed "impossible," the vice president urged his colleagues to keep trying.[59] It was an uphill struggle. As organizing director Cindy Estrada reported in 2010, the "new auto industry" had purposely located in "low-wage, non-union states," and the UAW faced a host of barriers, including hostile communities, weak labor movements, and a large and scattered workforce. Companies not only were reluctant to challenge local mores but also wanted to reduce labor costs. Although there was sympathy among workers, those with union backgrounds were screened out. Refusing to admit defeat, Estrada hoped that workers would reach a "tipping point" and speak out. "Despite the gains they have made in spreading fear," she concluded, "there is still great hope."[60]

At HMMA, complaints persisted. On Glassdoor, an employment review website, workers spoke out about demanding managers, long hours, and a lack of autonomy. Although the workweek was officially thirty-eight hours and forty-five minutes long, reality was very different. Summarizing the problems, one worker wrote: "Overtime and hard to make a work and life balance." Another added, "Expected to work extended hours and also on off days." Frequently changing shift assignments were also unpopular: "The downsides of working at Hyundai Motor Manufacturing Alabama would have to be the alternating of shifts every few months."[61] Other sources confirmed that working at HMMA was much harder than the dominant narrative allowed. While reluctant to criticize Hyundai, resident Gary Burton admitted that working in the plant was "challenging." Workers had to be extremely "disciplined" in order to cope, especially with the "fast pace." In 2015, even Rick Neal, HMMA's vice president of human resources, acknowledged that jobs were "hard work," and many could not survive. "The whole process is not easy," he explained in an interview. "It's very difficult and not everybody is cut out for it. A lot of folks who get hired think, 'I've got all these great wages and benefits and I'm just going to cruise.' And then they suddenly find out how difficult it is and they can't do the work or they can't follow the policies and pretty soon they are out the door."[62]

There were repeated protests about Korean managers. The complaints reflected cultural differences, as in Korea long hours and total commitment to the job were the norm. In the late 1970s, HMC employees worked from 8:00 a.m. to 8:00 p.m., six days a week, with mandatory overtime. Workers were typically in the factory for eighty-four hours a week. Managers worked even longer, often sleeping in the factory in temporary cots. Unlike the Japanese carmakers, women did work in Hyundai's factories, putting in at least nine hours a day. Mandatory hours had been reduced by the early 2000s, but devotion to the company and willingness to work overtime remained standard. In the United States, managers' expectations led to conflict. "Sometimes it seems Koreans see Americans as trained pets that are only alive to work," noted one employee. "10 hour work shifts Monday through Friday and sometimes Saturdays. 10 hours being actually working . . . so you're usually away from home more than 12 hours a day on average." Others repeatedly framed the problem in cultural terms. "HMMA is saturated with the Korean business/military culture and that brings numerous challenges," summarized another.[63]

HMMA tried to respond. In Quebec, communication with French-speaking employees had compounded the problem, but things were a little easier in Alabama. In an effort to reduce cultural clashes, the company sent employees on free trips to South Korea. By 2015, almost thirteen hundred HMMA workers had been on the weeklong tours, which were designed to allow them to "experience the Korean culture." As the plant employed close to four thousand people, and turnover was considerable, however, the majority of employees did not take part. Denying that employees were disgruntled, Hyundai claimed that Korean managers were fair. According to the company, the plant was "harassment-free, discrimination-free, and violence-free."[64]

Financial rewards also helped. Employees were provided with free uniforms, two weeks of paid vacation per year, and generous discounts—between 23 and 27 percent—on Hyundai cars. The company also paid over 90 percent of an employee's health insurance premiums for both single and family coverage and provided free life insurance and a 401(k) program. Some workers praised the extensive on-site facilities, which included a bank, gym, softball field, and two cafeterias. Above all, they applauded the pay, which was "good for the Area." By locating the plant in a poor area, Hyundai had a decisive advantage, with many workers putting up with the long hours and demanding environment due to the lack of alternatives. By 2015, after a decade of production, there had not been a major campaign to organize HMMA. Neal admitted that employees worked "substantial amounts of overtime," especially before the company added a third shift in 2012, which was designed to reduce the "fatigue factor." He stressed, however, that many production employees earned $75,000 a year after overtime, while maintenance workers made close to $100,000. "I don't think there is a private employer that pays as well as we do or offers the wide variety of benefits we provide," he boasted.[65]

The poverty of the area gave the company enormous advantages. In 2002, the average household income in Montgomery County was $34,500 a year, but assembly jobs at Hyundai averaged $55,000 (before overtime). In surrounding counties, incomes were even lower. Neighboring Lowndes County had a 28.9 percent unemployment rate and a median household income of $21,095, while Wilcox County had a 33.8 percent poverty rate and a household income of just $19,035.[66] As the *Mobile Register* put it, Wilcox was "Alabama's poorest county" and one of the most impoverished places in America. Demand for jobs at the plant was enormous, and most workers were reluctant to speak out. "We'll put an ad out there for a few Hyundai people," Castile noted in 2016, "and we'll get thousands of applications." HMMA, summarized one employee, was "great if you are ready to work hard."[67]

During the Great Recession, Hyundai hired more temporary workers, strengthening its position. In May 2015, HMMA employed 2,902 full-time workers along with 657 temporary employees and 48 Korean expatriates (there were also many Korean American managers). The changes gave Hyundai decisive advantages: temps lacked job security and often tried to please the company. If there was a prospect of organizing, Hyundai could make these workers permanent in order to—as Gary Casteel put it—"dampen their interest for unionization." For Casteel, temporary workers were the "cancer of the industry." The UAW was also hit hard by the recession, which led to widespread layoffs. By 2010, UAW records indicate that membership had dipped below 500,000—compared to 1.2 million in the early 1980s—undermining the union's capacity to organize.[68]

As the national economy tanked, budget-oriented Hyundai benefited. Between 2008 and 2010, its market share rose, surpassing 7 percent. In these years, Kia and Subaru were the only other carmakers to post an increase in U.S. sales. As it had shown with its warranty, Hyundai took risks to gain sales. In 2009, it surprised other companies by letting buyers return their vehicles within a year, at no cost, if they lost their job or income. At a time of acute job insecurity, it was a masterstroke. Helped by the move, HMC became the world's fifth largest automaker, ahead of Honda, Nissan, and Chrysler.[69] For a company that had been on its knees in the 1990s, this was a remarkable turnaround. As the *New York Times* noted, Hyundai went from "0 to 60 in a Recession," helped by aggressive marketing, keen pricing, and improved quality. By August 2010, with the national economy still weak, the *Wall Street Journal* reported that Hyundai's Montgomery plant was at "full capacity." During these years, HMC also opened factories in the Czech Republic (2008), Russia (2011), and Brazil (2012).[70]

Observing these developments, dominant voices proclaimed that HMMA was a great success. In 2014, the Montgomery Chamber of Commerce—using figures supplied by Hyundai—claimed that the plant and its suppliers had created 12,630 jobs, with an annual payroll of $485.5 million. The total economic impact was $4.82 billion (in terms of additional purchases of goods and services). According to the chamber, Hyundai was "the Deal of a Lifetime." Highlighting its ability to shape the narrative, HMMA also commissioned a study by M. Keivan Deravi, an economics professor at Auburn University, that used the same data.[71] According to the company's calculations, in 2014 Hyundai and its suppliers accounted for 2 percent of Alabama's entire gross domestic product. As supporters stressed, the Korean firms had more local content than their Japanese predecessors. Ten suppliers were located very near HMMA, some right next to the factory. Helped by these synergies, Hyundai America continued to grow, achieving a record 8.1 percent market share in 2016.[72]

By focusing on the plant's total economic impact, however, supporters overlooked that benefits were unevenly distributed. Rural areas, especially in the Black Belt, received few gains. None of the four automotive assembly plants in Alabama were located in the Black Belt, and all were beyond commuting distance for people living there. Residents were left wishing that the factories would "come a little closer." Even before Hyundai, Montgomery had been stronger economically than the Black Belt counties. "Montgomery County is part of the belt geographically," explained the *Montgomery Advertiser*, "but the activities of the Capital set it apart from the region economically." In Montgomery County, employment rates and incomes exceeded the state average, but the rest of the Black Belt lagged. Hyundai reinforced these patterns. In 2018, Todd Strange, who went on to become mayor of Montgomery, admitted that the Hyundai plant had failed to help the belt.[73]

It was a similar story with suppliers. According to a listing compiled by the EDPA in 2016, the vast majority of suppliers were located in Montgomery County or to the east of it—on the way to Kia's plant in Georgia—rather than in the poorer counties of the southwest. "We've been fortunate with the suppliers that have located here," admitted Lori Hugeley, an economic development official in Lee County, which bordered Georgia. Many suppliers were clustered around Lee County's largest city, Auburn, which attracted Koreans with its high-quality public schools, respected university, and proximity to Atlanta. Of sixty-two Hyundai suppliers listed by the chamber in 2016, just seven were located west of Interstate 65. Many Black Belt counties, including Choctaw, Greene, Hale, Marengo, Perry, Sumter, and Wilcox, had none. Jobs at suppliers paid less than assembly-line positions, and most were temporary.[74] Famous for the protests that led to the passage of the landmark 1965 Voting Rights Act, Selma—and Dallas County—also missed out. In 2014, the county was 80 percent black, and 36 percent of its residents lived in poverty. Conditions in the Black Belt remained "particularly bad," admitted Sheila Eckman. "You drive past these impoverished areas, with little shacks and everything, and mostly black people live there," she related. The age-old problem of the "two Alabamas" remained.[75]

The lack of change was significant. When the plant was announced, leaders had promised jobs for the poor. "You're going to have single moms who used to work two jobs a day now working one to provide for her family," claimed Siegelman. "She'll be able to raise her children with Alabama values and then send them off to college." Significantly, the governor pledged that there would be big gains for the Black Belt, including its most famous town. "Watch Selma," he declared the day after Hyundai's announcement.[76] The press piped a similar tune. "Hyundai Plant Expected to Bring Jobs to Black Belt," declared the *Decatur Daily*. Hyundai's arrival, added a hopeful *Selma Times Journal*, was "our World Series."[77]

Siegelman tried to deliver. When the plant was announced, he recognized that poorer counties had been bypassed by the industry. "I want to get another plant somewhere in west Alabama," he claimed. "I want everyone in this state to have a job." Insisting that the Hyundai announcement had "left a deep footprint," in April the governor embarked on a "Jobs Tour" of small cities to help them recruit new industries, particularly Hyundai suppliers. Known as Team Alabama, key members of the administration joined him. Many of the towns visited, however, were not in the Black Belt. It was crucial, Siegelman explained on a visit to Clanton—just outside Birmingham—that Alabama secure supplier jobs. "We didn't want Georgia or Mississippi to have a shot," he explained.[78]

Siegelman promised to keep working on economic development in poor areas. In November 2002, he was up for reelection, and the Hyundai announcement was expected to help him. Before the vote, the *Tuscaloosa News* claimed that the governor had an "exceptionally successful record of economic development," as Honda, Toyota, and Hyundai had all arrived during his term.[79] Weakened by a failed effort to set up a state lottery to fund college tuition, however, Siegelman was defeated by Bob Riley in a tight election that also featured allegations of vote tampering and a malfunctioning voting machine. His efforts to relaunch his political career were cut short by a 2006 conviction for bribery and mail and wire fraud. Although some saw his treatment as politically motivated—the Democrat was disliked by many in a state that was "bright red"—a federal appeals court upheld his conviction. In February 2017, he was released on probation. After Siegelman's defeat, Alabama's Republican governors—Riley, Robert Bentley, and Kay Ivey—showed less interest in bringing jobs to the Black Belt, where most voters were Democrats.[80]

In the longer term, the plant struggled to alter deep-seated patterns of inequality. In the Montgomery area, there were gains in employment and income levels, but state data were less impressive. Illustrating this, 2008 census data showed that 15.7 percent of Alabamians lived below the poverty line, placing the state in the bottom ten nationally. In 2006, Alabama's infant mortality rate was also the third highest in the nation. One plant, even if it was big and successful, could not turn around fundamental disparities. As Burton summarized, the plant had "helped, [but] it has not alleviated the poverty." Confirming this, in 2016 the proportion of Alabamians living in poverty had increased to 16.8 percent, one of the highest rates in the country.[81] Deindustrialization also continued. "Even with the tremendous success that we had," acknowledged Sewell, "we still had a net loss in terms of manufacturing jobs." Illustrating this, when HMMA was announced, manufacturing employed 309,700 workers in Alabama, but by 2017, the figure had dropped to 265,900. It was not surprising that Hyundai workers felt fortunate, especially in a state where manufacturing remained the biggest employer.[82]

For America's auto industry, HMMA was very significant. It took the industry into new areas and confirmed Alabama's status as a major player. In 2015, less than two decades after the first Mercedes M-Class had rolled off the line, Alabama was the fifth largest producer of cars and light trucks in the country. According to the EDPA, apart from the assembly plants, which employed thirteen thousand people, a further twenty-four thousand worked for suppliers.[83] Most outsiders did not realize what a sizeable industry this was—or that their car might be made in Alabama. Between 1997 and 2015, more than 9.3 million cars and light trucks were produced there, and the state ranked second in *Business Facilities'* Automotive Manufacturing Strength list, a prestigious accolade. In 2016, eleven different passenger vehicle models were made in Alabama, and the EDPA proclaimed that the state was "at the center of the new U.S. Auto Industry." Supporters noted that the sector had gone through the Great Recession with "not even a layoff," encouraging further investment.[84]

By the time HMMA made its first Sonata, Alabama was a drawing card for foreign manufacturers. When Kia Motors looked to set up its first U.S. plant, attention immediately focused on the state. The company's executives had watched the foundation of the Montgomery plant, and it exerted a big influence on Kia's decision-making process. In the end, the plant went to Georgia, but its location near the Alabama line was no accident. Synergies with Hyundai would be at the heart of the Korean wave's next phase.[85]

CHAPTER EIGHT

When Kia Came
to Georgia

On February 26, 2010, more than five hundred dignitaries from South Korea and the United States gathered in West Point, Georgia, for the opening of Kia Motors' first North American factory. Built on a 2,200-acre site, the $1.2 billion plant covered 2.4 million square feet and had the capacity to produce three hundred thousand vehicles a year. As *Automotive News* observed, the factory was "big by any standard." It created about three thousand jobs, with almost as many again provided by suppliers. The outcome was a massive boost to Troup County, a former textile area in western Georgia that had one of the highest unemployment rates in the state. It was also a proud moment for Governor George "Sonny" Perdue III, who been courting Kia since 2003, when he had first visited company officials in Korea. "Kia's decision to locate its first US manufacturing operation here in Georgia will be a milestone both for this company and our state," he declared at the ceremony.[1] Outside observers saw the plant as very significant. Dubbed a "defining moment for the region" by one state-level publication, Kia's arrival also attracted national and international press attention. "An increasing number of Asian carmakers are opening manufacturing operations in the U.S.," summarized the BBC, "particularly in the South."[2]

In many ways, Kia's story was even more remarkable than that of Hyundai. Both firms were upstarts, but Kia was smaller and lacked profile, particularly in the United States. When the American auto industry was at its peak in the 1960s, Kia was producing bicycles. It only started making cars in 1974, using foreign designs and parts. Between 1981 and 1986, Kia only made light trucks, while in 1997 it went bankrupt. At that time, Kia's share of the U.S. market was just 0.36 percent, about half that of Hyundai. For every Kia on American roads, there were twenty-two Toyotas.[3] Starting in the late 1990s, Kia's sales grew. Together with the partnership with Hyundai, this paved the way for overseas expansion, yet the move still carried risks. West Point was built during the depths of the global financial crisis, when many automakers were laying off workers. As Kia constructed the plant, GM and Chrysler stood on the brink of collapse. Kia opened the plant just a decade after entering the U.S. market, a much shorter period of time than its predecessors. It also located the factory in a state that other foreign automakers had spurned and in an area where workers lacked automotive experience.[4]

Kia's decision had profound implications. With the arrival of South Korea's second largest carmaker, the industry's third wave gathered pace. Across Georgia and Alabama, especially in the corridor between Montgomery and West Point, Korean suppliers arrived. The plant was a major economic boost for the Chattahoochee Valley region, drawing workers from at least ten counties in Georgia and Alabama. Perdue termed the Kia project "the largest single economic development announcement in the history of our state," while state officials described it as the "Super Bowl" of economic development. In 2006, *Business Facilities*, a national corporate publication, even termed the Kia agreement the "Economic Development Deal of the Year." Like Hyundai—and unlike the earlier Japanese and German transplants—Kia brought with it a newly built chain of parts factories, as well as locally made engines. Subsequent expansions created more jobs.[5]

Drawing on a substantial body of original interviews, as well as newly released archival papers and other records, this chapter examines how Kia came to Georgia and what it meant for the local communities involved.[6] It shows that Kia's decision was partly linked to a $410 million incentive package that it received from state and local authorities, as well as the cost advantages that a Deep South location offered.[7] These factors, however, were not the whole story. In the course of an extensive bidding war, Kia rejected a $1 billion incentive package from Mississippi; its choice was not just about money. A closer interrogation shows that an important role was also played by other factors, particularly the location of the site, which offered easy access to both Atlanta and Montgomery. Unique personal bonds, especially between Perdue and Ahn Byung Mo, CEO of Kia Motors America, were also crucial. "They don't teach in business school how important relationships are," summarized Craig Lesser, the commissioner of the Georgia Department of Economic Development, who oversaw the deal. "Governor Perdue was very receptive; Ahn wanted to meet with him from time to time, Governor Perdue was very open with him, very positive. I truly believe . . . the relationships that we formed, on multiple levels . . . were very, very fundamental in that deal." As the sources demonstrate, human agency was an important element in this story, including the extraordinary—and distinctive—tale of how the land was acquired. Rather than moving to a site that the state had prepared for industrial development—the standard arrangement—Kia (and especially Ahn) insisted on one with multiple landowners, producing human interactions that made this story unique. The topic of industrial recruitment has usually been viewed in economic terms, but this was a story about people as much as money. Some key participants even claimed that divine intervention had been involved.[8]

When the plant was built, the national press portrayed Kia's arrival in glowing terms. According to CNN, West Point had hit the "economic jackpot." Journalist Elise Zieger related how grateful locals had renamed their town "Kiaville" and spoke of the company as a "savior." Someone even erected a sign that read, "Thank you Jesus for bringing Kia to our town." According to this narrative, the plant had generated rapid growth, revitalized the downtown, and created hope. "The old downtown is new again," summarized Mayor Drew Ferguson IV. "It's an exciting time." Ebullient business publications portrayed Kia as a lucrative prize, while special features in the *New York Times* and *USA Today* were also very positive. At a time when most of America was gripped by recession, the small rural community of West Point had "somehow managed to draw the winning ticket in the nation's economic lottery."[9]

Closer probing reveals a different picture. The authorities went to extensive lengths to secure the plant, and Kia received tax breaks at the expense of the local public schools, which remained poorly performing. Many of the jobs went to residents of Alabama, which had not paid to secure the plant, generating resentment. Union members—most of them from Atlanta—also complained that Kia would not hire them. Despite some regeneration of the downtown, more than a decade later, West Point remained a poor, majority-black community; few residents got jobs at the plant, and Kia employees, especially white-collar staff, refused to live there. Outside reporters missed these limitations. The relationship between Korean managers and American workers was also strained. Troup County still had a high poverty rate, especially in the depressed mill villages that had been its economic heart. Furthermore, locals feared that the plant would close when the incentives ran out and worried that their economy had become too dependent on Kia. A closer examination of this key factory reveals that growth—while real and much-needed—had strict limits and was accompanied by significant tensions and costs.[10]

Founded in 1825 by Governor George Troup, who signed an act organizing Creek Indian lands into several new counties, Troup County had long been a strategic location. Positioned along the Atlanta and West Point rail line, LaGrange, the county seat, acted as a hospital center for the Confederacy in 1863–64, during and after the battles around Atlanta. After this, the county, which was framed by the Chattahoochee River and its tributaries, emerged as a textile hub. The area's growth was underpinned by Callaway Mills, which was run by various members of the Callaway family between 1900 and 1968.[11] During the textile industry's heyday after World War II, Callaway Mills employed over five thousand people in the area, while many more worked at textile-related companies such as International Playtex and West Point–Pepperell. When Milliken and Co. acquired Callaway Mills in 1968, however, about half the workforce was laid off, and the industry's decline accelerated in subsequent decades as imports proliferated and jobs were automated. In 2002, the *LaGrange Daily News* dubbed textiles a "dying industry," adding that mill closures had "crippled what was once a pillar of the South's economy." Based in Troup County, West-Point Stevens—a successor to West Point–Pepperell—filed for Chapter 11 bankruptcy in 2003 and closed many mills, including two in LaGrange and another in nearby Valley, Alabama. Between 2004 and 2009, Troup County's unemployment rate jumped from 6.6 to 14.6 percent. Conditions were even bleaker in neighboring Chambers County, Alabama, where unemployment topped 21 percent before Kia opened.[12] According to Ricky Wolfe, a former chairman of the Troup County Board of Commissioners, the area was "dying" before Kia arrived. "We were, as you know, textile oriented. . . . The store fronts were closing. I mean, it was a really tough, tough situation."[13]

Desperate for new investment, local leaders were elated when, in the fall of 2005, rumors began to circulate that an anonymous foreign company was interested in a "mega-site" in the western part of the state. The first clear evidence occurred on November 30, when Jim Ewing from the Department of Economic Development visited West Point and described a huge project that needed at least 1,000 acres of land plus interstate frontage and rail access. The eventual site was discussed, but Ewing was also keen on several other options, as they were more prepared for industrial development. On December 6, a small group of Kia managers arrived at LaGrange-Callaway airport, accompanied by consultants and Ewing's staff. Diethard Lindner, the chairman of the Development Authority of LaGrange, a group founded in 1973 to attract industry, met the delegation. Aware that a lot was at stake, local officials were sworn to secrecy. "Company will abandon Georgia if we cannot keep quiet," wrote Lindner. Those involved referred to the company as "Project G"; few knew that it was Kia.[14]

Still, in a small community, the visitors did not go unnoticed. On December 13, for example, Hyundai-Kia chairman Chung Mong-Koo, along with nine leading executives, arrived in Troup County by helicopter and toured the area in two unmarked vehicles, looking at sites in West Point and Hogansville, at opposite ends of the county. As *LaGrange Daily News* editor Andrea Lovejoy recalled, the delegation's use of helicopters and "big fancy black cars" produced "all kind of crazy rumors" among the perplexed and curious locals. While some feared that a prison might be built, others suspected that an Asian-based corporation was interested in constructing a factory. None anticipated the size of the investment—or guessed the suitor's identity.[15]

At the state level, however, officials had been wooing Kia for some time. Perdue visited South Korea, home to several corporations that had invested in Georgia, during his first year in office. Samsung Electronics America and Hyundai Motor America already had regional headquarters in Atlanta. Perdue's predecessors had worked hard to provide a probusiness climate, selling their state on the international stage in a way that typified the South's globalization. Governor from 1991 to 1999, Zell Miller laid some important groundwork, enlarging tax incentives to corporations, using the holding of the 1996 Olympic Games in Atlanta to publicize the state's growth ethic, and overseeing a "major overhaul" of economic development policy. Business recruitment efforts, he insisted, needed to move beyond their traditional "low-wage" focus and become more global. By 1994, Miller claimed that Georgia was the fastest-growing state east of the Colorado River, although his papers also recorded concern that the "bulk" of growth was concentrated around Atlanta.[16]

A native of Perry, in central Georgia, Perdue was especially keen to attract business beyond Atlanta and address the infamous "two Georgias" problem.[17] Like Miller, he traveled widely in search of investment.[18] On his initial visit to Korea, in October 2003, he called on Chairman Chung, a reclusive figure who rarely traveled internationally. "He was planting the first seeds," recalled Chris Clark, a former leader of the Department of Economic Development. In April 2002, Hyundai had announced its plant in Montgomery, about eighty miles from West Point, and Perdue knew that Kia was looking for a site for its first U.S. factory. Given the close links between the two brands—Hyundai owned 37 percent of Kia's stock, making it the company's largest shareholder—Perdue knew that Georgia was in the running. The sixty-five-year-old Chung was widely seen as the Hyundai Group's most powerful decision maker, while his son, Chung Eiu-Sun, was chairman of Kia. Lesser recalled that Perdue wanted the plant for political and economic reasons—as well as personal ones. "Not counting Florida, Georgia's the only southern state without a foreign automobile manufacturer, and the Governor . . . is going to be running for re-election," he related. "It was *very* important for him for not just political reasons but substantive reasons. It's a lot of jobs, associated with an automobile manufacturing facility, a lot of good jobs."[19]

A cornerstone of the South Korean economy, Kia Motors Corporation was founded in 1944. In its early years, the company concentrated on making bicycles. In the 1960s, Kia began making trucks that were based on Mazda designs. Car production followed in the 1970s but again relied heavily on foreign designs, particularly from Mazda and Ford. Entering the U.S. market in 1994, Kia gradually developed its own products. In 1998, Hyundai became the major shareholder in Kia, initiating cost savings, stabilizing its finances, and improving vehicle quality. Although the two companies had separate sales operations, they shared vehicle platforms and some design and development efforts, helping Kia to flourish. By 2005, Kia was selling over three hundred thousand vehicles a year in the United States, roughly the future capacity of West Point. Nevertheless, the company was an emerging force, and an American plant was a risk. Although it was building a factory in Slovakia, at

Georgia Governor George "Sonny" Perdue III, who played a key role in bringing Kia to West Point, Georgia. Courtesy of Richard B. Russell Library for Political Research and Studies, University of Georgia.

the time Kia's only foreign factories were joint ventures with local carmakers in Vietnam and China, and its global sales lagged well behind the major Japanese and American brands. Overseas expansion, however, protected Kia from currency fluctuations. In early 2006, just before the plant was announced, the South Korean won rose 3.2 percent compared to the U.S. dollar, reducing profits made overseas. "We need to expand more in the global market in order to escape foreign exchange risks," explained Kia vice president Choi Soon-Chul. The company's desire to expand and the growth that it was experiencing made it an attractive target for American politicians.[20]

Perdue was well-placed to take advantage. Prior to entering politics, he was a successful business owner in Houston County, with significant interests in agribusiness and transportation. Shaped by these experiences and responsive to the corporate interests that fueled the GOP's growth, Perdue was determined to make Georgia "an even more business-friendly state." He immediately made economic development a high priority. "As Governor, one of my main goals is a growing Georgia," he declared. "To strengthen our economy, it is important to grow existing Georgia businesses and attract new business to our state."[21] As a key part of this policy, the governor pursued an "aggressive international marketing strategy" that focused heavily on the automotive industry. Car plants were big political trophies, and as the *Atlanta Journal-Constitution* pointed out, Georgia had "missed out on six auto plants that had come South since 1993." The closest it came was in 2002, when Democratic governor Roy Barnes had tried to persuade DaimlerChrysler to build a factory near Savannah. Although the state offered $320 million in incentives—a move that Perdue criticized at the time—the company decided against building the facility, and Barnes lost his bid for reelection as the cleared site sat empty. Strategists knew that the political rewards—and personal validation—would be great if Perdue could land a car plant. "Once you get one," commented Mark Vitner, a Wachovia Corporation economist, "you're a hero."[22]

To improve his chances, Perdue made a number of important changes. In July 2004, he appointed Craig Lesser, a former radio host and Georgia Power executive, as the commissioner of the Department of Economic Development. A straight-talking New Yorker who had moved to Georgia in the 1970s, Lesser reorganized the department, creating a marketing division and establishing "a new brand for Georgia" that was promoted through increased advertising. Determined to secure more international investment, Lesser also traveled extensively, especially in Asia. These efforts achieved results. In 2005 the department helped 182 companies expand or locate facilities in Georgia, compared with 151 in 2004. These firms created 15,902 new jobs and attracted $2.68 billion in investment. Respected observers praised Georgia's efforts. As *Site Selection* magazine reported, under Perdue's stewardship the Peach State's business climate rose from twelfth in the nation in 2003 to seventh in 2004 and third in 2005.[23]

Perdue, however, also had to contend with bad news, especially in the automotive sector. Shortly before the Kia deal was finalized, Ford and General Motors announced that their long-standing Atlanta-area factories would close, resulting in the loss of around five thousand jobs. State officials offered Ford a $106 million package to keep its sixty-year-old Hapeville plant open, but the facility was shuttered in 2006 as the company downsized. Around the same time, "local corporate icons" BellSouth, Georgia-Pacific, and Scientific Atlanta "were absorbed by out-of-town concerns," and Atlanta lost its bid to secure the NASCAR Hall of Fame (which went to rival Charlotte). As a result, state officials were desperate for a flagship economic development.[24]

Perdue had interested Kia in Georgia, but a lot of work remained to be done. Bidding for a new automotive plant was a national event, and a wide variety of states were involved. Early in the process, Alabama alone submitted seven possible sites to Kia, which showed most interest in a location near Decatur. Several northern states also tried to compete, but Kia quickly gravitated to the South. In December 2005, *Automotive News* reported that Kia was also looking at sites in Chattanooga, Tennessee; Aiken, South Carolina; and Hopkinsville, Kentucky; as well as West Point. Strong competition subsequently came from Mississippi, where Governor Haley Barbour promoted sites in Meridian and Columbus. The Georgia team knew that they would have to bid to land Kia. "As long as competition was in the picture," recalled Lindner, "you couldn't ignore the incentives."[25]

Although Kia had plenty of alternatives, the corporation was very interested in West Point. In the late 1990s, Chairman Chung dispatched Ahn Byung Mo to find a plant site for Hyundai in America, and he spent a lot of time in Alabama. Driving regularly along I-85 between Atlanta airport and Montgomery, Ahn discovered the future Kia site in West Point, falling in love with the attractive open farmland. Ahn's personal connection with the site illustrated the importance of human variables—as well as economics—in this story. As Jane Fryer, president of the Troup County Chamber of Commerce, recalled, "Mr. Ahn . . . wanted this site. He had seen that site as he drove from the airport going to Hyundai, and he'd stop in LaGrange, get him a drink, and use the restroom. . . . He'd look out over there, and it was beautiful pastureland. . . . He would say to himself: 'That would be a beautiful place for a Kia plant. And it's in the good location, because it's close to the airport, [and] it's close to Hyundai.'" If the Kia plant were built at West Point, Ahn quipped to Lindner, he could drive straight to Atlanta airport, which offered nonstop flights to Seoul, without having to take a bathroom break. Although Georgia officials did not know at the time just how fond Ahn was of the location—and *Automotive News* did not report the story until later—his personal connection with it put them in a strong position. "That spot . . . was always in his mind," remembered Ray Coulombe, LaGrange's economic development manager. "We know now, what's in Mr. Ahn's mind, was going to get *done*." During their December 13 visit, the Kia managers, including Chung, had lunch with the local delegation and confirmed their interest in the West Point site. Although no deal had been made, the team set to work to secure the site for their secret client.[26]

The land that Ahn wanted, however, was controlled by thirty-six property owners, and in many cases it had been in the same family for generations. It was extremely rare for an industrial site to have so many owners. With Ahn adamant, the residents were told that the state wanted to purchase their land for economic development. At a meeting on December 22 between officials and the property owners, Drew Ferguson III, a West Point banker and chairman of West Point Development Authority, found "no interest" among the community members in selling. Ferguson remembered the difficult position he found himself in, as Kia wanted every property. "You could not lose one," he recalled, "without losing the whole project." There were other barriers, as Kia had selected a site containing farms, roads, and homes rather than one that was prepared for industrial development. Officials emphasized that the odds were against them. "We really didn't want to operate there," recalled Jim Ewing, the state's project manager, "because we saw all those houses. Everything about it to me looked insurmountable." Kia also wanted the deal sealed quickly, yet normally it took several years to negotiate such a large agreement, and that was with a preprepared site.[27]

Working almost nonstop, Ferguson set about changing the owners' minds.

To do so, he concentrated on getting to know them. "I *never* talked about money with them, until the end," he explained. Almost all the owners, he recalled, had family members who had lost jobs in the textile industry, and they understood that their community was dying. During his lengthy visits, Ferguson emphasized the project's benefits, gradually persuading the owners to sell. "I wanted my grandchildren to live here," explained owner Eddie Striblin, "but hopefully there will be jobs for them, which is more important." Others similarly put community needs ahead of their own, despite their "mixed emotions." It was also crucial that Ferguson, who was president of Capital City Bank in West Point, was a respected community figure. "My whole banking career prepared me to do that job," he reflected. "I knew people, I had the people skills, and I had a good solid reputation of a friend, and trustworthy."[28] Ferguson secured all thirty-six signatures by a March 5 deadline, jetting to Korea the next day to deliver the news. It was a remarkable turnaround, especially as one recalcitrant resident could have derailed the deal. Bearing this in mind, Ferguson—a self-professed "open Christian" who prayed throughout the negotiations—felt that divine intervention had occurred. "This was a project that was just sort of meant to be here," he asserted.[29]

Money, however, also played a role. The state got access to the land by paying more than $35 million, a generous amount. As Ferguson admitted, the landowners were paid "probably twice the appraised value," so they were able to move to better properties in the area. Some locals referred to them as "Kia millionaires."[30] Government agencies also had considerable authority; in 2005, the General Assembly granted the Department of Economic Development "broad new powers, including the ability to buy land and a multimillion-dollar pool of bond money to pay for it." Still, Ferguson's efforts were crucial. Kia had plenty of options, and a property dispute would have caused delays and negative publicity. Those close to the negotiations stressed that Kia was desperate to avoid such controversy.[31] The whole deal was also concluded covertly. "Imagine trying to get options on more than two dozen pieces of property without it becoming a news story," noted Lesser. Behind the scenes, Ferguson also helped the families find new properties and arranged for mortgage financing through his bank until state funds arrived.[32]

As the land was being acquired, state and local officials were meeting with Kia's representatives. Between December 2005 and March 2006, when the site announcement was made, officials held nearly fifty meetings in Georgia and at Kia's offices in Irvine, California. Progress was gradually made. At a meeting on January 5, for example, Lindner was designated as the community project coordinator, heading a team that included Ferguson, Fryer, and several local politicians. In the series of meetings that followed, the Georgians connected personally with Kia's managers. Noticing that the Koreans often chose southern food rather than the Asian snacks on offer, local greeters welcomed their guests with "a full-on Georgia barbecue spread, complete with Brunswick stew." "They cleaned their plates," recalled Fryer. State officials were similarly thoughtful. When they met with Ahn's team, the state delegation replaced the usual fleet of Fords with rented Kias, using the vehicles to drive to and from the site.[33] In order to give the visitors the best impression of the area, the Georgians entertained the Korean delegation at Callaway Gardens, a 14,000-acre resort outside West Point, and at the Hills and Dales estate, the Callaway family's opulent Italianate mansion in LaGrange. Visits to West Point were fleeting and focused on the site rather than the town.[34]

Members of the local team, who hailed from an area with just a handful of Korean residents, were also instructed how to behave. To avoid alienating their powerful guests, officials were sent extracts from Boye Lafayette De Mente's *Korean Etiquette and Ethics in Business*. Key instructions included carefully presenting business cards with the right hand—it was disrespectful to pass items with the left hand—as well as introducing the most senior individuals first. The Americans were also warned that Koreans were "clever, forceful negotiators" who liked to extract concessions after agreements were signed. "Every year Korea becomes more and more modern," warned the guide, "but it is important to recognize that modern does not equal Western."[35]

On several occasions, state leaders went to extraordinary lengths to accommodate their guests. "They bent over backwards, to do whatever it took to meet their expectations, to provide them with what they needed or wanted," recalled Andrea Lovejoy. On February 23, 2006, Chung Mong-Koo visited the site. Given the hierarchical nature of Korean corporate culture, it was a crucial moment. "One little thing could have gone wrong, and he could have stopped the whole project," admitted Fryer. She recalled some frenzied preparations before Chung's visit, with local authorities even enlisting inmates to help: "We had to get the cows off the property. . . . We had to have the prisoners out there to clean up the land, to get the cowpatties out." In addition, prisoners laid truckloads of gravel to ensure that Chung's car could get to the highest point of the site, where he would bless it from within a special tent. On the day, however, it rained heavily, worrying the local team. As Chung got to the tent, which was equipped with a special "throne," the rain stopped suddenly, and the sun came out. Fryer and others interpreted this coincidence as another positive omen. "The visit was a complete success," wrote Lindner.[36]

Apart from the land, state leaders knew that they needed a strong incentive package. Since the 1970s, when Ohio and Pennsylvania had competed for the Volkswagen plant, states had worked hard to generate well-paying automotive jobs. "Auto plants are among states' most coveted economic development coups," summarized the *Atlanta Journal-Constitution*. "Even the hint of a new auto plant can cause job-hungry states to scramble."[37] Aware of the precedents, Perdue used the $252 million deal that Alabama offered Hyundai as a particular "reference." That agreement placed Georgia in a strong position, as insiders knew that Kia wanted to be near HMMA but was unlikely to go to Alabama. "Hyundai had probably emptied the till in Alabama, as far as incentive money was concerned," summarized Cy Wood, the editor of the *Valley (Ala.) Times-News*, "so by going just a few miles over the state line into Georgia, there was *another* cash register there for incentives to locate a plant."[38] In all, local and state authorities provided Kia with $410 million worth of incentives, $258 million of it from state coffers. Crucially, the state purchased the site for $35.7 million and conducted the site preparation work, including grading, at a cost of $24.8 million. The Department of Transportation agreed to provide road improvements, including the creation of a new interchange and access road from I-85. The state would also spend $6.05 million on a rail spur to the site. Importantly, the company received a 100 percent abatement on state, county, and city property taxes for sixteen years, beginning in 2007. Troup County's Board of Education also agreed to waive half of Kia's property taxes from 2007 until 2016 and 25 percent of its school taxes from 2017 to 2022. Even Kia admitted that the property tax abatements alone were worth more than $130 million. Local authorities and utility providers also agreed to provide about $21 million in infrastructure improvements, mainly in upgrades to water, gas, power, and sewer facilities. Mike Dobbs summed up the thinking behind the document. "Sonny Perdue, the governor, wanted this industry very badly," he recalled, "and we did too."[39]

Apart from these major items, the thirty-eight-page incentives document included a wide range of miscellaneous inducements, including English and Korean classes for key employees, half the bill for the plant's ground-breaking party, and ten prestigious HOPE scholarships for the children of company officials. The state also waived residency requirements for company employees "and their family members" who enrolled in public educational institutions. Funding came from economic development bonds and One Georgia Authority grants. One Georgia, a state agency dedicated to encouraging economic development in rural areas, was slated to receive about $1.6 billion from the state's tobacco settlement.[40] Perhaps the most important item, however, was Georgia's $20 million commitment to construct and operate a 70,000-square-foot training center on the site. Aware that Kia's managers worried about staffing the plant, Perdue assured them that Georgia Quick Start would meet their needs. Part of the Technical College System of Georgia, Quick Start was a workforce training program that had been in operation since the late 1960s. A well-respected initiative, it became a cornerstone of Georgia's ability to attract outside industry. With an annual budget of over $11 million, Quick Start could train the large workforce that Kia needed. According to Lesser, this was a "huge element" of the deal.[41]

The incentives were important to Kia, and key state officials admitted that their bid would not have been competitive without them.[42] Perdue's papers show that Kia pushed hard for a better deal. The company opened talks on February 15, 2006, by requesting $337 million in state support, well above Georgia's offer of $204 million. Lesser also complained that Kia refused to give firm commitments about the number of supplier jobs that it would create. "Company has been very vague about suppliers saying only we will have some that may lead to 1000 hard extra jobs at 2 plants," he reported to Atlanta. Kia was in a strong position, pressing the state to increase its offer to $258 million. By using this figure rather than that of the total package, Perdue's team insisted that costs were on a par with the Hyundai agreement, which had not created as many jobs.[43] Local officials also pushed hard for the deal, agreeing to offer $150 million on top of the state's contribution. In the final round of negotiations, Lesser reported to Clark that he was having to rein in the local delegation: "The community has been very aggressive and supportive.... [T]hey're willing to do almost anything. We've advised them to be prudent." The local team still agreed to additional concessions, including waiving all city and county building permits during initial construction, supplying a sophisticated hazmat vehicle with a "fully trained" response crew, and providing a "rent-free" office building to temporarily house company employees.[44]

For many Koreans, this situation was ironic—and enjoyable. After the Korean War, Korea was virtually devastated, and the fledgling South Korean state depended heavily on U.S. aid. In 1961, South Korea's GNP was just eighty-two dollars per capita. Now, however, the tables were turned, the product of a sustained economic turnaround that was underpinned by the performance of the automotive and electronic sectors. "For Koreans," summarized Joshua Van Lieu, a Korean history specialist at LaGrange College, "there's more than a little bit of pride that, 'Now we can go to America, and save *them*, that they have to come to *us* now.'" According to Rev. James Yu, who had grown up in the devastated Korea of the 1950s, "Everything became rubble, broken. Nobody at that time . . . ever imagined that Korea will ever rise up again." Yu, who led a separate Korean congregation at a local Baptist church, was "proud" of Kia's success.[45]

As scholars have demonstrated, South Korea's "economic miracle" was based on the development of an export-driven economy. During the 1980s, exports comprised over 35 percent of GNP, and by 1990 South Korea was the tenth largest exporter in the world. An export strategy suited a nation that did not have a large domestic market or rich natural resources. Korea's growth was also influenced by rivalry with Japan, its despised colonial ruler. When Hyundai and Kia considered foreign investments, their decisions reflected the moves of their Japanese rivals, who already ran factories in the United States. As Eun Mee Kim has written, "Japanese colonialism (1910–45) left an indelible mark on the Korean economy." Korean automakers wanted to prove that they could operate successful U.S. plants, and they located in areas that avoided competition with the Japanese, especially for labor.[46]

When the plant opened, the Korean press related a sense of satisfaction. "Residents' support for Hyundai and Kia is absolute," noted *Chosŏn ilbo*, a prominent Seoul daily. "Signs all over town read, 'Thank you for sending Kia.'" The paper noted that productivity in West Point was higher than in Kia's domestic factories and stressed the benefits that Korean firms had brought to poor American states. It even asserted, "Korean companies flock to the most backward region of the United States," yet few Americans were aware of these views. Koreans who moved to Troup County, usually from Seoul, shared this shock at how small and rural the area was. "To me, Seattle is America, New York is America," commented Kilsup Yoon, who moved from Seattle to Georgia in 2011. "This is a different part of America, like seeing the countryside, with the pasture, and the horses." There was considerable culture shock; in 2000, for example, Asians comprised just 2 percent of the South's population, and most lived in urban areas.[47]

In the United States, the incentive deal attracted considerable attention. The *New York Times* called it "one of the biggest packages in memory." Ultimately, however, financial considerations could not explain Kia's decision. To try and beat Georgia, Mississippi offered an unprecedented $1 billion incentive package—including $240 million from Hurricane Katrina relief—if Kia came to Columbus. Reflecting a common view, Joe Max Higgins, head of economic development in the eastern Mississippi city, boasted that the plant could be bought. He compared the situation to shopping for shoes: "You go in and ask for size 8D in black with tassels, and they say, 'No, we don't have them,' and you leave to go to another store, but on the way out, a new delivery comes in." For Higgins, Mississippi was in a "war," and it was determined to win.[48]

This confidence was misplaced. Apart from incentives, the positioning of the West Point site was crucial. "It's just the location," summarized West Point mayor Billy Head, who helped negotiate the deal. "We are about 86 miles from Atlanta, and 86 miles from Montgomery." In contrast, Columbus, Mississippi, was not near an interstate; it was farther from major cities—especially Atlanta and Montgomery—and the area around it was rural. As *Automotive News* reported, concerns about the smaller population—Columbus was home to only twenty-six thousand people—led Kia to reject Mississippi's $1 billion offer. The West Point area contained thousands of displaced textile workers. Kia leaders knew that the plant could tap into plenty of employees, and Quick Start assuaged fears that they would not be qualified. Proximity to a major international port at Savannah—one of the busiest in the country—was also important. Being close to Hyundai was, however, vital. "Our first priority in selecting a site was to maximize synergy with Hyundai's Alabama plant," explained Kim Seung-Tack, who headed Kia's Global Strategy Group. "Other considerations included the availability of a qualified work force, logistics and transportation infrastructure, and the incentive package."[49]

The personal connections formed between company and state officials were again decisive. As Kia's key figure on the ground, Ahn Byung Mo had a soft spot for the West Point site—Head described him as "smitten" with the location. Ahn was a reserved man, and the bonds that he forged with the local team, particularly Perdue and Lesser, were vital. Rejecting Mississippi's offer, he cited the importance of these links: "It's like we are dating seriously and thinking of marriage. An increased dowry is not a factor. We fell in love."[50]

Other pressures pushed Kia to expand production abroad—and made Georgia attractive. In Korea, Kia had to deal with a unionized workforce that regularly struck for higher wages and better conditions. "For years," summarized *Automotive News* in 2004, "the Korean assembly lines of Kia and its parent Hyundai often have been stopped by workers who are part of one of the strongest labor unions in a country known for militant labor." In the summer of 1998, strikes in South Korea crippled exports, preventing the Hyundai group from meeting global demand.[51] As Kia looked for a U.S. site, the issue was urgent. In August 2005, the Korean Confederation of Trade Unions, which had more than twenty-seven thousand members at Kia, extended a strike in search of an 8.4 percent wage increase and improved bonus payments. More than 70 percent of Hyundai's 42,500-member union had also walked out. Some analysts saw labor militancy in South Korea as a "key hurdle" for the Hyundai group, which had ambitious global growth plans. In September, when Kia settled the dispute by giving workers a 6.9 percent wage hike, the company estimated that it had lost over $400 million. Managers looked to escape these problems. According to Nathan Jung, who had worked for Kia in Seoul, "In Korea the union is such a big headache for the employers, and always they're asking something more." In contrast, the American South was attractive because it was "union-free."[52]

As James Cobb and others have documented, the South also had a long history of attracting industry by selling the availability of "cheap, non-union labor." Most southern states were also right-to-work states. Georgia led the way; in 1947, straight after passage of the Taft-Hartley Act, which curtailed union rights nationally, the Peach State passed one of the first right-to-work laws.[53] To attract industry, Georgia's officials had long focused on the union issue. By the twenty-first century, the Department of Economic Development boasted that the Peach State had "the third-lowest manufacturing unionization rate in the U.S.," and companies that located there could rely on a "reliable workforce with low turnover rates in a right-to-work state." In 2008, less than 5 percent of Georgians belonged to unions, compared to 12.4 percent nationally (and more in traditional automotive states such as Michigan and Ohio).[54]

In Troup County, officials were even more candid. Since the 1970s, local boosters had lured around sixty companies—including ExxonMobil Chemical and Duracell—to a 2,500-acre industrial park in LaGrange. None of them were union. "We wanted nonunion; we felt very strongly [about] that," recalled Fryer, the long-serving president of the chamber of commerce. "We would not talk to anybody that we knew right off the bat was going to unionize, and today we still don't have any unionized companies here." As other local officials pointed out, Troup County had a long history of attracting industry on these grounds. "We're an antiunion community," summarized county commissioner Ricky Wolfe. "I think that's a plus." In their dealings with Kia, local officials aggressively sold their antiunion credentials and had the record to back them up.[55]

This pitch mattered. The union issue, recalled Lindner, had "a lot to do" with Kia's move to West Point, as the company wanted to escape the "highly unionized" environment in Korea. When Kia built its plant in Slovakia in 2004–5, managers made this clear, even though unions were what *Automotive News* called "the norm" in the central European country. "The management [of the Slovak plant] without labor unions is [Kia's] basic principle," commented Bae In-Kyu, president of Kia Motors Slovakia.[56] In Georgia, Kia did not discuss the union issue directly, yet management referred to workers as "team members" and "family," encouraging identification with the company. The support of state agencies for the firm's position also made unionization unlikely.[57]

Once Mississippi's offer was spurned, personal connections remained critical. In the closing days of negotiations, state officials met with Kia's representatives in Atlanta, determined to secure an agreement before the Koreans flew home. Drawing on Georgian hospitality, Lesser arranged for the two teams to meet at the Atlanta Fish Market one Friday night. The teams talked in the bar and then over dinner, relaxing as they hammered out the final terms. "We took the bar tab and wrote on the back of it the five or six things we had not agreed on, and beside each a number, the dollar figure we were apart on each issue," he recalled. "We slipped that tab back and forth across the table for about twenty minutes, each time crossing out the old number and writing a new one." Eventually, the two sides found common ground; they shook hands at 7:30 p.m. While the state had increased the size of its incentive package, Kia had firmed up its supplier numbers, agreeing to bring five major firms—and an extra twenty-six hundred jobs—to Georgia. After sending Perdue an email that read, "We have a deal," Lesser celebrated. "I felt great that night," he recalled. On March 12, the pair led a delegation of state and local officials to Seoul to sign the contract. The team only stayed in Korea for a day, but they visited Rolling Hills (Hyundai-Kia's five-star training center), had an eight-course dinner with Chairman Chung, and were ferried everywhere by private helicopter. It was quite an experience.[58]

In October 2006, Perdue and Chung hosted the official ground-breaking ceremony at the site, where farmland had been transformed into cleared and level dirt. Inside a tent full of dignitaries, the two leaders gave each other commemorative plaques and led a dirt-shoveling ceremony. The event was carefully managed, with local officials told to greet the Koreans but not to comment further. Those who gave speeches—such as Tim Duffey, the chairman of the Troup County Board of Commissioners—had their remarks prepared for them by the state. "They wanted it short and sweet," recalled Duffey. During the event, the local community also spent almost $24,000 on "in-kind" expenses, providing their overseas visitors with—among other things—personalized gifts, free golf carts, and high-speed internet access.[59] Related infrastructure improvements were soon under way. Costing $81 million, the new diamond-shaped interchange on Interstate 85 was a huge undertaking in its own right. The project included the construction of two new bridges, as well as 5 miles of new road. At its heart was Kia Boulevard, a landscaped thoroughfare that led directly to the plant. In December 2008, after eighteen months of work, the interchange was opened.[60]

Construction of the plant itself encountered some difficulties. In the spring of 2006, several Hyundai group executives became embroiled in a corruption scandal in Korea, stalling the decision-making process. In May, *Automotive News* reported that the West Point plant was surrounded by "uncertainty," as Chairman Chung had been indicted on embezzlement charges, while Kia boss Chung Eiu-Sun was also under investigation.[61] As a result, the ground-breaking ceremony, which was scheduled for April, had to be put back twice until Chung was released. Other problems, including "overcapacity in Asia and difficulty obtaining financing," held up construction of the plant, which was originally supposed to open in early 2009. Still, company and state officials argued that the delay—the factory opened in February 2010—was minor. Privately, however, state leaders knew that any holdup would cost Kia "substantial amounts of money." It also caused frustration and anxiety locally. As Duffey admitted, the embezzlement scandal "cast a shadow on the whole project," and rumors were rife that the plant would never open.[62]

In January 2008, however, a significant breakthrough occurred when officials proudly announced that Kia was "Now Hiring!" In an industry first, interested applicants had to apply exclusively online either from home or at one of Georgia's fifty-three Department of Labor Career Centers. The response illustrated the depressed economy, as Kia received 43,013 applications for 1,200 first-shift jobs. In the spring of 2010, the company also got 31,000 applications for 1,200 second-shift positions. "We were clearly heading, not downhill, we were already in the tank," admitted Drew Ferguson, referring to the area before Kia opened.[63] Some 97 percent of first-shift applicants had a high school education. "In my experience," commented Randy Jackson, Kia's human resources manager, "attracting such a high-quality pool of applicants in such large numbers so quickly is unprecedented." The state-funded Kia Georgia

Training Center was responsible for screening and training workers. The first building constructed on the site, the center housed advanced equipment, including welding and electronic labs and "state-of-the-art programmable logic controllers."[64]

Locating in the Deep South also brought ongoing economic benefits. Wages at Kia, while attractive to many, were lower than industry norms. Production workers started at $14.90 an hour and could progress to a top of $23.50 an hour. Jackson argued that Kia was justified in paying less than its competitors. "Toyota, Hyundai, Mercedes, Honda—anybody who's out there, you have to look at them," he explained. "But you also have to look at the maturity of their facilities. We have to compare ourselves to other start-ups." Toyota workers in Kentucky earned twenty-seven to thirty dollars an hour—comparable to the wages of UAW members—but employees in newer plants farther south made less. As the Big Three—and the UAW—steadily weakened, new factories could pay less.[65]

Many of those hired had worked in textiles, an industry that paid poorly by manufacturing standards. In addition, Kia liked these applicants because they had factory experience, including familiarity with shifts. Because unions had never organized much of the textile industry, displaced mill workers were also used to nonunion environments.[66] While Kia did not divulge the racial makeup of its workforce, the company hired many African Americans, particularly in production areas. Again, many of these workers came from textiles. In order to avoid EEOC charges, Kia had to ensure that its workforce reflected the racial makeup of the area. (In 2000, Troup County was 31.9 percent black.) Nevertheless, some local officials remembered that Kia's managers, accustomed to an ethnically homogeneous society, had arrived with very different racial attitudes. "When they came they would ask us, 'Do we have to hire black people, or do we have to pay black people the same?'" recalled Ray Coulombe, "and I said [laugh], 'Wait a minute, first of all, you can't talk like that around here,' and we gave them a culture primer." Learning local mores, managers adjusted.[67]

As promised, Kia brought with it many suppliers, and these jobs were also popular. Because Kia used a just-in-time production system, which relied on regular parts deliveries rather than holding large inventories, many suppliers established facilities near the plant. The first supplier to ink a deal, in August 2007, was Hyundai Mobis. The largest auto parts company in South Korea, Mobis constructed a 310,000-square-foot facility, which supplied a variety of major components, on the Kia site. In December 2007, Sewon Precision, another big Kia supplier, announced that it would build its first U.S. plant in LaGrange. These firms were soon joined by Sejong, a muffler-maker, and Glovis, which carried out predelivery work for Kia. By June 2008, following further announcements, Perdue claimed that the plant had created six thousand jobs.

"Automotive suppliers are flocking to West Georgia in order to provide services to Kia and the other automakers in the Southeast," he boasted.[68]

Latching on to these claims, the national media portrayed Kia's arrival as an unalloyed success story, describing West Point in a particularly positive light. One *New York Times* headline—"Auto Plant Breathes New Life into Mill Town That Was Fading Away"—was representative. In 2010, *USA Today* reporter Larry Copeland similarly claimed that the West Point area had a "new heart." Copeland cited projections that the plant would create twenty thousand new jobs over a nine-county area of Georgia and Alabama, generating an annual economic impact in Georgia alone of $4 billion a year. The press also claimed that an influx of Korean managers had increased cultural diversity in West Point, where a former KFC had become a popular Korean restaurant.[69]

This coverage went too far. The $4 billion figure came from a Georgia Tech study of the plant's projected impact, yet the state had commissioned this analysis. It was based on optimistic modeling that the twenty thousand new jobs would be created within two years. In fact, in 2011, even Kia claimed that it had created around ten thousand jobs, three thousand of them at the plant.[70] The number of new positions did not replicate the amount lost as other manufacturing industries, particularly textiles, collapsed over several decades. Many of those laid off by the mills were over forty-five and lacked high school diplomas, making them uncompetitive for automotive positions. As state labor commissioner Michael Thurmond explained, "Not everyone will benefit [from Kia] unless they are educated, skilled, or trainable." This proved to be the case. "That's one of the big criticisms," admitted former tax assessor David Noles, "because we had all those jobs, but very few people in Troup County were qualified for them."[71]

Still, many locals tried. The number of applicants for entry-level jobs at suppliers—where wages were lower—was indicative. In February 2009, more than three thousand people stood in line for hours to apply for six hundred jobs at Sewon that paid ten dollars an hour.[72] In November 2011, unemployment in the West Point area stood at 11 percent. While the figure was trending downward (it was 16 percent two years earlier), it remained high. Even Mayor Ferguson, an enthusiastic Kia supporter, admitted that the area had lost at least sixteen thousand jobs over the previous twenty years, more than the automaker had created. To be sure, conditions were much better than they would have been without Kia, but the situation was not as rosy as outside journalists—and Perdue's office—proclaimed. Most postindustrial towns, moreover, could not attract automotive plants; there were not enough to go around.[73]

Although cars were being built in Georgia again, experienced autoworkers were among the losers. In particular, displaced union members from the Ford and GM plants in Atlanta complained that they could not get hired. "I guess because of their ties with the UAW, we haven't been able to get anybody signed on at that [Kia] plant," charged Zane Payne, a union official in Atlanta. In response, Kia insisted that it would train workers from the bottom up, yet it did not address the union issue directly. Others did. Mikell Fryer, an official at the Georgia Department of Labor, admitted that former UAW members would not be considered because "Kia runs a nonunion assembly plant." Locally, it was well-known that the union workers were not welcome at Kia. "We had two automotive plants close in Atlanta during this process," related Lindner, "the Ford and General Motor plants, and . . . they [Kia] didn't want those folks."[74] The state was again very accommodating. In December 2011, a group of former GM and Ford workers sued the state because it had failed to release records about Kia's screening process. Soon afterward, the legislature amended the Open Records Act, inserting an exemption for records that related to a training program. This exemption was retroactive and could be used to withhold documents sought by a lawsuit. In November 2013, moreover, the Georgia Supreme Court ruled in favor of the state, decreeing that it did not have to divulge its records because they were trade secrets.[75]

The new jobs also had a cost. Some questioned the price of the incentive package, especially as Kia enjoyed generous waivers on property taxes. These breaks came at the expense of Troup County's schools, where ACT scores were below the state average (which was itself below national norms). In 2013–14, the graduation rate in Troup County's schools was 71 percent, much lower than the national average of 82 percent. "Troup's schools need improvement, not financial sacrifice," declared the *Atlanta Journal-Constitution*. When Kia made its announcement, a renowned annual ranking of education placed Georgia forty-first.[76] Tacitly admitting the problem, in 2015 Kia became a "founding investor" of the THINC College and Career Academy, a public charter school designed to increase the graduation rate and produce work-ready students. Locally, most residents defended the abatements, arguing that the tax value of the site had jumped. As Noles recalled, however, there were off-the-record complaints from existing employers, who had not been treated as generously, as well as from farmers. Property owners near the site were also unhappy, as they received no compensation and grumbled about increased traffic, noise, and roadside garbage. Apart from Kia, moreover, many suppliers received assistance. In June 2009, Kumho Tire Georgia and Sewon were awarded $3.8 million and $5 million, respectively, from One Georgia.[77]

Inside the plant, conditions were not as idyllic as the company claimed. Few workers were willing to publicly speak out, but in private forums, many complained about autocratic management, arduous rotating shifts, and the isolated location of the plant. There was also tension between Korean executives and local workers, as managers—most of them on short-term contracts from Seoul—put in extremely long hours and expected the same level of dedication from their employees.[78] Some Korean residents spoke to these issues.

"To Korean managers, not only blacks but the white people, they are lazy," explained Kilsup Yoon. "They don't have like hardworking mentality, so that's the biggest problem." In return, added Korean American Young Brown, locals saw the Koreans as "workaholics." Koreans, summarized Ricky Wolfe, were "extremely demanding to work for. It is their culture, and it is their style."[79]

Out in the community, there were other tensions. Many jobs went to Alabamians, who had not paid to secure the plant. Alabama officials claimed that one-quarter of Kia's workforce came from their state, but Georgia leaders insisted that the figure was lower. While Georgia's government wanted to prioritize its citizens, Kia insisted that all applicants were treated equally, even though the Quick Start program, funded by Georgia taxpayers, trained out-of-state hires. As the *Atlanta Journal-Constitution* noted bluntly, Alabama was "poised to horn in" on Georgia's "Kia party" "without paying a dime of incentives."[80] Across Georgia, some voters disparaged the incentive package on these grounds.[81] It was a criticism that irked those on the Alabama side of the line. "Instead of blaming people from Alabama for working in Kia," thought Cy Wood, "you ought to blame the people in Georgia who aren't qualified to work at Kia."[82]

The scramble for jobs revealed a bigger problem. As local officials admitted, the region around West Point had become too dependent on the automotive sector, a problem not recognized—at least publicly—by state leaders. "At one time it was all textile," related Fryer, "and we were leaning heavily that way. Now we're automotive, and if anything should happen—God forbid it ever happening—we're going to be where we were . . . when what happened with the textile industry." West Point's former vice mayor, Donald Gilliam, shared this concern: "Now, instead of textiles dominating . . . it's automotive dominated, so still we'll have basically all of our eggs in one basket." Many residents were worried, especially as the plant could close when the incentives stopped. Leaders of neighboring counties were also concerned. In Harris County, a new industrial park housed six companies, and five of them were Kia suppliers. "Part of the strategy is to diversify that business park," commented Colin Martin, the president of the chamber of commerce, "get some other businesses in there so that we're not quite so heavily dependent, not just on the automotive industry, but specifically the Kia plant."[83]

In West Point itself, the plant's benefits were not as great as the media reported. A lifelong resident, Gilliam, who was African American, was well aware of this. Despite the positive headlines, the city's population was not increasing, and Kia had not had a huge transformative impact. Between 2000 and 2010, West Point's population actually decreased, from 3,545 to 3,474, continuing a long-term pattern. "West Point, it's not growing," noted Gilliam. "If you don't grow, I don't see how you can be progressing." In 2014, the census estimated that West Point's population had increased slightly, to 3,770, but the city remained disproportionately poor and African American.[84] Over 33 percent of residents lived in poverty, and more than 60 percent of the population was black. Even white business leaders acknowledged the problems. "We still have a tremendous amount of poverty," admitted Drew Ferguson III.[85]

Poverty was especially evident in the desolate mill villages located just outside downtown, where low-income residents, most of them African American or Latino, congregated because the housing was cheap. Yet reporters who wrote about West Point failed to mention the mill villages. In these once-vibrant communities, most of the mills had been demolished, leaving empty blocks and few services or stores. Despite a limited revival, even downtown West Point had not recaptured its past glory, when it had supported a wide variety of retail outlets, including six furniture stores and major department store chains. None of these stores remained. The problems in West Point, which also lacked its own high school and had a shortage of good-quality housing, meant that few Kia employees lived there. This disappointed local people, particularly realtors. White-collar employees, especially Korean managers, gravitated to communities with stronger retail and educational facilities, particularly Auburn in Alabama and Newnan and Peachtree City in Georgia. "The Korean believes that Newnan or Auburn, those *city*, their education system is better than LaGrange or West Point," summarized Jung. Although Newnan was forty minutes away, Jung lived there. Kia staff stopped in West Point to eat at the city's two Korean restaurants—these were the Koreans noticed by the press—but they did not put down roots. As Yoon put it, "West Point doesn't have any culture. . . . No one regards that as a residential area. . . . It's so desolate, and you feel *so* bad."[86]

In other parts of the county, poverty was also a problem. Although it had a more vibrant downtown, LaGrange was home to several struggling mill villages. Between 2009 and 2013, census data showed that 23.6 percent of Troup County's residents lived below the poverty line, considerably higher than the state average of 18.2 percent. According to Alton West, LaGrange's African American community development director, the city had "its fair share" of poverty, "and maybe a little bit more." Like many residents, West had anticipated that Kia would lead to "more growth than it actually has." In 2018, LaGrange mayor Jim Thornton admitted that the city still had "a lot" of old mill village housing, much of it in "disrepair." Upgrading these neighborhoods, where most houses were privately owned, was a "hard struggle."[87]

Still, residents were appreciative. "It would have been rough without it [the Kia plant]," admitted Gilliam, "no doubt about that, especially with all the mills being dismantled." In most other southern textile communities, displaced mill workers faced long-term joblessness or found work in lower-paid industries, usually in the service sector. In 2012, the area also received a boost when Point University, a small private Christian college, moved its main campus from

The water tower in the city of West Point, Georgia, pictured in early 2020. Emblazoned with Kia's logo, the tower is visible to drivers on busy Interstate 85, as is the giant Kia plant nearby. Courtesy of Kaye Minchew.

East Point (part of Atlanta), basing itself in the old WestPoint Stevens headquarters. The college's move led to the refurbishment of several buildings, and there were plans to build a twelve-hundred-seat chapel. Although Kia's arrival had created tension and criticism—and its impact on the local community was more complex than the media suggested—overall it was a story of job creation and reindustrialization rather than the narrative of decline that is usually associated with the automobile industry, especially during the Great Recession.[88]

For Kia, the move to Georgia was undoubtedly successful. The factory originally produced the Kia Sorento, but subsequent expansions led to it also making the Kia Optima and Hyundai Santa Fe (reaffirming the importance of proximity to HMMA). On July 11, 2013, after just three and a half years of production, West Point made its one millionth vehicle. There were also expansions at suppliers, some of them assisted by LaGrange Development Authority bonds.[89] The Kia story also had broader economic—and political—consequences. As the *Journal-Constitution* reported, snaring the plant was an "election year bonus" for Perdue. The governor's local campaign manager, Colin Martin, described the announcement as "one of the very defining moments of his governorship. . . . It was electrifying." Georgia's first Republican governor since Reconstruction, Perdue won reelection in 2006 by an increased margin and subsequently enjoyed high approval ratings. Term-limited, he stood down in 2010 but was succeeded by another Republican, Nathan Deal.[90] Within the business community, the deal brought Georgia considerable kudos. In 2006, largely due to Kia, *Area Development* magazine gave Georgia its Gold Shovel award for job creation. Downplaying the costs of the deal, Perdue repeatedly used the case to defend his political record, proving—he argued—that serious investment could be attracted beyond Atlanta.[91]

The factory gave Kia visibility, helping it become one of the fastest-growing brands in the country. Between 2009 and 2016, Kia's share of the U.S. market rose from 2.83 to 3.62 percent. The massive plant—along with a water tower displaying the words "Kia, West Point, Georgia"—was clearly visible to drivers on I-85, a major regional artery. At night, rows of powerful lights illuminated the building, making it impossible to miss. Kia's website boasted that two popular models were made in the United States, and the company even parked a full-size Sorento inside Atlanta's international airport, along with a sign proclaiming: "Built with pride in West Point, Georgia."[92] At the 2015 Super Bowl, Kia advertised the new Sorento with a sixty-second spot featuring the movie actor Pierce Brosnan, while press releases emphasized that the vehicle was made in Georgia. Another Sorento commercial was filmed in Troup County, though "scenic locations" in LaGrange were prioritized over West Point. Kia's vehicles were a common sight on the area's roads, and Drew Ferguson III was among those who refused to drive anything else. "Without Kia," he declared in 2015, "this would literally be a ghost town." The remark epitomized how Kia had brought growth—and the return of economic dependence—to the West Point area.[93]

EPILOGUE

In the decade after Kia's arrival, America's other automakers continued to thrive. Even during the Great Recession, the worst global downturn since World War II, the sector advanced. In December 2008, at the height of the crisis, Toyota workers in America were training or cleaning—but they still had jobs. At other Japanese plants, the situation was similar. "They never had a layoff. . . . Everybody got, even if they cut back on their hours working, everybody still got a full paycheck," summarized Mike Woods, discussing Nissan's operations in Tennessee. The foreign-owned plants, added the *New York Times*, had "deep pockets and ample credit," so they fared better than GM and Chrysler, which had to be rescued by a $17 billion federal bailout. The buyout further strengthened the transplant sector's position. "When your competitor is struggling or goes out of business," commented scholar Matthew Slaughter, "that tends to be a good thing for you if you are one of the stronger companies like Toyota and Honda."[1]

Although subsequent crises tested the industry, it continued to grow. In March 2011, a tsunami brought the Japanese industry "to its knees," leading to temporary plant closures by Honda, Mitsubishi, Nissan, Subaru, and Toyota. In the United States, however, foreign automakers again stayed open. "Toyota, unofficially, has a no-layoff policy," recalled Georgetown manager Wayne Robey. "When they had the big tsunami in Japan . . . there were some parts that we got from there that we couldn't get. . . . And so there was some downtime then, but here again, no one gets laid off." Designed to increase workers' investment in their job, the strategy was a long-standing fixture of Asian carmakers. At a time when millions of American workers were retrenched, it was a powerful selling point.[2]

Even in difficult times, there were new arrivals. In 2008, Volkswagen announced that it would build a new plant in Chattanooga, creating over two thousand jobs. Again, there was fierce interstate bidding. The year before, Toyota had opened a plant in Tupelo, Mississippi, choosing the location over Chattanooga (which had also bid for Kia in 2005–6). Keen not to lose out, Republican governor Bill Haslam and U.S. senator Bob Corker helped arrange $577 million of incentives for VW. The company also chose the Tennessee site, however, because it had access to two major interstate highways, as well as proximity to major markets in Nashville and Atlanta. Once again, incentives were not the whole story.[3]

As the industry recovered from the Great Recession, other plants followed. In 2015, Volvo announced a plant in Berkeley County, South Carolina, its first in the United States. While the Deep South location had many precedents, this was the first transplant in a coastal area. Highlighting the industry's global nature, it was also the first time that a Chinese-owned automaker had opened a U.S. factory. (In 2010, Volvo had been acquired by Geely Motors.) Further investment by Chinese automakers and suppliers was anticipated, especially as China was now the world's largest auto market.[4] Avoiding competition with BMW, Volvo located its plant on the other side of the state. The company was lured to the area by a familiar range of factors, including generous incentives, a large and flat site, proximity to transport links (especially Interstate 26 and a major port), and the availability of "well-trained" workers. Managers also selected an area that locals described as economically "depressed," producing a scramble for jobs (and making unionization unlikely). "The South Carolina factory is very important for Volvo," explained North American CEO Lex Kerssemakers. "It is a very clear signal that we are dedicated to the U.S. market." Beginning production in 2018, the plant created four thousand jobs.[5]

The other major announcement occurred in Alabama, cementing its status as a new automotive powerhouse. In January 2018, Toyota and Mazda declared that they would build a $1.6 billion joint venture near Huntsville. Even before the plant was announced, Alabama tied with Tennessee as the fifth largest producer of vehicles in the country. The new facility added significantly to these numbers, as it was set to employ over four thousand people. To land the plant, Governor Kay Ivey offered $370 million in subsidies, including the key element of worker training. A location close to other transplants, especially Toyota's engine factory in Huntsville, was important. Suggesting personal connections, Aiko Toyoda also described the move as a homecoming. The industry's rise, concluded *Automotive News*, showed "no signs of letting up."[6]

Existing transplants also grew. Confounding the recession, there were major expansions by Hyundai in Alabama (2011), Nissan in Tennessee (2012), and Toyota in Kentucky (2013). In Smyrna, Nissan started to make the Leaf, an innovative and affordable electric vehicle (EV) that foretold the industry's future. The new lithium-ion battery plant was one of the first in the world to be operated by a mainstream automaker, and Nissan was also the first company to manufacture battery components and packs in the United States. Funding the plant cost $1.7 billion, most of which was provided by a United States Department of Energy loan. At the same time as EVs were being developed, buyers also flocked to high-end conventionally powered vehicles. Here again, the sector was a pioneer. In 2013, Toyota began to make Lexus models in Kentucky, the first time the luxury vehicles had been produced in America. Mercedes also began to make luxury AMG models in Alabama. After nervous starts, both plants had come a long way.[7]

As these expansions showed, the foreign-owned sector had some significant advantages. While the Detroit Three relied heavily on the North American market, the transplants exported more. Mercedes and BMW sent their American-made vehicles around the globe, giving the industry widespread recognition. Most were SUVs, and the sector also did well because it had anticipated the growth of these vehicles, developing pathbreaking models. "This SUV segment is the most growing segment in the last ... twenty years," summarized a senior Mercedes executive in 2018. Making more SUVs than the domestics, especially popular "crossover" models, the transplants thrived. In 2016 and 2017, on the back of booming SUV sales, Mercedes became the world's biggest luxury automaker.[8]

As the sector grew, it made history. In 2018, *Automotive News* reported the "latest milestone" in the sector's "steady rise," as foreign-owned plants were on track to account for more than half of North American production for the first time. In 2017, domestic manufacturers represented 50.7 percent of production, compared to 49.3 percent for foreign automakers. As recently as 2007, the figures were 63 and 37 percent. Demand for international nameplates was strong; in 2017, they had a 54.4 percent market share and made six of the top ten selling vehicles. Several of these models—including the Honda Civic, Nissan Rogue, Toyota Camry, and Toyota Corolla—were produced in the United States.[9]

Japanese companies remained the sector's heart. In 2017, the Japanese Automobile Manufacturers Association documented that its members produced nearly four million vehicles in the United States, a tenfold increase since the industry's birth. "From their initial investments in the early 1980s to the present, the history of Japanese-brand automakers in the U.S. is one of growth, economic and community integration," wrote director Manny Manriquez. According to the association, Japanese automakers supported 1.5 million direct, intermediate, or spinoff jobs in the United States. The top selling passenger cars in the country, the Civic and Camry, were made in foundational transplants. In 2017, Americans bought 764,000 of these two cars, more than twice Honda's total U.S. sales when HAM was established.[10]

The industry's growth also reframes scholarship. Most work has focused on the domestic companies, especially in the era before the foreign-owned plants arrived. Focusing heavily on communities in the upper Midwest, the existing narrative needs revision, especially given the foreign-owned sector's size and maturity. Overseas automakers took the industry into new parts of the United

States, making it much more geographically dispersed. Offering a story of growth, this industry also challenges the narrative of decline that dominates scholarship on the auto sector.[11] *America's Other Automakers* also challenges work that has been completed on the transplants, most of which has reached positive conclusions. This book is driven by a more critical argument, one that recognizes the industry's benefits *and* costs. There was more to this story than grateful communities and contented workers. Across the sector, residents opposed costly incentive packages, which were granted by some of the poorest states in the country. Local people worried about the negative impact of the plants, particularly increased traffic, pollution, and unsustainable growth. There were battles over land, as residents were pressured to sell by boosters, especially governors. Inside the plants, workloads were high and injuries common; many workers sought a better deal. At the newest plants, these tensions have continued. When Volvo announced its U.S. factory, not all locals shared Governor Nikki Haley's enthusiasm that this was a "great day in South Carolina." "We don't want congestion," summarized landowner Harold Fitzgerald, voicing familiar complaints.[12]

Even at "model" factories, labor tensions were a constant. "There's still . . . union interest out there," admitted Robey at Toyota in Kentucky, a prize-winning plant that was widely praised.[13] During and after the Great Recession, the industry hired more temps to slash production costs, contracting with third-party agencies like Yates Services and Kelly Services to do so. Although companies promised to make these workers permanent, most became stuck. Lacking job security, they exposed how many workers—even when they got jobs at the plants—were excluded from the industry's promise of upward mobility. "No one's really worried about the fact that you're so exhausted from working seven days a week, you're dependent on some drug to stay awake, or dependent on drugs to go to sleep, or for pain," summarized Chris Young, a per-matemp at Nissan. Adding to their problems, temps were usually unable to vote in NLRB elections because they were not "employees." According to historian Andrew C. McKevitt, these workers were part of the "precariat," a growing group in the neoliberal era who suffered from "helplessness and victimization."[14]

Responding to the complaints of temporary and permanent workers, the UAW ran two major campaigns after 2010, at VW in Chattanooga and at Nissan in Canton, Mississippi. The *Washington Post* called the VW drive a "big deal," especially as it came after "nearly three decades" of organizing in the sector. The 2017 Canton vote, added *The Guardian*, was "potentially historic," symbolizing labor's efforts to penetrate the South, where multinationals had flocked to take advantage of "lower wages and non-union workforces." Although neither campaign gave the UAW the big breakthrough it wanted, workers were given a stronger voice.[15]

Chattanooga was a close call. Like earlier organizing drives, it showed that transplant workers had plenty of grievances, particularly about fast-paced work and demanding managers. "It was their way or no way," summarized one. The UAW also worked hard—in cooperation with German unions—to extract a neutrality pledge from Volkswagen. With the company on the sidelines, the union seemed on the cusp of a long-awaited victory.[16] The UAW was unprepared, however, for the intense opposition it encountered from almost all of Tennessee's Republican politicians, as well as powerful conservative activists and national lobby groups. In emotive appeals, conservative leaders threatened that the plant would close if workers unionized. Corker and other Republicans intimated that Volkswagen would manufacture its new SUV—a crucial model—in Chattanooga rather than Mexico if the UAW was kept out. Republican leaders threatened to withhold state incentives if this was not the case. According to veteran organizer Larry Steele, such opposition was "not new" but became "more in the open" after 2010, when the Republicans swept Congress.[17] In February 2014, the union was narrowly defeated, 712 votes to 626. Encouraged by the close margin, the UAW fought on, later winning a ballot among skilled trades workers that helped to secure concessions from VW. In June 2019, however, the UAW lost another plant-wide vote 833–766 after facing fierce conservative opposition, particularly from governor Bill Lee. VW, moreover, increasingly deferred to local mores, claiming—like many automakers before it—that unionization was up to workers.[18]

As it fought on in Tennessee, the union faced other problems. Between 2017 and 2019, the UAW suffered from a series of corruption scandals involving the alleged misuse of union funds for personal expenses. In November 2019, the escalating scandal led to the resignation of UAW president Gary Jones, while six ex-officials pleaded guilty to corruption charges. In related developments, GM filed suit against Fiat Chrysler Automobiles, charging that the company bribed UAW officials in order to gain favorable labor contracts that disadvantaged GM. The UAW, summarized *Automotive News*, was in "crisis." Although the union took significant steps to address the issues, the allegations, which were well-publicized by the media, further hampered organizing. In particular, they helped validate conservative efforts to roll back labor rights.[19]

Events in Mississippi also proved frustrating for the union, partly because early signs were promising. Unlike Chattanooga, Canton had a majority-black workforce, and many African Americans—complaining about overbearing supervisors, heavy workloads, and racial discrimination—were particularly alienated. "They don't want that line to stop for nothing," summarized one supporter. Proceeding gradually, the UAW mobilized black workers with an innovative campaign that stressed that "Labor Rights are Civil Rights." Backing also came from powerful national politicians, including Bernie Sanders and DNC chair Tom Perez, as well as celebrities such as actor Danny Glover and musician Common.[20]

The union, however, confronted community and corporate opposition, a formidable combination. Led predominantly by Americans, Nissan responded with a fierce drive against the union, especially when it called a vote. The company utilized many of the techniques that it had perfected in Tennessee, including one-on-one meetings with workers and extensive use of in-plant television. Opposition also came from state and local elites, particularly Republicans. While the union mobilized many blacks, it had less support among whites. Struggling to respond, in August 2017, the UAW lost the vote by a two-to-one margin. The result, the *Detroit News* concluded, was a "devastating defeat." The votes confirmed how difficult it was to organize the new industry, especially as factories were designed so that employees came from a wide geographical area, worked in self-contained teams, and could easily be replaced. Their isolated location—and size—also posed difficulties.[21]

For the UAW, however, all was not lost, especially as the campaigns also confirmed that these workers had many grievances. Despite significant opposition, including threats to close the plants, many workers *still* backed the UAW. Even within these communities, there were plenty of workers, along with residents and unsuccessful job applicants, who did not view the plants in a glowing light. Workers continued to organize, and their efforts helped to keep wages at the plant high. Even at new transplants, wages stayed close to Big Three levels, despite reports of a small gap opening up in entry-level jobs. Things were not as simple as the industry claimed.[22]

The expansions also hurt the union, especially as the domestic companies continued to pink-slip staff. While the relationship between the two sectors was complex—and there was some truth to claims that foreign-owned plants had pushed the domestics to improve vehicle quality—there was no doubt the new industry did not just displace imports. As *Automotive News* put it, the growth of the transplants came "at the expense of the Detroit 3." In 1970, GM employed over four hundred thousand production workers in the United States, but by 2015, only fifty thousand remained. In 2008, top managers went to Washington, where they used to wield enormous power, "hat in hand" to ask for government loans, which averted bankruptcy but led to further job cuts. The foreign-owned plants, while not the only cause, were partly responsible. "They were nonunion, but they didn't make quite the [wage] scale we made," summarized a lifelong GM worker. "We're a shell of what we were. Transplants, imports, and automation is all part of what did that."[23]

The foreign-owned industry had inherent cost advantages. By hiring a new workforce and building greenfield plants, it gained a vital head start. At the Detroit Three, legacy costs, particularly the provision of pensions and health care for retirees, also added between $1,000 and $1,500 to the price of every car. At the foreign-owned plants, workers were newly hired and young, slashing these expenses. In 2008, Toyota U.S.A. supported just seven hundred retirees, compared to more than four hundred thousand at GM. "The transplants have an advantage over domestic producers," summarized the *Chicago Tribune*, "because their plants are newer and more efficient. In addition, the domestic companies have an older work force, with huge pension and health obligations."[24]

With its membership concentrated at the domestics, the UAW was a major casualty of these changes. Between 1990 and 2007, the Detroit Three closed twenty-nine North American factories. Over the same period, UAW membership tumbled from one million to four hundred thousand. In 1990, Owen Bieber admitted that the transplants, which his union had initially encouraged, had become "devastating." Even workers who kept their jobs faced concessionary demands. In 2007, GM placed new hires on separate contracts with lower pay and fewer benefits, a reflection of cost pressures. At the transplants, workers watched—helped by the rise of the Internet and social media—as their domestic counterparts endured layoffs and plant closings. In 2018, they noticed as GM cut another fourteen thousand workers and closed five plants. In the fall of 2019, they observed a month-long strike at GM as UAW members sought to limit concessions and plant closures. In contrast, their factories stayed open.[25]

In a fast-changing industry, however, the foreign-owned sector also faced uncertainty. As this book has highlighted, automaking—like its products—is mobile. During the Great Recession, foreign carmakers increasingly invested in Mexico, where they were lured by a familiar cocktail of financial incentives, worker training programs, and lower wages. By 2018, Honda, Mazda, Nissan, and Volkswagen were all producing vehicles in Mexico, while BMW and Toyota were building plants there. In the United States, many worried that transplants would leave their communities when incentives ran out—if not before.[26] As the *Washington Post*'s Matt McFarland has observed, the entire industry also faced an "uncertain future." Some experts believed that robotic vehicles were about to cause an epochal "disruption," while the car-sharing economy—led by Uber, Lyft, Car2go, and Zipcar—was growing rapidly, threatening traditional ownership patterns. Brash Tesla Motors' chief executive, Elon Musk, pledged to make millions of electric cars a year by 2025, pushing mainstream rivals to develop EVs.[27] Climate change also posed challenges. In 2019, *Automotive News* reported that the global auto industry was experiencing a "big push" into EVs. According to the International Energy Agency, the number of EVs on the world's roads was forecast to rise from 2 million in 2019 to 140 million by 2030. In Europe and China, automakers electrified in response to tightening regulations and received more generous government subsidies. Many transplants, however, made large SUVs and pickups, making them poorly positioned in a changing market.[28]

Other evidence, however, comforted the industry. As *Automotive News* reported in 2019, many young buyers were still attracted to car ownership—and dealerships—even if they needed their parents' help to buy vehicles. Experts pointed out the obstacles that existed before self-driving cars became safe, leaving their mass adoption in doubt. Ride sharing was largely limited to urban areas, where some studies indicated that it increased demand for private cars, particularly new models (which Uber often required). Ride-sharing schemes depended on cars, and driverless vehicles needed to be manufactured. Despite Musk's predictions, EVs also struggled to gain traction, particularly in the United States. In 2018, plug-in EVs comprised just 2 percent of the market.[29]

The industry also responded to new trends, especially as EV sales were predicted to rise. Nissan Leaf production in Tennessee was well-established, while Volvo had big plans for EVs in South Carolina. BMW and Mercedes also announced that they would make electric SUVs in their U.S. plants, mostly for export. In 2019, Vance received $1 billion to build EVs, part of Daimler's plans to electrify its entire vehicle lineup. Other transplants invested in hybrids, which were more accepted by American consumers. In 2019, Toyota pumped $238 million into Georgetown so that it could build new hybrids, including the RAV4. As the *Louisville Courier-Journal* reported, the move boosted the huge facility, especially as the crossover was a best seller.[30]

Ironically, demand for traditional vehicles, particularly large SUVs and pickups, also remained strong. In 2015, an unprecedented 17.4 million cars and light trucks were sold in the United States, and most were SUVs and pickups. Between 2016 and 2018, annual sales stayed above seventeen million, with light trucks continuing to boom. In 2018, for every EV sold, fifty conventionally powered vehicles hit the road. As *International Business Times* concluded in 2019, EVs were some way from "mass adoption." Big-engined vehicles remained especially popular. Highlighting this, as Mercedes electrified, it also announced that it would build an "ultraluxe" SUV in Alabama. Called the Maybach GLS, it cost $200,000 and was powered by a "560-plus" horsepower V-8 engine. The most expensive car to be made in America, it was expected to do well, particularly in the United States and China. "Luxury SUVs are taking off," summarized an analyst. "It's what a big section of the market wants."[31]

As the industry adapted to a changing market, the centrality of carmaking to the American story was reaffirmed. In the 2016 presidential election, Trump's shock victory drew heavily on his promises to bring back industrial jobs and put "America first." A symbol of America's industrial might, the auto industry—both domestic and foreign-owned—was at the heart of his plans. "Trump made US car production a key part of his campaign against Hillary Clinton and won in part with the backing of voters in states with the largest percentage of workers in the sector," summarized *The Guardian*. Automotive-heavy battleground states, including Michigan, Ohio, Pennsylvania, and Wisconsin, all turned red. Trump also swept the transplant belt in the lower Midwest and South. In Spartanburg, home to BMW's massive plant, he won 63 percent of the vote.[32]

The result put pressure on automakers to keep jobs in the United States. Just before Trump's inauguration, Ford canceled a $1.6 billion car plant in Mexico following his criticisms of outsourcing. The move sent "shock waves" through the industry. Trump also pledged to impose a "big border tax" on Toyota if it built a factory in Mexico and spoke out against BMW's plans to move there.[33] Once in office, Trump continued to prioritize the auto industry. "Perhaps no industry could be affected in more ways by the new administration than the auto business," summarized the *New York Times*. The president pressured carmakers to invest in the United States and claimed credit for outcomes even when the reasons for them were complex. In his 2018 State of the Union address, for example, Trump praised Toyota and Mazda's decision to set up their new U.S. plant. Valuable jobs, he insisted, were coming home. In 2019, the president also applauded Toyota's hybrid investment in Georgetown, again suggesting that his policies were responsible. Furthermore, Trump rolled back Obama-era climate change policies, seeking to undermine rules that allowed liberal states—particularly California—to set tighter rules on climate-warming car emissions.[34]

Trump also set about renegotiating NAFTA, pledging to pull the United States out of the treaty if necessary. This would allow the United States to apply tariffs on Mexican goods such as vehicles. As *Automotive News* put it, autos were the "critical issue" in the negotiations, which had "industry-shattering implications."[35] Renegotiating the deal, however, proved difficult. Throughout 2019, Trump urged a divided Congress to ratify his United States–Mexico–Canada Agreement (USMCA), which he pitched as "probably the largest trade deal ever made." USMCA largely preserved the structure and substance of NAFTA but added new features to protect U.S. industry. It required 40–45 percent of vehicle content to come from countries that paid autoworkers at least sixteen dollars an hour—a provision aimed at Mexico—and increased the portion that must originate from within North America from 62.5 to 75 percent. In addition, Mexican workers were given more rights to organize. The Democrats expressed misgivings about the deal, which lacked enforcement, and after the 2018 midterm elections they controlled Congress. In October 2019, *Automotive News Canada* noted that it remained an "open question" whether USMCA would be ratified, especially given the polarized political climate in the United States. In particular, the impeachment enquiry delayed ratification, leaving the industry "stuck in a waiting game." In January 2020, however, the United States Senate passed the deal 89–10 after Democrats negotiated new language that strengthened labor, environmental, and enforcement provisions. The tougher automotive content rules were also approved. On January 29, Trump—claiming that he had ended the NAFTA "nightmare" and asserting that more than seventy-six thousand auto jobs would now be created—signed the new law.[36]

Other parts of Trump's agenda worried the industry. In 2018, one in five cars made in the United States was exported, making the sector vulnerable to changes in trade policy. Relying on global supply chains, companies opposed tariffs on imported parts. Toyota estimated that the cost of its Kentucky-built Camry, which had 30 percent overseas content, would rise by $1,800 if subjected to new tariffs.[37] The industry fought back. In April 2019, Trump stepped away from threats to close the southern border after auto companies pointed out that U.S. plants that relied on Mexican parts would be crippled. The industry's power—and the fact that it was so global—meant that radical changes in trade policy were not achieved.[38]

As the sector faced the future, leaders were upbeat. The "international automakers" argued that they were responsible for the "reinvention" of America's auto industry, creating jobs, raising quality, and helping consumers. According to spokesperson John Bozella, they had "made the American auto industry the most vibrant and competitive in the world." In 2017, foreign automakers made 5.2 million vehicles in the United States, almost half of total production. If these vehicles were parked end to end, they would wrap around the globe. Since the foundation of Honda's plant in Ohio, the industry claimed that it had invested $82 billion into the American economy.[39]

Industry supporters elided costs. There was no mention of the jobs lost as transplants grew, of the expensive incentive packages, or of the opposition that the plants produced. Workplace injuries were not discussed, and labor battles were overlooked. The true amount of U.S. content—a complex measurement—was also glossed over. In 2017, the American Automotive Policy Council, a domestically led organization, asserted that Detroit Three vehicles had higher levels of domestic content (53 percent compared to 35 percent). In response, foreign-owned companies used higher numbers and stressed the scale of their investments in the United States, which were undoubtedly considerable. "We are local," they asserted.[40]

After more than four decades of growth, there was no disputing the foreign-owned sector's size or significance. Set up in 2015, "Here for America," a website sponsored by the foreign-owned industry, was designed to "increase public education" about the sector's importance. Pointing to the site, veteran employees acknowledged criticisms, especially about foreign ownership, yet reminded us of the industry's importance, especially on the ground. "Different ones try to put Toyota in a bad light," summarized Robey. "They say, 'Oh don't buy a Toyota, because it's a Japanese company, and all the profits go back to Japan.' . . . The company's owned by Japan, and by [the] Japanese, but there's so much benefit to us for it being here." As big as their domestic rivals, America's "other" automakers have a rich history, one worthy of serious—and further—exploration.[41]

NOTES

INTRODUCTION

1. "Honda of America Mfg., Inc." (company brochure), n.d. (ca. 1991–92), folder 23, box 255, John Glenn Papers, Ohio State University Archives, Columbus, Ohio (hereafter Glenn Papers); "Establishing Honda of America Manufacturing 1980," Honda Worldwide, accessed June 17, 2020,https://global.honda/heritage/episodes/1980 establishinghondaofamerica.html (chapter 8); "Made Over Here" (Honda advertisement), *Marysville Journal-Tribune*, November 9, 1982, 10; closing quotation in "Honda Auto Production Begins," *Marysville Journal-Tribune*, November 5, 1982, 4.

2. "Japanese Industry Puts Roots in Tennessee Soil," *Chicago Tribune*, March 3, 1985; Alexander, *Steps along the Way*, 129; "Free Toyota Tour" flyer, ca. June 2017 (Toyota Kentucky document); "About TMMK," Toyota Kentucky, accessed July 28, 2017, http:// toyotaky.com/boutdex.asp.

3. For a helpful overview of the emergence of the "transplant" sector, see Doron P. Levin, "'Transplant' Car Makers Redefine the Industry," *New York Times*, June 23, 1992, D7. As in Levin's article, the term "transplant" was sometimes put in quotation marks, partly because some top managers of these companies disliked it, arguing that they were part of the U.S. economy and created jobs for Americans. As the term was widely used in industry publications without quotation marks, however, it will also subsequently be employed here without them. For an example of its generic use, see "25 Years of Transplant Milestones," *Automotive News*, April 27, 1998.

4. Louis Uchitelle, "If Detroit Falls, Foreign Makers Could Be Buffer," *New York Times*, November 17, 2008, A1; "UAW: Organizing U.S. Transplants across South Key to Future," *Automotive News*, July 14, 2011; Micheline Maynard, "Shifting Michigan Southward," *New York Times*, June 22, 2005, C1.

5. Jacobs, *The New Domestic Automakers*, 1; Nick Bunkley, "Transplants Set to Dominate North American Production," *Automotive News*, January 15, 2018; Chappell, interview.

6. "Proceedings of the 29th UAW Constitutional Convention," June 18–23, 1989, 324, box 10, Convention Proceedings Papers, United Automobile Workers of America Papers, Walter P. Reuther Library, Wayne State University, Detroit, Michigan (hereafter Convention Proceedings Papers).

7. *The Harbour Report 2001*, 13; Patrick Jonsson, "America's 'Other' Auto Industry," *Christian Science Monitor*, December 2008; Dan Eaton, "Japan's Big 3 Automakers Built More Cars in U.S. Than Detroit 3 Last Year," *Columbus Business First*, June 1, 2016.

This statistic was based on cars. If trucks and SUVs were included, however, the Detroit Three retained their edge.

8. "About Mercedes-Benz U.S. International," Mercedes-Benz, accessed December 1, 2016, https://www.mbusi.com/about/mbusi-corporate-info/facts-figures; "BMW Manufacturing Announces New Milestone," BMW press release, April 7, 2010, BMW USA, accessed December 1, 2016, https://www.bmwusfactory.com/bmw_articles /bmw-manufacturing-announces-new-milestone-exports-over-one-million-vehicles -in-first-15-years-of-south-carolina-plant/.

9. Quoted in G. Chambers Williams III, "UAW Targets Canton Plant," *Rutherford County Daily News Journal*, September 3, 2012, 1.

10. An important recent addition to the field, Jacobs's *New Domestic Automakers* offers a sweeping survey of twenty foreign-owned auto factories. Data-heavy and lacking in human agency, the book does not explore in detail the causes and consequences of a particular company's decision to locate in a certain community. Aimed primarily at policymakers, it also contains almost no coverage of the tensions that the industry's growth produced.

11. Cobb, *The Selling of the South*, 2, 35; Atkins, *Covering for the Bosses*, 193–209 (quotation on 197); Jamie Butters, "Auto Union Works to Keep Status Quo," *Akron Beacon Journal*, September 6, 2003, D1; Sue Anne Pressley, "The South's New-Car Smell," *Washington Post*, May 11, 2001, A1 (closing quotations). Butters's long piece, which was widely circulated by news agencies, claimed that the transplants "have had almost no labor strife to speak of."

12. There are some works, especially of early transplants, that provide a more critical voice. See particularly Gelsanliter, *Jump Start*, and Hoyman, *Power Steering*, both of which explore the foundational Honda, Nissan, and Toyota plants (Hoyman's short book also examines the Saturn plant in Spring Hill, Tennessee). A critical overview of the sector has also been provided more recently by Anderson and McKevitt's essay, "From 'the Chosen' to the Precariat," 255–70. My book builds on these works, especially by extending the analysis past the first transplants and exploring the three waves of the industry's development in detail.

13. Price Smith, interview. These points are explored further below.

14. Bradford Wernie, "The Catch with NAFTA," *Automotive News*, September 19, 2016, 3; Ryan Beene, "Kia to Unveil Plans for Assembly Plant in Mexico," *Automotive News*, August 26, 2014; Martin, interview (quotation).

15. Boyle, *The UAW* (quotation). For important works on labor relations in the auto industry, particularly the upsurge in unionization that occurred in the North in the 1930s and 1940s, see particularly Fine, *Sit-Down*; Friedlander, *The Emergence of a UAW Local*; and Babson, *Building the Union*. For studies focused on northern autoworkers' experiences on the job, see especially Lichtenstein and Meyer, *On the Line*; Asher and Edsforth, *Autowork*.

16. For studies focused on decline, see, for example, Milkman, *Farewell to the Factory*; Dandaneau, *A Town Abandoned*; Dudley, *The End of the Line*; and Shotwell, *Autoworkers under the Gun*. On deindustrialization as a whole, a classic work is Bluestone and Harrison, *The Deindustrialization of America*. The quotations are from the book titles cited above.

17. Key works on the industry's problems in the early twenty-first century include Ingrassia, *Crash Course*, and Dewar, *A Savage Factory*. Other recent works on the industry's problems, especially the social tensions arising from its decline in Michigan, include Young, *Teardown*; Highsmith, *Demolition Means Progress*. For an apt illustration of press coverage of the northern industry's problems, see "Anatomy of Detroit's Decline," *New York Times*, December 8, 2013. The "postindustrial" quotation is in the subtitle of Dudley's *The End of the Line*.

18. For works in this vein, see particularly Perrucci, *Japanese Auto Transplants*, which covers several early factories; Kenney and Florida, *Beyond Mass Production*; Berggren, Bjorkman, and Hollander, *Are They Unbeatable?*

19. For a work that covers both transplants and joint ventures, see Green and Yanarella, *North American Auto Unions in Crisis*. For scholarship on transplants in unpublished dissertations, especially—again—from a management or organizational behavior perspective, see especially Daher, "Culture and Management Practices"; Lilleston, "Japanese Management"; McGehee, "The Impact."

20. In this vein, see Gelsanliter, *Jump Start*; Alexander, *Steps along the Way*, 129–34; Alexander, *Friends*, esp. 149–53.

21. Cobb, *The South and America*, 206–8 (quotation on 207).

22. Rubenstein, *The Changing US Auto Industry*, 229; Perrucci, *Japanese Auto Transplants*, 131; Gelsanliter, *Jump Start*, 78–79.

23. Cobb, *The Selling of the South*, 2, 35 (quotations in title); James C. Cobb, "Beyond the 'Y'All Wall': The American South Goes Global," in Cobb and Stueck, *Globalization and the American South*, 1–18.

24. Cobb, *The South and America*, 207; Jerry Grillo, "How Kia Came to Georgia," *Georgia Trend*, August 2009, 18–25.

25. Jung, interview; Dziczek, interview. Right-to-work laws ban compulsory union membership in workplaces.

26. Lesser, interview; Collins, interview (quotations).

27. McKevitt, *Consuming Japan*, 10. Writers have been articulating the contested idea of globalization for at least three decades, and there are of course multiple globalizations. I here concur with Cobb and Stueck's definition of globalization as "the transnational flow of people, capital, technology, and expertise that is initiated and sustained by the desire to capitalize on natural or human resources or attractive investment opportunities available somewhere else" (*Globalization and the American South*, xii).

28. Cobb and Stueck, introduction, xii (quotation); Stamper, interview. As outlined in the famous 1938 "Report on Economic Conditions of the South," which prompted President Franklin D. Roosevelt to characterize the South as "the nation's no. 1 economic problem," the South is here defined as encompassing the eleven states of the former Confederacy, plus Oklahoma (which became a state in 1907) and Kentucky. This definition also accords with the influential scholarship of the famous southern regionalist Rupert Vance, who argued that history, not geography, made the South. See Hulsemann, "Greenfields in the Heart of Dixie," 219–54, 220.

29. Bhagwati, *In Defense of Globalization*, 3; Zieger and Gall, *American Workers, American Unions*, 262. Bhagwati defines economic globalization as "integration of na-

tional economies into the international economy through trade, direct foreign investment (by corporations and multinationals), short-term capital flows, international flows of workers and humanity generally, and flows of technology" (3).

30. Bhagwati, *In Defense of Globalization*, esp. 3–8 ("defining issue" quotation on 3). The literature on globalization is vast. Bhagwati's book is a key work that argues that globalization has had largely positive consequences. For influential critical accounts, see Brecher, Costello, and Smith, *Globalization from Below*; Ritzer, *The McDonaldization of Society*; Pieterse, *Globalization and Culture*. For a helpful summary of key debates, see Zieger and Gall, *American Workers, American Unions*, 262–64.

31. Maynard, "Shifting Michigan Southward"; Chappell, interview; McAlinden, interview.

32. See, for example, Warren Brown, "UAW Loses Key Battle at Nissan Plant," *Washington Post*, July 28, 1989, A1; Tas Papathanasis, "Smyrna: The Crucible of American Labor," *Christian Science Monitor*, August 11, 1989.

33. Doron P. Levin, "Toyota Plant in Kentucky Is Font of Ideas for U.S.," *New York Times*, May 5, 1992; Lindsay Chappell, "In Georgetown, Toyota Became Global," *Automotive News*, October 29, 2007; "Overseas Manufacturing Operations," Toyota Global, February 17, 2017, accessed November 9, 2017, http://newsroom.toyota.co.jp/en /corporate/companyinformation/worldwide.

34. As detailed in chapter 1, Rolls-Royce had built small numbers of cars in Massachusetts between 1921 and 1931, but the BMW plant was much bigger and more significant.

35. Alan L. Adler, "Mercedes-Benz Move Just One in Wave from Foreign Automakers," undated *Associated Press* clipping, folder 62, box 5, Owen Bieber Papers, United Automobile Workers of America Papers, Walter P. Reuther Library, Wayne State University, Detroit, Michigan (hereafter Bieber Papers).

36. Von Kuenheim quoted in "Statement to U.S. News Media by Eberhard von Kuenheim," June 23, 1992, "BMW" folder, box 1, Liz Patterson Papers, South Carolina Political Collections Library, University of South Carolina, Columbia (hereafter Patterson Papers); "Economic Impact Analysis of the BMW Project for South Carolina" (South Carolina Development Board report), June 1992, file number 200545, Central Correspondence files, Jim Hodges Gubernatorial Papers, South Carolina Department of Archives and History, Columbia (hereafter Hodges Gubernatorial Papers).

37. Chappell, interview; Longgrear, interview.

38. McNair, interview; "State Economic Impact: Alabama," ca. 2017, Here for America, accessed January 30, 2018, http://hereforamerica.com/wp-content/uploads/2017 /05/AL-State-Report-2017.pdf.

39. Strange, interview; "About Hyundai Motor Manufacturing Alabama," Hyundai, accessed November 8, 2017, https://www.hmmausa.com/our-company/about -hmma/.

40. "About Hyundai Motor Manufacturing Alabama"; Lindsay Chappell, "Kia, Uncle Sam Vie for Hard Hats in Georgia," *Automotive News*, October 23, 2006, 34; McAlinden, interview; Bunkley, "Transplants Set to Dominate"; "The World's Biggest Automobile Companies," World Atlas, accessed December 19, 2019, https://www.worldatlas.com /articles/which-are-the-world-s-biggest-automobile-companies.html.

41. Butters, "Auto Union Works," D1; Sam Stockard, "As Nissan Goes, So Goes Ruth-erford County," *Rutherford County Daily News Journal*, March 21, 2000, 10; Reed quoted in Atkins, *Covering for the Bosses*, 196.

42. Douglas A. Fraser to Kiyoshi Kawashima, April 2, 1982, folder 24, box 140, Bieber Papers (quotation); "UAW Sets Demand That Japan Firms Build Autos in U.S.," *Wall Street Journal*, January 14, 1980; Fraser, interview, 213.

43. The UAW did have a presence at three joint ventures: a GM/Toyota plant in Fre-mont, California; a Ford/Mazda factory in Flat Rock, Michigan; and a Chrysler/Mit-subishi plant in Normal, Illinois. The union hoped that its presence would influence the unionization of the first transplants. This presence, however, was mainly due to prior bargaining arrangements with Big Three partners, and sole-owned transplants were a different situation. King, interview; Laarman, interview.

44. Jeffrey Ball, "Vote at Nissan Plant in Smyrna, Tenn., Is Key Union Test," *Wall Street Journal*, September 28, 2001, A4.

45. Casteel, interview; Bensinger, interview.

46. McNair, interview; Sewell, interview; "Mercedes-Benz U.S. International Eco-nomic Impact in Alabama: 2006"; "2014 Economic Impact: Honda Manufacturing of Alabama, LLC," both studies prepared for the EDPA by the Center for Business and Economic Research at the University of Alabama.

47. "Mercedes-Benz U.S. International Economic Impact in Alabama: 2006"; Jeff Amy, "Nissan Marking 10th Year in Canton," *Memphis Commercial Appeal*, May 25, 2013, 1.

48. Robey, interview; Armstrong, interview. I also draw here on my tours of the Kia factory in West Point, Georgia, on May 8, 2015, and the Toyota plant in Georgetown, Kentucky, on June 14, 2017.

49. Ghosn and Ries, *Shift*, 197; "Obama Administration New Path to Viability for GM and Chrysler," March 31, 2009, Obama White House, accessed November 25, 2016, https://www.whitehouse.gov/assets/documents/Fact_Sheet_GM_Chrysler_FIN.pdf; Dominic Rushe, "Fiat's Mexico Factories in Doubt as Trump Threatens New Tariffs," *The Guardian* (U.K.), January 10, 2017, 21.

50. "Honda of America Mfg., Inc." (company brochure), n.d. (ca. 1991–92), folder 23, box 255, Glenn Papers; Bieber, interview, 86.

CHAPTER 1: BUILD IT HERE

1. Jacobs, *New Domestic Automakers*, 51–52; Jerry Hirsch, "First Volkswagen Bee-tle Arrived in a U.S. Showroom 65 Years Ago," *Los Angeles Times*, January 31, 2014 (quotation).

2. For an account that portrays VW in Westmoreland as the "first" foreign manufac-turer to produce cars in the United States, see "Honda's First U.S.-Built Car Rolls Out," *New York Times*, November 2, 1982, D4.

3. Chappell, interview (quotation); Hulsemann, "Greenfields in the Heart of Dixie," 227, 249; Jacobs, *New Domestic Automakers*, 52.

4. Laarman, interview; Jacobs, *New Domestic Automakers*, 52.

5. "Karl Benz (1844–1929)," in *Encyclopaedia Britannica*, accessed November 13,

2017, https://www.britannica.com/biography/Karl-Benz; Jacobs, *New Domestic Automakers*, 17–20, 22–23.

6. Jacobs, *New Domestic Automakers*, 19, 24–28; "Rolls-Royce Here Called Insolvent; Cites Losses in Slump," *New York Times*, January 6, 1932, 23.

7. Jacobs, *New Domestic Automakers*, 17, 24.

8. Ingrassia, *Crash Course*, viii, 14, 22–23 (GM quotation), 24; Norton et al., *A People and a Nation*, 491 (Ford quotation); Foner, *Give Me Liberty!*, 722 (closing quotations).

9. Ingrassia, *Crash Course*, 32 (Wilson quotation), 33; Foner, *Give Me Liberty!*, 873, 878; UAW International Executive Board Minutes, January 26–29, 1973, box 18, 285, International Executive Board Minutes, United Automobile Workers of America Papers, Walter P. Reuther Library, Wayne State University, Detroit, Michigan (hereafter International Executive Board Minutes) ("settle" quotation); "A Declining Population in a Widespread City," *Forbes*, accessed September 12, 2016, http://www.forbes.com /pictures/emeh45jimm/a-declining-population-in-a-widespread-city-13 /#26e892841177.

10. Fine, *Sit-Down*; Halpern, *UAW Politics*, 256; Zieger and Gall, *American Workers, American Unions*, 109–10, 194, 196; International Executive Board Minutes, August 20, 26, September 9, October 5, 1964, 22, 30, box 14(closing quotations).

11. Benchich, interview.

12. Ingrassia, *Crash Course*, 30 (quotation), 36; Jacobs, *New Domestic Automakers*, 52.

13. Jacobs, *New Domestic Automakers*, 93, 108–9; "Toyota Company History," Toyota-USA, accessed November 13, 2017, http://corporatenews.pressroom.toyota .com/corporate/company+history/; *The Harbour Report a Decade Later*, 6–7 (quotation on 6).

14. *The Harbour Report a Decade Later*, 7 (quotations); Foner, *Give Me Liberty!*, 969–70; McAlinden, interview.

15. Leonard to Masao Yamamoto, January 23, 1973, folder 3, box 162, Leonard Woodcock Papers, United Automobile Workers of America Papers, Walter P. Reuther Library, Wayne State University, Detroit, Michigan (hereafter Woodcock Papers); Herman Rebhan to Leonard Woodcock, December 18, 1972, Woodcock Papers.

16. Leonard Woodcock to Masao Yamamoto, January 23, 1973, folder 3, box 162, Woodcock Papers.

17. Leonard Woodcock to Katsuji Kawamata, August 9, 1973; Herman Rebhan to Leonard Woodcock, December 18, 1972; and "Present Conditions of Japan's Direct Investment in the United States" (Japanese Ministry of Foreign Affairs Study), May 1973, all in folder 3, box 162, Woodcock Papers.

18. Jacobs, *New Domestic Automakers*, 93, 106–9; Eiji Toyoda to Leonard Woodcock, August 28, 1973, folder 3, box 162, Woodcock Papers (quotations).

19. Collin Gonze to Leonard Woodcock, June 23, 1976 ("rationalize" quotation); Helen M. Kramer to Howard Young, November 23, 1976, both in folder 5, box 162, Woodcock Papers (other quotations).

20. Lydia DePillis, "Tennessee Was Afraid of the United Auto Workers," *Washington Post*, February 18, 2014 (quotations by Kristin Dziczek); Chappell, interview.

21. Bhagwati, *In Defense of Globalization*, 3–8; "Remarks of Leonard Woodcock:

Toyota-Nissan Council Meeting," October 13–14, 1975, folder 5, box 162, Woodcock Papers (quotations).

22. "Restrict Auto Exports, UAW Exec Asks Japanese," *Asahi Evening News*, April 4, 1974; Leonard Woodcock to Ichiro Shioji, March 27, 1974, folder 4; closing quotation in "Remarks of Leonard Woodcock: Toyota-Nissan Council Meeting," October 13–14, 1975, folder 5, both in box 162, Woodcock Papers.

23. Leonard Woodcock to Ichiro Shioji, March 27, 1974, folder 4, box 162, Woodcock Papers.

24. International Executive Board Minutes, January 29–31, 1974, box 20, 6; Benchich, interview.

25. Herman Rebhan to Leonard Woodcock, April 10, 1974 (first quotation); "UAW Seeks Cutback of Exports to U.S.," *Japan Times*, April 3, 1974; "Restrict Auto Exports, UAW Exec Asks Japanese," *Asahi Evening News*, April 4, 1974 (second quotation), all in folder 4, box 162, Woodcock Papers.

26. "UAW and Foreign Car Firms at Odds over Union Efforts to Restrict Imports," *Wall Street Journal*, April 5, 1974 (quotations); "Statement Delivered by Ken Morris, Director, UAW Region 1B at the Third Annual Convention of the Jidosha Soren," September 19, 1974, folder 4, box 162, Woodcock Papers.

27. Leonard Woodcock to Hon. William E. Simon, May 18, 1976, folder 5, box 162, Woodcock Papers.

28. Toshio Nakamura to Leonard Woodcock, April 6, 1976, and Leonard Woodcock telegram, n.d., both in folder 5, box 162, Woodcock Papers; Agis Salpukas, "U.A.W. to Review Free-Trade Stand," *New York Times*, August 20, 1971, 41.

29. Reginald Stuart, "Car Makers in Plea on Imports," *New York Times*, February 12, 1980, D1; Paul E. Tsongas, "Did the Chrysler Bailout Work?," *New York Times*, August 2, 1983; Cowie, *Stayin' Alive*, 15, 303.

30. Clyde H. Farnsworth, "Rep. Vanik Warns Japan to Curb Auto Exports," *New York Times*, March 8, 1980, 28; Farnsworth, "Bill to Curb Car Imports Planned," *New York Times*, February 4, 1981, D3; "Glenn Proposes Measures to Help Ailing Auto Industry in U.S." (press release), June 11, 1980, folder 30, box 324, Daniel Doherty files, Glenn Papers; Clyde H. Farnsworth, "Japanese Warned of Car Quotas," *New York Times*, April 17, 1981, D1.

31. Department of Transportation data cited in Ed to John H. Glenn, February 4, 1981; "Glenn Cosponsors Bill Imposing Quota on Japanese Automobile Imports" (press release), February 5, 1981, both in folder 30, box 324, Daniel Doherty files, Glenn Papers. The figures quoted here include both truck and automobile production.

32. Senator John Glenn press release, October 25, 1980, folder 30, box 324, Daniel Doherty files, Glenn Papers; Clyde H. Farnsworth, "Car Import Issue Left to Reagan," *New York Times*, November 19, 1980, D5.

33. Minchin, *Empty Mills*, 111–12; Cowie, *Stayin' Alive*, 13–16.

34. Clyde H. Farnsworth, "U.S. Aide Calls Japan's Auto Curbs Noninflationary," *New York Times*, May 3, 1981, 7; "Glenn Praises Japan's Initiatives on Auto Imports" (press release), September 5, 1980, folder 30, box 324, Daniel Doherty files, Glenn Papers.

35. Jacobs, *New Domestic Automakers*, 95, 109; "Japanese Car Import Curb," *New*

York Times, October 21, 1982, D8; Steve Lohr, "Japan Set to Keep Limits on Exports of Its Cars to U.S.," *New York Times*, February 13, 1983, 1; "Ready or Not, Let Cars Compete," *New York Times*, July 27, 1983, A22.

36. Japanese newspapers quoted in Farnsworth, "U.S. Aide," 7.

37. Douglas Fraser oral history interviews with John Barnard, May 15, 29, June 6, 12, 22, 1990, 163–64, International Executive Board Oral Histories, United Automobile Workers of America Papers, Walter P. Reuther Library, Wayne State University, Detroit, Michigan (hereafter International Executive Board Oral Histories); Ingrassia, *Crash Course*, 103–104.

38. *The Harbour Report a Decade Later*, 17 (quotations); Lamar Alexander to John J. Da Ponte, May 21, 1984, folder 3, box 657, 1979–87, Lamar Alexander Gubernatorial Papers, Tennessee State Library and Archives, Nashville, Tennessee (hereafter Alexander Papers).

39. "UAW Sets Demand That Japan Firms Build Autos in U.S.," *Wall Street Journal*, January 14, 1980.

40. Jonathan Cutler, "UAW Should Organize Non-Union Automakers," *Fort Wayne (Ind.) Journal-Gazette*, December 11, 2008, A9 (quotation); Fraser oral history, 213.

41. Doug Fraser et al. to Presidents and Bargaining Committee Chairpersons, April 17, 1980, folder 56, box 6, Douglas A. Fraser Presidential Papers, United Automobile Workers of America Papers, Walter P. Reuther Library, Wayne State University, Detroit, Michigan (hereafter Fraser Presidential Papers).

42. Douglas A. Fraser et al. to Presidents and Bargaining Committee Chairpersons, April 14, 1980, folder 56, box 6, Fraser Presidential Papers (Fraser quotations); "Japan Labor Leaders Ask Toyota, Nissan to Produce Cars in U.S.," *Wall Street Journal*, February 4, 1980.

43. Interview with Doug Fraser, May 5, 1981, 60–62, transcript in folder 71, box 3, Douglas A. Fraser Personal Papers, Walter P. Reuther Library, Wayne State University, Detroit, Michigan (hereafter Fraser Personal Papers) (quotations).

44. Yasunobu, "Honda Ohaio"; "Japan Labor Leaders Ask Toyota, Nissan to Produce Cars in U.S.," *Wall Street Journal*, February 4, 1980 (Shioji quotations).

45. "UAW Sets Demand That Japan Firms Build Autos in U.S.," *Wall Street Journal*, January 14, 1980.

46. Clyde H. Farnsworth, "Vote Due on U.S. Auto Content Bill," *New York Times*, December 8, 1982, D1 ("bitterly contested" quotation); Robert D. Hershey Jr., "House Passes U.S. Auto Content Bill," *New York Times*, December 16, 1982, D1; Steve Lohr, "Bill on Auto Content Worries Japan," *New York Times*, November 5, 1983, 46 ("deep concern" quotation); Clyde H. Farnsworth, "House, 219–199, Votes to Require U.S.-Made Parts in Imported Cars," *New York Times*, November 4, 1983, A1.

47. Howard Young to Frank James, December 3, 1980, "Toyota 1980–83" folder, box 73, Fraser Presidential Papers; Ihara, *Toyota's Assembly Line*, ix–xiii.

48. *The Harbour Report a Decade Later*, 17.

49. Handwritten plant tour notes, n.d. (ca. 1980), "Toyota 1980–83" folder, box 73, Fraser Presidential Papers.

50. Interview with Doug Fraser, May 5, 1981, 60–62, transcript in folder 71, box 3, Fraser Personal Papers.

51. "Why Tension Grows around VW's New Plant," *Business Week*, February 6, 1978, 106.

52. "VW Chief Opens U.S. Plant, Keeps Fingers Crossed," *Los Angeles Times*, October 6, 1976, D9 (Schmücker quotation); "Ceremony Marks VW Plant Takeover," *Washington Post*, October 6, 1976, C9 (Shapp quotation).

53. Jerry Knight, "Volkswagen Begins Production of Cars in American Plant," *Washington Post*, April 11, 1978, D7; Jerry Knight, "VW Rabbit Output Starts at Snail's Pace," *Washington Post*, April 23, 1978, N1; John Holusha, "Volkswagen to Shut U.S. Plant," *New York Times*, November 21, 1987, 1 (quotation).

54. Knight, "Volkswagen Begins Production," D7; "Why Tension Grows," 106.

55. Jacobs, *New Domestic Automakers*, 50–52; Neal Gabler, "Volkswagen's Nazi-Era Blood Crimes," *The Nation*, January 4, 2016; Nicholas Colchester, "The Emigration of a German Miracle," *Financial Times* (U.K.), April 23, 1976.

56. Colchester, "The Emigration of a German Miracle"; Douglas A. Fraser to Jay D. Aldridge, March 16, 1979, folder 34, box 75, Fraser Presidential Papers (quotations).

57. Jacobs, *New Domestic Automakers*, 51–52; E. J. Moran's file notes, September 21, 1973, folder 27, box 12, Fraser Presidential Papers.

58. Carl H. Hahn statement, June 30, 1983, "Volkswagen, 1983–1986" folder, box 171, Bieber Papers (quotations); Jacobs, *New Domestic Automakers*, 53.

59. Unidentified VW official quoted in Joe Alex Morris, "VW Has Losses on U.S. Sales," *Los Angeles Times*, February 15, 1973.

60. Charles A. Vanik to Hon. William E. Simon, February 18, 1975 (first quotation); and Leonard Woodcock to Eugen Loderer, March 3, 1975, both in folder 27, box 12, Fraser Presidential Papers; Colchester, "The Emigration of a German Miracle."

61. Jacobs, *New Domestic Automakers*, 53; Colchester, "The Emigration of a German Miracle."

62. James A. Duerk to Jean C. Gordon, August 4, 1976 (first quotation); and James A. Rhodes to Ralph G. Bieber, August 3, 1976 (other quotations), both in folder 4, box 31, Ohio Department of Economic and Community Development Papers, Ohio History Connection, Columbus, Ohio (hereafter OED Papers).

63. Nicholas A. Panuzio to James A. Rhodes, May 4, 1976; Ohio Department of Economic and Community Development news release, June 30, 1975, folder 4, box 31, OED Papers.

64. Colchester, "The Emigration of a German Miracle"; Carl to Bolton F. Koch, April 26, 1976 ("odds" quotation); and Charles Bolton to James Duerk, April 22, 1976, both in folder 4, box 31, OED Papers (last quotation).

65. Knight, "Volkswagen Begins Production," D7; "Why Tension Grows," 106.

66. Bill Gernerd, "Shapp, Greenblat Tell How State Got Volkswagen Plant," *Allentown Morning Call*, May 11, 1985, W32.

67. Greater Cleveland Growth Association news release, June 2, 1976; James A. Duerk to James V. Stanton, April 16, 1976; and Ohio Department of Economic and Community Development news release, June 30, 1975, all in folder 4, box 31, OED Papers.

68. "Why Tension Grows," 106–7 (McLernon quotation 107); Associated Press summary, September 14, 1978, folder 35, box 75, Fraser Presidential Papers.

69. Knight, "VW Rabbit Output," N1 (first two quotations); Jacobs, *New Domestic*

Automakers, 53–55. New Stanton is the nearest sizeable town, whereas Westmoreland is the name of the county.

70. Jacobs, *New Domestic Automakers*, 53–55; Knight, "VW Rabbit Output," N1.

71. Colchester, "The Emigration of a German Miracle."

72. Jacobs, *New Domestic Automakers*, 53–55; "The Big Five Interviews," *Ward's Auto World*, December 1978, 102, 104 (quotations).

73. "Why Tension Grows," 106.

74. Ibid.; and Jean C. Gordon to Governor James Rhodes, July 8, 1976, folder 4, box 31, OED Papers.

75. "Why Tension Grows," 106–8.

76. Knight, "Volkswagen Begins Production," D7; Arthur J. Edmonds to Douglas Fraser, July 18, 1977, folder 35, box 75, Fraser Presidential Papers (quotation).

77. "Why Tension Grows," 107–8.

78. "Joint Memorandum of Plaintiffs and Defendant Volkswagen of America, Inc. Concerning Settlement," 2, 5–6, 9–10, October 1988 (quotations); and Dan Sherrick to Charles Bowling, Bill Casstevens, Jordan Rossen, and Dick Shoemaker, January 27, 1988, both in "Volkswagen, 1987–1992" folder, box 171, Bieber Papers.

79. Jordan Rossen to Charles Bowling, Bill Casstevens, and Dick Shoemaker, October 20, 1988; and Daniel W. Cooper to Jordan Rossen, October 14, 1988, both in "Volkswagen, 1987–1992" folder, box 171, Bieber Papers.

80. "UAW Begins Organizing VW," *Washington Post*, December 3, 1977, C9; "Westmoreland VW Workers Vote for UAW," *Washington Post*, June 10, 1978, D10 (Fraser quotation); Knight, "VW Rabbit Output," N1.

81. Associated Press summary, September 14, 1978, folder 35, box 75, Fraser Presidential Papers; "Rabbit Plant Restarts," *Washington Post*, October 17, 1978, D9 ("depleted" quotation); "Vote Ends Walkout at Pa. VW Plant," *Washington Post*, October 15, 1978, A4 ("developments" quotation); Frank James telephone memorandum to Douglas Fraser, October 9, 1978, folder 35, box 75, Fraser Presidential Papers; "The Big Five Interviews," *Ward's Auto World*, December 1978, 103 (closing quotations).

82. Toni Schmeucker to Douglas Fraser, October 4, 1978; and Eugene Lorenz to Cecil Hampton ("pattern" quotation), both in folder 35, box 75, Fraser Presidential Papers.

83. Frank James telephone memorandums to Douglas Fraser, October 9 and 16, 1978; and Ray Ross to Doug and Frank, October 16, 1978, all in folder 35, box 75, Fraser Presidential Papers. James's memos summarize the views of other staff, including Cecil Hampton, Dan Cooper, and Ray Ross.

84. Frank James telephone memorandum, October 19, 1978; and "Major Gains Achieved for UAW-VWOA Workers," *UAW Report*, October 4, 1978, both in folder 35, box 75, Fraser Presidential Papers.

85. Trumka, interview; Zieger, *The CIO*, 34–39, 147, 339.

86. Frank James to Doug Fraser, January 11, 1979; Carolyn to Frank, March 6, 1979 (first two quotations); and Frank to Doug, March 12, 1979 (third and fourth quotations), all in folder 34, box 75, Fraser Presidential Papers.

87. Douglas A. Fraser to Jay D. Aldridge, March 16, 1979, folder 34, box 75, Fraser Presidential Papers.

88. A. J. Schell to UAW Headquarters, June 12, 1979 (quotations); and A. J. Schell to Frank James, June 13, 1979, both in folder 34, box 75, Fraser Presidential Papers.

89. Jacobs, *New Domestic Automakers*, 56; Sheldon Friedman to Dick Shoemaker, May 8, 1990, "Volkswagen, 1987–1992" folder, box 171, Bieber Papers.

90. Jacobs, *New Domestic Automakers*, 55–56; Carl H. Hahn statement, June 30, 1983, "Volkswagen, 1983–1986" folder, box 171, Bieber Papers (quotations).

91. "VW of America Closes Plant in Pa. until Feb. Because of Slow Sales," *Washington Post*, January 22, 1983, D11 (quotation); "VW's U.S. Plant in 2-Week Closing," *New York Times*, April 25, 1987, F1; Holusha, "Volkswagen," 1; Volkswagen of America press release, November 20, 1987, "Volkswagen, 1987–1992" folder, box 171, Bieber Papers.

92. Holusha, "Volkswagen," 1 (O'Grady quotations); Volkswagen of America press release, November 20, 1987, "Volkswagen, 1987–1992" folder, box 171, Bieber Papers (VW quotation).

93. Elliott Anderson to Paul Lowry, July 18, 1990; and Sheldon Friedman to Dick Shoemaker, May 8, 1990, both in "Volkswagen, 1987–1992" folder, box 171, Bieber Papers.

94. Andrew Pollack, "Sony Is Said to Be in Deal for TV Plant," *New York Times*, April 17, 1990, D5; Jack Markowitz, "For Some, Myth Lasts 20 Years after VW," *Pittsburgh Tribune-Review*, August 28, 2008 (closing quotation).

95. Chappell, interview; Holusha, "Volkswagen," 1.

96. "UAW Scores VW Decision to End U.S. Auto Assembly" (UAW press release), November 20, 1987, "Volkswagen, 1987–1992" folder, box 171, Bieber Papers ("beacon" quotation); Richard Gazarik, "VW: Flop in New Stanton, Boom in Tennessee," *Pittsburgh Tribune*, June 16, 2013.

97. McAlinden, interview ("UAW plant" quotation); Chester B. Bahn, "Volkswagen's Union Workers Suffer Bad Rap," unidentified clipping; and Owen Bieber to Peter Laarman, May 26, 1988, both in "Volkswagen, 1987–1992" folder, box 171, Bieber Papers.

98. William C. Triplett II to United Auto Workers, November 29, 1978; and Frank James to Don Stillman, December 6, 1978 ("nice" quotation), both in folder 35, box 75, Fraser Papers.

99. Carl to Bolton F. Koch, April 26, 1976, folder 4, box 31, OED Papers.

CHAPTER 2: LAND ONLY

1. Paul Lienert, "Honda Maps an Ambitious Strategy," *Detroit Free Press*, December 29, 1985.

2. Chappell, interview (quotation); Toni Harrington to John Glenn, May 14, 1997, folder 26, box 296, Patricia Buckheit files, Glenn Papers; Jacobs, *New Domestic Automakers*, 2, 9.

3. James A. Duerk to Charles E. Webb, August 31, 1977, "Honda 1977" folder, box 30, OED Papers.

4. Clyde H. Farnsworth, "Unions and the Japanese," *New York Times*, November 17, 1980, D2 (first two quotations); John Holusha, "GM and Toyota Sign Auto Pact," *New York Times*, February 18, 1983, A1 (third quotation); Holusha, "Layoffs Are Just One UAW Problem," *New York Times*, January 24, 1982, 4.

5. Leonard Page to Joe Tomasi and Dick Martin, April 13, 1982 (first two quotations); and Doug Fraser to International Executive Board, March 22, 1982, both in folder 26, box 3, Fraser Presidential Papers (part 2). Also known as the Wagner Act (after its key sponsor, Senator Robert F. Wagner), the 1935 National Labor Relations Act was a landmark piece of legislation that encouraged collective bargaining through independent unions and greatly increased federal protections of union rights. The act also established the National Labor Relations Board to protect workers' rights. See Zieger, Minchin, and Gall, *American Workers, American Unions*, 79–81.

6. Chappell, interview; King, interview; Laarman, interview (closing quotation).

7. "Toyota's Entry into the United States," Toyota Global, accessed December 6, 2016, http://www.toyotaglobal.com/company/history_of_toyota/75years/text/taking_on_the_automotive_business/chapter2/section9/item5.html; Jacobs, *New Domestic Automakers*, 84.

8. Lienert, "Honda Maps" (Irimajiri quotation); Nobe, "Beikoku Honda"; "Honda of America Manufacturing, Inc.: A Brief History," n.d., folder 27, box 296, Patricia Buckheit files, Glenn Papers (last two quotations); WardsAuto, "U.S. Vehicle Sales Market Share by Company, 1961–2016," accessed April 27, 2018, http://wardsauto.com/datasheet/us-vehicle-sales-market-share-company-1961-2014.

9. "Honda of America Manufacturing, Inc." (first quotation); and "Written Statement of American Honda Motor Co., Inc. to the U.S. International Trade Commission Investigation," October 25, 1991, folder 28, both in box 296, Patricia Buckheit files, Glenn Papers; "Establishing Honda of America Manufacturing" (index); Yasunobu, "Honda Ohaio" ("one-way traffic" quotation on page 7 of translation).

10. "Establishing Honda of America Manufacturing" (chapter 2), https://global.honda/heritage/episodes/1980establishinghondaofamerica.html.

11. Ibid.; Yasunobu, "Honda Ohaio" (quotation on 5 of translation).

12. "Establishing Honda of America Manufacturing" (chapters 3 and 4).

13. Ibid. (chapter 4); Wolfgang Saxon, "Gov. James Rhodes Dies at 91," *New York Times*, March 6, 2001.

14. James A. Rhodes to Kihachino Kawashima, May 5, 1976 (quotations); and Soichiro Honda to James A. Rhodes, October 14, 1976, both in "Honda-1976" folder, box 30, OED Papers.

15. Frederick A. Sexton to Cedrick M. Shimo, March 10, 1977, "Honda-1977" folder, box 30, OED Papers.

16. E. B. Ransom to Who It May Concern, May 3, 1977; and Bricker, Evatt, Barton and Eckler (legal firm) to Richard A. Mercer, May 10, 1977, both in "Honda-1977" folder, box 30, OED Papers.

17. Fred A. Sexton to Kiyoshi Ikemi, May 17, 1977, "Honda-1977" folder, box 30, OED Papers. A foreign trade zone is an isolated policed area adjacent to a port of entry—such as an airport—where foreign goods can be unloaded or stored without being subject to import duties.

18. James A. Duerk to Charles E. Webb, August 31, 1977, "Honda—1977" folder, box 30, OED Papers (quotations); Jacobs, *New Domestic Automakers*, 85–86.

19. James A. Duerk to Kazuo Nakagawa, May 13, 1977 (first two quotations); James

A. Duerk to Hiroshi Suzuki, May 13, 1977 (third quotation); and H. Nakamura to James A. Rhodes, May 7, 1977 (fourth quotation), all in "Honda—1977" folder, box 30, OED Papers.

20. "Honda Motor Company" (contact list); and James A. Duerk to Masahiko Obi, May 13, 1977, both in "Honda—1977" folder, box 30, OED Papers.

21. Rick to J. Duerk and F. Sexton, May 10, 1977, "Honda—1977" folder, box 30, OED Papers.

22. Sidney B. Hopps to Nat Simon, September 20, 1977 (first two quotations); and Kaye Evans to Director Duerk, July 8, 1977 (third quotation), both in "Honda—1977"folder, box 30, OED Papers; "Former Governor Rhodes Returns to Scene of One of His Greatest Triumphs 20 Years Later," *Ohio Report*, October 8, 1997, 1–2; George J. Gibel, "No Major Problems Seen for Utility Service to Honda Site," *Marysville Journal-Tribune*, October 13, 1977, 1.

23. Masami Suzuki to James A. Rhodes, July 28, 1977 (first two quotations); and James A. Rhodes to Shigeyoshi Yoshida, July 29, 1977 (other quotations), both in "Honda—1977" folder, box 30, OED Papers.

24. James A. Rhodes to Masami Suzuki, August 2, 1977, "Honda—1977" folder, box 30, OED Papers.

25. Kazuo Nakagawa to Richard E. Dyck, August 23, 1977, "Honda—1977" folder, box 30, OED Papers (quotation); Jacobs, *New Domestic Automakers*, 85–86.

26. S. Yoshida to James Duerk, August 12, 1977 (first quotation); "Nissan, Honda Eyeing California for Auto Plants," *Japan Times*, June 9, 1977 (Fraser quotation), both in "Honda—1977" folder, box 30, OED Papers.

27. First quotation in "Remarks by Mr. Kawashima," October 11, 1977, "Honda—1977" folder, box 30, OED Papers; "Establishing Honda of America Manufacturing" (chapter 4, other quotations).

28. Lana Wetterman, "Mayor Critical of News Media for Distorted Honda Coverage," *Marysville Journal-Tribune*, November 5, 1982, 1 (Nuckles quotation); "Honda Auto Production Begins," *Marysville Journal-Tribune*, November 5, 1982, 4 (other quotations).

29. Lana Wetterman, "Mayor Critical of News Media for Distorted Honda Coverage," *Marysville Journal-Tribune*, November 5, 1982, 1; "Honda's U.S. Plant Brings Trouble, Not Prosperity, to Small Ohio Town," *Wall Street Journal*, October 5, 1982, 31 (quotations).

30. Gelsanliter, *Jump Start*, 160–61.

31. Ibid.; "Comments on Honda Issue," *Marysville Journal-Tribune*, November 12, 1982, 4 (Grimes quotations); "Honda's U.S. Plant Brings Trouble, Not Prosperity, to Small Ohio Town," *Wall Street Journal*, October 5, 1982, 31.

32. "Establishing Honda of America Manufacturing" (chapter 5); Lindsay Chappell, "Honda Talent Is Home-Grown," *Automotive News*, November 11, 2002.

33. First quotation in Yasunobu, "Honda Ohaio" (3 of translation); "Establishing Honda of America Manufacturing" (chapter 7); second quotation in "Establishing Honda of America Manufacturing" (chapter 8).

34. Lienert, "Honda Maps."

35. Zieger, *American Workers*, 178; Yoshida, "Honda."

36. International Executive Board Minutes, September 22–25, 1980, 418–19, box 9, Secretary-Treasurer's Papers.

37. International Executive Board Minutes, September 22–25, 1980, 419–20 (first quotation), 422–23 (other quotations), box 9, Secretary-Treasurer's Papers.

38. International Executive Board Minutes, September 14–16, 1981, 132–33, box 9, Secretary-Treasurer's Papers (first three quotations); Joyce, interview (fourth and fifth quotations); Kylie Conway, "UAW Leader Joe Tomasi Dies at 86," *NBC News*, August 7, 2007, http://nbc24.com/archive/uaw-leader-joe-tomasi-dies-at-86.

39. William C. Triplett II to Chet Hale, June 26, 1980, folder 25, box 140, Bieber Papers; Ferriss and Sandoval, *The Fight in the Fields*; "Stevens Boycott in Japan," *Newsweek*, November 14, 1977, 39.

40. William C. Triplett II to Chet Hale, June 26, 1980, folder 25, box 140, Bieber Papers (memorandum quotations); Yasunobu, "Honda Ohaio" (2 of translation).

41. "The Honda Philosophy at Work in the U.S."; Yasunobu, "Honda Ohaio" (3 of translation).

42. Gelsanliter, *Jump Start*, 98–99; S. Yoshida to Owen Bieber, February 12, 1986, folder 25, box 140, Bieber Papers ("anti" quotation); International Executive Board Minutes, September 22–25, 1980, 421, box 9, Secretary-Treasurer's Papers ("disturbed" quotation).

43. International Executive Board Minutes, September 14–16, 1981, 131, box 9, Secretary-Treasurer's Papers; Joyce, interview.

44. Gelsanliter, *Jump Start*, 99; Henry Scott Stokes, "U.S. Officials Brief Tokyo on Car Woes," *New York Times*, April 8, 1981, D14.

45. Frank Provenzano, "In Detroit, Dealers Sold on Imports," *Chicago Tribune*, July 15, 1990, 3; Rob Hotakainen, "No Mood to 'Buy US,'" *Fort Wayne (Ind.) Journal-Gazette*, December 7, 2014, H1 (Mondale and bumper sticker quotations); Chafe, *The Unfinished Journey*, 476; *The Harbour Report a Decade Later*, 34 (closing quotation).

46. HAM and UAW memorandum of agreement, April 21, 1982 (first quotation); S. Yoshida to Owen Bieber, February 12, 1986 (second and third quotations); Owen Bieber to Kiyoshi Kawashima, May 10, 1985 (fourth quotation), all in folder 24, box 140, Bieber Papers.

47. HAM and UAW memorandum of agreement, April 21, 1982, folder 24, box 140, Bieber Papers.

48. Clyde H. Farnsworth, "Honda Ends Opposition to Auto Union's Efforts," *New York Times*, April 23, 1982; Gelsanliter, *Jump Start*, 3, 101 (last quotation by Al Kinzer).

49. Steve Yokich to Owen Bieber, August 5, 1983, folder 24, box 140, Bieber Papers.

50. Leonard Page to Joe Tomasi, November 10, 1982, folder 24, box 140, Bieber Papers (quotation); Holusha, "Layoffs," 4.

51. Yoshida quoted in Yasunobu, "Honda Ohaio" (8 of translation); Steve Yokich to Owen Bieber, August 5, 1983, folder 24, box 140, Bieber Papers (Yokich quotation).

52. Leonard Page to Owen Bieber, November 10, 1983, folder 24, box 140, Bieber Papers (Page quotations); Robert D. Hershey Jr., "House Passes U.S. Auto Content Bill," *New York Times*, December 16, 1982, D1; Yasunobu, "Honda Ohaio."

53. Leonard Page to Owen Bieber, Steve Yokich, and Joe Tomasi, March 8, 1984 (quo-

tations); Leonard Page to Owen Bieber and Steve Yokich, March 8, 1984, both in folder 24, box 140, Bieber Papers.

54. Leonard Page to Owen Bieber and Steve Yokich, March 8, 1984 (quotation); and Leonard Page to Owen Bieber and Steve Yokich, March 19, 1984, both in folder 24, box 140, Bieber Papers.

55. "Marysville Plant Tour" (by Saturn employees), February 10, 1987, 29–30, folder 1, box 141, Bieber Papers.

56. Ibid.

57. Ibid.

58. S. Irimajiri to "All Associates" (first quotation); and "Honda of America Wage and Benefit History," September 1984 (last two quotations), both in folder 24, box 140, Bieber Papers.

59. Yasunobu, "Honda Ohaio" (5 of translation); Yoshida, "Honda."

60. Peter Perl, "Honda's Ideas Challenged," *Washington Post*, December 25, 1985, A1 (first two quotations); Warren Brown, "Honda Makes Inroads in U.S. by 'Doing Everything Right,'" *Washington Post*, April 14, 1985, D4 (other quotations).

61. "Honda of America Manufacturing, Inc."; Brown, "Honda Makes Inroads," D4.

62. Keith Robinson, "UAW Tries First Union Vote in Ohio Honda Plant," *The Journal*, November 24, 1985, 45, folder 24, box 140, Bieber Papers.

63. Owen Bieber to Kiyoshi Kawashima, May 10, 1985 (quotation); and Owen Bieber to Ray Majerus, January 8, 1985, both in folder 24, box 140, Bieber Papers.

64. Joseph Tomasi to Steve Yokich, September 10, 1985 (first quotation); and Peter Laarman to Steve Yokich, January 4, 1985 (second quotation), both in folder 24, box 140, Bieber Papers; Brown, "Honda Makes Inroads," D4; Perl, "Honda's Ideas Challenged," A1.

65. Owen Bieber to Kiyoshi Kawashima, May 10, 1985, folder 24, box 140, Bieber Papers.

66. Joseph Tomasi and Hugh Smith to Shige Yoshida, October 24, 1985 (quotations); Owen Bieber to Chairman Okamura, November 4, 1985; and "Election Date Set in Honda Organizing Drive," November 8 1985, all in folder 24, box 140, Bieber Papers.

67. Steve Yokich to Owen Bieber, September 23, 1985 (quotations); Owen Bieber to Chairman Okamura, November 4, 1985; and Owen Bieber to Chairman Okamura (unsent draft), November 4, 1985, all in folder 24, box 140, Bieber Papers.

68. "All Production and Maintenance Associates" (Honda document), October 29, 1985; and Shige Yoshida to All Associates and Your Families, November 5, 1985, both in folder 24, box 140, Bieber Papers. Honda claimed that the survey was completed by approximately 98 percent of the workforce.

69. Shige Yoshida to All Associates, October 30, 1985, folder 24, box 140, Bieber Papers.

70. Yasunobu, "Honda Ohaio" (pages 4 and 5 of translation); Gelsanliter, *Jump Start*, 35; Lindsay Chappell, "Whitlock to Leave Honda," *Automotive News*, April 17, 1995 ("combative" quotation); "What Management Personnel May or May Not Say or Do in Connection with Union Organizational Activities of Associates" (Honda document), ca. 1985, folder 24, box 140, Bieber Papers (last quotation).

71. Al Kinzer to Fellow Associates, November 20, 1985; and "Associates Being Called at Home" (Honda document), ca. November 1985, both in folder 24, box 140, Bieber Papers (quotation in second document).

72. Randy Limbird, "Group at Honda of America Tries to Keep All Unions Out," *Louisville Courier-Journal*, n.d. (Barker quotation); "The Associates of Honda Announce the Associates Alliance" (flyer), n.d., both in folder 24, box 140, Bieber Papers (other quotation).

73. Quotations in Leonard Page to Joe Tomasi, December 3, 1985, folder 24; Leonard Page to Owen Bieber, April 15, 1986, folder 25, both in box 140, Bieber Papers.

74. Quotations in "Unfair Labor Practice Charge," December 13, 1985, folder 24; and S. Yoshida to Owen Bieber, February 12, 1986, folder 25, both in box 140, Bieber Papers; Becker, interview.

75. Yoshida, "Honda"; Yasunobu, "Honda Ohaio" (9 of translation).

76. "UAW Will Appeal NLRB Honda Decision" (UAW press release), January 31, 1986, folder 25, box 140, Bieber Papers; Owen Bieber oral history interview with John Barnard, April 10–11, 1997, 87, box 1, International Executive Board Oral Histories.

77. Steve Yokich to Owen Bieber, March 14, 1986 (first quotation); and "UAW Withdraws Petition at Honda" (press release), March 17, 1986, both in folder 25, box 140, Bieber Papers; Yasunobu, "Honda Ohaio" (4 of translation, second and third quotations).

78. Yasunobu, "Honda Ohaio" (quotation on page 4 of translation); "Honda of America Manufacturing, Inc."; "Marysville Plant Tour," 2.

79. "UAW Withdraws Petition at Honda" (press release), March 17, 1986 (first quotation); and Steve Yokich to Owen Bieber, March 14, 1986, both in folder 25, box 140, Bieber Papers; Bieber oral history interview, 87 (second quotation).

80. Leonard Page to Owen Bieber and Steve Yokich, August 29, 1985; and Steve Yokich to Peter Laarman, October 2, 1985, both in folder 24; and quotations in Leonard Page to Dick Shoemaker, January 3, 1986, folder 25, all in box 140, Bieber Papers.

81. International Executive Board Minutes, August 31–September 1, 1987, 41, box 11, Secretary-Treasurer's Papers.

82. Leonard Page to Owen Bieber and Steve Yokich, August 29, 1985, folder 24; and Steve Yokich to Owen Bieber, March 14, 1986, folder 25, both in box 140, Bieber Papers.

83. International Executive Board Minutes, June 12–14, 1984, ii, box 10, Secretary-Treasurer's Papers.

84. Joseph Tomasi to Steve Yokich, September 10, 1985, folder 24 (Tomasi quotations); Jim Turner to Steve Yokich, March 6, 1986, folder 25 (Turner quotations), both in box 140, Bieber Papers.

85. Lienert, "Honda Maps."

86. Noboru Okamura to Owen Bieber, November 14, 1985; and Jim Turner to Steve Yokich, March 4, 1986 (quotations), both in folder 25, box 140, Bieber Papers.

87. Leonard Page to Joe Tomasi, February 25, 1986; and Leonard Page to Owen Bieber and Steve Yokich, September 5, 1986, both in folder 25, box 140, Bieber Papers.

88. S. Yoshida to Owen Bieber, February 12, 1986 (first two quotations); and Noburo Okamura to Owen Bieber, January 29, 1986 (third quotation), both in folder 25, box 140, Bieber Papers.

89. Steve Yokich to Owen Bieber, March 14, 1986 (first quotation); Jim Harbour, "The

Honda Way," *Automotive Industries*, August 1987, both in folder 25, box 140, Bieber Papers (other quotations).

90. "Plant Visit Summary: Honda of America Manufacturing, Marysville, Ohio," November 4, 1986, folder 1, box 141, Bieber Papers (first two quotations); "Marysville Plant Tour," 5, 27, 31 (other quotations on 31).

91. Louise Kertesz, "Japanese Rapped on Black Jobs," *Automotive News*, August 29, 1988; Yasunobu, "Honda Ohaio" (5 of translation).

92. Louis Uchitelle, "For Blacks, a Dream in Decline," *New York Times*, October 23, 2005 (statistic); Zieger, *For Jobs and Freedom*, 208–9, 224–30; Cowie, *Stayin' Alive*, 57–63.

93. "Demographic Info for JAPIA," February 5, 1977, "Honda—1977" folder, box 30, OED Papers.

94. McAlinden, interview; "Nissan, Honda Eyeing Calif. for Auto Plants," *Japan Times*, June 9, 1977, "Honda—1977" folder, box 30, OED Papers.

95. Douglas Frantz, "Honda to Pay 377 Women and Blacks for Hiring Bias," *Los Angeles Times*, March 24, 1988.

96. Dick Shoemaker to Ben Perkins, August 30, 1989 (first quotation); and Karlyn Barker, "National Urban League Issues Civil Rights Challenge," *Washington Post*, undated clipping, both in folder 25, box 140, Bieber Papers; "Marysville Plant Tour," 27 (other quotations).

97. Jim Turner to Steve Yokich, March 6, 1986; Linda Woods to UAW Headquarters, January 17, 1987 (Woods quotations); and Owen Bieber to Bill Casstevens, February 2, 1987 (closing quotation), all in folder 25, box 140, Bieber Papers.

98. "Marysville Plant Tour," 27; Bieber quoted in Peter Laarman to Owen Bieber, October 19, 1988, folder 58, box 32, Bieber Papers. The Laarman document includes extracts of the *Automotive News* interview referred to in the text.

99. Martin Whitfield, "Swindon Car Plant Will Be Non-Union," *The Independent* (U.K.), April 18, 1990 (first quotation); other quotations Jack Sizemore to Stan Marshall, November 29, 1993, folder 65, box 30, Bieber Papers.

100. "Proposal to Organize Nissan" (Greer, Margolis and Mitchell confidential document), April 16, 1991, folder 24, box 165 (first quotation); Greer, Margolis, Mitchell and Associates et al., "Organizing the Transplants: A Proposed Plan," January 14, 1993, 3, folder 65, box 30 (second quotation), both in Bieber Papers.

101. Dick Shoemaker to Owen Bieber, February 9, 1994, folder 65, box 30, Bieber Papers; Bieber quotations in Bieber oral history interview, 88.

102. Glenn quotation in John Glenn to Howard Paster, May 5, 1993, folder 27, box 296, Patricia Buckheit files; "Remarks of Senator John Glenn, Honda of America Visit, Marysville, Ohio," November 2, 1992, folder 13, box 538; Nocera and Clinton quotations in Barbara Nocera to Marcia L. Hale, April 21, 1993, folder 27, box 296, Patricia Buckheit files; "Honda of America Manufacturing, Inc."; *Detroit Free Press* quoted in "Honda North America, Inc. Issue Brief," ca. February 1995, folder 26, box 296, Patricia Buckheit files, all in Glenn Papers.

103. Harold Cassel to Lloyd Mahaffey, January 5, 1995 (first two quotations); Steve Yoder and Masao Yoshikawa to All MAP Associates, June 16, 1994 (third quotation), both in folder 2, box 141, Bieber Papers.

104. Ogino, "Naze Nikkei Maker"; Danny Hakim, "Auto Union and Honda Dispute Safety Record at Plants in Ohio," *New York Times*, June 26, 2002, 1 (quotations); *The Harbour Report: North America 2003*, 36.

105. Paul Magnusson and James B. Treece, "Honda, Is It an American Car?," *Business Week*, November 18, 1991, 105–12; Scott Whitlock to Stephen B. Shepard, November 13, 1991, folder 28, box 296, Patricia Buckheit files, Glenn Papers; Doron Levin, "Honda Blurs Line between American and Foreign," *New York Times*, March 14, 1990, A1; Steve Lohr, "Bill on Auto Content Worries Japan," *New York Times*, November 5, 1983; Bob Davis and Jacob M. Schlesinger, "Dispute on Parts for Cars Stalls Talks on Trade," *Wall Street Journal*, February 7, 1994, A2.

106. Danny Hakim, "Auto Union," 1 (quotations); Ogino, "Naze Nikkei Maker."

107. Whitfield, "Swindon Car Plant" ("associates" quotation); King, interview (second quotation); Fraser oral history interviews, 169.

108. Greer, Margolis, Mitchell and Associates et al., "Organizing the Transplants," 4 ("starting-point" quotation); UAW International Executive Board Minutes, September 16–17, 1986, 41, box 11, Secretary-Treasurer's Papers.

CHAPTER 3: THE JEWEL IN TENNESSEE?

1. Jenny Tenpenny, "World Watches Nissan Job 1," *Rutherford County Daily News Journal*, June 16, 1983, 1.

2. William Serrin, "Nissan Brings Foreign Ways to Tennessee," *New York Times*, April 20, 1981.

3. "Japanese Industry Puts Roots"; Alexander, *Steps along the Way*, 129 ("watershed" quotation); Lamar Alexander, "Nissan Comes to Tennessee," December 1980, folder 5, box 740, Alexander Papers. As Alexander acknowledged, Nissan was the largest investment outside of the financial services industry.

4. Elizabeth Murray, "Nissan Plant Tops in U.S.," n.d. (ca. 1992), unidentified clipping, "Nissan Northern America, Smyrna TN" folder, box 23, shipment 4, Bart Gordon Papers, Albert Gore Research Center, Middle Tennessee State University, Murfreesboro, Tennessee (hereafter Gordon Papers); Ghosn and Ries, *Shift*, 118 (quotation); "Governor Haslam, Commissioner Boyd Announce Nissan to Undergo Major Expansion at Smyrna Facility," *Targeted News Service* (U.S.), March 18, 2015. In 2015, Smyrna was producing around 650,000 vehicles a year.

5. Joey Ledford, "Automakers Empower South," *Atlanta Journal-Constitution*, January 11, 2004, C4 (first quotation); Micheline Maynard, "Shifting Michigan Southward," *New York Times*, June 22, 2005, C1; "Contribution of the Automotive Industry to the Economies of All Fifty States and the United States," Center for Automotive Research report, January 2015, accessed March 19, 2015, 6, 39, www.cargroup.org/?module=Publications; Pressley, "The South's New-Car Smell," A1 (closing quotation).

6. "Japanese Industry Puts Roots" (first quotation); John Holusha, "In Tennessee, the US and Japan Mesh," *New York Times*, June 16, 1983, A18; Kathy Sawyer, "Nissan's Tennessee Plant Cool to Labor Organizers," *Washington Post*, June 19, 1983, A2; Rowland Evans and Robert Novak, "Nissan's Non-Union 'Utopia,'" *Washington Post*, Sep-

tember 28, 1983; David A. Vise, "The Japanese Style Is Catching On in Tennessee," *Washington Post*, July 25, 1982, G1.

7. Lydia DePillis, "This Is What a Job in the U.S.'s New Manufacturing Industry Looks Like," *Washington Post*, March 9, 2014; Bill Vlasic, Hiroko Tabuchi, and Charles Duhigg, "An American Model for Tech Jobs?," *New York Times*, August 5, 2012, 1.

8. Casteel, interview; Evans and Novak, "Nissan's Non-Union 'Utopia'" (quotation); Lynne Wilbanks, "Mississippi Eyes Upcoming Union Vote at Nissan's Smyrna Plant," *Mississippi Business Journal*, September 3, 2001, 1.

9. Existing accounts of Nissan's arrival are limited. The most detailed is Gelsanliter, *Jump Start*, 45–58. A journalist, Gelsanliter provides valuable firsthand information but does not utilize archival records. For limited coverage, see also Cobb, *The South and America*, 207, and Jacobs, *New Domestic Automakers*, 94, both of which stress the role of financial incentives.

10. First and third Ishihara quotations in "Remarks by Takashi Ishihara," n.d. (ca. October 1980); "Briefing Paper / Governor Alexander Nissan," n.d.; and "historically significant" quotation in Takashi Ishihara, "Congratulations," *Rutherford County Daily News Journal*, October 20, 1983, 2, all in folder 5, box 740, Alexander Papers.

11. "News from the Office of the Governor" (Governor Alexander press releases), November 3 and 7, 1980, folder 5, box 740, Alexander Papers.

12. Jacobs, *New Domestic Automakers*, 93–94; Alexander, "Nissan Comes to Tennessee"; and "The Name Has Changed but the Product's the Same," *Rutherford County Daily News Journal*, October 20, 1983, both in folder 5, box 740, Alexander Papers; "Nissan Is Driven," *Time*, September 14, 1981.

13. "Remarks by Takashi Ishihara," n.d. (ca. October 1980); and "Statement from Governor Alexander," September 18, 1980, both in folder 5, box 740, Alexander Papers.

14. "Legislator Condemns Plan to Train Tennesseans in Japan," *Maryville (Tenn.) Times*, February 4, 1981 (Cotham quotation); Woods, interview.

15. "Governor's Briefing," August 25, 1976, folder 52, box 245, Ray Blanton Gubernatorial Papers, Tennessee State Library and Archives, Nashville (hereafter Blanton Papers); John Burgess, "Tennessee: Japan's Home away from Home," *Washington Post*, August 26, 1990; HJB-58, "A Resolution Relative to the Selection of Smyrna, Tennessee, by Nissan," February 5, 1981, folder 5, box 740, Alexander Papers ("citizen" quotation).

16. "Governor's Proposed Cuts in Education Are in Error," *Athens Post-Athenian*, February 11, 1981 (first quotation); Burgess, "Tennessee" (second quotation).

17. "Best thing" quotation in Alexander, "Nissan Comes to Tennessee"; and "first priority" quotation in Governor Alexander press conference, January 19, 1982, both in folder 5, box 740; "Governor Tells Newsmen: 1980 Industry Growth 'Astounding,'" *Milan Mirror-Exchange*, February 4, 1981; "Remarks of Governor Lamar Alexander," October 21, 1983, folder 5, box 740; and Lamar Alexander to Howard H. Baker Jr., November 29, 1982, folder 3, box 657, all in Alexander Papers.

18. "Gov. Alexander Gives First-Hand Report on Trade Trip to Japan," n.d. (ca. 1982), press clipping folder 9, box 805, Alexander Papers ("maples" quotation); "Japanese Industry Puts Roots"; Alexander, *Friends: Japanese and Tennesseans*, 17 ("dozens" quotation); Alexander, "Nissan Comes to Tennessee" (Zaitsu quotation); and "Remarks

of Governor Lamar Alexander," October 21, 1983, both in folder 5, box 740, Alexander Papers.

19. Kaichi Kanao to Governor Alexander, June 25, 1980, Jim Cotham to Lamar Alexander, July 9, 1980; and itinerary, July 14–16, 1980, all in folder 13, box 1010, Alexander Papers. The first two items above were marked "Strictly Confidential" and "Private and Confidential."

20. Lamar Alexander to T. F. Yukawa, July 29, 1985; and T. F. Yukawa to Lamar Alexander, July 10, 1985, both in folder 3, box 657; "News from the Office of the Governor," ca. October 1980, folder 4, box 894, all in Alexander Papers.

21. "Demonstration Deplorable," *Nashville Banner*, February 6, 1981, 8 (first two quotations); "News from the Office of the Governor," November 3, 1980, folder 5, box 740, Alexander Papers; "Waverly Residents Attend Nissan Ground-Breaking," *Waverly News-Democrat*, February 11, 1981 (other quotations); and "World Auto Leader Will Speak at Groundbreaking," *The Tennessean*, January 25, 1981.

22. Gelsanliter, *Jump Start*, 49; Alexander, *Steps along the Way*, 133 (quotations); "Datsun Talks," *Nashville Banner*, September 20, 1980; Woods, interview.

23. Alexander, *Steps along the Way*, 133 (first two quotations); Serrin, "Nissan"; "News from the Office of the Governor," November 3, 1980, folder 5, box 740, Alexander Papers; and "Waverly Residents Attend Nissan Ground-Breaking," *Waverly News-Democrat*, February 11, 1981 ("vital link" quotation).

24. "Nissan Training Center," January 1981–June 1983, folder 9, box 805, Alexander Papers; Vickie Gibson, "Nissan Coming to Rutherford," *Rutherford County Daily News Journal*, October 30, 1980; Cobb, *The South and America*, 207; Serrin, "Nissan."

25. "Cost Benefit Ratios of Nissan Project, Smyrna, Tennessee," Tennessee Department of Economic and Community Development Study, February 10, 1981, folder 9, box 805; and Sue Atkinson to Lewis Lavine, January 18, 1982, folder 5, box 740, both in Alexander Papers.

26. "Remarks by Takashi Ishihara, President, Nissan Motor Co.," n.d. (ca. October 1980), folder 5, box 740, Alexander Papers.

27. Serrin, "Nissan"; Woods, interview; "Remarks of Governor Lamar Alexander: Nissan Grand Opening," October 21, 1983, folder 5, box 740 ("things" quotation), Alexander Papers.

28. "Japanese Industry Puts Roots"; "A Resolution Relative to the Selection of Smyrna, Tennessee by Nissan Motor Manufacturing Corporation USA as the Location for a Plant and Corporate Headquarters," ca. 1980; and "News from the Office of the Governor" (Governor Alexander press release), December 10, 1980, both in folder 5, box 740, Alexander Papers; Daniel F. Cuff, "Tennessee's Pitch to Japan," *New York Times*, February 27, 1985; Lamar Alexander to Howard H. Baker Jr., January 15, 1981, folder 3, box 657, Alexander Papers (quotation).

29. "Japanese Industry Puts Roots" (first quotation); "Eduardo Lachica, "Tennessee's 'Hustle' Is Attracting Japanese Industry," *Nashville Banner*, March 4, 1981, folder 16, box 104 (second and third quotations); and "Remarks by Takashi Ishihara, President, Nissan Motor Co.," n.d. (ca. October 1980), folder 5, box 740 (fourth quotation), both Alexander Papers.

30. HJB-58, "A Resolution" (House of Representatives quotations); and John L. Parish to Currie B. Spivey Jr., August 4, 1982, folder 3, box 657, Alexander Papers.

31. Lamar Alexander to Takashi Ishihara, December 24, 1985, folder 3, box 657, Alexander Papers (first four Alexander quotations); Alexander, "Nissan Comes to Tennessee" (other Alexander quotations).

32. "Japanese Industry Puts Roots"; Woods, interview (first quotation); "Statement, James C. Cotham III, Commissioner, Tennessee Department of Economic and Community Development," ca. October 1980, folder 5, box 740 (second quotation); Sam Ridley to Takashi Ishihara, April 12, 1984, folder 3, box 657 (other quotations), both Alexander Papers.

33. "News from the Office of the Governor" (Governor Alexander press release), November 7, 1983, folder 5, box 740, Alexander Papers (first Alexander quotation); Alexander, *Steps along the Way*, 129; Hunt, interview (Hunt quotations); Sawyer, "Nissan's Tennessee Plant," 15, 17 (final two Alexander quotations).

34. Lamar Alexander to Jim Gentry, February 18, 1981 (first quotation); Lamar Alexander to Howard H. Baker Jr., November 29, 1982 (second quotation), both in folder 3, box 657, Alexander Papers.

35. "Nissan to Bring Changes," unidentified clipping, ca. 1983; first Ridley quotation in Ray Potter, "Smyrna Doesn't Want to Be a Small Detroit," unidentified clipping, ca. 1983, both in folder 6, box 12, Walter King Hoover Papers, Albert Gore Research Center, Middle Tennessee State University, Murfreesboro, Tennessee (hereafter Hoover Papers); Vickie Gibson, "Bureau on Record against Nissan," *Rutherford County Daily News Journal*, October 7, 1980 (Mitchell quotations); Sam Ridley to Takashi Ishihara, April 12, 1984, folder 3, box 657, Alexander Papers (final Ridley quotation).

36. Vickie Gibson, "State Decides on Road," *Rutherford County Daily News Journal*, January 27, 1987 (first quotation); Lamar Alexander to Miss Jamie Johns, April 15, 1981, folder 3, box 657, Alexander Papers (second quotation); and Barry Bryant and Terri Kaminski, "S.C. Firm Wins Nissan Contract," *Nashville Banner*, January 27, 1981 (third quotation).

37. Alexander, "Nissan Comes to Tennessee."

38. "Excerpt from I and A Meeting," December 5, 1980, folder 5, box 740 (McWherter and Griffin quotations); and Joel Kaplan, "Fight Staged over Nissan Tax Benefits," unidentified clipping dated March 4, 1981, folder 16, box 104, both Alexander Papers (Morton quotation). Despite these reservations, both men ultimately backed the package as a necessary evil.

39. "Nissan Training Plan by Lashlee Criticized," *Elizabethton Star*, February 5, 1981 (first two quotations); Ken Renner, "Nissan Training Aid Irks Assembly," *Knoxville Journal*, undated clipping (ca. February 1981) (third and fourth quotations), both in folder 16, box 104, Alexander Papers.

40. "Fair Funds Proposal Scored," *Knoxville Journal*, February 6, 1981 (first quotation); "Legislator Condemns Plan to Train Tennesseans in Japan," *Maryville (Tenn.) Times*, February 4, 1981 (second and third quotations); "Governor's Proposed Cuts in Education Are in Error," *Athens Post-Athenian*, February 11, 1981 (fourth quotation).

41. "A Tight Budget," *Johnson City Press-Chronicle*, February 4, 1981.

42. "Fair Funds Proposal Scored," *Knoxville Journal*, February 6, 1981.

43. "Democrats Criticize Promises to Nissan," clipping titled "C-A," February 5, 1981, folder 16, box 104, Alexander Papers.

44. Ishikawa, "Beikoku Keiei" (first quotation); Joel Kaplan, "Nissan Denies Bypassing Able Minority Applicants," unidentified clipping, n.d. (ca. October 1981), folder 16, box 104, Alexander Papers (Williams quotations).

45. Jerry L. Benefield to Jim Cooper, November 16, 1990, folder 15, box 13, Jim Cooper Papers, Albert Gore Research Center, Middle Tennessee State University, Murfreesboro, Tennessee (hereafter Cooper Papers); Robert E. Cole and Donald R. Deskins, "Racial Factors in Site Selection and Employment Patterns of Japanese Auto Firms in America," *California Management Review* 31, no. 1 (Fall 1988): 9–15, 21; "Proceedings of the 29th UAW Constitutional Convention," June 18–23, 1989, 325 (quotation); and "Proceedings of the 30th UAW Constitutional Convention," June 14–18, 1992, 248, both in box 10, Convention Proceedings Papers.

46. Alan Hall and Lisa Human, "Protest by Union Seen for Nissan Groundbreaking," *The Tennessean*, January 28, 1981 (quotations); "Foreign Autos Are Not Better," *Jackson Sun*, February 22, 1981.

47. "Boycott Datsun" (photograph), *Johnson City Press-Chronicle*, February 4, 1981 ("quality products" quotation); "Boos Greet Nissan Co.," *Union City Messenger*, February 4, 1981 (other quotations).

48. Charles W. Stevens, "Nissan Truck Plant Ground Breaking Rite Draws Angry Crowd," *Wall Street Journal*, February 5, 1981 (first two quotations); "Union Activity: Jeers, Rock Mar Ceremony," *Knoxville Journal*, undated clipping (third quotation), folder 16, box 104, Alexander Papers.

49. Mike Kopp, "Area Labor Union Officials Upset with Nissan Action," *Rutherford County Daily News Journal*, January 16, 1981; "Officer Injured by Rock," *Murfreesboro Journal*, February 3, 1981; "Governor Tells Newsmen: 1980 Industry Growth 'Astounding,'" *Milan Mirror-Exchange*, February 4, 1981 ("hit" quotation); "Boos Greet Nissan Co.," *Union City Messenger*, February 4, 1981; Charles W. Stevens, "Nissan Truck Plant Ground Breaking Rite Draws Angry Crowd," *Wall Street Journal*, February 5, 1981 (closing quotation).

50. "In Smyrna: Nissan U.S.A. Plant Site Dedicated Tuesday," *Smyrna Courier*, February 5, 1981 (first quotation); Albert Cason, "McMurray Steel Gets Nissan Pact," *The Tennessean*, February 28, 1981; Jayne Matthews, "Alexander Sees No Need to Meet with Protesters," *Murfreesboro Journal*, February 3, 1981; Steven Epley, "40,000 Applications Filed for Smyrna's Nissan Jobs," *Chattanooga News Free Press*, April 23, 1981 (second and third quotations).

51. "Disgraceful Spectacle," *Chattanooga News Free Press*, February 4, 1981 (first quotation); "Demonstration Deplorable," *Nashville Banner*, February 6, 1981 (second quotation); "In Smyrna: Nissan U.S.A. Plant Site Dedicated Tuesday," *Smyrna Courier*, February 5, 1981 (third and fourth quotations).

52. "Unions Get Official Criticism," *Murfreesboro Journal*, February 5, 1981 (quotation); Jet Henson to Lamar Alexander, February 4, 1981, folder 5, box 740; Lamar Alexander to Marvin T. Runyon, February 25, 1981, folder 3, box 657; "Gov. Alexander Gives

First-Hand Report on Trade Trip to Japan," undated press clipping, folder 9, box 805, all in Alexander Papers.

53. Lamar Alexander to Mitsuya Goto, January 3, 1983; Lamar Alexander to Mitsuya Goto, December 19, 1985; Mitsuya Goto to Lamar and Honey Alexander, December 10, 1985, all in folder 3, box 657, Alexander Papers.

54. Lamar Alexander to Mr. and Mrs. Takashi Ishihara, August 19, 1983; Takashi Ishihara to Lamar Alexander, September 12, 1983 (quotation); Lamar Alexander to Marvin Runyon, October 3, 1983, all in folder 3, box 657, Alexander Papers; "Dinner for Mr. and Mrs. Ishihara," October 21, 1983; and "Remarks of Governor Lamar Alexander: Nissan Grand Opening," October 21, 1983, both in folder 5, box 740, Alexander Papers.

55. Tenpenny, "World Watches," 1; "Cheers Greet First Smyrna-Built Truck," *The Tennessean*, June 17, 1983, B1; "Remarks of Governor Lamar Alexander," October 21, 1983, folder 5, box 740, Alexander Papers (Alexander quotations).

56. Sawyer, "Nissan's Tennessee Plant," A2 (first two quotations); Holusha, "In Tennessee," A18 (third quotation); Yoshida, "Honda" (fourth quotation).

57. "News from the UAW" (UAW press release), June 16, 1983, folder 11, box 155, Bieber Papers (Bieber quotations); Kathy Sawyer, "Auto Workers' Union Installs New President," *Washington Post*, May 20, 1983, A6; Zieger, *American Workers*, 67–68.

58. *The Harbour Report a Decade Later*, 34 (first three quotations); Bensinger, interview (fourth and fifth quotations).

59. Hans Greimel, "Takashi Ishihara" (obituary), *Automotive News*, May 19, 2008; Hunt, interview; "Remarks by Takashi Ishihara," n.d. (ca. October 1980) (Ishihara quotations); and "Briefing Paper / Governor Alexander Nissan," n.d., both in folder 5, box 740, Alexander Papers.

60. Alexander, "Nissan Comes to Tennessee" (quotation); Sam Ridley to Takashi Ishihara, April 12, 1984, folder 3, box 657, Alexander Papers.

61. Sawyer, "Nissan's Tennessee Plant," A2; Vise, "The Japanese Style," G1; International Executive Board Minutes, March 14–16, 1983, 169–170, box 10, Secretary-Treasurer's Papers (quotation).

62. International Executive Board Minutes, March 14–16, 1983, 170, box 10, Secretary-Treasurer's Papers (first quotation); Bieber oral history interview, 92; Vise, "The Japanese Style," G1 (second quotation); Jim Turner to Steve Yokich, August 26, 1986, folder 11, box 155, Bieber Papers; "Statistics of Japanese Auto Industry," September 25, 1973, folder 3, box 162, Woodcock Papers.

63. Leonard Page to Dick Martin et al., June 6, 1983; and Jim Turner to Steve Yokich, August 26, 1986, both in folder 11, box 155, Bieber Papers; "Statement from Governor Alexander," May 11, 1984; and "Nissan Adds Night Shift" (Nissan press release), June 3, 1985 (quotation), both in folder 5, box 740, Alexander Papers.

64. "Workers Mistreated at Nissan's Tennessee Plant," *The Progressive*, press release, May 7, 1987, folder 12, box 155, Bieber Papers; John Junkerman, "Nissan, Tennessee: It Ain't What It's Cracked Up to Be," *The Progressive*, June 1987, 17–18.

65. Junkerman, "Nissan, Tennessee," 16–20 (first two quotations on 17, 20); Gelsanliter, *Jump Start*, 64–65; Lynn Agee to Jim Turner, March 13, 1987, folder 12, box 155, Bieber Papers; "Union a Thorn in Nissan's Crown," *Chicago Sun-Times*, May 18, 1987;

Randy Hilman, "Overwork, Intimidation Claimed at Nissan," *The Tennessean*, May 7, 1987 (third quotation); "Nissan Denies Magazine's Report That Tenn. Crews Are Overworked," *Detroit Free Press*, May 8, 1987.

66. Frank Joyce to Owen Bieber, May 13, 1987, folder 12, box 155, Bieber Papers (first and second quotations); International Executive Board Minutes, June 1–17, 1986, 143–44, box 11, Secretary-Treasurer's Papers (third quotation).

67. Frank Joyce to Owen Bieber, May 13, 1987, folder 12 (quotation); Jerry L. Benefield to James M. Turner, January 3, 1989, folder 15; and Steve Yokich to Owen Bieber, August 15, 1988, folder 13, all in box 155, Bieber Papers.

68. Ben Perkins to Steve Yokich, March 16, 1988; and Steve Yokich to Jim Turner, February 23, 1988, both in folder 13, box 155, Bieber Papers.

69. Steve Yokich to Owen Bieber, August 15, 1988, folder 13; Ben Perkins to Steve Yokich, January 24, 1989, folder 15, both in box 155, Bieber Papers.

70. John Junkerman, "Nissan" (unpublished draft article), folder 12, box 155, Bieber Papers; International Executive Board Minutes, August 31–September 1, 1987, 60–61, box 11, Secretary-Treasurer's Papers (quotations); Laurie A. Graham, "How Foreign-Owned Auto Plants Remain Union-Free," *New Labor Forum* 17, no. 3 (Fall 2008): 58–66, 62–64.

71. Steve Yokich to UAW Officers, June 20, 1988; "Nissan Plant" (UAW memo), June 16, 1988; and Dan Whittle, "Nissan Picketers Oppose Union," *Rutherford County Daily News Journal*, June 9, 1988 (quotations), all in folder 13 (Nissan correspondence, 1988), box 155, Bieber Papers.

72. Don Ephlin to Steve Yokich, February 13, 1989 (first quotation); "Nissan Has Six Times as Many Worker Comp Cases as Ford Glass Plant," UAW flyer, ca. 1989; and Phil West, "Union, Nissan Face Off," *Knoxville News*, May 7, 1989 (second and third quotations), all in folder 15 (Nissan correspondence, 1989), box 155, Bieber Papers.

73. International Executive Board Minutes, May 30–June 1, 1989, 36–37, 50, box 11, Secretary-Treasurer's Papers; Ben Perkins to Steve Yokich, June 2, 1989; and Ben Perkins to Steve Yokich, June 7, 1989, both in folder 15, box 155, Bieber Papers.

74. James Risen, "UAW Rejected at Nissan Plant in Major Defeat," *Los Angeles Times*, July 28, 1989; Mike Silverstein to Dick Shoemaker, August 2, 1989, folder 14 (first quotation); "Statement by Nissan Motor Manufacturing USA in Response to Questions Regarding Safety," ca. May 1989, folder 15; and Dan Whittle, "Nissan Picketers Oppose Union," *Rutherford County Daily News Journal*, June 9, 1988, folder 13 (second and third quotations), all in box 155, Bieber Papers; Steele, interview (fourth and fifth quotations).

75. Lynn Agee to Ben Perkins and Jordan Rossen, October 24, 1989, folder 14 (first two quotations); and Frank Mirer to Dick Shoemaker, n.d., folder 13, both in box 155, Bieber Papers; Gelsanliter, *Jump Start*, 198; Kenney and Florida, *Beyond Mass Production*, 266 (third quotation).

76. Rubenstein, *Making and Selling Cars*, 173; Dan Whittle, "Nissan Picketers Oppose Union," *Rutherford County Daily News Journal*, June 9, 1988 (first two quotations); Chappell, interview (third quotation).

77. "Participative Management at Nissan," May 22, 1989 (company flyer), folder 15, box 155, Bieber Papers; Lindsay Chappell, "Jerry Benefield," *Automotive News*, May 19,

2008 (first quotation); Jerry L. Benefield to James M. Turner, January 3, 1989, folder 15 (second quotation); "Statement by Gail O. Neuman," May 18, 1989, folder 15; and Ben Perkins to Steve Yokich, March 16, 1988, folder 13 (third quotation), all in box 155, Bieber Papers.

78. Sweeney, interview; Leonard Page to Owen Bieber and Steve Yokich, December 7, 1988, folder 16, box 156, Bieber Papers; "New UAW Division," *New York Times*, September 7, 1989.

79. John Holusha, "Union Rebel: Jerry Tucker," *New York Times*, October 23, 1988; Bieber oral history interview, 94 (Bieber quotations). On the UAW's involvement in the introduction of "team production," see Mike Parker and Jane Slaughter, "Behind the Scenes at Nummi Motors," *New York Times*, December 4, 1988, 2; Merrill Goozner, "Confrontation and Cooperation on the Auto Front," *Chicago Tribune*, June 18, 1989, 1. For critiques of these systems, especially by industrial relations scholars, see Mike Parker and Jane Slaughter, "Management-by-Stress: The Team Concept in the US Auto Industry," *Science as Culture* 1, no. 8 (1990): 27–58; Laurie Graham, "Inside a Japanese Transplant: A Critical Perspective," *Work and Occupations* 20, no. 2 (May 1993): 147–73. For a defense of team production at NUMMI, see Bruce Lee, "Workers at Our Plant Aren't Anxious, They're Proud," *Washington Post*, October 29, 1988, A25.

80. "Landmark Dates" (Nissan document), May 1989; "Nissan Expansion to Create 2,000 New Jobs" (Nissan press release), April 3, 1989 (Kume quotation), both in folder 15, box 155, Bieber Papers.

81. Gelsanliter, *Jump Start*, 199 (first quotation); Janet Braunstein, "Nissan Considers Second U.S. Plant," *Detroit Free Press*, October 10, 1990 (second quotation).

82. Woods, interview; Members of Nissan In-Plant Organizing Committee to Owen Bieber, ca. July 1990, folder 16; Carlton Horner to Steve Yokich, July 29, 1986, folder 11 (quotation); and Tom Groom to All Managers, June 1, 1988, folder 13, all in box 155, Bieber Papers.

83. *The Harbour Report a Decade Later*, 270 (first quotation); Bieber oral history interview, 88 (Bieber quotations).

84. Syler, interview (first quotation); Laird, Long and Sylvester analysis of the 1989 Nissan campaign, March 18, 1991, folder 24, box 165, Bieber Papers (second quotation); Dziczek, interview (third quotation).

85. Lamar Alexander to Howard H. Baker Jr., June 16, 1982 (quotation); Lamar Alexander to Takashi Ishihara, November 29, 1982; and Lamar Alexander to Howard H. Baker Jr., November 29, 1982, all in folder 3, box 657, Alexander Papers.

86. Risen, "UAW Rejected" (first quotation); International Executive Board Minutes, March 12–13, 1990, 89, box 11, Secretary-Treasurer's Papers (Yokich quotation); "Nissan, Bridgestone Subsidiaries in U.S.," *Daily Labor Report*, January 9, 1990 (Neuman quotation).

87. Frank Mirer to Stan Marshall, October 2, 1989, folder 14; Ben Perkins to Owen Bieber, Stan Marshall, and Dick Shoemaker, March 7, 1994, folder 16 (quotation); Rosetta Tibbs to Ben Perkins, May 18, 1994, folder 16; and Tim Martin, "Nissan to Announce Altima Recall," *The Tennessean*, March 14, 1994, folder 16, all in box 155, Bieber Papers.

88. John J. Hodorowicz, "Nissan Employees Had No Voice, Lost Jobs," *Rutherford*

County Daily News Journal, August 28, 2001, x; Ghosn and Ries, *Shift*, vii–xviii (first quotation on xvii), 120 (second, third, fourth, and fifth quotations), 121; *The Harbour Report 2001*, 15, 26, 30; Steele, interview (sixth quotation).

89. Steele, interview (first quotation); Dale Russakoff, "The Union Gap," *Washington Post*, July 20, 2006, D1 (second quotation); Ghosn and Ries, *Shift*, 118 (third quotation); Terril Yue Jones, "UAW Loses Bid to Enter Nissan Plant," *Los Angeles Times*, October 4, 2001.

90. Ogino, "Naze Nikkei Maker" (quotations); Steele, interview; Bensinger, interview.

91. Gelsanliter, *Jump Start*, 208, 239; Ernest J. Yanarella and William C. Green, "Building Other People's Cars: Organized Labor and the Crisis of Fordism," in Green and Yanarella, *North American Auto Unions*, 1–15; Laarman, interview.

92. Janet Braunstein, "Nissan Considers Second U.S. Plant," *Detroit Free Press*, October 10, 1990 (Benefield quotations); Laarman, interview (other quotations).

93. "Nissan Workers Reject Union," *Fort Lauderdale Sun Sentinel*, July 28, 1989, 3D; *The Harbour Report: Competitive Assessment*, 6–7, 72–73 (quotations on 6).

94. "News from Nissan" (Nissan Motor Manufacturing Corporation USA press release), August 20, 1982, folder 5, box 740, Alexander Papers; Peter Laarman to Owen Bieber, October 19, 1988, folder 58, box 32, Bieber Papers (first quotation); "The Case for Saving the Big Three" (Economic Strategy Institute report), 1992, folder 32, box 255, Laura Beers files, Glenn Papers (second quotation); Jerry Dubrowski, "U.S. Costs Attracting Foreign-Car Factories," *Washington Times*, October 29, 1993, E1.

95. "Draft Remarks of Owen Bieber," February 27, 1990, 12–15, folder 40, box 15 (Bieber quotations); and "Draft Remarks of Owen Bieber, IPS Conference," August 21, 1990, folder 24, box 16, both in Bieber Papers; *The Harbour Report a Decade Later*, 273–74 (Iacocca quotations); "Detroit's Big Three: Are America's Carmakers Headed for the Junkyard?," *The Economist*, April 14, 1990, 79; Laarman, interview (closing quotation).

96. "News from the Office of the Governor" (press release), November 3, 1980, folder 5, box 740, Alexander Papers.

97. Serrin, "Nissan" (quotation); Smyrna population figures at the U.S. Census Bureau, http://quickfacts.census.gov/qfd/states/47/4769420.html; Al Gore interview with Tony Badger, April 10, 2005 (in author's possession).

CHAPTER 4: "TOYOTA, A BIG YES"?

1. Jacobs, *New Domestic Automakers*, 111; Collins quotations in Martha Layne Collins to Sandra Goodwyn, October 31, 1986, "Toyota 4" folder, box 64, Governor's Correspondence files, Martha Layne Collins Papers, Kentucky Department for Libraries and Archives, Frankfort, Kentucky (hereafter Collins Papers).

2. Martha Layne Collins to Barclay B. McCoy, February 18, 1986, "Toyota 4" folder, box 64, Collins Papers.

3. Collins, interview.

4. Kevin Kerfoot, "Oh, What a Feeling—Again!," *Georgetown News and Times*, November 28, 1990, 1; Lamar Alexander to Takashi Ishihara, December 24, 1985, folder 3, box 657, Alexander Papers (quotation).

5. Jacobs, *New Domestic Automakers*, 107–9, 112 (quotation on 107); William E. Osos to Owen Bieber, June 8, 1988, folder 16; and Paul Prather, "First Test Car Rolls out of Toyota Plant," *Lexington Herald-Leader*, n.d. (ca. early June 1988), folder 16, both in box 165, Bieber Papers.

6. Aaron M. Kessler, "With a Hush, an American Lexus Plant Goes to Work," *New York Times*, November 13, 2015, B1; "Free Toyota Tour" flyer, ca. June 2017 (Toyota Motor Manufacturing Kentucky, Inc., document), copy in author's possession; "About TMMK," Toyota Kentucky, accessed July 28, 2017, http://toyotaky.com/boutdex.asp.

7. Chappell, interview; "Toyota Plants Capture Top J. D. Power and Associates Awards," PR Newswire, May 17, 2001, accessed December 14, 2016, http://www .prnewswire.com/news-releases/toyota-plants-capture-top-jd-power-and -associates-awards-71865672.html; "Toyota Kentucky Brings Home Platinum Plant Quality Award," accessed December 14, 2016, http://toyotaky.com/detailnews. asp?PRID=617.

8. Lindsay Chappell, "Georgetown's Extreme Makeover," *Automotive News*, June 12, 2006.

9. *The Harbour Report: Competitive Assessment*, 43–45, 51 ("best" quotation); *The Harbour Report 2001*, 30; *The Harbour Report 2003*, 31.

10. Doron Levin, "Toyota Plant in Kentucky Is Font of Ideas for U.S.," *New York Times*, May 5, 1992 (quotations); Toni Harrington to John Glenn, May 14, 1997, folder 26, box 296, Patricia Buckhart files, Glenn Papers.

11. Levin, "Toyota Plant"; Chappell, "Georgetown's Extreme Makeover" ("crown jewel" quotation); Lindsay Chappell, "In Georgetown, Toyota Became Global," *Automotive News*, October 29, 2007 ("mother plant" quotation); Jeremy W. Peters, "Hardly a Union Hotbed," *New York Times*, September 4, 2007, C1 (final two quotations).

12. Jon Newberry, "Toyota's Second Home: Kentucky," *Cincinnati Post*, March 3, 2006, A1; Greg Paeth, "Birth of a Plant Meant the Rebirth of a County," *Cincinnati Post*, February 24, 2007, A11; Sanford Nowlin, "Toyota Driving Force in Kentucky Boom," *San Antonio Express-News*, October 13, 2002, A1.

13. "Working Together to Build the Best Vehicle," *Georgetown News and Graphic*, April 30, 1994. For upbeat scholarly studies, see Haywood, "A Report," 17; Haywood, "Toyota Motor Manufacturing," 155–66; Fraas, *The Public Papers*, 9; Bailey, "Courting Toyota," 5.

14. Chappell, "In Georgetown" (quotations); Levin, "Toyota Plant." The expert referred to is Sean McAlinden, who is quoted in Levin's article and identified as a senior researcher at the University of Michigan.

15. For early accounts that cover the mixed reaction, see Gelsanliter, *Jump Start*, 81–90; Perrucci, *Japanese Auto Transplants*, 84–86, 92–96.

16. Micheline Maynard and Nick Bunkley, "As Auto Prosperity Shifts South, Two Towns Offer a Study in Contrasts," *New York Times*, December 5, 2006, C1 (Cuneo quotation); "Toyota, a Big Yes," *Georgetown News and Times*, December 12, 1985, 1; Mary Branham, "After Long Wait: Shovels Now Turn," *Georgetown News and Times*, May 6, 1986, 10 (closing quotation).

17. Peter Laarman to Owen Bieber, January 27, 1987, folder 58, box 32, Bieber Papers (quotation); Joyce, interview.

18. For accounts—all of them pretty brief—that stress the importance of the Toyota incentives, see Rubenstein, *The Changing US Auto Industry*, 229; Cobb, *The South and America*, 207; Perrucci, *Japanese Auto Transplants*, 131; Gelsanliter, *Jump Start*, 78–79; Thompson, "The Toyota Decision," 21–23.

19. Jacobs, *New Domestic Automakers*, 111; Lesser, interview; Collins, interview.

20. Jacobs, *New Domestic Automakers*, 101–6; "75 Years of Toyota," Toyota website, accessed December 15, 2016, http://www.toyota-global.com/company/history_of_toyota/75years/text/taking_on_the_automotive_business/chapter1/section1/item1 .html.

21. Jacobs, *New Domestic Automakers*, 106–9; McAlinden, interview; WardsAuto, "U.S. Vehicle Sales."

22. Eiji Toyoda to Leonard Woodcock, August 28, 1973, folder 3, box 162, Woodcock Papers; *The Harbour Report a Decade Later*, 34; "75 Years of Toyota," chap. 1, sec. 1, item 2 (quotations).

23. "75 Years of Toyota," chap. 1, sec. 3, item 1; Rubenstein, *The Changing US Auto Industry*, 228; Jacobs, *New Domestic Automakers*, 109.

24. "A Financial Profile of Toyota," *Japanese Motor Business*, March 1987; and "Update on Toyota," *Japanese Motor Business*, December 1987, 15, both in folder 9, box 165, Bieber Papers; Chris Rose, "Yen Surges to All Time High in US," *Georgetown News and Times*, April 22, 1986, 6.

25. "75 Years of Toyota," chap. 1, sec. 3, item 3 (quotations); Rubenstein, *The Changing US Auto Industry*, 229; *The Harbour Report a Decade Later*, 59.

26. Collins, interview; Fraas, "'All Issues Are Women's Issues,'" 213; Andy Mead, "Jubilant Crowd Jams Scott Gym," *Lexington Herald-Leader*, December 13, 1985, B1; Lusby, interview (quotations).

27. "Toyota Motor Manufacturing, U.S.A. Fact Sheet," ca. 1987, "Toyota" folder, box 64, Collins Papers; Cobb, *The South and America*, 207; Mary Branham, "Toyota Pact Signed," *Georgetown News and Times*, March 4, 1986, 1; Branham, "Businesses to Relocate," *Georgetown News and Times*, May 27, 1986, 1.

28. Kansas, for example, reportedly offered a sweetened deal that included industrial revenue bonds to pay for the plant, generous property tax savings, extensive tax credits, and job training funds. For more on how other states offered "larger packages," see Cheryl Truman, "State Officials Feared Losing Toyota to Tennessee at the Last Minute," *Lexington Herald-Leader*, December 15, 1985, A1; Jacobs, *New Domestic Automakers*, 111; Milward and Newman, "State Incentive Packages," 203–22, 212. The quotation above is from Jacobs, *New Domestic Automakers*, 111.

29. Mary Branham, "Knicely Germinated Japan Idea" and "Collins Excited at Prospect of Japanese Investment," both *Georgetown News and Times*, April 22, 1986, 2; "75 Years of Toyota," chap. 1, sec. 3, item 3 (quotation); Collins, interview; James A. Kurz, "Cherry Blossom Time in the Bluegrass: The Coming of the Toyota Motor Corporation of Japan to Kentucky," unpublished University of Kentucky paper, December 1985, 39, James C. Klotter Personal Papers, History Department, Georgetown College, Georgetown, Kentucky (hereafter Klotter Papers). Copies of all documents cited from this collection are in the author's possession.

30. Collins, interview (first quotation); Branham, "After Long Wait," 10; Toyota offi-

cial quoted in *Louisville Courier-Journal*, October 14, 1986, B12, cited in Perrucci, *Japanese Auto Transplants*, 68; T. W. Samuels Jr. to Martha Layne Collins, December 18, 1985, "Toyota 3" folder, box 64, Collins Papers (closing quotation).

31. Mary Branham, "Toyoda's Visit Cordial," *Georgetown News and Times*, March 18, 1986, 1, 6; Branham, "Toyota Gives $1 Million," *Georgetown News and Times*, May 6, 1986, 1; Collins, interview (quotations); Fraas, "'All Issues,'" 225–48.

32. Prather, interview; David Rushling, "Knicely Speaks at Clark Meeting," *Georgetown News and Times*, February 25, 1986, 1, 7; Maynard and Bunkley, "As Auto Prosperity Shifts," C1; Jacobs, *New Domestic Automakers*, 111; Lamar Alexander to Mitsuya Goto, December 19, 1985, folder 3, box 657, Alexander Papers.

33. Rushling, "Knicely Speaks," 1, 7 (Knicely quotation); Prather, interview (second and third quotations); "Resources for Economic Development, Georgetown, Kentucky," 1989 (Kentucky Cabinet for Economic Development brochure), 11, Kentucky Room, Scott County Public Library (closing quotation); I. Ogiso to Don Stillman, July 26, 1988, folder 8; and Don Stillman to Dick Shoemaker, September 20, 1988, folder 16, both in box 165, Bieber Papers.

34. This conclusion is based on the author's detailed reading of the thousands of letters that Governor Collins received about the Toyota project, especially when the news was announced.

35. James J. Coleman to Martha Layne Collins, December 11, 1985; and John David Cole to Martha Layne Collins, December 13, 1985, both in "Toyota 2" folder; and Dick Mayer to Martha Layne Collins, October 20, 1986, "Toyota 4" folder, all in box 64, Collins Papers.

36. "Collins Unhappy with Early Release," *Georgetown News and Times*, December 12, 1985, 6; Truman, "State Officials," A1; "Scott Confirmed as Toyota Site," *Lexington Herald-Leader*, December 10, 1985, A1 (Collins quotation); James E. Huddleston to Martha Layne Collins, December 25, 1985, "Toyota" folder, box 64, Collins Papers.

37. "Quality of Life Would Remain About the Same," *Georgetown News and Times*, December 10, 1985, 4 (Mooney quotations); Mary Branham, "Pollock Excited at Prospect," *Georgetown News and Times*, December 12, 1985, 5 (Pollock quotations).

38. Price Smith, interview (first and second quotations); Cheryl Truman, "Rural Scott Hopes to Win Industrial Prize," *Lexington Herald-Leader*, November 17, 1985, A1; Apple, interview (third and fourth quotations).

39. Lusby, interview; Mary Branham, "Scott Population to Grow," *Georgetown News and Times*, July 29, 1986, 1; "History of Georgetown, KY," Georgetown / Scott County website, accessed December 15, 2016, http://www.georgetownky.com/History/history -new; Apple, Johnston, and Bolton Bevins, *Scott County Kentucky*, 49, 399. There is dispute about whether Craig actually discovered the bourbon process—or if there was a single "inventor" of bourbon—but he was among those prosecuted for not paying the whiskey tax. See Apple, Johnston, and Bolton Bevins, *Scott County Kentucky*, 60.

40. Robey, interview; Andy Mead and Cheryl Truman, "Toyota Brings on Land Boom in Scott," *Lexington Herald-Leader*, December 22, 1985, A1; "Letters," *Georgetown News and Times*, May 20, 1986, 9 (Brown quotation); Collins, interview (Collins quotations); Roger Nesbitt, "Scott Residents Offer Mixed Views on Plant," *Lexington Herald-Leader*, December 4, 1985, A1.

41. Roger Nesbitt, Andy Mead, and Art Jester, "Way Appears Clear for Deal on Plant Land," *Lexington Herald-Leader*, December 7, 1985, A1; Hank Bond and Mary Branham, "Road Apparently Cleared for Industrial Location," *Georgetown News and Times*, December 10, 1985, 1 (first quotation); "Property Acquisition in Litigation," *Georgetown News and Times*, January 14, 1986, 5 (second and third quotations); Price Smith, interview (fourth quotation). According to the *Lexington Herald-Leader*, Billy Singer did not want to sell either but felt that he could not "stand in the way of something that will be worth a billion dollars to the state of Kentucky." The Singers also received $819,600 for their land. See Nesbitt, Mead, and Jester, "Way Appears Clear."

42. Price Smith, interview.

43. Mary Branham, "Cemeteries to Be Moved," *Georgetown News and Times*, December 31, 1985, 1 (quotation); Branham, "Businesses to Relocate," 1.

44. Mary Branham, "Traffic Concerns Voiced at Meeting," *Georgetown News and Times*, January 7, 1986, 1, 6.

45. Mary Branham, "Growth in Plans," *Georgetown News and Times*, August 12, 1986, 1.

46. Branham, "After Long Wait," 10; Branham, "Traffic Concerns," 1, 6 (first two quotations); Mary Branham, "Way Cleared for Toyota," *Georgetown News and Times*, January 14, 1986, 1–2 (third quotation).

47. Mary Branham, "Zone Change Recommended for Toyota Site," *Georgetown News and Times*, January 28, 1986, 1, 10; Branham, "Treatment Plant Location Nearly Finalized," *Georgetown News and Times*, February 18, 1986, 1, 12 (quotations); Branham, "Treatment Plant Decision Postponed," *Georgetown News and Times*, May 20, 1986, 2; Branham, "Permit Granted for Treatment Plant," *Georgetown News and Times*, July 1, 1986, 1, 2.

48. Mary Branham, "Hearing Held on Air Pollution," *Georgetown News and Times*, June 17, 1986, B1 (quotations); "Suit Seeks Building Delay," *Georgetown News and Times*, July 22, 1986, 1; Branham, "Knox Rules for State; Building Can Begin," *Georgetown News and Times*, July 29, 1986, 1; Knox, interview. Hammond headed the Kentucky Building Trades Council, AFL-CIO.

49. "Summary of Results of Toyota Impact Survey—Selected Variables," July 1986, University of Kentucky Survey Research Center study, 5–8, Kentucky Room, Scott County Public Library. The survey used random digit dialing to ensure that all residential numbers had an equal chance of being called. The counties surveyed were Scott, Bourbon, Clark, Fayette, Franklin, Grant, Harrison, Owen, and Woodford. The overall response rate was 66 percent. Respondents had to choose from the following responses: "strongly agree," "agree," "disagree," "strongly disagree," and "don't know."

50. "Summary of Results of Toyota Impact Survey—Selected Variables," July 1986, 5–10.

51. Ibid.

52. Stamper, interview; Apple, interview; Jacobs, *New Domestic Automakers*, 104.

53. Roller and Twyman, *The Encyclopedia of Southern History*, 680; John Connor Sr. to Senator Wendell Ford, January 12, 1987; and Pearl Branham to Governor Martha Collins, January 20, 1987, both in "Toyota" folder; and Johnny Brown to Senator Wendell H. Ford, October 24, 1986, "Toyota 4" folder, all in box 64, Collins Papers.

54. See, for example, Martha Layne Collins to Mr. and Mrs. Charles K. Carpenter, February 7, 1986, "Toyota" folder, box 64, Collins Papers.

55. Mary Branham, "Toyota Decision Opens Many Doors," *Georgetown News and Times*, February 4, 1986, 1 (first Collins quotation); Branham, "Toyota Gives $1 Million," 1 (Toyoda quotations); Collins, interview (final two Collins quotations). For Toyota's obviation of its wartime history, see "75 Years of Toyota," chap. 2, sec. 5.

56. Branham, "Zone Change," 1, 10 (Sexton quotation); Branham, "Toyota Decision," 1; Sen. Ed Ford, "Ford's Footnotes," *Georgetown News and Times*, February 18, 1986, 4; Gelsanliter, *Jump Start*, 143; Alecia Swasy, "Toyota Deal: Did Kentucky Give Away Too Much?," *Lexington Herald-Leader*, August 24, 1986, A1.

57. Jean Elkins to Gov. Martha Layne Collins, n.d. (ca. May 1986); W. Frank Burberry to Governor Collins, June 12, 1986; and Martha Layne Collins to Jean, May 15, 1986, all in "Toyota 1"folder; John F. Smahaj to Gov. Collins, September 29, 1986, "Toyota 4" folder, all in box 64, Collins Papers.

58. Jack Brammer and John Winn Miller, "Toyota Incentives Legal, Court Rules," *Lexington Herald-Leader*, June 12, 1987, 1, 16.

59. *Gordon Taub v. Commonwealth of Kentucky and Martha Layne Collins*, 842 F.2d 912 (6th Cir. 1988); Knox, interview (quotation).

60. Leonard R. Bauer to Martha Layne Collins, August 27, 1986, "Toyota 4" folder, box 64, Collins Papers (first two quotations); Gelsanliter, *Jump Start*, 87–88 (third and fourth quotations on 88).

61. Gelsanliter, *Jump Start*, 87–88 (quotations); C. Theodore Koebel et al., "Impacts of the Toyota Plant on Scott County, Kentucky" (study prepared by the University of Louisville for the Kentucky Department of Local Government), January 15, 1987, 5, Kentucky Room, Scott County Public Library; "Toyota in Kentucky" (staff report), *Lexington Herald-Leader*, November 27, 1990, A6.

62. "An Investment in Kentucky's Future" (UAW advertisement), *Georgetown News and Times*, January 14, 1986, 5 (first two quotations); I. Ogiso to Don Stillman, July 26, 1988, folder 8, box 165; and Owen Bieber to Bill Osos, March 17, 1988, folder 62, box 6 (Bieber quotation), both in Bieber Papers; Mary Branham, "Toyota: When the Snow Is Melted," *Georgetown News and Times*, February 18, 1986, 1, 3 ("freshmen" quotation).

63. Bieber oral history interview, 90; Owen Bieber to Masami Iwasaki, September 30, 1987; Masami Iwasaki to Owen Bieber, November 13, 1987, both in folder 62, box 6, Bieber Papers.

64. Masami Iwasaki to Owen Bieber, October 16, 1987 (first quotation); and Owen Bieber to Bruce Lee, November 4, 1987 (second quotation), both in folder 62, box 6, Bieber Papers.

65. Isomura quoted in I. Ogiso to Don Stillman, July 26, 1988, folder 8, box 165, Bieber Papers; Bieber quotation in Bieber oral history interview, 90. Ogiso was a leader in the Japanese Automobile Workers' Union (JAW) and met with Isomura on the UAW's behalf.

66. Don Stillman to Dick Shoemaker, September 20, 1988, folder 16, box 165, Bieber Papers (first three quotations); Chappell, "In Georgetown" ("worried" quotation); "Labor Letter," *Wall Street Journal*, December 29, 1987 (closing quotation).

67. "Fact Sheet: Hiring Process for Group Leaders, Team Leaders, and Team Mem-

bers" (Toyota document), January 1990, "Toyota" folder, Klotter Papers (first three quotations); Robey, interview (other quotations); Laarman, interview.

68. Leonard Page to Mike Nicholson, September 27, 1988, folder 8, box 165; Bill Young to Bill Osos, January 24, 1988; and Sheila Corn to James Planck, September 8, 1987 (quotation), both in folder 62, box 6, all in Bieber Papers.

69. Mr. and Mrs. William Mattingly to Martha Layne Collins, September 13, 1986, "Toyota 4" folder; and Larry D. Lee to Martha Layne Collins, February 3, 1986, "Toyota" folder, both in box 64, Collins Papers; "Interview: Meet a Japanese Auto Industry Executive in the U.S.," Japanese Automobile Manufacturers Association (JAMA), *Forum*, July 1988, 10, folder 8, box 165, Bieber Papers (Kusunoki quotations).

70. "UAW—Toyota Los Angeles—Hyatt" (meeting notes), May 31, 1988, folder 9, box 165, Bieber Papers.

71. "UAW—Toyota Los Angeles—Hyatt" (meeting notes), July 26, 1988, folder 9, box 165, Bieber Papers.

72. Norman Minch, "Clark to Close Plant in Georgetown," *Georgetown News and Times*, February 18, 1986, 13; "Clark: End of an Era," *Georgetown News and Times*, February 18, 1986, 1; Lusby, interview (closing quotation). The $12 million figure is based on a one-year period. After serving as Georgetown's vice mayor, Lusby became Scott County's executive judge. Elected in 1990, Lusby was still in the position when I interviewed him in June 2017.

73. Alecia Swasy, "Toyota May Seek State Aid for Training at Engine Plant," *Lexington Herald-Leader*, November 10, 1987, A1; Wells, interview; McIntyre, interview; McAlinden, interview (closing quotation).

74. Koebel et al., "Impacts of the Toyota Plant," 26–27 (first two quotations); Apple, Johnston, and Bolton Bevins, *Scott County Kentucky*, 336–37; McIntyre, interview (third quotation); Gossey, interview; *1980 Census of Population: General Population Characteristics Kentucky* (Washington, D.C.: U.S. Government Printing Office, 1982), 19–14.

75. Wells, interview; William E. Osos to Owen Bieber, June 8, 1988; and Prather, "First Test Car" ("forever" quotation), both in folder 16, box 165, Bieber Papers; Robey, interview.

76. "Georgetown Needs By-Pass," *Georgetown News and Times*, January 10, 1990, 2A; "The True Figures?," *Georgetown News and Times*, January 17, 1990, 2A–3A (quotation); Apple, Johnston, and Bolton Bevins, *Scott County Kentucky*, 401.

77. "Toyota's Announcement Renews County's Golden Opportunity," *Georgetown News and Times*, November 28, 1990, 2A (first two quotations); "Council Made Right Decision," *Georgetown News and Times*, December 13, 1989, 2A (third quotation); Prather, interview.

78. Hank Bond and Mary Branham, "Japanese Anxious to Adapt to Culture," *Georgetown News and Times*, January 14, 1986, 1; "We Feel Most Welcome in Our Old Kentucky Home," *Georgetown News and Times*, January 21, 1986, 5 (first two quotations); "Back in 1957 We Brought Our First Two Cars to America," *Georgetown News and Times*, May 6, 1986, 9 (third and fourth quotations); Peter T. Kilborn, "Buoyed on Prosperity Since Toyota Moved In," *New York Times*, February 23, 1991, 9; Kristi Lopez, "Cho

Finds Good Friends and Good Fishing in Scott County," *Georgetown News-Graphic*, April 30, 1994, 2B; Robey, interview (closing quotation).

79. Bernice Bowers, "Inside Japan," *Georgetown News and Times*, March 11, 1986, 8; Apple, Johnston, and Bolton Bevins, *Scott County Kentucky*, 400; Kilborn, "Buoyed on Prosperity," 9; *1980 Census of Population*, 19–14; "Quick Facts," United States Census Bureau, accessed August 23, 2017, https://www.census.gov/quickfacts/fact/chart/georgetowncitykentucky,scottcountykentucky/RHI225216#viewtop.

80. Bryon Brewer, "How One Big Company Changed a Little Town Forever," *Georgetown News and Graphic*, April 30, 1994, 8A; Denise Keenan, "Toyota Annexed," *Georgetown News and Times*, April 21, 1987, 1; Gelsanliter, *Jump Start*, 127–28; Prather, interview (quotations).

81. Stephen Peterson, "Toyota Opens New Power Train Plant," *Georgetown News and Times*, December 6, 1989, 1; Kerfoot, "Oh, What a Feeling," 1; Dave Lavender, "Production Begins in Toyota Expansion," *Georgetown News-Graphic*, March 2, 1994, 1; Liz Caras Petros, "Toyota Introduces Camry Wagon," *Lexington Herald-Leader*, February 8, 1992, A7; Petros, "Toyota Plans $90 Million Expansion," *Lexington Herald-Leader*, January 28, 1992, 1; Conner, interview.

82. Lavender, "Production Begins," 1; "Collins Coming to County," *Georgetown Graphic*, February 6, 1992, 1; "Karen Griffith Knows Firsthand" (Toyota advertisement), *Georgetown News-Graphic*, February 26, 1994, 8; Maynard and Bunkley, "As Auto Prosperity Shifts," C1. The J. D. Power award was given to the plant that produced vehicles with the fewest reported problems in North America.

83. Conner, interview; Robey, interview; Wells, interview. This paragraph also draws on my tour of Toyota's Georgetown plant, completed on June 14, 2017 (notes in author's possession).

84. Apple, interview (quotation); Danny Hakim, "Auto Union and Honda Dispute Safety Record at Plants in Ohio," *New York Times*, June 26, 2002, 1; Steele, interview.

85. Ihara, *Toyota's Assembly Line*, ix–xiii (quotation on x), 164.

86. Bill Young to Toyota Team Members, November 9, 1989; and "Summary of Wages and Benefits for Toyota Workers at Georgetown, KY," ca. 1992 (quotations), both in folder 17, box 165, Bieber Papers.

87. Bill Young to Friend, November 14, 1989 (first two quotations); and Charles Wolfe, "Court Rules Handbooks Don't Block Worker Firings," unidentified clipping (other quotation), both in folder 17, box 165, Bieber Papers. "At Will" employees were not supposed to be fired for refusing to break a law or exercising a legal right, although some were.

88. Martha Layne Collins to Don Rostenkowski, July 10, 1987; and Kristian Coulter to Gerald Ford and Mitch McConnell, January 24, 1986, "Tobacco 1" folder, both in box 63; Martha Layne Collins to Norma Wood Saunders, October 16, 1986, "Toyota 4" folder, box 64 (Collins quotation), all in Collins Papers; Robey, interview.

89. "Introducing the Truth Team," undated flyer (ca. 1990); and "Would You Like to Help the UAW Destroy Your Job?," Truth Team flyer, January 29, 1990, both in folder 17, box 165, Bieber Papers.

90. William E. Osos to Owen Bieber, November 20, 1989; and Alex M. Warren Jr.

to William E. Brock, October 23, 1989 (quotations), both in folder 16, box 165, Bieber Papers.

91. Dick Shoemaker to Owen Bieber, March 4, 1990 (first quotation); and Dick Shoemaker to Bill Osos, March 10, 1990 (second quotation), both in folder 17, box 165, Bieber Papers; Jena McGregor, "The Biggest Mass Layoffs of the Past Two Decades," *Washington Post*, January 28, 2015.

92. Stamper, interview; Judy Harden organizing report, March 31, 1992, folder 17, box 165, Bieber Papers (quotation).

93. Ichiro Ogiso to Don Stillman, August 1, 1989; Owen Bieber to Bill Osos, August 14, 1989, both in folder 16, box 165; Owen Bieber to Odessa Komer, March 17, 1988, folder 62, box 6, all in Bieber Papers.

94. Mark Allan Long to Benjamin C. Perkins, May 6, 1992, folder 24, box 165, Bieber Papers.

95. Honda North America, Inc., issue brief, ca. February 1995, folder 26, box 296, Patricia Buckhart files, Glenn Papers; International Executive Board Minutes, September 14–15, 1992, 14, box 18, Secretary-Treasurer's Papers (Bieber quotation); Warren Brown, "Toyota to Produce More in U.S., Canada," *Washington Post*, September 14, 1994, A7 (other quotation).

96. UAW Membership Charts in "Membership 1994; Charts Representing, 1981–1994" folder 61, box 5; Dick Shoemaker to Owen Bieber, February 9, 1994, folder 65, box 30, both in Bieber Papers.

97. Bieber oral history interview, 90 (Bieber quotation); Jeremy W. Peters, "Hardly a Union Hotbed," *New York Times*, September 4, 2007, C1.

98. Patton and Patton, "Dynamics of Growth and Change," 123–52, 134; Trey Crumbie, "Scott County's Population Growth Brings Benefits, Challenges," *Lexington Herald-Leader*, January 8, 2017; Maynard and Bunkley, "As Auto Prosperity Shifts," C1; Conner, interview.

99. Apple, interview; Price Smith, interview (first quotation); Wells, interview; Prather, interview (second quotation).

100. Chappell, "In Georgetown"; Chappell, interview; King, interview.

101. "Kentucky Wants a $1.6 Billion Toyota-Mazda Plant," *Lexington Herald-Leader*, August 8, 2017; *Automotive News Economic Development Guide*, July 2017, 24.

102. Lesser, interview; Musgrove, interview; "City of Greer Joint Statement," September 20, 1993, "City of Greer Joint Statement" folder, box 1, Carroll A. Campbell Gubernatorial Papers, South Carolina Department of Archives and History, Columbia, South Carolina (hereafter Campbell Gubernatorial Papers).

CHAPTER 5: A "SUCCESS STORY"?

1. Doron P. Levin, "Toyota Is Said to Pick Site in Kentucky," *New York Times*, December 4, 1985, 1 (first quotation); Chappell, interview (other quotation).

2. Pressley, "The South's New-Car Smell," A1 (first and second quotations); *The Harbour Report: North America 2003*, 9 (third quotation).

3. "BMW of North America, Inc. Press Information," June 23, 1992, "BMW" folder, box 1, Patterson Papers; "Statement to U.S. News Media"; Hall et al., *Like a Family*.

4. "Production Overview: BMW U.S. Factory," BMW website, accessed February 7, 2017, https://www.bmwusfactory.com/manufacturing/production-overview /?r=1486423034303#stats; Ely Portillo, "BMW's Success Story Spurs North Carolina Officials to Lure an Automaker," *Charlotte Observer*, November 14, 2014; WardsAuto, "U.S. Vehicle Sales"; Jack Ewing, "Who May Suffer the Most from Auto Tariffs?," *New York Times*, July 4, 2018, 1.

5. Chappell, interview (first quotation); Spartanburg County homepage, accessed February 9, 2017, http://www.spartanburgcounty.org/; Portillo, "BMW's Success Story" (second quotation); David Wren, "BMW's Greer Plant Leads U.S. in Car Exports," *Charleston Post and Courier*, February 15, 2017; Ana Swanson, "As Trump Hits China, Detroit Braces for Pain," *New York Times*, July 13, 2018, 1.

6. Chappell, interview; Campbell quotations from "Bullets for the Governor: BMW Presentation to Foreign Media," November 12, 1994, 2, 3, 14, box 9, Carroll A. Campbell Jr. Papers, South Carolina Political Collections Library, University of South Carolina, Columbia, South Carolina (hereafter Campbell Papers); Micheline Maynard, "Shifting Michigan Southward," *New York Times*, June 22, 2005, C1 (other quotation).

7. "BMW of North America, Inc. Press Information"; Interview with Mrs. Iris Campbell and son Mike Campbell, March 20, 2000, 11, Governor's Mansion Oral History Project, South Carolina Political Collections Library, accessed June 17, 2020, https://digital.tcl.sc.edu/digital/collection/scpcot/id/11/.

8. Sean Loughlin, "Union Leaders Attacking BMW," *Spartanburg Herald-Journal*, March 31, 1993; and Lee Ann Fleet, "Union to Protest BMW Plant, Raises Environment Issue," *Greenville News*, March 24, 1993, 1A.

9. Doron Levin, "This Is How BMW Became the Top-Selling Luxury Car Company in the U.S.," *Fortune*, May 12, 2015 (quotation); Jacobs, *New Domestic Automakers*, 155; WardsAuto, "U.S. Vehicle Sales."

10. "BMW of North America, Inc. Press Information"; Jacobs, *New Domestic Automakers*, 155–56.

11. "Bullets for the Governor," 16, 19; Jacobs, *New Domestic Automakers*, 156–57 (quotation on 156).

12. "Bullets for the Governor," 16, 19 (quotation); Jacobs, *New Domestic Automakers*, 156–57.

13. Henry Eichel, "S.C. Played Ardent Suitor to BMW," *Charlotte Observer*, June 24, 1992, 1A; Chuck Carroll and Betsy Teter, "BMW: How We Did It," *Spartanburg Herald-Journal*, June 24, 1992.

14. Carroll and Teter, "BMW: How We Did It."

15. Carroll A. Campbell Jr. to Larry Wilson, April 23, 1987; and Carroll A. Campbell Jr. to James N. Strausbaugh, February 20, 1987 (quotations), both in box 1, Economic Development Project Files, Campbell Gubernatorial Papers.

16. "Strategy for a Public Relations and Press Campaign in German-Speaking Countries," n.d. (quotations); and "International Business Development Activity Report," February 23, 1988–April 25, 1988), both in box 1, Economic Development Project Files, Campbell Gubernatorial Papers.

17. David L. Headrick to Robert Chapman, March 8, 1989, box 3, Economic Development Administrative Reference Files, Campbell Gubernatorial Papers.

18. "The South Carolina Economy: Perspectives and Possibilities" (South Carolina State Development Board report), October 6, 1986, 1, 4, 7, 10, box 1, Economic Development Project Files, Campbell Gubernatorial Papers.

19. "From Start to Finish: A Detailed Chronology of Events Leading to BMW's Decision," June 23, 1992, "Background Briefing Information" folder, box 1, Press Office files, Campbell Gubernatorial Papers.

20. Ibid.

21. Fred Baldwin, "South Carolina Wins the Prize," *Appalachia* (Journal of the Appalachian Regional Commission) 25, no. 4 (Fall 1992), 3; and Jim DuPlessis, Tim Flach, and Anne Perry, "Upstate Wins Race," *Greenville News*, June 23, 1992, A1.

22. Eichel, "S.C. Played Ardent Suitor," 1A (first two quotations); "Economic Impact Analysis."

23. "Statement to U.S. News Media"; Lee Ann Fleet, "What's State's Return on Incentive Package?," *Greenville News*, June 24, 1992, "BMW" folder, box 1, Patterson Papers; Leonard Page to Owen Bieber, February 2, 1993, folder 23, box 1, Bieber Papers.

24. "Economic Impact Analysis."

25. Ibid. (quotations); Eichel, "S.C. Played Ardent Suitor," 1A.

26. Bernd Pischetsrieder to Carroll A. Campbell Jr., March 20, 1992, Correspondence files, box 4, Economic Development Division files, Campbell Gubernatorial Papers.

27. "From Start to Finish: A Detailed Chronology of Events Leading to BMW's Decision," June 23, 1992, "Background Briefing Information" folder, box 1, Campbell Gubernatorial Papers.

28. "BMW Might Be Shifting Eyes to Spartanburg County," *Associated Press*, March 31, 1992 ("big" quotation); Carroll and Teter, "BMW: How We Did It" ("hesitant" quotation).

29. "Bullets for the Governor," 7–18, 38–39 (quotations on 9, 17), 49; Jacobs, *New Domestic Automakers*, 157, 159.

30. "BMW of North America, Inc. Press Information."

31. Jacobs, *New Domestic Automakers*, 157, 159; Nelson quoted in Carroll and Teter, "BMW: How We Did It."

32. "BMW of North America, Inc. Press Information."

33. "Bullets for the Governor," 37, 41; BMW quoted in Fleet, "Union to Protest BMW Plant."

34. "BMW of North America, Inc. Press Information"; Jacobs, *New Domestic Automakers*, 157.

35. "Bullets for the Governor," 32; Fred Monk, "Painful Trend Will Continue," *The State*, July 7, 1996; John Monk, "Roger Milliken," *The State*, October 7, 2001; "Statement to U.S. News Media"; Derrick, interview.

36. Maunula, *Guten Tag*, 2 (quotation); Marko Maunula, "Hoechst," in *South Carolina Encyclopedia*, accessed December 11, 2017, http://www.scencyclopedia.org/sce/entries/hoechst/.

37. "Bullets for the Governor," 20–24, 35 (quotation), 36, 53, 54; "Bavaria Meets the Blue Ridge," *U.S. News and World Report*, July 6, 1992, 20.

38. "Remarks by Governor Carroll A. Campbell, Jr. to BMW," December 10, 1992, box 8, Campbell Papers.

39. Carroll A. Campbell Jr. to Eberhard von Kuenheim, March 23, 1992, Correspondence files, box 4, Economic Development Division files, Campbell Gubernatorial Papers.

40. Baldwin, "South Carolina Wins the Prize" (quotation); Eichel, "S.C. Played Ardent Suitor," 1A.

41. Carroll A. Campbell Jr. to Dr. Bernd Pischetsrieder, March 17, 1992, Correspondence files, box 4, Economic Development Division files, Campbell Gubernatorial Papers; Betsy Teter and Adam C. Smith, "Runway May Be Extended for Big Planes," *Spartanburg Herald-Journal*, April 2, 1992.

42. "From Start to Finish: A Detailed Chronology of Events Leading to BMW's Decision," June 23, 1992, "Background Briefing Information" folder, box 1, Campbell Gubernatorial Papers.

43. Interview with Mrs. Iris Campbell and son Mike Campbell, 11. Carroll Campbell was diagnosed with Alzheimer's disease in 2001, ending his political career. He died in 2005.

44. Eichel, "S.C. Played Ardent Suitor," 1A.

45. See, for example, "Union Hits at BMW Plans for US Plant," *Financial Times*, July 29, 1992.

46. "Strategy for a Public Relations and Press Campaign in German-Speaking Countries," n.d., box 1, Economic Development Project files, Campbell Gubernatorial Papers (first quotation); "Bullets for the Governor," 25, 27 (second quotation).

47. *Europe* magazine quotation in "Quotes for Tucker," January 15, 1993, "Quotes for Tucker Eskew" folder, box 1, Campbell Papers; and Fleet, "Union to Protest BMW Plant"; Joyce, interview.

48. "Bullets for the Governor," 45; Fred Monk, "Unions Spreading False Information, Campbell Says," *The State*, April 3, 1993 (quotation).

49. Loughlin, "Union Leaders Attacking BMW"; Nicole Sterghos, "Unions Attack BMW," *Spartanburg Herald-Journal*, March 24, 1993, 1A (quotation); Doron P. Levin, "What BMW Sees in South Carolina," *New York Times*, April 11, 1993, F5.

50. "The Case for Saving the Big Three" (Economic Strategy Institute report), 1992, folder 32, box 255, Laura Beers files, Glenn Papers; quotation from *The Encyclopedia of Southern Culture*, cited in Loughlin, "Union Leaders Attacking BMW"; Ogino, "Naze Nikkei Maker"; Cobb, *The Selling of the South*, esp. 2–3.

51. Don Stillman to Stan Marshall, July 30, 1992, folder 23, box 1, Bieber Papers.

52. "Union Hits at BMW Plans for US Plant," *Financial Times*, July 29, 1992 (first and last quotations); "IG Metall Criticizes BMW-Manager" (translation of IG Metall press item), July 28, 1992 (other quotations), folder 23 (BMW South Carolina Plant, Union Talks, 1992–94), box 1, Bieber Papers.

53. Owen Bieber to Eberhard von Kuenheim, August 27, 1992, folder 23, box 1, Bieber Papers.

54. Von Kuenheim quoted in Klaus Zwickel to Eberhard von Kuenheim, August 7, 1992; and Owen Bieber to Eberhard von Kuenheim, December 11, 1992 (Bieber quotations), both in folder 23, box 1, Bieber Papers.

55. Klaus Zwickel to Owen Bieber, December 17, 1992, folder 23, box 1, Bieber Papers.

56. Eberhard von Kuenheim to Owen Bieber, December 22, 1992; and Don Stillman to Owen Bieber, January 6, 1993, both in folder 23, box 1, Bieber Papers.

57. Carol Smith, "Fluor Daniel Wins $100-Million BMW Contract to Build Auto Plant in S.C.," *Los Angeles Times*, October 2, 1992; Don Stillman to Owen Bieber and Stan Marshall, September 18, 1992, folder 23, box 1, Bieber Papers (quotation).

58. "Issue" quotation in "The Unions Come Calling," *Orangeburg (S.C.) Times and Democrat*, n.d., box 25, Campbell Papers (reprinting of editorial from *The State*); Loughlin, "Union Leaders Attacking BMW" ("substandard" quotation); Nicole Sterghos, "Unions Press Campbell on BMW," *Spartanburg Herald-Journal*, March 26, 1993, A14; and Fleet, "Union to Protest BMW Plant" (last quotation).

59. Frank Joyce to Owen Bieber, January 12, 1993, folder 23, box 1, Bieber Papers; Loughlin, "Union Leaders Attacking BMW" (Perkins quotation).

60. Owen Bieber to "Stan," September 30, 1993, folder 62, box 5, Bieber Papers (Bieber quotation); Fleet, "Union to Protest BMW Plant" (other quotations).

61. Monk, "Unions Spreading False Information"; "What Is Labor After in Efforts at BMW," *Greenwood Index-Journal*, undated clipping, box 25, Campbell Papers; and Betsy Teter, "Unions Misfire with First Shot against BMW," *Spartanburg Herald-Journal*, April 4, 1993.

62. Campbell quotations in "The Unions Come Calling," *Orangeburg Times and Democrat*, undated clipping (reprinting of editorial from *The State*); and Eskew quoted in Brigid Schulte, "Congress Invoked in BMW Fight," *Charlotte Observer*, March 31, 1993, IB, both in box 25, Campbell Papers; Sterghos, "Unions Attack BMW" (closing quotation).

63. Levin, "What BMW Sees," F5; Chappell, interview; Lindsay Chappell, "Some Managers Come from Outside, Some Others Are Snatched," *Automotive News*, June 13, 2005 (closing quotation).

64. Jim Clarke, "BMW Gives Employees Sense of Pride in Work," *Los Angeles Times*, May 29, 1994 (Hitt quotation); Levin, "What BMW Sees," F5 (other quotations); Chappell, interview.

65. Clarke, "BMW Gives Employees"; "UAW Officials Vow to Organize Workers at Transplant Plants," *Oklahoma City Journal Record*, May 18, 1995 ("screen" quotation); Leonard Page to Owen Bieber, February 2, 1993, folder 23, box 1, Bieber Papers ("anti-union" quotation).

66. Leonard Page to Owen Bieber, February 2, 1993, folder 23, box 1, Bieber Papers; Joyce, interview.

67. Walter C. Jones, "South Invites Vehicle Plants," *Savannah Morning News*, April 20, 2002, 1A (Hennett quotation); Sterghos, "Unions Press Campbell on BMW"; "Patterson Welcomes BMW" (press release), June 22, 1992 (first two Patterson quotations); and "Jobs, Economic Growth" (Patterson handwritten notes), n.d. (closing Patterson quotation), both in box 1, Patterson Papers.

68. See, for example, "City of Greer Joint Statement," September 20, 1993, "City of Greer Joint Statement" folder, box 1, Campbell Gubernatorial Papers.

69. Faye Patton to Governor Carroll Campbell, August 23, 1992 (first two quotations); Kathryn W. Hill and William J. Hill to Governor Carroll Campbell, August 18, 1992; Rhonda David to Governor Carroll Campbell, August 21, 1992 (closing quota-

tion), all in "Flatwood Road Community" folder, box 5, Economic Development Division files, Campbell Gubernatorial Papers.

70. Douglas McKay III to James D. Fortner, September 14, 1992, "Flatwood Road Community" folder, box 5, Campbell Gubernatorial Papers.

71. Bryan L. DuCayne to Your Honor, December 13, 1993, Correspondence files, box 5, Economic Development Division files, Campbell Gubernatorial Papers; Ernest F. Hollings to Edward E. Saleeby, November 18, 1993, box 9, 103rd Congress files (quotation), Ernest F. Hollings Papers, South Carolina Political Collections, University of South Carolina, Columbia; Monk, "Painful Trend Will Continue."

72. Jones, "South Invites Vehicle Plants," 1A; David Green, "The Price?," *Spartanburg Herald-Journal*, April 2, 1992.

73. Adam C. Smith, "What Drives Spartanburg's Leadership?," *Spartanburg Herald-Journal*, April 12, 1992, B1; Levin, "What BMW Sees," F5.

74. Fleet, "What's State's Return?"

75. Levin, "What BMW Sees," F5.

76. Pressley, "The South's New-Car Smell," A1; Ballenger quoted in Clarke, "BMW Gives Employees."

77. Levin, "What BMW Sees," F5 (first quotation); "Production Overview: BMW U.S. Factory," BMW website, accessed February 7, 2017, https://www.bmwusfactory.com/manufacturing/production-overview/?r=1486423034303#stats (second quotation); "BMW of North America, Inc. Press Information."

78. Jim Hodges to Karen Daily, June 18, 2001, file number 112660; Charles S. Way Jr. to Dr. Helmut Leube, July 29, 2002, file number 200641; and Jim Hodges to Jack F. Mayer, January 15, 2002, file number 200545, all in Central Correspondence files, Hodges Gubernatorial Papers.

79. Jack F. Mayer to Jim Hodges, January 25, 2002, file number 200545, Central Correspondence files, Hodges Gubernatorial Papers; Robert J. Edsall to Governor James Hodges, August 28, 2001; Robert J. Edsall, "State Gives Away Tax Income to BMW," *Greenville News*, August 27, 2001; and Jim Hodges to Robert J. Edsall, September 14, 2001, all in file number 117229, Central Correspondence files, Hodges Gubernatorial Papers.

80. Cobb, *The South and America*, 207; Jacobs, *New Domestic Automakers*, 2, 160. According to Jacobs, to qualify as a "new domestic" automaker, a producer had to meet or exceed the 62.5 percent domestic content requirement under the Canada–United States Trade Pact of 1965 and NAFTA (1994), thus qualifying for a waiving of all duties on imported parts; and manufacture 62.5 percent or more of the vehicles it sold in the United States or Canada in a given year in either of these two nations (*New Domestic Automakers*, 8).

81. Charles Pope and R. A. Zaldivar, "S.C.'s Poverty Persists While Income Rises," *The State*, September 30, 1997, A1; Alemayehu Bishaw and John Iceland, "Poverty 1999: Census 2000 Brief," U.S. Census Bureau Report, May 2003, accessed April 12, 2018, https://www.census.gov/prod/2003pubs/c2kbr-19.pdf; "Labor Force, Employment and Unemployment for South Carolina in 1992"; and "Labor Force, Employment and Unemployment for South Carolina in 1998," South Carolina Department of Employment and Workforce, Bureau of Labor Statistics, accessed April 12, 2018, https://jobs.scworks

.org/vosnet/analyzer/results.aspx?enc=HofuwY22SoLTS/uC+bpmi7ntbB42L7XyypLjx +HEeKO=; Peter Applebome, "Reminders of Its Old Poverty Hit South," *New York Times*, September 10, 1991, A1; Joyce, interview.

82. Minchin, *Empty Mills*, 211–45; Raynor, interview (quotation); "Labor Force, Employment."

83. Joyce, interview.

CHAPTER 6: SURPRISING THE WORLD

1. Chuck Carroll, "Mercedes; Campbell Wary of Unionism," *Spartanburg Herald-Journal*, April 9, 1993; Chappell, interview; Martin, interview; Campbell quoted in "A Champion's Effort," *Spartanburg Herald-Journal*, November 10, 1993, A8. Kurt Martin is a pseudonym.

2. Sewell, interview; Eckman, interview; "Surprised" quotation in "20th Celebration: Birth of Alabama Auto," Mercedes-Benz U.S. International, accessed December 8, 2017, https://mbusi.com/about/20th-celebration/20th-celebration-economy.

3. "Economic Impact Analysis of the Mercedes-Benz A.G. MPV Production Facility," n.d., folder 10, SG14281, Alabama Governors' Papers (Jim Folsom Jr.), Alabama Department of Archives and History, Montgomery, Alabama (hereafter ADAH).

4. "Contribution of the Automotive Industry to the Economies of All Fifty States and the United States" (Center for Automotive Research report), January 2015, 6, 39, accessed March 19, 2015, www.cargroup.org/?module=Publications; McNair, interview; Longgrear, interview; Strange, interview (last two quotations).

5. Chappell, interview; Eckman, interview.

6. "Remarks by Dr. Dieter Zetsche," September 30, 1993, folder 10 (quotations); "All Activity Report" (Mercedes-Benz newsletter), folder 12, both in SG14281, Alabama Governors' Papers (Forrest "Fob" James), ADAH; Martin, interview (closing quotations).

7. "Mercedes-Benz Project, Inc." (Mercedes-Benz press release), n.d., folder 10, SG14281, Alabama Governors Papers (Jim Folsom Jr.), ADAH.

8. "Mercedes-Benz Focuses on Globalization" (Mercedes-Benz document), n.d., folder 10, SG14281, Alabama Governors Papers (Jim Folsom Jr.), ADAH.

9. Ibid.; Martin, interview (closing quotation).

10. "Remarks by Dr. Dieter Zetsche," September 30, 1993 ("education" and "members" quotations); and "Mercedes-Benz Selects Tuscaloosa, Alabama for New Passenger Vehicle Manufacturing Facility" (Mercedes-Benz press release), n.d. (other Mercedes quotations), both in folder 10, SG14281, Alabama Governors Papers (Jim Folsom Jr.), ADAH; Helene Cooper and Michael J. McCarthy, "Mercedes Plant Said to Be Set for Alabama," *Wall Street Journal*, September 29, 1993, A5 (closing quotation).

11. Chappell, interview; "Decision Near on Mercedes Site," *New York Times*, September 29, 1993, D3; Sewell, interview; Castile, interview; Siegelman quoted in Ted Pratt and Michael Tomberlin, "$600 Million Project to Double Production at Vance Site," *Birmingham News*, August 29, 2000, 1A.

12. Cooper and McCarthy, "Mercedes Plant," A5 (first quotation); Lee H. Warner to

Jim Hayes, February 10, 2000, folder "H," SG25926, Senior Advisor Subject files, Alabama Governors Papers (Don Siegelman), ADAH (second quotation).

13. "Century of Growth: Alabama Grew, but Not Like Others," *Birmingham News*, December 30, 1999, 10A; "Table 22: Population of the 100 Largest Urban Places: 1990," U.S. Census Bureau, accessed December 12, 2017, https://www.census.gov/population/www/documentation/twps0027/tab22.txt; Julie Bosman, "Atlanta Looks to Sum Itself Up in Just Six Words," *New York Times*, November 17, 2005.

14. "Mercedes-Benz Selects Tuscaloosa," n.d. (Werner quotations); "Remarks by Dr. Dieter Zetsche," September 30, 1993 (Zetsche quotations), folder 10, SG14281, Alabama Governors Papers (Jim Folsom Jr.), ADAH; Peter Applebome, "South Raises Stakes in Fight for Jobs," *New York Times*, October 4, 1993, A12 (Applebome quotation); Allen R. Myerson, "O Governor, Won't You Buy Me a Mercedes Plant?," *New York Times*, September 1, 1996, F1; Longgrear, interview.

15. Jacobs, *New Domestic Automakers*, 172; Sewell, interview; Myerson, "O Governor," F1; "Feel Good about Mercedes Effort" (editorial), *Charleston Post and Courier*, October 1, 1993, 16A (first quotation); "A Champion's Effort," *Spartanburg Herald-Journal*, November 10, 1993, A8 (other quotations).

16. Don Phillips, "Jim Folsom, 79, Colorful Governor of Alabama in '40s and '50s, Dies," *Washington Post*, November 22, 1987 (first quotation); Dunlap, interview; Ed Castile to Jimmy Baker, January 26, 1995, folder 7, SG14281, Alabama Governors Papers (Forrest "Fob" James), ADAH (second quotation).

17. "Mercedes Expects Thousands of Job Seekers," *Montgomery Advertiser*, August 11, 1994, 11A; "Training Facility and Training" (extract of Project Rosewood agreement), September 29, 1993, folder 7 (quotations), SG14281, Alabama Governors Papers (Forrest "Fob" James), ADAH; Myerson, "O Governor," F1.

18. "Mercedes-Benz Selects Tuscaloosa"; Myerson, "O Governor," F1.

19. Jacobs, *New Domestic Automakers*, 172; Sewell, interview (quotations); Dunlap, interview; Benjamin Forgey, "The Rich Deposits of Birmingham's History," *Washington Post*, March 4, 1995, C1.

20. Carroll, "Mercedes; Campbell Wary" (quotation); International Executive Board Minutes, May 30–June 1, 1989, 36–37, box 11, Secretary-Treasurer's Papers.

21. Myerson, "O Governor," F1 (first quotation); Martin, interview; Keyes, interview.

22. Paul Tosto and Fred Monk, "Mercedes Bypasses S.C.," *The State*, September 30, 1993, 8A (Zehentner quotations); Chappell, interview; Jacobs, *New Domestic Automakers*, 172 ("second child" quotation); Sewell, interview.

23. Martin, interview.

24. Ted Pratt, "Honda Greets First 17 Workers," *Birmingham News*, November 10, 2000, 1B; "Mercedes-Benz 'Plants Seed' for Future at Groundbreaking" (Mercedes-Benz press release), May 3, 1994 (Zetsche quotations); and "Mercedes-Benz Project, Inc." (Mercedes-Benz press release), n.d., both in folder 10, SG14281, Alabama Governors Papers (Jim Folsom Jr.), ADAH; Martin, interview; Armstrong interview (closing quotation).

25. "Mercedes Jobs Attract 7,000," *Montgomery Advertiser*, August 17, 1994, 5B; "Mercedes Sets Deadline for Job Seekers," *Montgomery Advertiser*, August 13, 1994, 10A;

Walter C. Jones, "South Invites Vehicle Plants," *Savannah Morning News*, April 20, 2002, 1A.

26. Lindsay Chappell, "Alabama's Challenge: Find Enough Auto Workers," *Automotive News*, May 6, 2002; Martin, interview; Castile, interview; "Training Outline" (Mercedes-Benz document), November 1994, folder 7, SG14281, Alabama Governors Papers (Forrest "Fob" James), ADAH ("team" quotation).

27. "Remarks by Dr. Dieter Zetsche," September 30, 1993 (quotation); "Mercedes-Benz Plant in Tuscaloosa: Fact Sheet," n.d., both in folder 10, SG14281, Alabama Governors Papers (Jim Folsom Jr.), ADAH.

28. Chappell, "Alabama's Challenge"; Sewell, interview; "About Mercedes-Benz U.S. International: Facts & Figures," Mercedes-Benz U.S. International, accessed December 13, 2017, https://mbusi.com/about/mbusi-corporate-info/facts-figures (penultimate quotation); Armstrong, interview (closing quotation).

29. Armstrong, interview; Keyes, interview; Longgrear, interview.

30. Ed Castile to Billy Joe Camp, August 27, 1993, folder 10, SG14281, Alabama Governors Papers (Jim Folsom Jr.), ADAH (first quotation); "MB Project," December 12, 1994, folder 12, SG14281, Alabama Governors Papers (Forrest "Fob" James), ADAH (other quotations).

31. Ed Castile to Jimmy Baker, January 26, 1995, folder 7, SG14281, Alabama Governors Papers (Forrest "Fob" James), ADAH (first quotation); "Welcome to Mercedes-Benz U.S. International, Inc. (MBUSI), Tuscaloosa County, Alabama," Mercedes-Benz U.S. International, accessed December 13, 2017, https://mbusi.com/ (closing quotation).

32. Eddie Curran, "Alabamians Seem to Accept Incentives for Auto Plant," *Mobile Register*, April 2, 2002, 5B; Bailey, Kennedy, and Cohen, *The American Pageant*, 992–93; Michael Byrne, "Election Imperils Progress for Workers," *AFL-CIO News*, November 14, 1994, 1.

33. Strange, interview; Lindsay Chappell, "Alabama Politics Ensnare Mercedes Project," *Automotive News*, February 28, 1994.

34. Chappell, "Alabama Politics Ensnare" (Parsons quotation); Myerson, "O Governor," F1 (Torbert quotation).

35. David Firestone, "Bastion of Confederacy Finds Its Future May Hinge on Rejecting the Past," *New York Times*, December 5, 1999, 29 (quotations); Brian Lyman, "Alabama State Leaders Silent on Confederate Flag," *Montgomery Advertiser*, June 23, 2015; "Alabama Capitol Won't Fly Confederate Flag," *New York Times*, May 1, 1993, 7. The flag's removal also reflected pressure from African American groups.

36. Chris Bence to Fob re "Mercedes," September 8, 1994 (quotations); and Donald J. Claxton to Fob James, August 5, 1994, both in folder 16, SG14281, Alabama Governors Papers (Forrest "Fob" James), ADAH.

37. Chris to Governor James, May 16, 1997, folder 2, SG14281, Alabama Governors Papers (Forrest "Fob" James), ADAH; Martin, interview (closing quotations).

38. Bob Davis and Chris Bence to Governor Fob James, December 12, 1994 (quotation); and "MB Project," December 12, 1994, both in folder 12, SG14281, Alabama Governors Papers (Forrest "Fob" James), ADAH.

39. Ed Castile to Charles Snyder, November 15, 1994, folder 14, SG14281, Alabama Governors Papers (Jim Folsom Jr.), ADAH.

40. "Benz Debt 'Crippling' Tuscaloosa," *Montgomery Advertiser*, September 22, 1994 (quotation); Robert DeWitt, "Mercedes Costs Worry City Council," *Tuscaloosa News*, September 23, 1994.

41. "They Promised Too Much," *Wirtschaftswoche*, April 1995, English translation, folder 2, SG14281, Alabama Governors Papers (Forrest "Fob" James), ADAH; Myerson, "O Governor," F1.

42. Andreas Renschler to Fob James, April 19, 1995, folder 2, SG14281, Alabama Governors Papers (Forrest "Fob" James), ADAH.

43. "Mercedes-Benz U.S. International: Message Points for Media Inquiries on New Administration," February 1995, folder 2, SG14281, Alabama Governors Papers (Forrest "Fob" James), ADAH.

44. Chris Bence to Governor James, May 16, 1997, folder 2, SG14281, Alabama Governors Papers (Forrest "Fob" James), ADAH; Myerson, "O Governor," F1 (closing quotation).

45. James Barrett to Dr. H. Gzik, April 20, 1993; Owen Bieber to Mercedes-Benz AG, April 20, 1993; and Owen Bieber et al. to Helmut Werner, September 27, 1993 (first three quotations), all in folder 62, box 5, Bieber Papers; Keyes, interview (other quotation).

46. Bobby Lee Thompson to Ted Letson, August 11, 1994, folder 62, box 5, Bieber Papers.

47. Jacobs, *New Domestic Automakers*, 173; Robyn Meredith, "A Union March on Alabama," *New York Times*, June 29, 1999, C1.

48. Meredith, "A Union March," C1; Dunlap, interview; Pratt and Tomberlin, "$600 Million Project."

49. Lindsay Chappell, "Hyundai Goes Low on U.S. Wages," *Automotive News*, May 26, 2003 (McAlinden quotations); Chappell, "Hyundai's Wages Are among the Lowest," *Automotive News*, January 19, 2004 (other quotation); Jerry Dubrowski, "U.S. Costs Attracting Foreign-Car Factories," *Washington Times*, October 29, 1993, E1.

50. Meredith, "A Union March," C1 (Hallmark quotation); Dunlap, interview; Pratt and Tomberlin, "$600 Million Project"; Keith Bradsher, "Union Moves to Hold Vote at Nissan Plant in Tennessee," *New York Times*, August 15, 2001, 1.

51. Longgrear, interview; Myerson, "O Governor," F1 (third and fourth quotations); Jacobs, *New Domestic Automakers*, 173; Todd Kieffman, "Plans Dazzle Family," *Montgomery Advertiser*, April 2, 2002, 1A; Pratt and Tomberlin, "$600 Million Project" (Hubbert quotation).

52. Pratt and Tomberlin, "$600 Million Project" (Hicks quotation); Lindsay Chappell, "Transplant Growth Lures, Stymies UAW," *Automotive News*, August 27, 2001.

53. "Rural Ala. Auto Plant Turns UAW Battleground," *Detroit News*, October 27, 2003 (quotations); Rick Popely, "UAW May Have to Turn to the South," *McClatchy-Tribune Business News*, July 16, 2006, 1.

54. Popely, "UAW," 1.

55. Ibid.; Longgrear, interview.

56. Popely, "UAW," 1; Casteel, interview; Martin, interview; Armstrong, interview (closing quotation); Longgrear, interview.

57. Armstrong, interview (first quotation); "UAW President Dennis Williams," UAW, accessed February 16, 2017, https://uaw.org/executive-board/uaw-president-dennis -williams/; Doron Levin, "UAW Wants to Unionize Mercedes-Benz Plant in Alabama," *Fortune*, October 7, 2014 (other quotation).

58. Mike Ramsey, "UAW Plans to Set Up Local Units near VW and Daimler Plants," *Wall Street Journal*, July 11, 2014, B4 (first two quotations); Levin, "UAW Wants to Unionize" (Zetsche quotation); Casteel, interview.

59. "MBUSI: Facts and Figures," Mercedes-Benz U.S. International, accessed February 14, 2017, https://www.mbusi.com/about/mbusi-corporate-info/facts-figures; *The Harbour Report 2002*, 10; WardsAuto, "U.S. Vehicle Sales."

60. "Advisory Opinion No. 99–62" (Alabama Ethics Commission), December 1, 1999, container 7, folder 28, SG25744, Alabama Governors Papers (Don Siegelman), ADAH (first three quotations); Sewell, interview; Castile, interview.

61. Jerry Underwood, "Boom Bypasses State's Rural Areas," *Birmingham News*, November 12, 1999, 1E; Keyes, interview; "Alabama Educational Attainment, 2012–2016," U.S. Census Bureau, accessed July 24, 2018, https://www.census.gov/search-results .html?page=1&stateGeo=non . . . p=SERP&q=education+ranking&search.x=0&search. y=0&search=submit; "Percentage of People in Poverty by State Using 2- and 3-Year Averages: 2013–2014 and 2015–2016," U.S. Census Bureau, accessed July 24, 2018, https:// www.census.gov/library/publications/2017/demo/p60-259.html.

62. Chappell, "Alabama's Challenge"; Don Siegelman to Terry Everett, May 23, 2001, folder 12, box 26, SG25686, Alabama Governors Papers (Don Siegelman), ADAH; Sewell, interview; "State and Area Employment, Hours, and Earnings (Manufacturing, Alabama)," Bureau of Labor Statistics, accessed January 12, 2018, https://data.bls.gov/ timeseries/SMS01000003000000001?amp%253bdata_tool=XGtable&output_view=- data&include_graphs=true.

63. "We're 49th: No High School Diploma Means Life of Poverty," *Birmingham News*, December 26, 2000, 14A (first quotation); "Century of Growth: Alabama Grew, but Not Like Others," *Birmingham News*, December 30, 1999, 10A.

64. "US Steel Idling Alabama Mill; About 1,100 Jobs Affected," *Associated Press State Wire: Alabama*, August 17, 2015; Dunlap, interview.

65. *The Harbour Report 2001*, 8, 13 (quotation); Honda North America, Inc., issue brief, ca. February 1995, folder 26, box 296, Patricia Buckheit files, Glenn Papers.

66. Ogino, "Naze Nikkei Maker," 57–59; Lindner, interview.

CHAPTER 7: Y'ALL COME?

1. "Hyundai to Build Alabama Plant," *New York Times*, April 2, 2002, C2 (first quotation); George Talbot, "Hyundai's Plant Coming to Alabama," *Mobile Register*, April 2, 2002, 1A; "About HMMA," Hyundai Motor Manufacturing Alabama, accessed December 22, 2017, https://www.hmmausa.com/our-company/about-hmma/ (closing quotation); McNair, interview.

2. "Board Grants Authority to Close Hyundai Deal," *Anniston Star*, April 12, 2002; "Dealers: New Product Will Help Reach Hyundai's Goal," *Automotive News*, February 3, 2003.

3. "Board Grants Authority to Close Hyundai Deal," *Anniston Star*, April 12, 2002 (Siegelman quotations); "Dealers: New Product"; Burton, interview; Todd Kieffman, "Plans Dazzle Family," *Montgomery Advertiser*, April 2, 2002.

4. Strange, interview; Bob Johnson, "Governor Announces Initiatives to Help Existing Industry," *Tuscaloosa News*, April 9, 2002 (Riggs quotations); and Mary Orndorff, "Carmaker Offered Test Drives, Tours to State's Congressional Delegation," *Birmingham News*, April 2, 2002, 4A (Henry quotation).

5. "The *Tuscaloosa News* on Hyundai Announcement," *Talladega (Ala.) Daily Home*, April 7, 2002.

6. Jacobs, *New Domestic Automakers*, 2, 195; "About HMMA"; "Hyundai Motor Manufacturing Alabama, LLC Information Sheet," October 2017, Hyundai Motor Manufacturing Alabama, accessed December 22, 2017, https://www.hmmausa.com/wp -content/uploads/2017/10/Fact-Sheet-10_16_2017.pdf.

7. For a definition and history of Alabama's Black Belt, including coverage of its endemic poverty, see Terance L. Winemiller, "Black Belt Region in Alabama," in *Encyclopedia of Alabama*, accessed January 17, 2018, http://www.encyclopediaofalabama.org /article/h-2458.

8. Eckman, interview (quotations); Jonathan McElvy, "Siegelman Makes Trek to Selma in Order to Reap His Rewards," *Selma Times-Journal*, April 12, 2002; Tim Reeves, "Political Windfall," *Clanton (Ala.) Advertiser*, April 7, 2002.

9. Jacobs, *New Domestic Automakers*, 183–85; Steers, *Made in Korea*, 72–93.

10. Jacobs, *New Domestic Automakers*, 111; Amsden, *Asia's Next Giant*, v, 180, 266, 267.

11. Michael Tomberlin and Kim Chandler, "Hyundai Chooses Montgomery Site," *Birmingham News*, April 2, 2002, 1A; Jacqueline Kochak, "Hyundai Looks at Opelika," *Dothan (Ala.) Eagle*, September 8, 2001; John Daly and Mitch Moxley, "How Hyundai Became the Auto Industry's Pacesetter," *Globe and Mail*, April 29, 2010.

12. Tomberlin and Chandler, "Hyundai Chooses," 1A; Jacobs, *New Domestic Automakers*, 186–90 ("issues" quotation, 189); Kochak, "Hyundai Looks"; Daly and Moxley, "How Hyundai" (closing quotation); Strange, interview. A chaebol is a family-controlled business conglomerate in South Korea.

13. Daly and Moxley, "How Hyundai"; Kochak, "Hyundai Looks"; WardsAuto, "U.S. Vehicle Sales"; "Alabama Wins Coveted Carmaker," *Birmingham News*, April 2, 2002, 4A ("phoenix" quotation).

14. Jacobs, *New Domestic Automakers*, 193; "La. Makes Bid for Automobile Plant," *New Orleans Times-Picayune*, October 19, 2001; "Alabama Wins Coveted Carmaker."

15. Talbot, "Hyundai's Plant Coming."

16. "Talking Points for Entering Final Phase of Site Selection," February 25, 2002, folder 3 (Hyundai), SG25914, Alabama Governors Papers (Don Siegelman), ADAH (first quotation); Ellen McNair, "Recruiting Hyundai: The Montgomery Experience," HMMA Presentation, ca. 2014 (copy supplied to author by the Montgomery Chamber of Commerce) (second quotation); Musgrove, interview.

17. Lindsay Chappell, "Miss. Officials Defend Nissan Incentive Deal," *Automotive News*, May 27, 2013; Musgrove, interview (quotation); Jeff Amy, "Nissan Marking 10th Year in Canton," *Memphis Commercial Appeal*, May 25, 2013, 1.

18. Musgrove, interview; Talbot, "Hyundai's Plant Coming"; and John Porretto, "Mississippi Spent Big, Lost Hyundai," *Mobile Register*, April 2, 2002, 8B.

19. "Hyundai to Build Alabama Plant," *New York Times*, April 2, 2002, C2; Dana Beyerle, "Incentive Package Enticed Hyundai," *Tuscaloosa News*, April 5, 2002; Talbot, "Hyundai's Plant Coming."

20. Talbot, "Hyundai's Plant Coming" (first two quotations); Jacobs, *New Domestic Automakers*, 195; Laurie L. Ogle, "One Land Dispute Down, One to Go," *Elizabethtown (Ky.) News-Enterprise*, March 19, 2002 ("significantly" quotation); Mabry, interview.

21. Jacobs, *New Domestic Automakers*, 195; Castile, interview (quotations); "Hyundai Forecasts Record Year," *Automotive News*, November 20, 2002.

22. "Talking Points for Entering Final Phase of Site Selection," February 25, 2002 (first two quotations); and Don Siegelman to Mong Koo Chung, March 14, 2002, "Talking Points for Entering Final Phase of Site Selection," February 25, 2002 (third quotation), both in folder 3 (Hyundai), SG25914, Alabama Governors Papers (Don Siegelman), ADAH.

23. Mary Orndorff, "Carmaker Offered Test Drives," *Birmingham News*, April 2, 2002, 4A; Jeff Amy, "Stars to Fall on State License Plates in 2002," *Mobile Register*, September 23, 2000, 3A. A state law prevented Siegelman from removing the "Heart of Dixie" altogether (it was now contained in a heart symbol that was only three-fourths of an inch wide). Siegelman also supported failed efforts to change the state song from "Alabama" to "Stars Fell on Alabama."

24. Amy, "Stars to Fall."

25. Hugeley, interview; Hyundai Motor Company to Alabama and Opelika Officials, November 19, 2001 (Confidential), folder 4 (Hyundai), SG25914, Alabama Governors Papers (Don Siegelman), ADAH (quotations).

26. Hyundai Motor Company to Alabama and Montgomery Officials, November 19, 2001 (Confidential); McNair, "Recruiting Hyundai."

27. McNair, interview (first two quotations); Mary Orndorff, "Carmaker Offered Test Drives," *Birmingham News*, April 2, 2002, 4A (third quotation); McNair, "Recruiting Hyundai."

28. Beyerle, "Incentive Package"; Tomberlin and Chandler, "Hyundai Chooses"; Hugeley, interview (quotation).

29. Dana Beyerle, "State Unveils Hyundai Incentives," *Florence (Ala.) Times Daily*, April 5, 2002; "Summary of Incentives Available to Project Beach," December 12, 2001, folder 4 (Hyundai), SG25914, Alabama Governors Papers (Don Siegelman), ADAH; McNair, interview; Daly and Moxley, "How Hyundai"; Strange, interview (closing quotations).

30. John Mohr, "Honda Manufacturing of Alabama," in *Encyclopedia of Alabama*, accessed April 24, 2018, http://www.encyclopediaofalabama.org/article/h-3657; Samuel L. Webb and Margaret E. Armbrester, "Don Siegelman (1999–2003)," in *Encyclopedia of Alabama*, accessed January 17, 2018, http://www.encyclopediaofa labama.org /article/h-3300.

31. Dong-Jin Kim to Don Siegelman, October 19, 2001, folder 3 (Hyundai), SG25914, Alabama Governors Papers (Don Siegelman), ADAH.

32. Robert C. Farnell to Marilyn, October 31, 2001, folder 3 (Hyundai), SG25914, Alabama Governors Papers (Don Siegelman), ADAH; John Mohr, "Hyundai Motor Manufacturing Alabama," in *Encyclopedia of Alabama*, accessed January 16, 2018, http://www.encyclopediaofalabama.org/article/h-3658; Don Siegelman to Mong Koo Chung, February 23, 2002, folder 3 (Hyundai), SG25914, Alabama Governors Papers (Don Siegelman), ADAH (quotation).

33. Don Siegelman to Mong Koo Chung, March 14, 2002, and Don Siegelman to Dong-Jin Kim, March 14, 2002, both in folder 3 (Hyundai), SG25914, Alabama Governors Papers (Don Siegelman), ADAH.

34. Jeff Sessions and Richard Shelby to Mong-Koo Chung, March 12, 2002; Don Siegelman to Thomas C. Hubbard, May 15, 2002 (quotation), both in folder 3 (Hyundai), SG25914, Alabama Governors Papers (Don Siegelman), ADAH.

35. Jeff Stonerock to Dave Echols, October 31, 2001, folder 3 (Hyundai), SG25914, Alabama Governors Papers (Don Siegelman), ADAH.

36. C. J. Schexnayder, "Richard Shelby," in *Encyclopedia Alabama*, accessed January 17, 2018, http://www.encyclopediaofalabama.org/article/h-3865; Richard Shelby to Mong Koo Chung, February 26, 2002, folder 3 (Hyundai) (first quotation); Frank D. McPhillips to Don Siegelman, March 16, 2002, folder 4 (Hyundai), both in SG25914, Siegelman Papers, ADAH (second and third quotations).

37. "Alabama Congressman Courts Hyundai," *Athens (Ala.) News Courier*, November 4, 2001; Mary Orndorff, "Carmaker Offered Test Drives," *Birmingham News*, April 2, 2002 (quotation); Tim Reeves, "Political Windfall," *Clanton (Ala.) Advertiser*, April 7, 2002.

38. Steers, *Made in Korea*, 148–152; Doron Levin, "Hyundai Seeking U.S. Plant," *Pittsburgh Post-Gazette*, January 25, 2002, B11.

39. Levin, "Hyundai Seeking U.S. Plant," B11; Dziczek, interview.

40. McNair, interview (first quotation); McNair, "Recruiting Hyundai" (second quotation); Dunlap, interview (other quotation).

41. Castile, interview; Eckman, interview; *The Harbour Report: North America 2003*, 7–9; Steele, interview.

42. Hyundai Motor Company to Alabama and Montgomery Officials, November 19, 2001 (Confidential) (quotations); "Project V" memo, n.d., folder 4 (Hyundai), SG25914, Alabama Governors Papers (Don Siegelman), ADAH.

43. "Highlights of Project Agreement by and between the State of Alabama and Honda Manufacturing of Alabama, LLC," folder 31, box 5, SG25742, Alabama Governors Papers (Don Siegelman), ADAH; "Our Company," Honda Manufacturing of Alabama Timeline, Honda Manufacturing Alabama, accessed April 27, 2018, https://www.hondaalabama.com/our-company.

44. Jay Reeves, "Odyssey Begins," *Mobile Register*, April 26, 2000, 7B; and Mary Lett, "Honda's a Reality in Lincoln," *Montgomery Advertiser*, April 25, 2000, 5B (quotation).

45. "Project Diamond Agreement," folder 24, container 9 (call number SG25746), Alabama Governors Papers (Don Siegelman), ADAH (first two quotations); "Alabama's Road to Car Manufacturing," *Birmingham Post-Herald*, April 2, 2002, A3; *The Har-*

bour Report: North America 2003, 9; Pressley, "The South's New-Car Smell," A1 (closing quotation).

46. Ted Pratt, "Honda Greets First 17 Workers," *Birmingham News*, November 10, 2000, 1B.

47. McNair, interview (quotations); "About Hyundai Motor Company"; Steers, *Made in Korea*, 90–91.

48. Tomberlin and Chandler, "Hyundai Chooses," 1A; Talbot, "Hyundai's Plant Coming" (first two quotations); McNair, interview.

49. Bob Ingram, "Hyundai Facility to Have Major Impact," *Daphne Bulletin*, April 10, 2002; "The *Tuscaloosa News* on Hyundai Announcement"; "Alabama Wins Coveted Carmaker"; Warren Brown, "The Industry Isn't Going South, It's Just Moved There," *Washington Post*, April 23, 2006, G2.

50. "The *Tuscaloosa News* on Hyundai Announcement"; Tomberlin and Chandler, "Hyundai Chooses," 1A (Camp quotation).

51. Tomberlin and Chandler, "Hyundai Chooses," 1A (Siegelman quotation); Dong-Jin Kim to Don Siegelman, October 19, 2001, folder 3 (Hyundai), SG25914, Alabama Governors Papers (Don Siegelman), ADAH (Kim quotation).

52. Frank D. McPhillips to Don Siegelman, March 16, 2002, folder 4 (Hyundai), SG25914, Alabama Governors Papers (Don Siegelman), ADAH.

53. Mohr, "Hyundai"; Burton, interview; anonymous worker quotation in "Hyundai Motor Reviews," accessed March 19, 2015, http://www.glassdoor.com/Reviews/Hyundai-Motor-Manufacturing-Alabama-Reviews-E39713.htm.

54. John F. Knight Jr. and Hank Sanders to Don Siegelman, June 24, 2002; Don Siegelman to Hank Sanders, June 27, 2002, both in folder 3 (Hyundai), SG25914, Alabama Governors Papers (Don Siegelman), ADAH.

55. Tommy Gallion to Rex Bush, June 24, 2002, folder 3 (Hyundai), SG25914, Alabama Governors Papers (Don Siegelman), ADAH.

56. David Zaslawsky, "Celebrating Ten Years of Hyundai Production in Alabama," *Montgomery Business Journal*, May 2015, 49; Castile, interview; Chappell, "Some Managers Come from Outside."

57. Zaslawsky, "Celebrating Ten Years," 42; Popely, "UAW," 1 (quotations); Mohr, "Hyundai."

58. Popely, "UAW," 1; Casteel, interview.

59. Department Reports, 34th UAW Constitutional Convention, June 12–15, 2006, 105, 106, box 2, "UAW Constitutional Convention Materials, 2002–2010," Convention Proceedings Papers.

60. Ibid., 102–3.

61. "Hyundai Motor Reviews"; Zaslawsky, "Celebrating Ten Years," 44. Glassdoor is a popular website where employees and former employees provide anonymous reviews of companies and their management. While sites of this nature need to be treated cautiously, the reviews on this site are checked and verified, and results are widely reported. Because Hyundai workers were not allowed to talk to the media or academics about their jobs, it was also impossible to conduct on-the-record interviews with them. Hyundai also received positive comments, especially about pay.

62. Burton, interview; Zaslawsky, "Celebrating Ten Years," 42 (Neal quote).

63. Steers, *Made in Korea*, 80; "Hyundai Motor Reviews."

64. Zaslawsky, "Celebrating Ten Years," 48.

65. "Hyundai Motor Reviews"; Mohr, "Hyundai"; Zaslawsky, "Celebrating Ten Years," 42–44 (Neal quotations on 42).

66. Talbot, "Hyundai's Plant Coming"; Tomberlin and Chandler, "Hyundai Chooses," 1A.

67. Karen Tolkkinen, "Hard Times in Wilcox: Alabama's Poorest County," *Mobile Register*, December 24, 2001 (first quotation); Castile, interview; "Hyundai Motor Reviews" (closing quotation).

68. Casteel, interview (quotations); Zaslawsky, "Celebrating Ten Years," 44; Submitted Resolutions, 35th UAW Constitutional Convention, June 14–17, 2010, 43, 58, box 2, "UAW Constitutional Convention Materials, 2002–2010," Convention Proceedings Papers.

69. "Hyundai to Tap a Kia Plant," *Wall Street Journal*, August 31, 2010; Nick Bunkley, "Hyundai's Safety Net Proves Attractive in Uncertain Times," *New York Times*, February 5, 2009, B3.

70. Nick Bunkley, "From 0 to 60 in a Recession," *New York Times*, September 22, 2009, B1 (first quotation); "Hyundai to Tap a Kia Plant" (second quotation); "About Hyundai Motor Company."

71. McNair, "Recruiting Hyundai"; "Hyundai Motor Manufacturing Alabama 2014 Economic Impact: Executive Summary," copy supplied to author by the Montgomery Chamber of Commerce; M. Keivan Deravi, "Hyundai Motor Manufacturing Alabama: Economic Impact Study," Auburn University at Montgomery, August 2015, copy supplied to the author by the Montgomery Mayor's Office.

72. "Hyundai Motor Manufacturing Alabama 2014 Economic Impact"; Deravi, "Hyundai Motor Manufacturing Alabama"; WardsAuto, "U.S. Vehicle Sales."

73. Mike Cason, "Honda News Highlights Black Belt's Plight," *Montgomery Advertiser*, May 9, 1999, 1A (quotations); Strange, interview.

74. "Hyundai Suppliers in Alabama," ca. 2016, document supplied to the author by the Montgomery Chamber of Commerce; Hugeley, interview; "Announced New and Expanding Industry—City of Auburn, 1994–2016," document supplied to the author by the City of Auburn.

75. Eckman, interview (first two quotations); "Rural Alabama Needs Attention" (editorial), *Montgomery Advertiser*, January 15, 2000, 8A (third quotation); and "Challenge: Helping Rural Counties," *Mobile Register*, March 13, 2000, 6A; Hank Sanders and Faya Rose Toure, "Still Waiting in Selma," *New York Times*, March 6, 2015; Richard Fausset, "Film Shows a Selma Some Would Rather Not Revisit," *New York Times*, December 25, 2014, A17; Garrow, *Protest at Selma*.

76. Tim Reeves, "Political Windfall," *Clanton Advertiser*, April 7, 2002 (first two quotations); and McElvy, "Siegelman Makes Trek" (third quotation).

77. "Hyundai Plant Expected to Bring Jobs to Black Belt," *Decatur (Ala.) Daily*, April 3, 2002 (first quotation); Jonathan McElvy, "Selma Will Receive Great Deal of Employment from Hyundai," *Selma Times Journal*, April 5, 2002 (second quotation).

78. Tim Reeves, "Political Windfall," *Clanton (Ala.) Advertiser*, April 7, 2002 (first quotation); "Governor Don Siegelman's Jobs Tour Preliminary Report," April 30, 2002,

folder 3 (Hyundai), SG25914 (other quotations), Alabama Governors Papers (Don Siegelman), ADAH.

79. "The *Tuscaloosa News* on Hyundai Announcement."

80. Webb and Armbrester, "Don Siegelman (1999–2003)"; Adam Cohen, "The Strange Case of an Imprisoned Alabama Governor," *New York Times*, September 10, 2007, A28 (quotation); Kim Chandler, "Siegelman, Scrushy Guilty of Bribery," *Birmingham News*, June 30, 2006, 1A; Rob Holbert, "Siegelman after Prison Out Seeking His Truth," *Lagniappe* (Mobile, Ala.), November 29, 2017.

81. "Hyundai Motor Manufacturing Alabama 2014 Economic Impact"; "Infant Mortality Rate—2006," and "Persons below Poverty Level—2008," in "State Rankings—Statistical Abstract of the United States," U.S. Census Bureau, accessed January 12, 2018, https://www.census.gov/library/publications/2009/compendia/statab/129ed/rankings.html; Minchin and Salmond, *After the Dream*, 293; Burton, interview (closing quotation); "Percentage of People in Poverty by State."

82. Sewell, interview (quotations); "Alabama Statewide Manufacturing Figures," 2002–2017, Bureau of Labor Statistics, accessed January 12, 2018, https://data.bls.gov/timeseries/SMS01000003000000001?amp%253bdata_tool=XGtable&output_view=-data&include_graphs=true; "Largest Industries by State, 1990–2013," Bureau of Labor Statistics, accessed January 12, 2018, https://www.bls.gov/opub/ted/2014/ted_20140728.htm.

83. "Alabama's Automotive Industry" (EDPA study), August 2015, 1–3; Jacobs, *New Domestic Automakers*, 2.

84. "Alabama's Automotive Industry," 1–3; "Alabama Is at the Center of the New U.S. Auto Industry," ca. 2016, brochure supplied to the author by the EDPA; Sewell, interview (closing quotation).

85. Wood, interview.

CHAPTER 8: WHEN KIA CAME TO GEORGIA

1. Lindsay Chappell, "Kia, Uncle Sam Vie for Hardhats in Georgia," *Automotive News*, October 23, 2006, 34 (first quotation); April Wortham, "New Kia Plant Will Resemble Hyundai's," *Automotive News*, May 14, 2007, 46H; "Kia Manufacturing Plant Opening Celebrated in West Point," press release, Georgia Department of Economic Development, February 26, 2010 (second quotation), http://www.georgia.org/newsroom/press-releases/kia-manufacturing-plant-opening-celebrated-in-west-point/.

2. Karen Kennedy, "The Kia Effect: A Defining Moment for the Region," *Georgia Trend* 23 (August 2008): 73–75 (first quotation on 73), 78–82; "Kia Motors to Open First U.S. Plant," *BBC News*, March 13, 2006, http://newsvote.bbc.co.uk/2/hi/business/4801558.stm (second and third quotations); "Kia Picks Georgia for Site of U.S. Plant," *Calgary Herald*, March 14, 2006, D3.

3. Jacobs, *New Domestic Automakers*, 183–85; WardsAuto, "U.S. Vehicle Sales"; "Auto Sales, Sales and Share of Total Market by Manufacturer," *Wall Street Journal*, April 3, 2018. Between 1981 and 1986, the South Korean government prohibited Kia from making cars on the grounds that the industry was too competitive. See Jacobs, *New Domestic Automakers*, 185–86.

4. "Youngster Kia Feels Its Way among the U.S. Boulders," *Automotive News*, April 24, 1996; Lindner, interview; WardsAuto, "U.S. Vehicle Sales"; "Hyundai's U.S. Market Share from 1999–2012," Hyundai America, accessed April 24, 2018, http://hyundai america.us/an-american-success-story/u-s-demand-sales-market-share/; "Chrysler Is Largest Manufacturer to File for Bankruptcy," AutoNews.com, May 1, 2009, http://www.autonews.com/article/20090501/OEM/305019874/

5. Walter Woods, "Kia Breaks Ground for Plant," *Atlanta Journal-Constitution*, October 21, 2006, B1 (first quotation); Andrea Lovejoy, "It's Official," *LaGrange Daily News*, March 13, 2006 (second quotation); Lindsay Chappell, "Suppliers Are Linchpin of Hyundai Plant," *Automotive News*, May 5, 2003, 18N; "Automotive Manufacturing: Georgia," Georgia Power Community and Economic Development, 2014, 4, http://web .archive.org/web/20151201125709/selectgeorgia.com/publications/Automotive -Industry-Report.pdf (third quotation).

6. This chapter draws on over thirty interviews, as well as many written sources, particularly Governor Perdue's recently donated papers at the University of Georgia and the personal files of key economic development figures that were shared with me (copies in the author's possession). I garnered information on Kia and its decision-making process from industry publications, as well as from a tour of the West Point plant that Kia gave me on May 8, 2015 (notes in the author's possession).

7. Micheline Maynard and Jeremy W. Peters, "2 Asian Automakers Plan Ventures," *New York Times*, March 14, 2006, C1; Lindner, interview; Jerry Grillo, "How Kia Came to Georgia," *Georgia Trend*, August 2009, 18–25.

8. Lindsay Chappell, "Miss. Raises the Ante for Kia," *Automotive News*, March 6, 2006, 1, 39; Walter Woods, "Mississippi Ponies Up $1 Billion Bid for Kia," *Atlanta Journal-Constitution*, March 10, 2006, A1; Lesser, interview (first and second quotations); Lindner, interview; Ewing, interview; "Project Chronology," ca. 2005–6, Ray Coulombe Personal Papers, Rabun Gap, Georgia (hereafter Coulombe Papers).

9. Elise Zieger, "Town Hits Economic Jackpot to Become 'Kia-Ville,'" *Money and Main St.* (CNN.com), July 9, 2009, http://www.cnn.com/2009/LIVING/worklife/07/08 /fortunate.town/index.html (first through sixth quotations); Larry Copeland, "Kia Breathes New Life into Old Georgia Textile Mill Town," *USA Today*, March 25, 2010, 5A; Michael Luo, "Auto Plant Breathes New Life into Mill Town That Was Fading Away," *New York Times*, April 22, 2009, A12 (seventh quotation). For an example of positive business reaction, see Kennedy, "Kia Effect."

10. "Our Opinions: Education Takes a Back Seat to Kia," *Atlanta Journal-Constitution*, March 28, 2006, 10A; Dan Chapman, "West Point, Region Eager to Reap Kia Plant's Yield," *Atlanta Journal-Constitution*, November 8, 2009, 1A; Gilliam, interview; Yoon, interview.

11. Kaye Lanning Minchew, "Troup County," in *New Georgia Encyclopedia*, http:// www.georgiaencyclopedia.org/articles/counties-cities-neighborhoods/troup-county; Kaye Lanning Minchew, "Callaway Family," in *New Georgia Encyclopedia*, http://www .georgiaencyclopedia.org/articles/history-archaeology/callaway-family.

12. Joel Martin, "Troup Learns Lesson of Declining Textile Industry," *LaGrange Daily News*, February 3, 2002, 8; "Dying Textiles," *LaGrange Daily News*, February 3, 2002, 7 (first and second quotations); Joel Martin, "Textile Plants to Close," *LaGrange*

Daily News, January 10, 2004, 1; "Unemployment Rate in Troup County, GA (GATROU-P5URN)," U.S. Bureau of Labor Statistics via FRED, Federal Reserve Bank of St. Louis, https://fred.stlouisfed.org/series/GATROU5URN; "Unemployment Rate in Chambers County, AL (ALCHAM7URN)," U.S. Bureau of Labor Statistics via FRED, Federal Reserve Bank of St. Louis, https://fred.stlouisfed.org/series/ALCHAM7URN.

13. Wolfe, interview (quotations); Dobbs, interview.

14. Diethard Lindner, "Timeline," ca. 2005–6, Diethard Lindner Personal Papers, LaGrange, Georgia (hereafter Lindner Papers) (second quotation); "Kia Timeline," *LaGrange Daily News*, March 19, 2006 (first and third quotations); Fryer, interview.

15. Lovejoy, interview (quotations); Coulombe, interview; "Project Chronology," Coulombe Papers.

16. "Remarks by Governor Zell Miller," January 12, 1994, folder 1, box 37, subseries A; "The Korean Business Community in Georgia" and "Korean Population," September 1995, both in folder 6, box 237, subseries D; "Remarks by Governor Zell Miller, Gov's Economic Development Conference," May 19, 1993 (quotations), folder 75, box 68, subseries B, all in series IV, Zell Miller Papers, Richard B. Russell Library for Political Research and Studies, University of Georgia, Athens.

17. In an article published in 1985, Charles F. Floyd, a University of Georgia economist, identified the existence of "the 'two Georgias' problem." Disputing favorable Sun Belt–style publicity that emphasized how much Georgia was growing, Floyd emphasized that growth was concentrated in 14 metropolitan counties, predominantly in the Atlanta metropolitan area, with the other 145 counties lagging behind. While some of its conclusions were challenged, the article raised awareness of Georgia's uneven economic development. See Charles F. Floyd, "The 'Two Georgias' Problem," *Georgia Business and Economic Conditions* 45 (March–April 1985): 3–13; Bartley, *The Creation of Modern Georgia*, 233.

18. By October 2007, Perdue had made twelve international trips in search of new investment, with Asia and the Americas dominating his itinerary. See "Governor Perdue Leads Business Delegation to Japan and Korea," October 5, 2007, document 100507, ER1023, subseries A, series VII, George Ervin "Sonny" Perdue Official Papers, Richard B. Russell Library for Political Research and Studies, University of Georgia, Athens (hereafter Perdue Papers). At the time of writing, many of Governor Perdue's press releases were still available online in an archived version of his administration's website (http://sonnyperdue.georgia.gov/00/channel_createddate/0%/2c2095%2c78 006749_79685623%2c00.html). I used the copies preserved in the Perdue Papers, and these are the basis of the citations here.

19. Grillo, "How Kia Came to Georgia" (first quotation); Talbot, "Hyundai's Plant Coming"; Lindsay Chappell, "With Chung Sprung, Kia's Georgia Plant Plan Moves Ahead," *Automotive News*, August 7, 2006, 16; Lesser, interview (second and third quotations).

20. Steers, *Made in Korea*, 57–58, 73, 78, 84; Jacobs, *New Domestic Automakers*, 184; Micheline Maynard with Don Kirk, "Hyundai Predicts a Tripling of Sales in the U.S. by 2010," *New York Times*, September 21, 2002, C3; "Governor Announces Plans for Kia Groundbreaking Ceremony," October 2, 2006, document 102006; and "Governor Perdue, Chairman Chung Break Ground for New Kia Motors Plant," governor's press re-

lease, October 20, 2006, document 102006 (quotation), both in ER1022, subseries A, series VII, Perdue Papers; "Kia Motors to Open First U.S. Plant," *BBC News*, March 13, 2006.

21. "Georgia Wins Vaunted Silver Shovel Award," June 12, 2009, document 061209, ER1026, subseries A, series VII (first quotation); "Talking Points—Oakland Meadows Business Park Dedication," May 10, 2003, document 050903, ER97, subseries A, series I (second and third quotations), both in Perdue Papers.

22. "Georgia Shatters Economic Development Records in FY2006," August 3, 2006, document 080306, ER1022, subseries A, series VII, Perdue Papers (first quotation); Walter Woods, "$160,000 per Job to Land Kia," *Atlanta Journal-Constitution*, March 14, 2006, 1A (second, third, and fourth quotations).

23. Lesser, interview; "Governor Perdue Recommends Ken Stewart as GDEcD Commissioner," December 18, 2006, document 121806 (quotation); "Georgia Jobs and Investments Surge Thirty-Five Percent in 2005," February 1, 2006, document 020106; and "Governor Perdue Announces HP to Locate Data Centers in Metro Atlanta," May 17, 2006, document 051706, all in ER1022, subseries A, series VII, Perdue Papers.

24. Maynard and Peters, "2 Asian Automakers," C1; Walter Woods, "Key State Booster Resigns," *Atlanta Journal-Constitution*, December 19, 2006, C1 (quotations).

25. "Better Off without Kia? ADO Head," *Decatur (Ala.) Daily*, March 21, 2006; "Kia's Eye on Ga. for Plant," *Atlanta Journal-Constitution*, January 10, 2006, D1; Woods, "Mississippi Ponies Up," A1; Lindner, interview (quotations).

26. Lindsay Chappell, "Kia's New U.S. Plant Is No Windfall for U.S. Suppliers," *Automotive News*, April 3, 2006, 1, 39; "Kia Timeline"; Fryer, interview (first quotation); Lindner, interview; Coulombe, interview (second and third quotations).

27. "Kia Timeline" (first quotation); Ferguson III, interview (second and third quotations); Ewing, interview (fourth and fifth quotations); Lesser, interview.

28. Ferguson III, interview (first, fifth, and sixth quotations); Woods, "Kia Breaks Ground," B1 (second and third quotations); Jennifer Shrader, "Kia 'Means Almost Everything to the Community,'" *Automotive News*, March 16, 2006, 1, 2 (fourth quotation, 1).

29. Ferguson III, interview (quotations); Walter Woods, "Perdue Revels in Big Win," *Atlanta Journal-Constitution*, March 15, 2006, 1C.

30. Ferguson III, interview (first quotation); Ed Smith, interview (second quotation).

31. Woods, "Key State Booster Resigns," C1; Ferguson III, interview.

32. Lesser, interview (quotation); "Site Acquisition and Development Agreement," March 2, 2006, 20, "Kia" folder, box 2, subseries A, series I, Perdue Papers.

33. "Kia Timeline"; Walter Woods, "Passion, Luck Helped Land Kia," *Atlanta Journal-Constitution*, March 26, 2006, 1Q (quotations); Fred Barnes, "The Other American Auto Industry," *Weekly Standard*, December 22, 2008, 22.

34. "Project Chronology," Coulombe Papers; Minchew, "Callaway Family"; Kaye Lanning Minchew, "Callaway Gardens," in *New Georgia Encyclopedia*, http://www.georgiaencylopedia.org/articles/geography-environment/callaway-gardens.

35. Brown, interview; "South Korea—Business and Social Etiquette," n.d. (quotations), "Kia Automotive" folder, vertical files, Troup County Archives, LaGrange, Georgia; De Mente, *Korean Etiquette*.

36. Lovejoy, interview (first and fourth quotations); Fryer, interview (second and third quotations); "Timeline," Lindner Papers (fifth quotation); "Project Chronology," Coulombe Papers.

37. "VW Chief Opens U.S. Plant," *Los Angeles Times*, October 6, 1976, D9; J. Scott Trubey and Greg Bluestein, "Competing for More Korean Cars," *Atlanta Journal-Constitution*, September 29, 2013, D1.

38. Tommy Hills to Charlie Gatlin, February 1, 2006, "Kia" folder, box 2, subseries A, series I, Perdue Papers (first quotation); Wood, interview (second and third quotations).

39. Tommy Hills to Charlie Gatlin, February 1, 2006; and "Site Acquisition and Development Agreement," esp. 7–16, both in "Kia" folder, box 2, subseries A, series I; "Fact Sheet: Kia to Build Assembly Plant," March 13, 2006, document 031306, ER1022, subseries A, series VII, all in Perdue Papers; Dobbs, interview (quotations).

40. "Site Acquisition and Development Agreement," March 2, 2006, 19–20 (quotation on 20); "Project 0515 Funding Estimates," January 2006; and "Economic Development Bond Fund Needs," March 13, 2006, all in "Kia" folder, box 2, subseries A, series I; "Governor Announces Over $13.4 Million in OneGeorgia Awards," December 1, 2008, document 120108, ER1025, subseries A, series VII, all in Perdue Papers; James Barlament, "HOPE Scholarship," in *New Georgia Encyclopedia*, http://www.georgia encyclopedia.org/articles/education/hope-scholarship.

41. "Fact Sheet: Kia to Build Assembly Plant," March 13, 2006, document 031306, ER1022; and "Kia Georgia Training Center Opens in West Point," March 25, 2008, document 032508, ER1025, both subseries A, series VII; "Site Acquisition and Development Agreement," March 2, 2006, 16–18, "Kia" folder, box 2, subseries A, series I, all in Perdue Papers; Mary Downing Koon, "Quick Start," in *New Georgia Encyclopedia*, http://www .georgiaencyclopedia.org/articles/business-economy/quick-start; Lesser, interview (quotation).

42. Susanna Capelouto, "Kia Plant Provides Jobs in Georgia," *Morning Edition*, November 16, 2009, http://www.npr.org/templates/story/story.php?storyId=120448228; Tentler, interview.

43. Craig Lesser to Chris Clark, February 16, 2006, "Kia" folder, box 2, subseries A, series I, Perdue Papers (quotation).

44. Ibid. (first quotation); Jeff Lukken et al. to Byung Mo Ahn, February 7, 2006, Lindner Papers (second and third quotations).

45. Kim, *Big Business, Strong State*, 1; Steers, *Made in Korea*, 47–48; Van Lieu, interview (first and second quotations); Yu, interview (third and fourth quotations).

46. Kim, *Big Business, Strong State*, esp. 3 (first quotation), 89–92 (second and third quotations on 89), 104–105, 169; Song, *The Rise of the Korean Economy*; Amsden, *Asia's Next Giant*.

47. "Hyundai-Kia Beltway," *Chosŏn ilbo*, July 16, 2011 (first, second, and third quotations); "West Point," *Tonga ilbo*, October 17, 2006; Yoon, interview (fourth and fifth quotations); Reimers, "Asian Immigrants in the South," 100–134, esp. 106–7. I would like to thank Professor Joshua Van Lieu for providing translations of the above articles from Korean newspapers. The translations are contained in his presentation "Havens

and Gateways: LaGrange, Korea, and the Currents of World History," LaGrange College, February 12, 2012 (in the author's possession).

48. Maynard and Peters, "2 Asian Automakers," C2 (first quotation); Woods, "Mississippi Ponies Up," A1 (second and third quotations).

49. Head, interview (first and second quotations); Chappell, "Miss. Raises the Ante," 1, 39; Ken Krizner, "Kia Is the Latest Foreign Automaker to Site Plant in Southern U.S.," *Expansion Management* 21 (September/October 2006): 42–44 (third and fourth quotations on 42).

50. Head, interview (first quotation); Chappell, "Kia's New U.S.," 1, 39; Lovejoy, "It's Official" (second quotation).

51. Peter Chang, "The Expanded European Union," *Automotive News*, April 19, 2004 (first and second quotations); "Chung Is Confident Kia Can Help Hyundai," *Automotive News*, November 23, 1998, 30.

52. "Hyundai Motor Union Extends Strike," *Automotive News*, August 25, 2005 (first quotation); "Kia Motors, Union Agree to Wage Deal," *Automotive News*, September 13, 2005; Jung, interview (second and third quotations).

53. Cobb, *The Selling of the South*, 96–102 (quotation on 98); Bartley, *The Creation of Modern Georgia*, 205; Zieger, Minchin, and Gall, *American Workers, American Unions*, 152–59, 250.

54. "Industries in Georgia: Automotive," Georgia Department of Economic Development, http://www.georgia.org/industries/automotive/ (quotation); Cobb, *The South and America*, 206.

55. Fryer, interview (first and second quotations); Noles, interview; Wolfe, interview (third and fourth quotations).

56. Lindner, interview (first and second quotations); Chang, "The Expanded European Union" (third and fourth quotations).

57. Corinne Hodges to the author, August 21, 2015 (first quotation); "Welcome to Kia Motors Manufacturing Georgia," KMMG (second quotation), http://www.kia.com/us/en/content/why-kia/built-in-the-usa/overview. At the time, Hodges was head of public relations at the plant.

58. Grillo, "How Kia Came to Georgia" (first through fourth quotations); Lesser, interview (fifth quotation); Lovejoy, interview; "Timeline," Lindner Papers.

59. Woods, "Kia Breaks Ground," B1; Duffey, interview (first quotation); "Community 'In-Kind' Efforts," Lindner Papers (second quotation).

60. "Contract Awarded for I-85 West Point Interchange Project," May 31, 2007, document 053107, ER1023; and "Governor Perdue Announces Opening of I-85 Interchange and Roads in Troup to Serve New Kia Motors Facility," December 10, 2008, document 121008, ER1025, both in subseries A, series VII, Perdue Papers.

61. Lindsay Chappell, "Uncertainty Surrounds Kia's U.S. Plants," *Automotive News*, May 22, 2006, 8.

62. Chappell, "With Chung Sprung"; Craig Simons, "Kia Plant Stuck in Slow Lane," *Atlanta Journal-Constitution*, August 30, 2007, A1 (first quotation); "Site Acquisition and Development Agreement," 20, "Kia" folder, box 2, subseries A, series I, Perdue Papers (second quotation); Duffey, interview (third quotation).

63. Kevin Duffy, "Eager Workers Line Up for Kia," *Atlanta Journal-Constitution*, January 9, 2008, C1 (first quotation); "Kia Now Accepting Job Applications for Georgia Auto Plant," January 8, 2008, document 010808, ER1025, subseries A, series VII, Perdue Papers; Ferguson III, interview (second quotation); Copeland, "Kia Breathes New Life," 5A; "From KMMG Website (timeline)," Lindner Papers.

64. "Kia Builds Its Future with the State of Georgia," Georgia Department of Economic Development, November 2010, www.georgia.org/wp-content/uploads/2013 /09/Case-Study-Kia-11.2010.pdf (first and second quotations); Craig Lesser, "Lure More Than Money," *Atlanta Journal-Constitution*, March 24, 2006, A15 (third quotation).

65. April Wortham, "Kia Restricts Hiring at Ga. Plant to Web Applicants," *Automotive News*, January 21, 2008, 28H (quotations); Lindsay Chappell, "Transplant Wage 'Parity' Issue Derails Bailout," *Automotive News*, December 12, 2008.

66. Minchin, *Empty Mills*, 3, 22; Rob Richardson, "Kia Jobs: Textile Workers Fit Bill," *Hogansville Home News*, March 30, 2006, 1A, 2A; Ferguson III, interview.

67. "Troup Population: 58,779," *LaGrange Daily News*, March 23, 2001, 1; Ferguson III, interview; Coulombe, interview (quotations). The reflections offered here about the racial makeup of the workforce are also based on my May 2015 tour of the West Point plant.

68. "Top Tier Supplier Signs On for Kia Facility," August 8, 2007, document 080807, ER1023, subseries A, series VII, Perdue Papers; April Wortham, "Korean Supplier Follows Kia to Georgia," *Automotive News*, December 20, 2007; "Leading Kia Muffler Supplier to Locate in Troup County," November 20, 2007, document 112007, ER1024; "Top-Tier Kia Supplier to Locate New Facility in Harris County," May 20, 2008, document 052008, ER1025; and "Auto Supplier DongNam Tech to Locate in Columbus," June 12, 2008, document 061208, ER1025 (quotation), all in subseries A, series VII, Perdue Papers.

69. Luo, "Auto Plant Breathes New Life," A12 (first quotation); Zieger, "Town Hits Economic Jackpot"; Copeland, "Kia Breathes New Life," 5A (second quotation).

70. Georgia Tech study summarized in "Kia Now Accepting Job Applications for Georgia Auto Plant," January 8, 2008, document 010808 ; and "Kia Manufacturing Plant Opening Celebrated in West Point," February 26, 2010, document 022610, both in ER468 (news releases), series VII, subseries A, Perdue Papers; Jeanne Bonner, "Kia's Impact Wide in West Georgia," *Georgia Public Broadcasting*, November 30, 2011, http://www.gpb.org/news/2011/11/30/kias-impact-wide-in-west-georgia.

71. Minchin, *Empty Mills*, 1–2, 211–45; Copeland, "Kia Breathes Life," 5A (first quotation); Noles, interview (second and third quotations).

72. April Wortham, "'Now Hiring' Sign Draws Thousands to Ga. Parts Plant," *Automotive News*, February 12, 2009.

73. Bonner, "Kia's Impact"; Joel Martin, "Jobless Rate Concerns County," *LaGrange Daily News*, August 1, 2009; Copeland, "Kia Breathes New Life," 5A; Ferguson III, interview.

74. Matt Wilson, "Georgia Auto Plant Closings Leave Lingering Void," *Chattanooga Times Free Press*, June 2, 2009 (first quotation); Richardson, "Kia Jobs," 1A (second

quotation); "Kia Plant Shuns Atlanta Auto Workers," 11Alive.Com (Atlanta NBC affiliate), May 31, 2012, copy in author's possession; Lindner, interview (third and fourth quotations).

75. Jeanne Bonner, "Union Workers Sue over Kia Hiring," *Georgia Public Broadcasting*, May 23, 2012, http://www.gpb.org/news/2012/05/23/union-workers-sue-over -kia-hiring; Kate Brumback, "Georgia Court Rules for Governor, Kia in Open Records Case," *Athens Banner-Herald*, November 18, 2013.

76. "2014 4-Year Cohort Graduation Rate," Georgia Department of Education, October 30, 2014, http://www.gpee.org/fileadmin/files/PDFs/2014-year_Cohort_Grad -Rate.pdf; "U.S. High School Graduation Rate Hits Record High," *National Public Radio*, December 15, 2015, http://www.npr.org/sections/ed/2015/12/15/459821708/u-s -high-school-graduation-rate-hits-new-record-high; Wolfe, interview; "Education Takes a Back Seat to Kia," *Atlanta Journal-Constitution*, March 28, 2006, A10 (quotation); "Results of the 2006 Smartest State Award," *Morgan Quinto Press*, http://www .morganquitno.com/edrank06.htm.

77. THINC College and Career Academy fact sheet, 2016, http://www.thincacademy .net/wp-content/uploads/FACT-SHEET-2016.pdf; "Founding Investors," THINC College and Career Academy, http://www.thincacademy.net/our-investors/founding -investors/ (quotation); Noles, interview; "Governor Announces $16.2 Million in One-Georgia Awards," June 24, 2009, document 062409, ER 1026, subseries A, series VII, Perdue Papers.

78. For mixed reviews of working at Kia in Georgia, see the many reviews at "Kia Motors Manufacturing Georgia," Glassdoor, http://www.glassdoor.com/Reviews/Kia -Motors-Manufacturing-Georgia-Reviews-E360325.htm. Some typical comments: "Work schedule is tough and time off is hard to get unless your manager is friendly. Stress can be almost unbearable at times"; and "Long hours and mandatory overtime. Very little cohesion between Korean and US management." Although some workers were even more critical, Kia also received positive comments, especially about pay and benefits. Kia required all of its employees to sign nondisclosure agreements in which they pledged not to talk to the media or academics about their jobs, making it impossible to conduct on-the-record interviews with them.

79. Yoon, interview (first and second quotations); Yu, interview; Jung, interview; Brown, interview (third quotation); Wolfe, interview (fourth quotation).

80. Kevin Duffy, "Eager Workers," C1; Walter Woods, "Ala. Poised to Horn In on State's Kia Party," *Atlanta Journal-Constitution*, October 20, 2006, A1 (quotations).

81. "What If Kia Goes Belly Up?," *LaGrange Daily News*, December 13, 2008; and Jim Mason to the editor, "Readers Write," *Atlanta Journal-Constitution*, March 16, 2006, A18.

82. Wood, interview (quotations); Lovejoy, interview.

83. Fryer, interview (first and second quotations); Gilliam, interview (third quotation); Martin, interview.

84. Gilliam, interview (quotations); "West Point, Georgia Population: Census 2010 and 2000," U.S. Census, http://censusviewer.com/city/GA/West%20Point; "Annual Estimates of Resident Population: April 1, 2010 to July 1, 2014," West Point City, Georgia, U.S. Census, American Fact Finder, https://factfinder.census.gov.

85. "Annual Estimates of Resident Population"; Ferguson III, interview (quotation).

86. "Poverty Status in the Last 12 Months," 2009–13 American Community Survey five-year estimates, Troup County, Georgia, U.S. Census, *American Fact Finder*, https://factfinder.census.gov; Ferguson, interview; Jung, interview (first quotation); Yoon, interview (second quotation).

87. "Poverty Status"; West, interview; Thornton, interview.

88. Gilliam, interview (first and second quotations); Head, interview; Minchin, *Empty Mills*, 223–25, 285–90.

89. "Timeline," Lindner Papers; Matthew Strother, "Kia Suppliers May Receive $176 Million," *LaGrange Daily News*, December 4, 2012; "Our History," KMMG, http://www.kmmgusa.com/about-kmmg/our-history/.

90. Walter Woods, "Georgia Wins Kia Plant," *Atlanta Journal-Constitution*, March 13, 2006, A1 (first quotation); Martin, interview; Matthew C. Hulbert, "Sonny Perdue (b. 1946)," in *New Georgia Encyclopedia*, http://www.georgiaencyclopedia.org/articles/government-politics/sonny-perdue-b-1946.

91. "Georgia Shatters Economic Development Records in FY2006," August 3, 2006, document 080306, ER1022; "Georgia Wins Prestigious Gold Shovel Award," July 30, 2007, document 073007, ER1023; "Governor Perdue's State of the State Address," January 10, 2007, document 011007, ER1023; "Governor Perdue Marks Final Sine Die of Administration," April 29, 2010, ER1027, all in subseries A, series VII, Perdue Papers.

92. WardsAuto, "U.S. Vehicle Sales"; "About KMMG: A Message from President and CEO Shin," KMMG, http://www.kmmgusa.com/about-kmmg/our-message/; Min-Ji Jung, "Built in the U.S.A.," *Kia Buzz*, http://kia-buzz.com/built-in-the-u-s-a/. This paragraph also draws on my plant visit.

93. "Pierce Brosnan Makes 'Perfect Getaway' in All-New 2016 Sorento during Kia Motors' Super Bowl Commercial," *India Automobile News* (New Delhi), January 27, 2015; "Kia Commercial Filmed in Troup," *LaGrange Daily News*, October 21, 2009 (first quotation); Ferguson III, interview (second and third quotations).

EPILOGUE

1. Woods, interview (first quotation); Clifford Krauss, "Foreign Automakers in the U.S. Cut Back," *New York Times*, December 22, 2008, B1 (other quotations); Louis Uchitelle, "U.S. Layoffs Increase as Businesses Confront Crisis," *New York Times*, October 26, 2008.

2. Robey, interview; "Quake and Tsunamis Affect Japan's Auto Industry," *Autotrader*, March 2011, accessed January 24, 2018, https://www.autotrader.com/car-reviews/quake-and-tsunamis-affect-japans-auto-industry-80268; John Holusha, "Japan's Productive Car Unions," *New York Times*, March 30, 1993, D1.

3. "VW Picks Tennessee as Site for a Car Plant," *New York Times*, July 16, 2008, C6; Lydia DePillis, "Union Vote at VW Plant Is Seen as Bellwether," *Washington Post*, February 14, 2014, A1.

4. Aaron M. Kessler, "Volvo's $500 Million Assembly Plant in South Carolina to Create 2,000 Jobs," *New York Times*, May 12, 2015, 3; Ana Swanson, "As Trump Hits China, Detroit Braces for Pain," *New York Times*, July 13, 2018, 1.

5. "Well trained" and "depressed" quotations in "Volvo Bringing First U.S. Factory, Thousands of Jobs, to Berkeley County," *ABC News*, May 11, 2015, accessed January 29, 2018, http://www.crda.org/news/local_news/volvo-bringing-first-u-s-factory -thousands-of-jobs-to-berkeley-county/; Brenda Rindge, "Volvo Plant in Berkeley County to Invest $1B," *Charleston Post and Courier*, September 18, 2017; Phil LeBeau, "Volvo Expanding US Production Plans in South Carolina," *CNBC*, September 19, 2017, accessed January 24, 2018, https://www.cnbc.com/2017/09/19/volvo-expanding-us -production-plans-in-south-carolina.html (last two quotations).

6. Kim Chandler and Tom Krisher, "New Toyota-Mazda Plant Will Bring 4,000 Jobs," *Winston-Salem Journal*, January 11, 2018, A9; Nick Bunkley, "Transplants Set to Dominate North American Production," *Automotive News*, January 15, 2018 (quotation).

7. "Nissan to Add 800 Jobs," *Chattanooga Times Free-Press*, October 20, 2012; Cheryl Jensen, "Nissan Battery Plant Begins Operations in Tennessee," *New York Times*, December 13, 2012; Bill Vlasic, "Toyota Said to Plan Lexus Plant in Kentucky," *New York Times*, April 19, 2013, 1.

8. Sholnn Freeman, "Detroit Waves Flag That No Longer Flies," *Washington Post*, August 19, 2006, A1; Fred Barnes, "The Other American Auto Industry," *Washington Examiner*, December 22, 2008; "Hyundai's U.S. Operations Contribute More Than 94,000 Private Sector Jobs," Center for Automotive Research press release, http://www.cargroup.org/?module=News&event=View&newsID=10; Elisabeth Behrmann, "Mercedes Plans More SUVs," *Automotive News*, January 17, 2018, accessed January 24, 2018, http://www.autonews.com/article/20180117/COPY01/301179951/mercedes-plans-more -suvs?cciid=email-autonews-asdetroit; Martin, interview.

9. Bunkley, "Transplants Set to Dominate"; "Auto Industry Begins 2017 with a Steady Pace," AIADA Report, February 2, 2017, accessed April 27, 2018, https://www.aiada.org /news/market-watch/auto-industry-begins-2017-steady-pace.

10. "35 Years of Manufacturing and R & D in America," JAMA Report, http://www .jama.org/2017-2018-contributions-report-highlights-35-years-jama-members -manufacturing-presence-america/ (Manriquez quotation on 2); Laurence Iliff, "How Camry Fought Off Civic," *Automotive News*, January 8, 2018, 3; Jacobs, *New Domestic Automakers*, 84.

11. For the emphasis on decline, see, for example, Milkman, *Farewell to the Factory*; Dandaneau, *A Town Abandoned*.

12. The positive tone is epitomized by Jacobs, *New Domestic Automakers*, as well as by the powerful economic and political elites who recruited—and defended—the industry, especially in the local press. These voices have also been included throughout this study. Quotations in "Volvo Bringing First U.S. Factory."

13. Robey, interview; Stamper, interview; Bensinger, interview.

14. Anderson and McKevitt, "From 'the Chosen' to the Precariat," 264–65; Young quoted in Lydia DePillis, "This Is What a Job in the U.S.'s New Manufacturing Industry Looks Like," *Washington Post*, March 9, 2014. McKevitt's definition of "precariat" draws on the work of British economist Guy Standing, who identifies a growing "precariat" in Europe whose members are a product of neoliberal globalization. This group "feel their lives and identities are made up of disjointed bits, in which they cannot con-

struct a desirable narrative or build a career." See Guy Standing, "Who Will Be a Voice for the Emerging Precariat?," *The Guardian*, June 1, 2011.

15. Damian Paletta, "UAW Faces Another Southern Setback," *Wall Street Journal*, March 15, 2014; Lydia DePillis, "Why Volkswagen Is Helping to Organize Its Own Plant," *Washington Post*, February 11, 2014 ("big deal" quotation); DePillis, "Union Vote at VW Plant," A1 (other *Post* quotation); Mike Elk, "Nissan Attacked for One of the 'Nastiest Anti-Union Campaigns' in Modern US History," *The Guardian*, August 1, 2017 (last two quotations).

16. Mike Ramsey, "VW Chops Labor Costs in the U.S.," *Wall Street Journal*, May 23, 2011; Mike Elk, "The Battle for Chattanooga," *In These Times*, March 13, 2014 (Ed Hunter quotation); Bensinger, interview.

17. King, interview; Steven Greenhouse, "Automaker Gives Its Blessings, and G.O.P. Its Warnings," *New York Times*, February 12, 2014, 3; Lydia DePillis, "Sen. Bob Corker Can't Stand the United Auto Workers," *Washington Post*, February 14, 2014, A1; Steele, interview (quotation); Silvia, "The United Auto Workers' Attempts."

18. DePillis, "Union Vote at VW Plant," A1; Jamie McGee, "Chattanooga VW Workers Vote against Joining UAW," *Jackson Sun*, June 16, 2019, A6; Larry Vellequette, "Tenn. Governor's Visit Strikes Anti-Union Tone," *Automotive News*, May 6, 2019, 9.

19. Michael Martinez, "New UAW Boss Aims to Contain the Crisis," *Automotive News*, November 11, 2019, 1 (quotation); Richard Gonzales, "UAW President Gary Jones Abruptly Resigns amid Corruption Scandal," *NPR*, November 20, 2019, https://www.npr.org/2019/11/20/781479446/uaw-president-gary-jones-abruptly-resigns-amid-corruption-scandal; Katie Johnson, "Under Trump, Labor Protections Stripped Away," *Boston Globe*, September 3, 2018.

20. Hearn, interview (quotation); Bernie Sanders, "Why I Proudly Support Nissan Workers' Fight to Unionize," *The Guardian*, August 3, 2017; Mike Elk, "Mississippi Nissan Workers Hope for Historic Win," *The Guardian*, July 24, 2017. This paragraph also draws on my visit in May 2016 to the UAW's offices in Canton, which were decorated with materials carrying the "Labor Rights Are Civil Rights" slogan.

21. Elk, "Nissan Attacked"; Wells Jr., interview; Keith Laing, "UAW Regional Director Up for Top Post," *Detroit News*, December 1, 2017, A12 (quotation).

22. Paletta, "UAW Faces Another Southern Setback"; Bensinger, interview; King, interview; Casteel, interview; David Barkholz, "UAW Has Allies in Transplant Drive," *Automotive News*, December 27, 2010.

23. Bunkley, "Transplants Set to Dominate" (first quotation); Chappell, interview; Benchich, interview (second quotation); "Ford Tops GM in U.S. Factory Jobs," *Automotive News*, February 15, 2015.

24. Patrik Jonsson, "America's 'Other' Auto Industry," *Christian Science Monitor*, December 5, 2008, 1; William Neikirk, "Auto Industry on Road South," *Chicago Tribune*, December 4, 1991, 1 (quotations); "25 Years of Transplant Milestones," *Automotive News*, April 27, 1998.

25. Gina Chon and Stephen Power, "German Auto Makers Rev Up U.S. Output," *Wall Street Journal*, August 14, 2007, A6; Paul C. Judge, "Vehicle Sales Gained 3.2% in January," *New York Times*, February 6, 1990, D6 (Bieber quotation); Chappell, interview; James McCarten, "Trump Uses State of the Union Speech to Urge Congress to Ap-

prove USMCA," *Automotive News Canada*, February 5, 2019; Hannah Lutz, "GM Q3 Earnings Fall 8.7%," *Automotive News Canada*, October 29, 2019.

26. Laurence Iliff, "Booming Bajio," *Automotive News*, January 8, 2018, 4, 24; Fryer, interview; Gilliam, interview.

27. Matt McFarland, "Cadillac Enlists Lust, Hedonism and Car-Sharing," *Washington Post*, October 24, 2015 (first quotation); Lee Gomes, "Self-Driving Cars," *New York Times*, July 10, 2016, 7 (other quotation); Drew Harwell, "Electric-Car Rivals Like the 'Tesla Killer' Are Exactly What Elon Musk Wants," *Washington Post*, January 15, 2015.

28. Larry Vellequette, "EV Conundrum," *Automotive News*, March 4, 2019, 1 (quotation), 24; Nick Gibbs, "New EVs, New Doubts," *Automotive News*, March 11, 2019, 3.

29. Jackie Charniga, "Debt-Saddled Buyers Lean on Mum, Dad," *Automotive News*, March 10, 2019; David Muller, "Younger Buyers Still Want the Dealership," *Automotive News*, August 12, 2019; Gomes, "Self-Driving Cars," 7; Emily Badger, "More Rides to Hail May Mean More Traffic to Bear," *New York Times*, October 17, 2017, B4; Pete Bigelow, "Tesla Trims Work Force as Challenges Grow," *Automotive News*, January 21, 2019, 84; Gibbs, "New EVs, New Doubts," 3.

30. Felix Richter, "Infographic," *International Business Times* (U.S.), January 9, 2019; Gibbs, "New EVs, New Doubts," 3; Grace Schneider, "Toyota to Invest $238 Million," *Louisville Courier-Journal*, March 13, 2019; Hans Greimel, "China's EV Startups," *Automotive News*, August 20, 2018.

31. Michael Wayland, "'17 Sales Soften," *Automotive News*, January 8, 2018, 1, 33; "It's Not an Industry in Crisis Anymore," *Automotive News*, January 26, 2018; David Phillips, "U.S. Sales Rise 2.2% in December," *Automotive News*, January 3, 2019; Richter, "Infographic" (first quotation); Gibbs, "New EVs, New Doubts," 3; Urvaksh Karkaria, "A U.S.-Built Benz with a History-Making Price," *Automotive News*, March 18, 2019, 1, 33 (last three quotations, last two by Tim Urquhart).

32. Dominic Rushe, "Fiat's Mexico Factories in Doubt," *The Guardian*, January 10, 2017, 21 (quotation); "US Election 2016: Trump Victory in Maps," *BBC News*, accessed January 29, 2018, http://www.bbc.com/news/election-us-2016-37889032; Jack Ewing, "Who May Suffer the Most from Auto Tariffs?," *New York Times*, July 4, 2018, 1.

33. Iliff, "Booming Bajio," 4 (first quotation), 24; Motoko Rich, "Surprised Toyota Gets the Twitter Treatment," *New York Times*, January 7, 2017, 12 ("border tax" quotation).

34. Bill Vlasic, "Worried Car Industry Braces for Change," *New York Times*, December 9, 2016, 19 (quotation); "President Donald Trump's 2018 State of the Union Address," January 30, 2018; Coral Davenport, "California and 23 States Sue U.S. in War on Auto Emissions," *New York Times*, September 21, 2019, 17.

35. "Trump's NAFTA Partners Stand Their Ground against New Auto Rules," *Automotive News*, January 23, 2018 ("critical issue" quotation); "What Is the Future of NAFTA?," *Automotive News*, November 17, 2017 ("industry-shattering" quotation).

36. Ana Swanson, "In Search for Leverage, Trump May Be Undercutting His Own Trade Deals," *New York Times*, April 15, 2019 ("largest trade deal" quotation); McCarten, "Trump Uses State of the Union Speech" (second quotation); John Irwin, "USMCA Delay Is Holding Back $8B in Parts Orders," *Automotive News Canada*, October 2019 (closing quotation); Emily Cochrane, "Senate Passes Revised NAFTA," *New*

York Times, January 16, 2020; "U.S. Senate Approves North American Trade Deal Replacing NAFTA," *Automotive News Canada*, January 16, 2020; Justin Sink, "Trump Signs New USMCA Trade Deal," *Automotive News*, January 29, 2020 ("nightmare" quotation).

37. Jim Tankersley and Ana Swanson, "Moves to Modify Deals on Trade and Tariffs Put Carmakers in Jam," *New York Times*, May 11, 2018, 3; Jamie Lincoln Kitman, "The Jobs Lost to Auto Tariffs," *New York Times*, July 9, 2018, 21; Tiffany Hsu, "G.M. Says New Wave of Trump Tariffs Could Force U.S. Job Cuts," *New York Times*, June 30, 2018.

38. "Trump Dials Back Mexico Border Threat," *Automotive News*, April 3, 2019; Tankersley and Swanson, "Moves to Modify Deals," 3.

39. "About Us," Here for America, accessed January 29, 2018, www.hereforamerica. com; "International Automakers and Dealers in America," Here for America impact study, 2018, accessed April 16, 2019, www.hereforamerica/wp-contents/uploads /2018/12/HereForAmerica2018.pdf; "Foreign Carmakers in the U.S.," *New York Times*, June 14, 2018 (Bozella quotation).

40. "State of the U.S. Automotive Industry 2017," American Automotive Policy Council report, 19, accessed January 30, 2018, www.americanautocouncil.org/ . . . /2017%20 Economic%20Contribution%20Report.pdf; "Here for America," Here for America (homepage), accessed April 23, 2019, www.hereforamerica.com (closing quotation).

41. "About Us," Here for America; "International Automakers and Dealers in America"; Robey, interview (closing quotations).

BIBLIOGRAPHY

MANUSCRIPTS

Athens, Georgia

Richard B. Russell Library for Political Research and Studies, University of Georgia

Zell Miller Papers

George Ervin "Sonny" Perdue Official Papers

Columbia, South Carolina

South Carolina Department of Archives and History

Carroll A. Campbell Gubernatorial Papers

Jim Hodges Gubernatorial Papers

South Carolina Political Collections Library, University of South Carolina

Carroll A. Campbell Jr. Papers

Governor's Mansion Oral History Project

Ernest F. Hollings Papers

Liz Patterson Papers

Columbus, Ohio

Ohio History Connection

Ohio Department of Economic and Community Development Papers

Ohio State University Archives

John Glenn Papers

Detroit, Michigan

Walter P. Reuther Library, Wayne State University

UNITED AUTOMOBILE WORKERS OF AMERICA PAPERS

Convention Proceedings Papers

Douglas A. Fraser Personal Papers

Douglas A. Fraser Presidential Papers

International Executive Board Minutes

International Executive Board Oral Histories
Owen Bieber Papers
Secretary-Treasurer's Papers
Leonard Woodcock Papers

Frankfort, Kentucky

Kentucky Department for Libraries and Archives

Martha Layne Collins Papers

Georgetown, Kentucky

James C. Klotter Personal Papers, History Department, Georgetown College

Scott County Public Library

Toyota vertical files

LaGrange, Georgia

Diethard Lindner Personal Papers, shared with the author

Troup County Archives

KIA AUTOMOTIVE VERTICAL FILES

Montgomery, Alabama

Alabama Department of Archives and History

Alabama Governors Papers
Jim Folsom Jr. Gubernatorial Papers
Forrest "Fob" James Gubernatorial Papers
Don Siegelman Gubernatorial Papers

Murfreesboro, Tennessee

Albert Gore Research Center, Middle Tennessee State University

Jim Cooper Papers
Bart Gordon Papers
Walter King Hoover Papers

Nashville, Tennessee

Tennessee State Library and Archives

Lamar Alexander Gubernatorial Papers
Ray Blanton Gubernatorial Papers

Rabun Gap, Georgia

Ray Coulombe Personal Papers, shared with the author

David Andrea, Ann Arbor, Michigan, May 5, 2016
Lindsey Apple, Georgetown, Kentucky, June 14, 2017
Jason Armstrong, July 2, 2018 (telephone interview)
Joe Atkins, May 11, 2016 (telephone interview)
Craig Becker, Washington, D.C., April 21, 2015
Al Benchich, Detroit, Michigan, June 8, 2017
Richard Bensinger, April 26, 2016 (telephone interview)
Young Brown, LaGrange, Georgia, November 19, 2015
Elizabeth Bunn, Washington, D.C., October 11, 2013
Debbie Burdette, LaGrange, Georgia, November 20, 2015
Gary Burton, June 26, 2018 (telephone interview)
Sanchioni Butler, Canton, Mississippi, May 9, 2016
Gary Casteel, May 6, 2016 (telephone interview)
Ed Castile, Montgomery, Alabama, April 15, 2016
Jason Catchings, Canton, Mississippi, May 10, 2016
Washad Catchings, Canton, Mississippi, May 10, 2016
Lindsay Chappell, Brentwood, Tennessee, April 19, 2016
Martha Layne Collins, June 19, 2017 (telephone interview)
Jack Conner, Georgetown, Kentucky, June 12, 2017
Ray Coulombe, Rabun Gap, Georgia, November 18, 2015
Butler Derrick, Easley, South Carolina, April 13, 2011
Mike Dobbs, LaGrange, Georgia, November 12, 2015
Tim Duffey, LaGrange, Georgia, November 16, 2015
Phillip Dunlap, Auburn, Alabama, April 13, 2016
Kristen Dziczek, Ann Arbor, Michigan, May 5, 2016
Sheila Eckman, Auburn, Alabama, April 13, 2016
Jim Ewing, November 20, 2015 (telephone interview)
Drew Ferguson III, West Point, Georgia, November 13, 2015
Susan Ferguson, LaGrange, Georgia, November 10, 2015
Frank Figgers, Canton, Mississippi, May 10, 2016
Jane Fryer, LaGrange, Georgia, November 10, 2015
Donald Gilliam, West Point, Georgia, November 19, 2015
Willie Gossey, June 19, 2017 (telephone interview)
Tom Hall, LaGrange, Georgia, November 9, 2015
Billy Head, West Point, Georgia, November 13, 2015
Eric Hearn, Canton, Mississippi, May 10, 2016
Lori Hugeley, Opelika, Alabama, April 12, 2016
Keel Hunt, Murfreesboro, Tennessee, April 22, 2016
E. Carl Johnson, April 28, 2016 (telephone interview)
Frank Joyce, June 7 and 11, 2017 (telephone interviews)
Nathan Jung, LaGrange, Georgia, April 14, 2016
Lisa Keyes, July 3, 2018 (telephone interview)
Bob King, Ann Arbor, Michigan, June 7, 2017
David Knox, Georgetown, Kentucky, June 16, 2017

Peter Laarman, June 11, 2017 (telephone interview)
Craig Lesser, Atlanta, Georgia, November 20, 2015
Diethard Lindner, LaGrange, Georgia, November 9, 2015
Dara Longgrear, June 28, 2018 (telephone interview)
Andrea Lovejoy, LaGrange, Georgia, November 9, 2015
Jeff Lukken, LaGrange, Georgia, November 11, 2015
George Lusby, Georgetown, Kentucky, June 12, 2017
Colin Martin, July 5, 2018 (telephone interview)
Kurt Martin (pseudonym), May 15, 2018 (telephone interview)
Sean McAlinden, Ann Arbor, Michigan, May 5, 2016
Reuben McIntyre, June 18, 2017 (telephone interview)
Ellen McNair, Montgomery, Alabama, April 15, 2016
Nita Miller, Canton, Mississippi, May 10, 2016
Chris Milton, Canton, Mississippi, May 9, 2016
Jeffrey Moore, Canton, Mississippi, May 9, 2016
Ronnie Musgrove, Jackson, Mississippi, May 10, 2016
David Noles, LaGrange, Georgia, November 12, 2015
Travis Parks, Canton, Mississippi, May 10, 2016
Tom Prather, Georgetown, Kentucky, June 13, 2017
Harris Raynor, Union City, Georgia, June 18, 2010
Wayne Robey, Georgetown, Kentucky, June 15, 2017
Patricia Ruffin, Canton, Mississippi, May 10, 2016
Steve Sewell, Birmingham, Alabama, April 12, 2016
James Sims, Canton, Mississippi, May 9, 2016
Ed Smith, Auburn, Alabama, November 19, 2015
Price Smith, Georgetown, Kentucky, June 16, 2017
Trent Smith, Canton, Mississippi, May 9, 2016
Kim Stamper, Georgetown, Kentucky, June 15, 2017
Larry Steele, May 9, 2016 (telephone interview)
Todd Strange, June 28, 2018 (telephone interview)
John Sweeney, Washington, D.C., July 15, 2013
Kent Syler, Murfreesboro, Tennessee, April 19, 2016
Larry Tate, Canton, Mississippi, May 11, 2016
Tod Tentler, LaGrange, Georgia, November 10, 2015
Jim Thornton, June 27, 2018 (telephone interview)
Richard Trumka, Washington, D.C., April 23, 2015
Joshua Van Lieu, LaGrange, Georgia, November 11, 2015
Karen Wells, Georgetown, Kentucky, June 15, 2017
Willard "Chip" Wells Jr., Canton, Mississippi, May 10, 2016
Alton West, LaGrange, Georgia, November 16, 2015
Ernest Whitfield, Canton, Mississippi, May 10, 2016
Ricky Wolfe, LaGrange, Georgia, November 16, 2015
Cy Wood, Lanett, Alabama, November 13, 2015
Mike Woods, Smyrna, Tennessee, April 22, 2016

Kilsup Yoon, LaGrange, Georgia, November 17, 2015
James Yu, LaGrange, Georgia, April 14, 2016

NEWSPAPERS AND JOURNALS

Agence France-Presse
Akron (Ohio) Beacon Journal
Allentown Morning Call
Anniston Star
Appalachia
Asahi Evening News
Associated Press
Associated Press State Wire: Alabama
Athens (Ala.) News Courier
Athens Banner-Herald
Athens Post-Athenian
Atlanta Journal-Constitution
BBC News
Birmingham News
Birmingham Post-Herald
Boston Globe
Business Week
Calgary Herald
California Management Review
Charlotte Observer
Charleston Post and Courier
Chattanooga News Free Press
Chattanooga Times Free Press
Chicago Sun-Times
Chicago Tribune
Chosŏn ilbo
Christian Science Monitor
Cincinnati Post
Clanton (Ala.) Advertiser
Columbus Business First
Daily Labor Report
Daphne Bulletin
Decatur (Ala.) Daily
Demopolis Times
Detroit Free Press
Detroit News
Dothan (Ala.) Eagle
domain-b (India)
Economic Development Quarterly

Economic Development Review
Economist
Elizabethton (Tenn.) Star
Elizabethtown (Ky.) News-Enterprise
Europe
Expansion Management
Financial Times
Financial Times (U.K.)
Florence (Ala.) Times Daily
Forbes
Fortune
Fort Lauderdale Sun Sentinel
Fort Wayne (Ind.) Journal-Gazette
Forum
Georgetown Graphic
Georgetown News and Graphic / George-
    town News-Graphic
Georgetown News and Times
Georgia Business and Economic
    Conditions
Georgia Public Broadcasting
Georgia Trend
Globe and Mail
Greenville News
Greenwood (S.C.) Index-Journal
The Guardian
The Guardian (U.K.)
Harvard Business Review
Hogansville Home News
Huffington Post
The Independent (U.K.)
International Business Times (U.S.)
International Herald Tribune
In These Times
Jackson Sun
Japan Times
Johnson City Press-Chronicle
The Journal
Kaigai rodo jiho

Knoxville Journal
Knoxville News
Lagniappe (Mobile, Ala.)
LaGrange Daily News
Lexington Herald-Leader
Los Angeles Times
Louisville Courier-Journal
Marysville Journal-Tribune
Maryville (Tenn.) Times
McClatchy-Tribune Business News
Memphis Commercial Appeal
Milan Mirror-Exchange
Mississippi Business Journal
Mobile Register
Montgomery Advertiser
Montgomery Business Journal
Morning Edition (NPR)
Murfreesboro Journal
Nashville Banner
The Nation
New Labor Forum
Newsweek
New Orleans Times-Picayune
New York Times
Ohio Report
Oklahoma City Journal Record
Orangeburg (S.C.) Times and Democrat
Ottawa Citizen
Pittsburgh Post-Gazette
Pittsburgh Tribune

Pittsburgh Tribune-Review
PR Newswire
The Progressive
Reuters
Rutherford County Daily News Journal
San Antonio Express-News
Sanken ronshu
Savannah Morning News
Selma Times-Journal
Shokun!
Smyrna Courier
Spartanburg Herald-Journal
The State
Talladega (Ala.) Daily Home
Targeted News Service (U.S.)
The Tennessean
Tonga ilbo
Troup Trends
Tuscaloosa News
Union City Messenger
U.S. News and World Report
USA Today
Wall Street Journal
Washington Examiner
Washington Post
Waverly News-Democrat
Weekly Standard
Winston-Salem Journal
Wirtschaftswoche

TRADE AND UNION JOURNALS

AFL-CIO News
Area Development
Automotive News
Automotive News Canada
Autotrader
Business Facilities

India Automobile News (New Delhi)
Japanese Motor Business
Site Selection
UAW Report
Ward's Auto World

REPORTS

Haywood, Charles F. "A Report on the Significance of Toyota Motor Manufacturing
Kentucky, Inc. to the Kentucky Economy." Gatton College of Business and Economics, University of Kentucky, 1998.

The Harbour Report a Decade Later: Competitive Assessment of the North American Automotive Industry, 1979–1989. Rochester, Mich.: Avon Printing Company, 1990.

The Harbour Report: Competitive Assessment of the North American Automotive Industry, 1989–1992. Madison Heights, Mich.: E and G Printing Services, 1992.

The Harbour Report 2001. Troy, Mich.: Harbour and Associates, 2001.

The Harbour Report 2002. Troy, Mich.: Harbour and Associates, 2002.

The Harbour Report: North America 2003. Troy, Mich.: Harbour and Associates, 2003.

BOOKS, ARTICLES, CHAPTERS, AND DISSERTATIONS

Alexander, Lamar. *Friends, Japanese and Tennesseans: A Model of U.S.-Japan Cooperation*. Tokyo: Kodansha International, 1986.

———. *Steps along the Way: A Governor's Scrapbook*. Nashville: Thomas Nelson, 1986.

Amsden, Alice H. *Asia's Next Giant: South Korea and Late Industrialization*. New York: Oxford University Press, 1989.

Anderson, David M., and Andrew C. McKevitt. "From 'the Chosen' to the Precariat: Southern Workers in Foreign-Owned Factories Since the 1980s." In *Reconsidering Southern Labor History: Race, Class, and Power*, edited by Matthew Hild and Keri Leigh Merritt, 255–70. Gainesville: University Press of Florida, 2018.

Apple, Lindsey, Frederick A. Johnston, and Ann Bolton Bevins. *Scott County Kentucky: A History*. Georgetown, Ky.: Scott County Historical Society, 1993.

Asher, Robert, and Ronald Edsforth, eds. *Autowork*. Albany: State University of New York Press, 1995.

Atkins, Joseph B. *Covering for the Bosses: Labor and the Southern Press*. Jackson: University Press of Mississippi, 2008.

Babson, Steve. *Building the Union: Skilled Workers and Anglo-Gaelic Immigrants in the Rise of the UAW*. New Brunswick, N.J.: Rutgers University Press, 1991.

Bailey, Eric. "Courting Toyota, Selling Kentucky: Conflict and Relationship Building in the Establishment of Toyota Motor Manufacturing of Kentucky, 1984–1989." Master's thesis, Eastern Kentucky University, 2011.

Bailey, Thomas A., David M. Kennedy, and Lizabeth Cohen. *The American Pageant*. Boston: Houghton Mifflin, 1998.

Bartley, Numan V. *The Creation of Modern Georgia*. 2nd ed. Athens: University of Georgia Press, 1990.

Bates, Beth Tompkins. *The Making of Black Detroit in the Age of Henry Ford*. Chapel Hill: University of North Carolina Press, 2012.

Berggren, Christian, Torsten Bjorkman, and Ernst Hollander. *Are They Unbeatable? Report from a Fieldtrip to Study Transplants, the Japanese Owned Auto Plants in North America*. Stockholm: Royal Institute of Technology, 1991.

Bhagwati, Jagdish. *In Defense of Globalization*. New York: Oxford University Press, 2004.

Bluestone, Barry, and Bennett Harrison. *The Deindustrialization of America: Plant Closings, Community Abandonment, and the Dismantling of Basic Industry*. New York: Basic Books, 1982.

Boyle, Kevin. *The UAW and the Heyday of American Liberalism, 1945–1968*. Ithaca, N.Y.: Cornell University Press, 1995.

Brecher, Jeremy, Tim Costello, and Brendan Smith. *Globalization from Below: The Power of Solidarity*. Cambridge, Mass.: South End Press, 2000.

Chafe, William H. *The Unfinished Journey: America Since World War II*. 3rd ed. New York: Oxford University Press, 1995.

Clemens, Paul. *Made in Detroit: A South of 8 Mile Memoir*. New York: Doubleday, 2005.

Cobb, James C. *The Selling of the South: The Southern Crusade for Industrial Development, 1936–1980*. Baton Rouge: Louisiana State University Press, 1982.

——— . *The South and America Since World War II*. New York: Oxford University Press, 2011.

Cobb, James C., and William Stueck. Introduction to *Globalization and the American South*, edited by James C. Cobb and William Stueck, xi–xvi. Athens: University of Georgia Press, 2005.

Cole, Robert E., and Donald R. Deskins. "Racial Factors in Site Selection and Employment Patterns of Japanese Auto Firms in America." *California Management Review* 31, no. 1 (1988): 9–22.

Cowie, Jefferson. *Stayin' Alive: The 1970s and the Last Days of the Working Class*. New York: New Press, 2010.

Daher, Najy "Nick." "Culture and Management Practices: A Study of Japanese Automotive Companies Operating in the United States, 1980–1995." PhD diss., University of Maryland, 2012.

Dandaneau, Steven P. *A Town Abandoned: Flint, Michigan, Confronts Deindustrialization*. Albany: State University of New York Press, 1996.

De Mente, Boye Lafayette. *Korean Etiquette and Ethics in Business*. 2nd ed. Lincolnwood, Ill., 1994.

Dewar, Robert J. *A Savage Factory: An Eyewitness Account of the Auto Industry's Self-Destruction*. Bloomington, Ind.: AuthorHouse, 2009.

Dudley, Kathryn Marie. *The End of the Line: Lost Jobs, New Lives in Postindustrial America*. Chicago: University of Chicago Press, 1994.

Esch, Elizabeth D. *The Color Line and the Assembly Line: Managing Race in the Ford Empire*. Oakland: University of California Press, 2018.

Feldman, Richard, and Michael Betzold, eds. *End of the Line: Autoworkers and the American Dream*. New York: Weidenfeld and Nicolson, 1988.

Ferriss, Susan, and Ricardo Sandoval. *The Fight in the Fields: Cesar Chavez and the Farmworkers Movement*. New York: Harcourt Brace, 1997.

Fine, Sidney. *Sit-Down: The General Motors Strike of 1936–1937*. Ann Arbor: University of Michigan Press, 1969.

Foner, Eric. *Give Me Liberty! An American History*. 2nd ed. New York: W. W. Norton, 2009.

Fraas, Elizabeth. "'All Issues Are Women's Issues': An Interview with Governor Martha Layne Collins on Women in Politics." *Register of the Kentucky Historical Society* 99, no. 3 (Summer 2001): 225–48.

——— , ed. *The Public Papers of Governor Martha Layne Collins, 1983–1987*. Lexington: University Press of Kentucky, 2006.

Friedlander, Peter. *The Emergence of a UAW Local, 1936–1939: A Study in Class and Culture*. Pittsburgh: University of Pittsburgh Press, 1975.

Garrow, David J. *Protest at Selma: Martin Luther King, Jr., and the Voting Rights Act of 1965*. New Haven, Conn.: Yale University Press, 1978.

Gelsanliter, David. *Jump Start: Japan Comes to the Heartland*. New York: Farrar, Straus and Giroux, 1990.

Ghosn, Carlos, and Philippe Ries. *Shift: Inside Nissan's Historic Revival*. New York: Doubleday, 2005.

Green, William C., and Ernest J. Yanarella, eds. *North American Auto Unions in Crisis: Lean Production as Contested Terrain*. Albany: State University of New York Press, 1996.

Hall, Jacquelyn Dowd, James Leloudis, Robert Korstad, Mary Murphy, Lu Ann Jones, and Christopher B. Daly. *Like a Family: The Making of a Southern Cotton Mill World*. Chapel Hill: University of North Carolina Press, 1987.

Halpern, Martin. *UAW Politics in the Cold War Era*. Albany: SUNY Press, 1988.

Hamper, Ben. *Rivethead: Tales from the Assembly Line*. New York: Warner Books, 1991.

Haywood, Charles F. "Toyota Motor Manufacturing, Kentucky, and the Kentucky Economy." In *Japan in the Bluegrass*, edited by P. P. Karan, 155–66. Lexington: University Press of Kentucky, 2001.

Highsmith, Andrew R. *Demolition Means Progress: Flint, Michigan, and the Fate of the American Metropolis*. Chicago: University of Chicago Press, 2015.

Hoyman, Michele. *Power Steering: Global Automakers and the Transformation of Rural Communities*. Lawrence: University Press of Kansas, 1997.

Hulsemann, Karsten. "Greenfields in the Heart of Dixie: How the American Auto Industry Discovered the South." In *The Second Wave: Southern Industrialization from the 1940s to the 1970s*, edited by Philip Scranton, 219–54. Athens: University of Georgia Press, 2001.

Ihara, Ryoji. *Toyota's Assembly Line: A View from the Factory Floor*. Melbourne: Trans Pacific Press, 2003.

Ingrassia, Paul. *Crash Course: The American Automobile Industry's Road from Glory to Disaster*. New York: Random House, 2010.

Ishikawa, Mamoru. "Beikoku Keiei ni Chosen suru Nissan no Jikken" (Nissan's experiment that challenges American management). *Ekonomisuto* 61, no. 44 (1983): 44–51.

Jacobs, A. J. *The New Domestic Automakers in the United States and Canada: History, Impacts, and Prospects*. Lanham, Md.: Lexington Books, 2016.

Jenkins, Davis. "Japanese Transplants and the Work System Revolution in U.S. Manufacturing." PhD diss., Carnegie Mellon University, 1995.

Keeran, Roger. *The Communist Party and the Auto Workers Unions*. Bloomington: Indiana University Press, 1980.

Kenney, Martin, and Richard Florida. *Beyond Mass Production: The Japanese System and Its Transfer to the U.S.* New York: Oxford University Press, 1993.

Kim, Eun Mee. *Big Business, Strong State: Collusion and Conflict in South Korean Development, 1960–1990*. Albany: State University of New York Press, 1997.

Lichtenstein, Nelson. *State of the Union: A Century of American Labor*. Princeton, N.J.: Princeton University Press, 2002.

Lichtenstein, Nelson, and Stephen Meyer, eds. *On the Line: Essays in the History of Auto Work*. Urbana: University of Illinois Press, 1989.

Lilleston, Judith Anne. "Japanese Management in the United States Auto Industry: Can It Be Transported? Nissan: A Case Study." PhD diss., City University of New York, 1993.

Maunula, Marko. *Guten Tag, Y'All: Globalization and the South Carolina Piedmont, 1950–2000*. Athens: University of Georgia Press, 2009.

McCartin, Joseph A. *Collision Course: Ronald Reagan, the Air Traffic Controllers, and the Strike That Changed America*. New York: Oxford University Press, 2011.

McGehee, Ronnie Lynn. "The Impact of a Large Automotive Manufacturing Plant on Demographic Expansion and Educational Changes in a Mississippi School District." PhD diss., Mississippi State University, 2007.

McKevitt, Andrew C. *Consuming Japan: Popular Culture and the Globalizing of 1980s America*. Chapel Hill: University of North Carolina Press, 2017.

Milkman, Ruth. *Farewell to the Factory: Auto Workers in the Late Twentieth Century*. Berkeley: University of California Press, 1997.

Milward, H. Brinton, and Heidi Hosbach Newman. "State Incentive Packages and the Industrial Location Decision." *Economic Development Quarterly* 3, no. 3 (1989): 203–22.

Minchin, Timothy J. *"Don't Sleep with Stevens!": The J. P. Stevens Campaign and the Struggle to Organize the South, 1963–80*. Gainesville: University Press of Florida, 2005.

———. *Empty Mills: The Fight against Imports and the Decline of the U.S. Textile Industry*. Lanham, Md.: Rowman and Littlefield, 2013.

———. *Labor under Fire: A History of the AFL-CIO Since 1979*. Chapel Hill: University of North Carolina Press, 2017.

Minchin, Timothy J., and John A. Salmond. *After the Dream: Black and White Southerners Since 1965*. Lexington: University Press of Kentucky, 2011.

Nobe, Eiichi. "Beikoku Honda Yorinseisan no 25nen wo Furikaette" (Notes from Honda's first 25 years in auto manufacturing in the United States). *Sanken ronshu* 37 (2009): 1–11.

Norton, Mary Beth, David M. Katzman, David W. Blight, Howard P. Chudacoff, Thomas G. Paterson, William M. Tuttle Jr., and Paul D. Escott. *A People and a Nation: A History of the United States*. 6th ed. Boston: Houghton Mifflin, 2001.

Ogino, Noburo. "Naze Nikkei Maker ga Target ka" (Why are Japanese manufacturers targets?). *Kaigai rodo jiho* 25, no. 14 (2001): 57–59.

Patton, Janet W., and H. Milton Patton. "Dynamics of Growth and Change in Georgetown, Kentucky." In *Japan in the Bluegrass*, edited by P. P. Karan, 123–52. Lexington: University Press of Kentucky, 2001.

Perrucci, Robert. *Japanese Auto Transplants in the Heartland: Corporatism and Community*. New York: Aldine De Gruyter, 1994.

Pieterse, Jan Nederveen. *Globalization and Culture: Global Melange*. Lanham, Md.: Rowman and Littlefield, 2009.

Reimers, David M. "Asian Immigrants in the South." In *Globalization and the Ameri-*

can South, edited by James C. Cobb and William Stueck, 100–134. Athens: University of Georgia Press, 2005.

Ritzer, George. *The McDonaldization of Society: Revised New Century Edition*. Thousand Oaks, Calif.: Pine Forge Press, 2004.

Roller, David C., and Robert W. Twyman, eds. *The Encyclopedia of Southern History*. Baton Rouge: Louisiana State University Press, 1979.

Rubenstein, James M. *The Changing US Auto Industry: A Geographical Analysis*. London: Routledge, 1992.

———. *Making and Selling Cars: Innovation and Change in the U.S. Automotive Industry*. Baltimore, Md.: Johns Hopkins University Press, 2001.

Russ, Jonathan S. "Made in the USA: Honda and Toyota as Transplant Automobile Manufacturers in the United States." PhD diss., University of Delaware, 1996.

Russo, John, and Sherry Lee Linkon. "Collateral Damage: Deindustrialization and the Uses of Youngstown." In *Beyond the Ruins: The Meanings of Deindustrialization*, edited by Jefferson Cowie and Joseph Heathcott, 201–18. Ithaca, N.Y.: ILR Press, 2003.

Scranton, Philip, ed. *The Second Wave: Southern Industrialization from the 1940s to the 1970s*. Athens: University of Georgia Press, 2001.

Shotwell, Gregg. *Autoworkers under the Gun: A Shop-Floor View of the End of the American Dream*. Chicago: Haymarket Books, 2011.

Silvia, Stephen J. "The United Auto Workers' Attempts to Unionize Volkswagen Chattanooga." *ILR Review* 71, no. 3 (May 2018): 600–624.

Song, Byung-Nak. *The Rise of the Korean Economy*. 3rd ed. New York: Oxford University Press, 1997.

Steers, Richard M. *Made in Korea: Chung Ju Yung and the Rise of Hyundai*. New York: Routledge, 1999.

Thompson, James A. "The Toyota Decision." *Economic Development Review* 7, no. 4 (Fall 1989): 21–23.

Thornton, J. Mills, III. *Dividing Lines: Municipal Politics and the Struggle for Civil Rights in Montgomery, Birmingham, and Selma*. Tuscaloosa: University of Alabama Press, 2002.

Vlasic, Bill. *Once upon a Car: The Fall and Resurrection of America's Big Three Automakers—GM, Ford, and Chrysler*. New York: Harper Luxe, 2011.

Widick, B. J., and Eli Ginzberg, eds. *Auto Work and Its Discontents*. Baltimore, Md.: Johns Hopkins University Press, 1976.

Windham, Lane. *Knocking on Labor's Door: Union Organizing in the 1970s and the Roots of a New Economic Divide*. Chapel Hill: University of North Carolina Press, 2017.

Yasunobu, Misato. "Honda Ohaio no Jikken Houkoku" (Report on an experiment at Honda Ohio). *Shokun!* 18, no. 5 (1986): 194–201.

Yoshida, Nobuyoshi. "Honda jo wo Semeru UAW no Shousan!?" (UAW's prospects of victory in attacking the Honda castle). In *Soshite Honda wa Tonda: Honda Kokusai Senryaku no Himitsu* (And then, Honda took off: Secrets of Honda's international strategy), 131–48. Tokyo: Jitsugyo no Nihonsha, 1986.

Young, Gordon. *Teardown: Memoir of a Vanishing City.* Berkeley: University of California Press, 2013.

Zieger, Robert H. *American Workers, American Unions.* 2nd ed. Baltimore, Md.: Johns Hopkins University Press, 1994.

——. *The CIO, 1935–1955.* Chapel Hill: University of North Carolina Press, 1995.

——. *For Jobs and Freedom: Race and Labor in America Since 1865.* Lexington: University Press of Kentucky, 2007.

Zieger, Robert H., and Gilbert J. Gall. *American Workers, American Unions.* 3rd ed. Baltimore, Md.: Johns Hopkins University Press, 2002.

Zieger, Robert H., Timothy J. Minchin, and Gilbert J. Gall. *American Workers, American Unions.* 4th ed. Baltimore, Md.: Johns Hopkins University Press, 2014.

INDEX

Hyundai Motor Company (*continued*)
156–59; and local support, 146, 155–56,
159–61; managerial philosophy of, 158–59;
mentioned, vii, 60, 82, 108, 127, 142, 146,
185; and the U.S. market, 145–48, 160–61.
See also Hyundai Motor Manufacturing
Alabama (HMMA)
Hyundai Group, 147, 168, 177
Hyundai–Kia group, 7–8, 148, 167, 178
Hyundai Mobis, 180
Hyundai Motor Manufacturing Alabama
(HMMA), 145–7, 155–63, 174, 185. *See also*
Hyundai Motor Company

Iacocca, Lee, 38, 82
IG Metall, 117–18, 141–42
Ikemi, Kiyoshi, 39
Imports, in U.S. auto market, 10, 15–16, 19; and
foreign–owned auto plants, 8, 10, 82, 88,
131, 192; reaction against, 18–23, 46, 61–62,
195, 196
Incentives, 3, 4, 5, 7–8, 9, 33, 117, 193; at
BMW, 108–9, 112–114; at Honda, 36, 41; at
Hyundai, 151–52, 154–55; at Kia, 165, 170,
173–74, 176; at Mercedes, 127, 130–31, 140; at
Nissan, 61, 65, 215n9; opposition to, 68–70,
86, 95–98, 102, 108–9, 121, 126, 134–35, 137–
38, 147, 156, 166, 182–83, 190, 196; at Toyota,
86, 87, 89, 106, 224n18; at Volkswagen,
26–27, 188
Industrial Review of Japan, 16
Industrial Training Service (Tenn.), 62, 68–69
Ingrassia, Paul, 15, 199n17
Injuries, and car plants, 51, 57–59, 75, 76,
77–78, 103–104, 121, 140, 190, 196. *See also*
Workloads; Speed-ups
Irimajiri, Shoichiro, 37, 44, 50
Ishihara, Takashi, 61–67, 72–74, 80, 84
Isomura, Iwao, 98, 100
Ivey, Kay, 162, 188
Iwasaki, Masami, 98

J.D. Power and Associates, 85, 102
Jackson, Randy, 179–80
Jacobs, A.J., 2, 84, 109, 124, 148, 198n10, 255n12
James, Forrest "Fob", 134–38, 152
James, Frank, 31, 34
Japanese Automobile Manufacturers
Association (JAMA), 2, 17–19, 189
Japanese Automobile Workers Union (JAW),
45

Japanese Ministry of International Trade and
Industry, 18
Japanese, sentiment against 3, 18, 42–43, 46–7,
61, 67, 71, 86, 93, 95–97; and the UAW, 18, 22
Johns, Jamie, 68
Johnson, Lyndon Baines, 61–62
Jones, Brereton, 101
Jones, Gary, 191
Jones, Truman, 71–72
Joyce, Frank, 45, 75, 117, 119, 125
Jung, Nathan, 5, 177, 184
Junkerman, John, 74–75

Kaigai rodo jiho, 81, 144
Karan, P.P., 86
Kawamata, Katsuji, 16
Kawashima, Kiyoshi, 1, 37–39, 42, 51
Kelly Services, 190
Kennedy, Robert, 135
Kenney, Martin, 77
Kentucky Fried Chicken (KFC), 90–91, 102, 181
Kentucky Planning and Zoning Commission,
93–94, 96
Keyes, Lisa, 132, 134, 138, 143
Kia Motors, 6, 8, 187–88; in Georgia, vii, 7–8,
164–86; and local concerns, 166, 179,
181–84; and local support, 164–66, 176–77,
179, 181, 184–85; mentioned, 60, 108, 145,
148, 160, 161, 163, 179–80, 176–77, 178; and
the U.S. market, 164–65, 186
Kim, J.H., 151
Kim, Seung–Tack, 176
King, Bob, 138, 158
Kinzer, Al, 118–20
Knicely, Carroll, 89–90
Knox, David, 95, 97
Komer, Odessa, 54
Korean Confederation of Trade Unions, 177
Kramer, Helen, 17
Kume, Yutaka, 78–79
Kusunoki, Kaneyoshi, 99

Laarman, Peter, 36, 81, 86
Labor Notes, 78
Labor tensions, 8–9, 29–32, 190–92; at BMW,
118–19, 121; at Honda, 51, 57–58; at Hyundai,
157–59; at Kia, 181–83; at Mercedes–Benz,
134, 138, 140; at Nissan, 61, 70–71, 73–76,
80–81; at Toyota, 97–100, 103–4
LaGrange (Ga.) Development Authority, 185
Lashlee, Frank, 68–69

Team Production Systems, 23, 75, 78, 88, 120, 221n79
Temporary workers, 140, 161, 190, 255–56n14. *See also* "Precariat"
Tennessee Occupational Safety and Health Administration (TOSHA), 76–77
Tensions, caused by sector, viii, 3, 6, 8, 12, 19, 198n10; at BMW, 109, 121–25; at Honda, 34, 42–49, 55–59; at Hyundai, 156–59; at Kia, 166, 181–84; at Mercedes, 127, 134–38, 142–43; at Nissan, 61, 67, 73–76; at Toyota, 86, 92–98, 101, 103, 105–6; at Volkswagen, 28–32. *See also* Opposition
Tesla Motors, 193
Textile industry, 45, 87, 108, 111, 122, 124; decline of 20, 110, 120, 143, 164, 166, 167; and growth of foreign-owned auto plants, 114, 115–16, 172, 176, 180, 181, 183–84
Tomasi, Joe, 44–47, 51–54
Toshiba Corporation, 65–66
Toyoda, Eiji, 16, 21, 88, 96, 98
Toyoda, Shoichiro, 89–90
Toyota Motor Company, 5, 7, 10, 15–17, 88, 98, 187–88, 192–93, 195, 196; Camry model, 21, 85, 87, 100–1, 189, 196; Corolla model, 15, 87–88, 189; Corona model, 15–16, 32; in Kentucky, 1, 6–7, 82, 84–106, 188–89, 194–95; Lexus division, 85, 109, 189; and local opposition, 86, 92–97, 101, 105–6; and local support, 85–86, 91–92, 100–102, 105–6; mentioned, vii, 25, 27, 37, 44, 57, 60, 81, 107–8, 124, 127, 155, 164, 180; production system of, 85, 88, 91, 100, 106; and the UAW, 21–23, 97–103; and the U.S. market, 84–85, 87–88, 189
Toyota Motor Manufacturing (TMM), 98–106. *See also* Toyota Motor Company
Trade Act (1974), 22
Troup County (Ga.) Board of Commissioners, 167, 178
Trump, Donald, 10, 194–96
Tucker, Jerry, 78, 221n79
Turner, Jim, 54–56, 74–75
Tuscaloosa News, 149, 155, 162

Uber, 193–94
Union avoidance, 5, 8–9, 57, 76, 80, 69, 131, 177–78, 188, 191–92; in Alabama, 138–39, 141–42, 154, 158; at BMW, 108, 110, 116–21, 125; at Honda, 41–44, 48–57; at Hyundai, 153–54; in Kentucky, 98–99, 104–105; at Kia, 177, 181–82; at Mercedes-Benz, 128, 131, 138–40;

at Nissan, 61, 66, 73–81, 192; in South Carolina, 117–21; at Toyota, 97–103
United Automobile Workers (UAW), viii, 2, 3, 8–10, 12, 14, 22, 30, 59, 78, 81, 85, 131, 154, 180–82, 191, 193; alienates Japanese automakers, 18–19; and BMW, 117–21; encourages Japanese auto plants in U.S., 12, 16–23; and Honda, 36, 42, 44–59; and Hyundai, 157–58, 160; and Kia, 181–82; and Mercedes, 138–42; and Nissan, 61, 70, 72–82; organizing drives of, 51–55, 58, 73–81, 103–5, 190–92; and Toyota, 86, 91, 98–100, 102–3; and Volkswagen, 30–34; and women workers, 54, 56, 105
University of Kentucky, 85, 90, 95
Urban League, 29, 56, 70
U.S. Clean Air Act (1970), 38
USA Today, 166, 181

Van Lieu, Joshua, 175, 251n47
Vanik, Charles A., 20, 25
Volkswagen AG, 2, 22, 25, 27, 29–30, 31, 32–33, 187, 190–91, 193; abandoned plant in New Jersey, 11–12, 24–25; Beetle model, 11–12, 24–25; and local opposition, 27–33; mentioned, 36, 40, 60, 62, 108; in Pennsylvania, 10–12, 23–34, 201n2; Rabbit model, 24, 27–28, 32, 34
Voluntary export restraint (VER), 20–21, 88
Volvo, 188, 190, 194
Von Kuenheim, Eberhard, 7, 114–19

Wall Street Journal, 19, 43, 71, 129, 160
Wallace, George, 135, 238n35
Washington Post, 27, 30, 50, 60–61, 105, 107, 155, 190, 193
Wells, Karen, 100, 103
Werner, Helmut, 128–31, 138
West Point-Pepperell, 166, 167
Whitlock, Scott, 52, 58
Wilkinson, Wallace, 96, 101
Williams, Dennis, 141–42
Wolfe, Ricky, 167, 178, 183
Women workers, 54–56, 72–73, 100–101, 105, 135, 158–59
Wood, Cy, 174, 183
Woodcock, Leonard, 16–19, 21
Woods, Mike, 62, 65–66, 187
Workloads, complaints about, 10, 51, 57–58, 74, 78, 80–81, 141, 190, 191. *See also* Speed-ups; Injuries

Since 1970: Histories of Contemporary America

Printed in the United States
By Bookmasters